Wireless LAN Glossary

802.11: The general standard, developed by the IEEE (Institute of Electrical and Electronics Engineers — the folks who create many of the standards for networking equipment), for wireless local-area networks. Within the 802.11 standard are various substandards, including 802.11b (11 Mbps using the 2.4 GHz spectrum), 802.11a (54 Mbps using the 5 GHz spectrum), 802.11g (54 Mbps using the 2.4 GHz spectrum), and 802.11n (100+ Mbps using the 2.4 GHz spectrum).

access point, or AP: A wireless LAN base station that connects a wired network (like the wired Ethernet connection on a broadband modem) to the wireless network. The AP contains a radio transceiver (which transmits and receives radio signals), and most APs contain a router that directs your networked devices' data to and from the Internet.

Bluetooth: A standard system for wireless personal-area networks, or PANs. Bluetooth provides speeds of up to 723 Kbps at short ranges (typically less than 10 meters). PAN technologies, like Bluetooth, are complementary to LAN technologies (like 802.11), and are typically used to connect peripheral devices, like keyboards to computers or wireless headsets to mobile phones.

Ethernet: A standard data communications protocol enabling computers and computer peripheral devices, such as printers, to interface with one another and across networks for the exchange of information. The most common variation of Ethernet found in home networks is the 100 Mbps 100BaseT variant, although dozens of other variations exist with speeds up to 1000 Mbps.

IP address: The "phone number" of the Internet, the IP address is used to identify computers and devices connected to the Internet and allows traffic to be routed across the Internet. Most wireless home networks have two IP addresses: a *public* IP address (used by your modem and access point or router) that identifies your network to other computers on the Internet, and a set of *private* IP addresses, used only within your network. Your access point (or separate router, if you have one) translates between your public and private IP addresses to send data to the right computer within your network.

LAN (local-area network): A computer data communications network used within a limited physical location, like a house.

network adapter (also network interface card, or NIC): A device that connects to an internal bus in a PC, which provides an interface between the computer or device and the LAN. For wireless networks, network adapters typically connect to the PC Card bus or to the USB bus of the device being networked.

network address translation (NAT): A process performed within your access point (or separate router, if you use one) to translate, or create a tie, between your internal network's "private" IP addresses and the public IP address assigned to your network by the ISP. A NAT router is a device that performs this translation and lets devices on your network using nonroutable private IP addresses communicate with devices on the Internet.

service set identifier (SSID): Also referred to as ESSID, network name, service area, and other names, this term identifies a specific wireless LAN. To connect to a network, a device must "know" the SSID of the network.

Wi-Fi protected access (WPA): An improvement to WEP, WPA adds — among other changes — a key (TKIP, or *temporal key integrity protocol*) that changes dynamically over time, which eliminates the greatest shortcoming of WEP. WPA is the minimum level of security you should choose, if at all possible. WPA-Enterprise adds 802.1X authentication to make the network even more secure.

Wi-Fi protected access 2 (WPA2): WPA2 adds even further enhancements to WPA, including AES (Advanced Encryption Standard), which makes the encryption key almost impervious to current cracker attacks.

Wired Equivalent Privacy (WEP): The encryption system used by wireless LANs to provide security on the network. WEP uses an encryption *key* (which can be 40 or 108 bits long — these keys are often referred to as 64- and 128-bit keys because of some extra bits used in the WEP system) to encrypt data flowing across the network. Without the WEP encryption key, unauthorized users see only garbled data and cannot read what is being sent across the network.

wireless Ethernet bridge: A device that connects to an Ethernet port on a networked device (like a PC, game console, or networked audio system) and provides network adapter functionality for that device.

wireless LAN repeater: A device that extends the range of a wireless LAN by receiving signals from an access point (and other devices on a wireless LAN) and retransmitting them. A wireless LAN repeater is often placed in a separate part of the house and is used to allow devices that are too far from the access point to "get on" the wireless LAN.

Wireless Home Networking For Dummies, 2nd Edition

Cheat Sheet

Wireless LAN Technologies

Wireless LAN Technology	Frequency	Maximum Speed	Compatibility	Availability
802.11b (Wi-Fi)	2.4 GHz	11 Mbps	802.11g	Now
802.11a	5 GHz	54 Mbps	None	Now
802.11g	2.4 GHz	54 Mbps	802.11b (at 11 Mbps)	Now
Pre-802.11n	2.4 GHz	100 Mbps+	802.11g (at 54 Mbps) / 802.11b (at 11 Mbps)	Now
802.11n	2.4 GHz or 5 GHz	100 Mbps+	802.11g (at 54 Mbps) / 802.11b (at 11 Mbps)	2006 or later

Wireless Home Network Equipment Requirements

Stuff You Need	Quantity You Need
Broadband DSL or cable modem connection	One
Wireless LAN access point (AP)	One (or maybe more if you have a big house)
Cat 5e patch cable*	Two: A short one, to connect AP to broadband modem, and a 100-foot one, for troubleshooting and emergencies
Wireless LAN network adapters	One per computer
Wireless Ethernet bridge	One per other networked device with Ethernet port (for example, Xbox)
Home network router	One (optional; usually included in access point)
Wireless repeater	One or more (optional)

*Make sure that your broadband router, AP, and other gear comes with a Cat 5e patch cable, or be sure to buy one separately in addition to the cable you need in order to connect the AP to the broadband router (if your AP doesn't come with a cable).

For Dummies: Bestselling Book Series for Beginners

Wireless Home Networking

FOR

DUMMIES®

2ND EDITION

Wireless Home Networking

FOR

DUMMIES®

2ND EDITION

by Danny Briere, Pat Hurley, and Edward Ferris

Wiley Publishing, Inc.

Wireless Home Networking For Dummies,® 2nd Edition

Published by
Wiley Publishing, Inc.
111 River Street
Hoboken, NJ 07030-5774
www.wiley.com

WILEY

About the Authors

Danny Briere founded TeleChoice, Inc., a telecommunications consulting company, in 1985 and now serves as CEO of the company. Widely known throughout the telecommunications and networking industry, Danny has written more than 1,000 articles about telecommunications topics and has authored or edited eight books, including *Internet Telephony For Dummies, Smart Homes For Dummies,* 2nd Edition, *HDTV For Dummies, Windows XP Media Center Edition 2004 PC For Dummies, Wireless Network Hacks & Mods For Dummies,* and *Home Theater For Dummies* (all published by Wiley Publishing, Inc.). He is frequently quoted by leading publications on telecommunications and technology topics and can often be seen on major TV networks providing analysis on the latest communications news and breakthroughs. Danny lives in Mansfield Center, Connecticut, with his wife and four children.

Pat Hurley is director of research with TeleChoice, Inc., specializing in emerging telecommunications technologies, including all the latest access and home technologies: wireless LANs, DSL, cable modems, satellite services, and home networking services. Pat frequently consults with the leading telecommunications carriers, equipment vendors, consumer goods manufacturers, and other players in the telecommunications and consumer electronics industries. Pat is the co-author of *Internet Telephony For Dummies, Smart Homes For Dummies,* 2nd Edition, *HDTV For Dummies, Windows XP Media Center Edition 2004 PC For Dummies, Wireless Network Hacks & Mods For Dummies,* and *Home Theater For Dummies* (all published by Wiley). He lives in San Diego, California, with his wife, beautiful daughter, and two smelly and unruly dogs.

Edward Ferris is a consultant and manager of information systems with TeleChoice, Inc., specializing in wired and wireless networking and security technologies, including all the latest VoIP technologies: SIP, vPBX, Hybrid PBX, QoS, and packet labeling and switching. Ed frequently consults with companies looking to tighten information security and expand network operations. He has written many training and technology manuals for corporate use and has created custom training materials and seminars for numerous applications and business processes. He lives in Norwood, Massachusetts, with his wife and three children.

Authors' Acknowledgments

Danny wants to thank his wife, Holly, and kids, for their infinite patience while he and Pat wrestled with this book toward the finish line. He agrees that the wireless Webcam in the shower was not a good idea. (Just kidding.) He also wants to thank his sister, Michelle, for all her hard work over the years that has made it possible to continue to survive in this crazy business environment — we could not have made it without her. He also wants to note that he got his pot rack (see *Smart Homes For Dummies,* 2nd Edition, for details). Now, if we can only talk her into the 42-inch Samsung HDTV he wants.

Ed wants to thank his wife, Maureen (Moe), for letting him take all the extra time to write instead of painting the house, mowing the lawn, and putting the kids to bed at night and for generally letting him get away with locking himself in the basement for untold hours to "create!" He also wants to thank her for all her support as a test subject and pre-editor of everything he types. Without her to say "Okay, now it makes sense to me," much of the instructional material in this book would not have gotten done.

Pat, as always, thanks his wife, Christine, for providing her impeccable "Can I write this wisecrack and not get in trouble?" judgment, and for her ability to restrain her desire to knock him over the head with a big frying pan when deadlines and late-night writing intrude on their domestic tranquility. He also wants to thank her for letting him hog the computers *and* the sofa while writing.

Danny and Pat want to thank the following people and organizations for their support in writing this book: Doug Hagan and Mehrshad Mansouri, at NET-GEAR; Dana Brzozkiewicz, at Lages & Associates, for ZyXEL; Trisha King, at NetPR, for SMC Networks; Fred Bargetzi, at Crestron; Shawn Gusz, at G-NET Canada (still waiting to try Auroras in our cars!); Karen Sohl, at Linksys; Keith Smith, at Siemon; Darek Connole and Michael Scott, at D-Link; Jeff Singer, at Crestron: Amy K Schiska-Lombard, at Sprint; Brad Shewmake, at Kyocera Wireless; James Cortese, at A&R Partners, for Roku; Bryan McLeod, at Intrigue Technologies (now part of Logitech); Bill Bullock, at Full Mesh Networks; Stu Elefant, at Wireless Security Corporation (now part of McAfee); Craig Slawson, at CorAccess (good luck, too!); and others who helped get the content correct for our readers.

Thanks also to our acquisitions editor, Melody Layne, who by now knows, from here to eternity, every product that will be wirelessly enabled, and to our project editor, Rebecca Whitney, who has the patience of a saint. Melody has been working with us on digital-homes titles for long enough that we would all feel old if we dwelled upon it. Thanks, Melody, for hanging in there with us.

Publisher's Acknowledgments

We're proud of this book; please send us your comments through our online registration form located at www.dummies.com/register/.

Some of the people who helped bring this book to market include the following:

Acquisitions, Editorial, and Media Development

Project Editor: Rebecca Whitney

Acquisitions Editor: Melody Layne

Technical Editor: Dan DiNicolo

Editorial Manager: Jodi Jensen

Media Development Supervisor: Richard Graves

Editorial Assistant: Amanda Foxworth

Cartoons: Rich Tennant
(www.the5thwave.com)

Composition Services

Project Coordinator: Kathryn Shanks

Layout and Graphics: Carl Byers, Lauren Goddard, Joyce Haughey, Stephanie D. Jumper, Erin Zeltner

Proofreaders: Leeann Harney, Dwight Ramsey, TECHBOOKS Production Services

Indexer: TECHBOOKS Production Services

Publishing and Editorial for Technology Dummies

    Richard Swadley, Vice President and Executive Group Publisher

    Andy Cummings, Vice President and Publisher

    Mary Bednarek, Executive Acquisitions Director

    Mary C. Corder, Editorial Director

Publishing for Consumer Dummies

    Diane Graves Steele, Vice President and Publisher

    Joyce Pepple, Acquisitions Director

Composition Services

    Gerry Fahey, Vice President of Production Services

    Debbie Stailey, Director of Composition Services

Contents at a Glance

Table of Contents

Introduction

*W*elcome to *Wireless Home Networking For Dummies,* 2nd Edition. Wireless networking for personal computers isn't really a new idea; it has been around since the late 1990s. The emergence of an industry standard, however, has caused the use of wireless networking technology to explode.

One of the most appealing things about the current crop of wireless networking equipment is the ease with which you can set up a home network, although its reasonable price may be its most attractive aspect. Setting up a wireless home network can be both inexpensive and easy. In some cases, it's almost as simple as opening the box and plugging in the equipment; however, you can avoid many "gotchas" by doing a little reading beforehand. That's where this book comes in handy.

About This Book

If you're thinking about purchasing a wireless computer network and installing it in your home, this is the book for you. Even if you have already purchased the equipment for a wireless network, this book will help you install and configure the network. What's more, this book will help you get the most out of your investment after it's up and running.

With *Wireless Home Networking For Dummies,* 2nd Edition, in hand, you have all the information you need to know about the following topics (and more):

- ✔ Planning your wireless home network
- ✔ Evaluating and selecting wireless networking equipment for installation in your home
- ✔ Installing and configuring wireless networking equipment in your home
- ✔ Sharing an Internet connection over your wireless network
- ✔ Sharing files, printers, and other peripherals over your wireless network
- ✔ Playing computer games over your wireless network

✔ Connecting your audiovisual gear to your wireless network

✔ Securing your wireless network against prying eyes

✔ Discovering devices that you can connect to your wireless home network

System Requirements

Virtually any personal computer can be added to a wireless home network, although some computers are easier to add than others. This book focuses on building a wireless network that connects PCs running the Windows operating system (Windows 2000 and XP) or the Mac OS X. If you're using a wireless network on Windows 98 or Me or on Mac OS 9, you can operate a wireless system with the system, but we doubt that you will use it much longer because these systems are less and less able to handle the rapidly increasing requirements of applications and the Internet. As a result, we focus mostly on the most recent operating systems (or OSes) — the ones that have been launched within the past five years or so. Wireless networking is also popular among Linux users, but we don't cover Linux in this book.

Because wireless networking is a relatively new phenomenon, the newest versions of Windows and the Mac OS do the best job of helping you quickly and painlessly set up a wireless network. However, because the primary reason for networking your home computers is to make it possible for all the computers (and peripherals) in your house to communicate, *Wireless Home Networking For Dummies,* 2nd Edition, gives you information about connecting computers that run the latest versions of Windows and the most widely used version of the Mac OS. We also tell you how to connect computers that run some of the older versions of these two operating systems.

How This Book Is Organized

Wireless Home Networking For Dummies, 2nd Edition, is organized into several chapters that are grouped into five parts. The chapters are presented in a logical order — flowing from planning to installing to using your wireless home network — but feel free to use the book as a reference and read the chapters in any order you want.

Part I: Wireless Networking Fundamentals

Part I is a primer on networking and on wireless networking. If you have never used a networked computer — much less attempted to install a network — this part of the book provides background information and technogeek lingo that you need in order to feel comfortable. Chapter 1 presents general networking concepts; Chapter 2 discusses the most popular wireless networking technology and familiarizes you with wireless networking terminology; and Chapter 3 introduces you to several popular alternatives to wireless networking.

Part II: Making Plans

Part II helps you plan for installing your wireless home network. Chapter 4 helps you decide what to connect to the network and where to install wireless networking equipment in your home, and Chapter 5 provides guidance on making buying decisions.

Part III: Installing a Wireless Network

Part III discusses how to install a wireless network in your home and get the network up and running. Whether your computers are Apple Macintosh running the Mac OS (see Chapter 8) or PCs running a Windows operating system (see Chapters 6 and 7), this part of the book explains how to install and configure your wireless networking equipment. In addition, Part III includes a chapter that explains how to use your wireless home network to share a single Internet connection (see Chapter 9). The last chapter in this part covers securing your wireless home network (see Chapter 10).

Part IV: Using a Wireless Network

After you get your wireless home network installed and running, you'll certainly want to use it. Part IV starts by showing you the basics of putting your wireless network to good use: sharing files, folders, printers, and other peripherals (see Chapter 11). We spend some time discussing other cool things you can do over a wireless network, including playing multiuser computer games (see Chapter 12), connecting your audiovisual equipment (see Chapter 13), and operating various types of smart-home conveniences (see Chapter 14).

Bluetooth-enabled devices are becoming more prevalent these days, so you don't want to miss Chapter 15 — or Chapter 16, for that matter, where we describe how to use wireless networking to connect to the Internet through wireless *hot spots* (wireless networks you can connect to when you're on the road — for free or a small cost) in coffee shops, hotels, airports, and other public places. How cool is that?

Part V: The Part of Tens

Part V provides four top-ten lists that we think you'll find interesting — ten frequently asked questions about wireless home networking (see Chapter 17); ten troubleshooting tips for improving your wireless home network's performance (see Chapter 18); ten devices to connect to your wireless home network — sometime in the future (check out Chapter 19); and the top ten sources for more information about wireless networking (turn to Chapter 20).

Icons Used in This Book

All of us these days are hyperbusy people, with no time to waste. To help you find the especially useful nuggets of information in this book, we have marked the information with little icons in the margin.

As you can probably guess, the Tip icon calls your attention to information that saves you time or maybe even money. If your time is really crunched, you may try just skimming through the book and reading the tips.

The little bomb in the margin should alert you to pay close attention and tread softly. You don't want to waste time or money fixing a problem that could have been avoided in the first place.

This icon is your clue that you should take special note of the advice you find there — or that this paragraph reinforces information that has been provided elsewhere in the book. Bottom line: You will accomplish the task more effectively if you remember this information.

Face it, computers and wireless networks are high-tech toys — we mean *tools* — that make use of some pretty complicated technology. For the most part, however, you don't need to know how it all works. The Technical Stuff icon identifies the paragraphs you can simply skip if you're in a hurry or you just don't care to know.

Where to Go from Here

Where you should go next in this book depends on where you are in the process of planning, buying, installing, configuring, or using your wireless home network. If networking in general and wireless networking in particular are totally new to you, we recommend that you start at the beginning, with Part I. When you feel comfortable with networking terminology, or you just get bored with the lingo, move on to the chapters in Part II about planning your network and selecting equipment. If you already have your equipment in hand, head to Part III to get it installed — and secured (unless you *like* the idea of your neighbor or even a hacker being able to access your network).

The wireless industry is changing fast. We provide regular updates on this book at www.digitaldummies.com so that you can see what changes, as it changes, chapter by chapter.

Happy wireless networking!

Part I
Wireless Networking Fundamentals

The 5th Wave   By Rich Tennant

EXPERIMENTING WITH THE WIRELESS LASER BEAM NETWORK

"Okay–did you get that?"

In this part . . .

*I*f you have never used a networked computer or you're installing a network in your home for the first time, this part of the book provides all the background info and down-and-dirty basics that will have you in the swing of things in no time. Here, you can find general networking concepts, the most popular wireless networking technology, wireless networking terminology, and several popular alternatives to wireless networking.

Chapter 1

Introducing Wireless Home Networking

In This Chapter

▶ Jump-starting your wireless revolution at home

▶ Comparing wired and wireless networks — and why wireless wins!

▶ Picking out a wireless standard to meet your needs

▶ Choosing the right wireless equipment

▶ Planning for your wireless home network

*W*elcome to the wireless age! Nope, we're not talking about your grandfather's radio — we're talking about just about everything under the sun — truly. What's not going wireless? Wanna say your refrigerator? Wrong — it is. How about your stereo? Yup, that too. Watches, keychains, baby video monitors, high-end projectors — even your thermostat is going wireless and going digital. It's not just about computers any more! Your entire world is going wireless, and in buying this book, you're determined not to get left behind. Kudos to you!

A driving force behind the growing popularity of wireless networking is its reasonable cost: You can save money by not running network wiring all over your house, by spending less on Internet connections, by sharing peripherals (such as printers and scanners), and by using your PC to drive other applications around your home, like your home entertainment center, or to talk on the phone. This book helps you spend your money wisely by helping you decide what you need to buy and helping you choose between the products that are on the market. Wireless networks are not only less expensive than more traditional wired networks, but are also much easier to install. An important goal of this book is to provide you with "the skinny" on how to install a wireless network in your home.

Whether you have one computer or several, you have several good reasons to want a personal computer network that until recently just didn't exist. The plummeting cost of wireless technologies, combined with their fast-paced technical development, has meant that more and more manufacturers are getting on the home networking bandwagon. That means that more applications around your house will try to ride your wireless backbone — by talking among themselves and to the Internet. So, wireless is here to stay and is critical for any future-proofed home.

Nothing But Net (work): Why You Need (Or Want) One

Wireless home networking isn't just about linking computers to the Internet. Although that task is important — nay, critical — in today's network-focused environment, it's not the whole enchilada. Of the many benefits of having wireless in the home, most have one thing in common: sharing. When you connect the computers in your house through a network, you can share files, printers, scanners, and high-speed Internet connections between them. In addition, you can play multiuser games over your network, access public wireless networks while you're away from home, check wireless cameras, use Internet Voice over IP (VoIP) services, or even enjoy your MP3s in your stereo system from work — really!

Reading *Wireless Home Networking For Dummies,* 2nd Edition, helps you understand how to create a whole-home wireless network to reach the nooks and crannies of your house. Wireless home networks don't have to be all about your PC. The big initial reason that people have wanted to put wireless networks in their homes has been to "unwire" their PCs, especially laptops, to enable more freedom of access in the home. But, just about every major consumer goods manufacturer is hard at work wirelessly enabling its devices so that they too can talk to other devices in the home.

Along these lines, we encourage you to think of your wireless home network as another utility network in your house — just like electricity or just like water. Rather than have outlets or spigots, your connection is in the air floating around your head. If you have a device that has the right protocols and passwords — and is in range — it can log on to this wireless *backbone* in your home. Over this backbone can ride data, running between computers and the Internet; MP3s, going from your stereo to your car; videos, from the Internet to your TV set; phones on your regular phone lines or over the Internet; and more. As you find more and more consumer devices sporting wireless interfaces, you can be happy that you have a wireless home network for them to log on to and link to your other devices and network connections — and your PC!

File sharing

As you probably know, computer *files* are created whenever you use a computer. If you use a word processing program, such as Microsoft Word, to write a document, Word saves the document on your computer's hard drive as an electronic file. Similarly, if you balance your checkbook by using Intuit Quicken, this software saves your financial data on the computer's drive in an electronic file.

A computer network lets you share those electronic files between two or more computers. For example, you can create a Word document on your computer, and your spouse, roommate, child, sibling, or whoever can pull the same document up on her computer screen over the network. With the right programs, you can even view the same documents at the same time!

But, here's where you get into semantics: What's a computer? Your car has more computing and networking capability than the early moon rockets. Your stereo is increasingly looking like a computer with a black matte finish. Even your refrigerator and microwave are getting onboard computing capabilities — and they all have files and information that need to be shared.

The old way of moving files between computers and computing devices involved copying the files to a floppy disk and then carrying the disk to the other computer. Computer geeks call this method of copying and transferring files the *sneakernet* approach. In contrast, copying files between computers is easy to do over a home network and with no need for floppy disks (or sneakers). It's almost as simple as copying files from your computer's hard drive to a floppy disk.

What's interesting is that more computers and devices are getting "used to" talking to one another over networks in an automated fashion. A common application is *synchronization*, where two devices talk to one another and make the appropriate updates to each other's stored information so that they're current with one another. Rockford Corporation (www.omnifimedia.com), for example, offers MP3 servers for cars that have wireless connectivity built in so that when your car returns home, it can "talk" to your wireless home network and computers and add any new CDs to its hard drives that your spouse may have added while you were gone. That way, you always have your music, "podcasts," and audiobooks at your fingertips — literally.

Printer and peripheral sharing

Businesses with computer networks have discovered a major benefit: sharing printers. Companies invest in high-speed, high-capacity printers that are shared by many employees. Sometimes an entire department shares a single printer or perhaps a cluster of printers is located in an area of the office set aside for printers, copy machines, and fax machines.

Just like in a business network, all the computers on your home network can share the printers on your network. The cost-benefit of shared printers in a home network is certainly not as dramatic as in a business, but the opportunity to save money by sharing printers is clearly one of the real benefits of setting up a home network. Figure 1-1 depicts a network through which three personal computers can share the same printer.

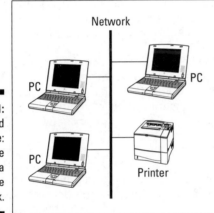

Figure 1-1:
Share and share alike: Share one printer via your home network.

Other peripherals, such as extra storage for your computers or for all those MP3s that someone in the household might be downloading, also are great to share. Anything connected to your PCs or which has a network port (we talk about these in great detail throughout the book) can be shared anywhere on your wireless network.

Internet connection sharing

Another driving reason behind many homeowners' interest in wireless home networking is a desire to share an Internet connection. As the Internet becomes a critical part of day-to-day living — from kids doing their homework to your managing your bank account — it's only natural that more than one person in the household wants to get online at the same time. And, with the sudden interest in *broadband connections* — cable, digital subscriber line (DSL), and satellite modems — for Internet connections, we can guess that the demand at home has only soared.

High-speed *(broadband)* Internet service is very appealing. Not only is the connection to the Internet as much as 50 times or more faster than a dial-up connection, with sharing enabled over your wireless network, all the computers connected to the network can access the Internet at one time through the same broadband service for one monthly fee. (It can be as low as $14.95 per month in some areas.) And, you can surf and talk on the phone at the same time. No more having your dial-up connection tie up your phone line!

Modem types

Your wireless network helps you distribute information throughout the home. It's independent of the method you use to access your outside-of-home networks, like the Internet. Whether you use a dial-up connection or broadband, your wireless home network will be applicable.

- **Dial-up modem:** This device connects to the Internet by dialing an Internet service provider (ISP), such as America Online (AOL) or EarthLink, over a standard phone line.

- **Cable modem:** This type of modem connects to the Internet through the same cable as cable TV. Cable modems connect to the Internet at much higher speeds than dial-up modems and can be left connected to the Internet all day, every day.

- **DSL modem:** Digital subscriber line modems use your phone line, but they permit the phone to be free for other purposes — voice calls and faxes, for example — even while the DSL modem is in use. DSL modems also connect to the Internet at much higher speeds than dial-up modems and can be left connected 24 and 7.

- **Broadband wireless modem:** The same wireless airwaves that are great for around the house communications are great for connecting to the Internet as well. Although the frequency may be different and the bandwidth much less, broadband wireless modems give you connectivity to your home's wireless net, in a similar fashion as DSL and cable modems.

- **Satellite modem:** Satellite modems tie in to your satellite dish and give you two-way communications even if you're in the middle of the woods. Although they're typically not as fast as cable modems and DSL links, they're better than dial-up and available just about anywhere in the continental United States.

- **Fiber optic modem:** We're at the front end of the fiber-fed revolution as the telephone and cable companies push to outcompete each other by installing extremely high-capacity fiber optic lines in homes to allow all sorts of cool applications. Until now, the broadband access link has been the limiting bottleneck as wireless networks tried to communication with the Internet. With fiber optics, you could see the broadband access capacity equal that of your wireless network.

Phone jacks versus a network

Most homes built in the past 20 years have a phone jack (outlet) in the wall in every room in the house where you would likely use your computer. Consequently, connecting your computer to the Internet via a dial-up modem over a telephone line doesn't require a network. You simply run a phone line from your computer's modem to the phone jack in the wall and you're in business.

However, without a network or Internet connection sharing turned on at the computer, the connection cannot be shared between computers; only one computer can use a given phone line at any given time. Not good.

With a wireless home network, we can help you extend that modem connection throughout the home. The same is true with your broadband modem — it can be shared throughout the home.

Sure, you could have more than one cable or DSL modem in your house, but don't bother. Because of their speed (bandwidth), cable and DSL modems can easily handle the Internet traffic generated by many individual computers, just like a 50-lane interstate can handle lots of cars at one time. Use a network to connect multiple computers to a cable modem or DSL modem to share an Internet connection.

When configuring your PCs on a network, you can buy equipment that lets you connect multiple computers to a regular or high-speed modem through the phone lines — or even through the coaxial wiring or the power lines — in your house. No matter what the physical connection is among your networked devices, the most popular language (or *protocol)* used in connecting computers to a broadband modem is to use a network technology known as Ethernet. *Ethernet* is an industry standard protocol used in virtually every corporation and institution; consequently, Ethernet equipment is plentiful and inexpensive. The most common form of Ethernet networking uses special cables known as *Category 5 UTP* (or unshielded twisted pair). These networks are named after their speed — most are 100 Mbps (much faster than alternative networks that run over powerlines or phone lines) and are called 100BaseT (you also find 1000BaseT networks, which run at 1 *giga*bit per second. Figure 1-2 illustrates a network that enables three personal computers to connect to the Internet through a DSL or cable modem (it works the same for a satellite or dial-up modem).

See Chapter 4 for more information about planning and budgeting for your network and Chapter 5 for help in selecting your wireless networking equipment.

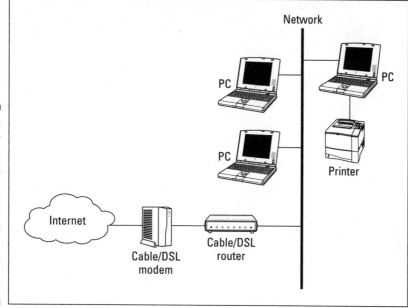

Figure 1-2:
Internet for all: Set up a network that enables many PCs to connect to the Internet through a DSL or cable modem.

Phone calling for free

With some new wireless phone capabilities, you can get rid of the static of your cordless phone and move digital over your wireless home network, thus saving money on calls by using less-expensive, Internet-based phone calling options. What started as a hobbyist error-prone service has grown into a full-fledged worldwide phenomenon — phone calling over the Internet is now ready for prime time.

- ✔ **Free and for-fee services are available.** Services like Vonage (`www.vonage.com`) and Skype (`www.skype.com`) allow you to use your regular phones to call over the Internet for free or low-cost monthly services.

- ✔ **Add-ons to popular software programs are available.** Internet calling and even videoconferencing has been added to instant messaging programs like AOL Instant Messenger (AIM) so that you can talk to the people you used to only "IM" with.

- ✔ **New devices make it simple.** New devices, such as the Olympia DualPhone (`www.dualphone.net`), are designed to ease access to these Internet calling services — so that you don't have to don a headset every time you want to make a phone call.

The best part is that it's all moving toward wireless too. Throw away that old cordless phone and replace it with a new wireless handset or a neat Wi-Fi phone that you can take on the road to make free calls from any Wi-Fi network on the road.

The convergence of wireless and Voice over IP is one of the major megatrends going on in the telecommunications and Internet markets today — you can bet that you want it in your home too!

Home arcades and wireless to go

If you aren't convinced yet that a wireless home network is for you, we have four more points that just may change your mind. Check them out:

- **Multiuser games over the network:** If you're into video games, multiplayer card games, or role-playing games, you may find multiuser games over the network or even over the Internet fascinating. Chapter 12 discusses how to use your wireless network to play multiuser games.

- **Audio anywhere in the household:** Why spend money on CDs and keep them stacked next to your stereo? Load them on your PC and make them wirelessly available to your stereo, your car, your MP3 player that you take jogging, and lots more. Check out Chapter 13 for more info on how to use your wireless network to send audio and video signals around the house.

- **Check your home wireless cam:** You can check out your house from anywhere in the house — or in the world — with new wireless cameras that hop on your home network and broadcast images privately or publicly over the Internet. Want to see whether your kids are tearing apart the house while you're working in your office downstairs? Just call up your wireless-networked camera and check them out. (In our generation, we always said, "Mom has eyes in the back of her head"; this generation will probably think that Mom is omniscient!)

- **Wireless on the go:** This concept is great if you have a portable computer. Many airports, hotels, malls, and coffee shops have installed public wireless networks that enable you, via hot spots, to connect to the Internet (for a small fee, of course). See Chapter 16 for more information about using wireless networking while away from home.

Wired versus Wireless

Ethernet is the most-often-used method of connecting personal computers to form a network because it's fast and its equipment is relatively inexpensive.

In addition, Ethernet can be transmitted over several types of network cable or sent through the air by using wireless networking equipment. Many new computers have an Ethernet connection built in, ready for you to plug in a network cable. The most popular wireless networking equipment transmits a form of Ethernet — simply using radio waves rather than Category 5e cables.

Installing wired home networks

Even though we're talking mostly about wireless networks in this book and how great they are, we would be misleading you if we told you that wireless is the only way to go. Wireless and wired homes each have advantages.

Wired homes are

- ✔ **Faster:** Wired lines can reach speeds of 1000 Mbps, whereas wireless homes tend to be in the 10 Mbps to 100 Mbps range. Both wireless and wired technologies are getting faster and faster, but wired will always be ahead.

- ✔ **More reliable:** Wireless signals are prone to interference and fluctuations, and degrade quickly over short distances; wired connections typically are more stable and reliable all over your home.

- ✔ **More secure:** You don't have to worry about your signals traveling through the air and being intercepted by snoopers, as you do with unsecured wireless systems.

- ✔ **Economical over the long term:** The incremental cost of adding Cat 5e voice and data cabling and RG-6 coaxial cabling into your house — over a 30-year mortgage — will be almost nothing each month.

- ✔ **Salable:** More and more home buyers are not only looking for well-wired homes but also discounting homes without the infrastructure. As good as wireless is, it isn't affixed to the house and is carried with you when you leave. Most new homes have structure wiring in the walls.

 If you're building a new home or renovating an old one, we absolutely recommend that you consider running the latest wiring in the walls to each of your rooms. That doesn't mean that you won't have a wireless network in your home — you will. It just will be different than if you were wholly reliant on wireless for your networking.

If you choose to use network cable, it should ideally be installed in the walls, just like electrical and phone wiring. Network jacks (outlets) are installed in the walls in rooms where you would expect to use a computer. Connecting your computer to a wired network is as easy as plugging a phone into a phone jack — after the wiring is in place, that is.

Without question, the most economical time to install network cable in a home is during the home's initial construction. In upscale neighborhoods, especially in communities near high-tech businesses, builders often wire new homes with network cable as a matter of course. In most cases, however, the installation of network cable in a new home is an option or upgrade that's installed only if the new owner orders it and pays a premium. Installing a structured wiring solution for a home can cost at least $2,000–$3,000, and that's for starters.

Although the installation of network cable in an existing home certainly possible, it's much more difficult and expensive than installing cable during construction. If you hire an electrician to run the cable, you can easily spend thousands of dollars to do what would have cost a few hundred dollars during your home's construction. If you're comfortable drilling holes in your walls and crawling around in attics and crawl spaces, you can install the cabling yourself for the cost of the cable and outlets.

The reality is that no home will ever be purely wireless or wireline (wired). Each approach has benefits and costs, and they coexist in any house. If you're building a new house, most experts tell you to spend the extra money on a structured wiring solution because it adds value to your house and you can better manage all the wiring in your home. We agree. But no wiring solution can be everywhere you want it to be. Thus, wireless is a great complement to your home, which is why we advocate a whole-home wireless network for your entire home to use.

Installing wireless home networks

If you're networking an existing home or are renting your home, wireless has fabulous benefits:

- **Portable:** You can take your computing device anywhere in the house and be on the network. Even if you have a huge house, you can interconnect wireless access points to have a whole-home wireless network.

- **Flexible:** You're not limited to where a jack is on the wall; you can network anywhere.

- **Cost effective:** You can start wireless networking for a couple of hundred dollars. Your wiring contractor can't do much with that!

- **Clean:** You don't have to tear down walls or trip over wires when they come out from underneath the carpeting.

What's more, there's really no difference in how you use your networked computer, whether it's connected to the network by a cable or by a wireless networking device. Whether you're sharing files, a printer, your entertainment system, or the Internet over the network, the procedures are the same on a wireless network as on a wired network. In fact, you can mix wired and wireless network equipment on the same network with no change in how you use a computer on the network.

It's time for the fine print. We would be remiss if we weren't candid and mention any potential drawbacks to wireless networks compared with wired networks. The possible drawbacks fall into four categories:

✔ **Data speed:** Wireless networking equipment transmits data at slower speeds than wired networking equipment. Wired networks are already networking at gigabit speeds, although the fastest current wireless networking standards (in the best situations) top out at 54 Mbps. (Some vendors have proprietary extensions that take the speed higher, but even these top out at a little more than 100 Mbps in the best scenarios.) But, for almost all the uses we can think of now (with the possible exception of high-definition video), this rate is plenty fast. Your Internet connection probably doesn't exceed a few Mbps in speed (though those lucky folks who get fiber optic lines run to their homes may exceed this rate by a big margin!), so your wireless connection should be more than fast enough.

✔ **Radio signal range:** Wireless signals fade when you move away from the source. Some homes, especially older homes, may be built from materials that tend to block the radio signals used by wireless networking equipment, which causes even faster signal degradation. If your home has plaster walls that contain a wire mesh, the wireless networking equipment's radio signal may not reach all points in your home. Most modern construction, however, uses drywall materials that reduce the radio signal only slightly. As a result, most homeowners can reach all points in their home with one centralized wireless *access point* (also called a *base station*) and one wireless device in or attached to each personal computer. And, if you need better coverage, you can just add another access point — we show you how in Chapter 18 — or you can upgrade to a newer technology, like 802.11n (when available), which promises farther coverage within your home.

✔ **Radio signal interference:** The most common type of wireless networking technology uses a radio frequency that's also used by other home devices, such as microwave ovens and portable telephones. Some wireless home network users, as a consequence, experience network problems (the network slows down or the signal is dropped) caused by radio signal interference.

✔ **Security:** The radio signal from a wireless network doesn't stop at the outside wall of your home. A neighbor or even a total stranger could access your network from an adjoining property or from the street unless you implement some type of security technology to prevent unauthorized access. To prevent unauthorized access, you can safeguard yourself with security technology that comes standard with the most popular wireless home networking technology. However, it's not bulletproof, and it certainly doesn't work if you don't turn it on. For more information on wireless security, go to Chapter 10.

For our money, wireless networks compare favorably with wired networks for most homeowners who didn't have network wiring installed when their houses were built. As we mention earlier in this chapter, even if you do have network wires in your walls, you probably want wireless just to provide the "untethered" access it brings to laptops and handheld computers.

Picking a Wireless Standard

The good news about wireless networks is that they come in multiple flavors, each with its own advantages and disadvantages. The bad news is that trying to decide which version to get when buying a system can get confusing. The good news is that, very rapidly, the dropping prices of the wireless systems and fast-paced development is creating dual- and tri-mode systems on the market that can speak many different wireless languages.

Here are the three major wireless systems now on the market:

- **802.11a:** Wireless networks that use the Institute of Electrical and Electronics Engineers (IEEE) 802.11a standard use the 5 GHz radio frequency band. Equipment of this type is among the fastest wireless networking equipment widely available to consumers.

- **802.11b:** Wireless home networks that use the 802.11b standard use the 2.4 GHz radio band. This standard is the most popular in terms of numbers of installed networks and numbers of users.

- **802.11g:** The latest member of the 802.11 wireless family to hit the mainstream, 802.11g has rapidly taken over the market. In many ways, 802.11g offers the best of both worlds — backward compatibility with 802.11b networks (it too operates over the 2.4 GHz radio frequency band) and the speed of 802.11a networks. And, the cost of 802.11g has dropped so precipitously that it's hardly more expensive than 802.11b, when you take into account rebates and incentive programs. For this reason, 802.11g has become the de facto solution that most users now buy.

A new standard, 802.11n, just being developed as this book goes to press. The first Pre-N units are on the streets, and they're fabulous in terms of speed, coverage, and ease of setup (we love the Belkin Wireless Pre-N Router [www.belkin.com]). There's still much to be determined about 802.11n as we write — including whether it will operate in the 2.4 or 5GHz range. Still, as this information becomes available, we expect it to be very popular with many wireless applications — and it will most likely support backward compatibility with 802.11b/g networks too.

Equipment that's based on the 802.11a standard doesn't interoperate with equipment based on the 802.11b/g standards. Several manufacturers sell equipment, however, that supports *both* approaches — the best of all worlds. And, if you really want to make sure that you're covered, check out dual-mode, tri-standard 802.11a/b/g wireless networking equipment that's on the streets. It's more expensive, but you maximize your options as well.

Equipment supporting all three finalized standards — 802.11a, 802.11b, and 802.11g — can carry the Wi-Fi logo — a trademark that's short for *wireless fidelity* — that's licensed for use by the Wi-Fi Alliance trade group, based on equipment that passes interoperability testing.

The terms surrounding wireless networking can get complex. First, the order of lettering isn't really right because 802.11*b* was approved and hit the market before 802.11*a*. Also, you see the term *Wi-Fi* used frequently. (In fact, we thought about calling this book *Wi-Fi For Dummies* because the term is used so much.) Wi-Fi refers to the collective group of 802.11 specifications: 802.11a, b, and g. You may sometimes see this group also named *802.11x* networking, where x can equal a, b, or g. To make matters more confusing, a higher-level parent standard named 802.11 predates 802.11a, b, and g and is also used to talk about the group of the three standards. Technically, it's a standards group over several other emerging specifications as well. For simplicity in this book, we use 802.11 and Wi-Fi synonymously to talk about the three standards as a group. We could have used 802.11x, but we want to save a number of *x*s (for our wives).

For the most part, 802.11b equipment is being phased out. If you're buying all new gear, 802.11g or 802.11a (plus some "prestandard" 802.11n stuff) are your real choices. You can still find a few bits of 802.11b gear, but it's mostly sold to fit into older 802.11b networks. If you already have some gear that's 802.11b, don't despair — it still works fine in most cases, and you can upgrade your network to 802.11g bit by bit (pun intended!) without worrying about compatibility. In this section, we still discuss 802.11b, even though it's increasingly not something you're likely to consider.

The differences between these three standards fall into five main categories:

- ✔ **Data speed:** 802.11a and 802.11g networks are almost five times faster than the older 802.1b networks. However, 802.11b networks are faster than most broadband Internet connection. If all you're doing is sharing a 2 or 3 Mbps Internet connection, you can probably get by with 802.11b. If you're doing more with your network (like sharing files), you may want to go with a faster technology like 802.11g or a. (By comparison, the new 802.11n standard is expected to provide speeds even faster than 802.11a/g — perhaps as fast as 100 or 200 Mbps!)

- ✔ **Price:** 802.11a and g networking equipment is typically more expensive than similar 802.11b equipment, but the price differential is minimal.

802.11b equipment has been on the market longer than 802.11a and g with hundreds of products in the marketplace. As a result, 802.11b will probably remain the least expensive version of Wi-Fi for some time. As we mention earlier in this chapter, 802.11g products cost barely more than comparable 802.11b products and will soon replace almost all 802.11b products in vendors' line-ups.

✔ **Radio signal range:** 802.11a wireless networks tend to have a shorter maximum signal range than 802.11b and g networks. The actual distances vary depending on the size and construction of your home. In most modern homes, however, all three of the competing standards should provide adequate range.

✔ **Radio signal interference:** The radio frequency band used by both 802.11b and 802.11g equipment is also used by other home devices, such as microwave ovens and portable telephones, resulting sometimes in network problems caused by radio signal interference. Few other types of devices now use the radio frequency band employed by the 802.11a standard.

✔ **Interoperability:** Because 802.11a and 802.11b/g use different frequency bands, they can't communicate over the same radio. Several manufacturers, however, have products that can operate with both 802.11a and IEEE 802.11b/g equipment simultaneously. By contrast, 802.11g equipment is designed to be backward compatible with 802.11b equipment — both operating on the same frequency band. The forthcoming 802.11n products will interoperate with each other after the standards are finalized, but will support backward compatibility to 802.11b/g if the standard falls in the 2.4GHz range as expected.

Think of dual-mode, multistandard devices as being in the same vein as AM/FM radios. AM and FM stations transmit their signals in different ways, but hardly anyone any more buys a radio that's only AM because almost all the receiving units are AM/FM. The user selects which band she wants to listen to at any particular time. With an 802.11a/b/g device, you can also pick the band that you want to transmit and receive in.

We expect that 802.11g products will be, at minimum, the standard device deployed in most home networks. Adding 802.11a to the mix hasn't been necessary to this point, but having an 802.11 a/b/g device will enable the home network to be able to communicate with the protocols it senses. We would be tempted to tell you not to worry about 802.11a at all — given how much 802.11g has dominated the market — but there are lots of outstanding efforts in the 5GHz range and involving 802.11a for delivering video around the house by set-top manufacturers that it's hard to make a blanket Tony Soprano "fuggettaboutit" statement.

For most home networks, 802.11g wireless networks are the best choice because they're relatively inexpensive, offer the best data speed, and provide more than adequate range for most homes. It's a great way to get started, and you don't need to worry about upgrading from 802.11b to g later on. However, keep an eye on the 802.11n products and their compatibility and price differential with 802.11g — that could be likewise attractive. If you find after reading more about these technologies in this book that 802.11b or a is best for you, that's okay too. The reality is, however, that the combined 802.11a/b/g units "future-proof" you the best if you want to go in that direction. So, you can take either fork in the wireless road. Buy low-cost 802.11g units now and upgrade to a nice 802.11n unit in a few years when costs have come down and all the kinks are worked out. Or, buy one of the 802.11n products that are available now and upgrade that product as needed.

Planning Your Wireless Home Network

Installing and setting up a wireless home network can be ridiculously easy. In some cases, after you unpack and install the equipment, you're up and running in a matter of minutes. To ensure that you don't have a negative experience, however, you should do a little planning. The issues you need to consider during the planning stage include the ones in this list:

✔ Which of your computers will you connect to the network (and will you be connecting Macs and PCs or just one or the other)?

✔ Will all the computers be connected via wireless connections, or will one or more computers be connected by a network cable to the network?

✔ Which wireless technology — 802.11a, 802.11b, or 802.11g — will you use? (Or will you use all of them? Or, will you use 802.11n when it's standardized and available?)

✔ Which type of wireless adapter will you use to connect each computer to the network?

✔ How many printers will you connect to the network?

✔ How will each printer be connected to the network — by connecting it to a computer on the network or by connecting it to a print server?

✔ Will you connect the network to the Internet through a broadband connection (cable or DSL) or dial-up? If so, will you share the Internet connection through a cable/DSL/satellite/dial-up router or by using Internet connection-sharing software?

✔ What other devices might you want to include in your initial wireless network? Do you plan on listening to MP3s on your stereo? How about downloading movies from the Internet (instead of running out in the rain to the movie rental store!)? Will you be using VoIP with your network?

✔ How much money should you budget for your wireless network?

✔ What do you need to do to plan for adequate security to ensure the privacy of the information stored on the computers connected to your network?

We discuss all these issues and the entire planning process in more detail in Chapter 4.

Choosing Wireless Networking Equipment

For those of us big kids who are enamored with technology, shopping for high-tech toys can be therapeutic. Whether you're a closet geek or (cough) normal, a critical step in building a useful wireless home network is choosing the proper equipment.

Before you can decide which equipment to buy, take a look at Chapter 4 for more information about planning a wireless home network. Read Chapter 5 for a more detailed discussion of the different types of wireless networking equipment. Here's a quick list of what you need:

✔ **Access point:** At the top of the list is at least one wireless *access point* (AP), also sometimes called a *base station.* An AP acts like a wireless switchboard that connects wireless devices on the network to each other and to the rest of the network. You gotta have one of these to create a wireless home network. They range from about $30 to $300, with prices continually coming down (prices predominantly are in the $40–$60 range). You can get APs from many leading vendors in the marketplace, including Apple (www.apple.com), D-Link (www.d-link.com), Linksys (www.linksys.com), NETGEAR (www.netgear.com), and Belkin (www.belkin.com). We give you a long list of vendors in Chapter 20, so check that out when you go to buy your AP.

For wireless home networks, the best AP value is often an AP that's bundled with other features. The most popular APs for home use also come with one or more of these features:

- **Network hub or switch:** A *hub* connects wired PCs to the network. A *switch* is a "smarter" version of a hub that speeds up network traffic. (We talk more about the differences between hubs and switches in Chapter 2.)

- **DHCP server:** A *Dynamic Host Configuration Protocol* (DHCP) server assigns network addresses to each computer on the network; these addresses are required for the computers to communicate.

- **Network router:** A *router* enables multiple computers to share a single Internet connection. The network connects each computer to the router, and the router is connected to the Internet through a broadband modem.

- **Print server:** Use a *print server* to add printers directly to the network rather than attach a printer to each computer on the network.

In Figure 1-3, you can see an AP that also bundles in a network router, switch, and DHCP server. You may increasingly see more features added that include support for VoIP routing as well. We talk about more features for your AP in Chapter 5.

TECHNICAL STUFF

The Intel Centrino chip

You may start hearing the term *Centrino* with respect to wireless products. No, it isn't a new atomic particle, but, rather, the new Intel wireless-enabled chip — the chip that will bring wireless connectivity to most laptops on the planet. Representing Intel's best technology for mobile PCs, the Intel Centrino mobile technology includes a new mobile processor, related chipsets, and 802.11 wireless network functions that have been optimized, tested, and validated to work together. If you're in the market for a laptop, you're confronted with a flood of advertising regarding the Centrino chipset. With Intel Inside and wireless at that, you can expect that when your children's friends come to your home for a sleepover, they can wirelessly connect their laptops back to their own homes so that they can say good-night to Mommy.

Figure 1-3:
Look for an AP that bundles a network router, switch, and DHCP server.

✔ **Network interface adapters:** As we mention earlier in this chapter, home networks use a communication method *(protocol)* known as *Ethernet.* The communication that takes place between the components of your computer, however, doesn't use the Ethernet protocol. As a result, for computers on the network to communicate through the Ethernet protocol, each of the computers must translate between their

Connecting to your wireless home network via your PDA or cell phone

One of the few areas of personal computing where Microsoft Windows has not been the dominant software is the area of handheld computers. The PDA devices from Palm became the first big success story in handheld computers in the early 1990s and have maintained their leadership position ever since. Handhelds from Hewlett-Packard (formerly Compaq) and other manufacturers based on the Microsoft Windows Mobile Operating System are finally giving Palm a run for its money. Even though Pocket PCs are still (on the average) more expensive than Palm PDAs, they boast computing power more akin to a full-size PC, running scaled-down versions of the most popular Windows-based application software.

Handheld computers running the Windows Mobile operating system are perfect candidates for wireless network connectivity. By definition, handheld computers are highly portable.

Here are a couple of reasons that going wireless with Windows Mobile may be worth the trouble. You can

- ✔ **Wirelessly synchronize** your address book, calendar, inbox, and other applications on your Pocket PC with your desktop computer from anywhere in your house without needing to plug into the docking station.

- ✔ **Access the Internet** from your Pocket PC, both over your wireless home network and

at wireless hot spots, such as in Starbucks coffee shops and in many airports and hotels.

- ✔ **Connect to other Pocket PC devices.** For example, mobile businesspeople can exchange files or even electronic business cards via a wireless connection.

- ✔ **Download MP3 files** to play on your Pocket PC.

The thought of being able to access your e-mail or browse the Internet on your handheld while sipping a latté in Starbucks is compelling. After you get your handheld set up with a wireless connection, synchronizing your calendar and phone list becomes a snap. But, you need a Secure Digital Input/Output (SDIO) card in order to do it. See Chapter 2 for more details about this new category of wireless network adapter. Chapter 7 walks you through the process of installing wireless network adapters and getting your PDA ready for Internet access.

More and more cell phones are coming out with Bluetooth embedded as well as Wi-Fi on board. You can do everything you can do with a PDA on some of these phones, which makes them your music-playing, phone talking, Internet browsing, photo-sharing iPod/cell phone/PDAs all-in-one devices (and it doesn't weigh a ton!).

---

internal communications protocol and Ethernet. The device that handles this translation is a *network interface adapter,* and each computer on the network needs one. Prices for network interface adapters are typically much less than $30, and most new computers come with one at no additional cost.

A network interface adapter that's installed inside a computer is usually called a *network interface card* (NIC). Many computer manufacturers now include as a standard feature an Ethernet NIC with each personal computer.

✓ **Wireless network interface adapter:** To wirelessly connect a computer to the network, you must obtain a wireless network interface adapter for each computer. Prices range between $50 and $150. A few portable computers now even come with a wireless network interface built in. They're very easy to use; most are adapters that just plug in.

The four most common types of wireless network interface adapters are

- **PC Card:** This type of adapter is often used in laptop computers because most laptops have one or two PC Card slots. Figure 1-4 shows a PC Card wireless network interface adapter.

Figure 1-4: A PC Card wireless network interface adapter.

- **SDIO card:** A *Secure Digital Input Output* (SDIO) card adapter is smaller than a PC Card adapter and enables you to link a Pocket PC or other palm-size computer to your network. Many high-end personal digital assistants (PDAs) now even come with wireless capability built-in, obviating the need for a wireless adapter.

- **USB:** A *Universal Serial Bus* (USB) adapter connects to one of your computer's USB ports; these USB ports have been available in most computers built in the past four or five years.

- **ISA or PCI adapter:** If your computer doesn't have a PC Card slot, SDIO card slot, or USB port, you have to either install a network interface card or a USB card (for a USB wireless network interface adapter) in one of the computer's internal peripheral expansion receptacles (slots). The expansion slots in older PCs are Industry Standard Architecture (ISA) slots. The internal expansion slots in newer PCs and Apple Macintosh computers follow the Peripheral Component Interconnect (PCI) standard.

More and more PDAs, laptops, and other devices are shipping with wireless already onboard, so you don't need an adapter of any sort. It just comes with the wireless installed in the device. We tell you how to get your wireless-enabled devices onto your wireless backbone in Part II of this book.

Chapter 2

From a to g and b-yond

*U*ntil very recently, networked computers were connected only by wire: a special-purpose network cabling. This type of wiring has yet to become a standard item in new homes, but we're getting closer, with more people asking to have a home wired from the start. That's a different book: *Smart Homes For Dummies* (also from Wiley and which we hope you consider when you're buying a new home). The cost of installing network cabling after a house is already built is understandably much higher than doing so during initial construction. By contrast, the cost of installing a wireless network in a particular home is a fraction of the cost of wiring the same residence — and much less hassle. As a result, because more and more people are beginning to see the benefits of having a computer network at home, they're turning to wireless networks in growing numbers. Many of us can no longer recall life without wireless phones; similarly, wireless computer networking is fast becoming the standard way to network a home.

That's not to say that it's easy, though. Face it: Life can sometimes seem a bit complicated. The average Joe or Jane can't even order a cup of java any more without having to choose between an endless array of options: regular, decaf, half-caf, mocha, cappuccino, latté, low fat, no fat, foam, no foam, and so on. Of course, after you get the hang of the lingo, you can order coffee like a pro. That's where this chapter comes in — to help you get used to the networking lingo that's slung about when you're planning, purchasing, installing, and using your wireless network.

Like so much alphabet soup, the prevalent wireless network technologies go by names like 802.11a, 802.11b, and 802.11g, employ devices such as APs and PC Cards, and make use of technologies with cryptic abbreviations (TCP/IP,

DHCP, NAT, MIMO, WEP, and WPA). Pshew. Whether you're shopping for, installing, or configuring a wireless network, you will undoubtedly run across some or all of these not-so-familiar terms and more. This chapter is your handy guide to this smorgasbord of networking and wireless networking terminology.

If you're not the least bit interested in buzzwords, you can safely skip this chapter for now and go right to the chapters that cover planning, purchasing, installing, and using your wireless network. You can always refer to this chapter whenever you run into some wireless networking terminology that throws you. If you like knowing a little bit about the language the locals speak before visiting a new place, read on.

Networking Buzzwords You Need to Know

A computer *network* is composed of computers or network-accessible devices — and sometimes other peripheral devices, such as printers — connected in a way that they transmit data between participants. Computer networks have been commonplace in offices for nearly 20 years, but with the advent of reasonably priced wireless networks, computer networks are becoming increasingly common in homes. Now, we mere mortals can share printers, surf the Internet, play multiplayer video games, and stream video like the corporate gods have been doing for years.

A computer network that connects devices in a particular physical location, such as in a home or in a single office site, is sometimes called a *local-area network* (LAN). Conversely, the network outside your home that connects you to the Internet and beyond is called a *wide-area network* (WAN).

In a nutshell, computer networks help people and devices share *information* (files and e-mail) and expensive *resources* (printers and Internet connections) more efficiently.

Workstations and servers

Each computer in your home that's attached to a network is a *workstation*, also sometimes referred to as a *client* computer. The Windows operating system (OS) refers to the computers residing together on the same local-area network as a *workgroup*. A Windows-based computer network enables the workstations in a workgroup to share files and printers that are visible through the *Network Neighborhood* (or *My Network Places*). Home networks based on the Apple Macintosh OS offer the same capability. On a Mac, just use the finder to navigate to the *Network*.

Some networks also have *servers,* which are special-purpose computers or other devices that provide one or more services to other computers and devices on a network. Examples of typical servers include

- **File server:** A *file server* makes storage space on hard disks or some other type of storage device available to workstations on the network. Although the situation isn't common, more folks are using file servers to centralize all their media, like digital audio and pictures. Common in-home applications of a file server today are consumer devices such as the Linksys Media Center Extender (www.linksys.com), wireless game adapters, or the Turtle Beach Systems AudioTron (www.turtlebeach.com; $269) MP3 servers that enable you to play your MP3s over your stereo wirelessly.

- **Network Attached Storage (NAS) Server:** A specialized kind of file server, an *NAS* device is basically a small, *headless* (it doesn't have a monitor or keyboard) computing appliance that uses a big hard drive and a special operating system (usually Linux) to create an easy-to-use file server for a home or office network. The Buffalo Technology LinkStation Network Storage Center (www.buffalotech.com) is a good example of an NAS device appropriate for a home network.

- **Print server:** A *print server* is a computer or other device that makes it possible for the computers on the network to share one or more printers. You don't commonly find a print server in a home network, but some wireless networking equipment comes with a print server feature built in, which turns out to be very handy.

- **E-mail server:** An *e-mail server* is a computer that provides a system for sending e-mail to users on the network. You may never see an e-mail server on a home network. Most often, home users send e-mail through a third-party service, such as America Online (AOL), EarthLink, MSN Hotmail, and Yahoo!.

- **DHCP server:** Every computer on a network, even a home network, must have its own, unique network address in order to communicate with the other computers on the network. A *Dynamic Host Configuration Protocol* (DHCP) server automatically assigns a network address to every computer on a network. You most often find DHCP servers in another device, like a router or an AP.

You can find many types of client computers — network-aware devices — on your network, too. Some examples include

- **Gaming consoles:** The Microsoft Xbox (www.xbox.com), Sony PlayStation 2 (www.playstation.com), and Nintendo GameCube (www.nintendo.com) have adapters for network connections or multi-player gaming and talking to other players while gaming. Cool! Read more about online gaming in Chapter 12.

- **Wireless network cameras:** The Panasonic KX-HCM280 and KX-HCM270 Network Cameras (www.panasonic.com/consumer_electronics/gate/cameras.asp) enable you to not only view your home when you're away but also pan, tilt, scan, and zoom your way around the home. *That's* a nanny-cam.

✔ **MP3 players:** Turtle Beach Systems' AudioTron (www.turtlebeach.com) enables you to use wireless technology to stream music from your computer or file server to your home stereo system. The system uses a computer on your home network as a source, which stores your CDs in the MP3 (or other) electronic format, and attaches just like a CD or DVD player to your home entertainment system.

Most consumer manufacturers are trying to network-enable their devices, so expect to see everything from your washer and dryer to your vacuum cleaner network-enabled at some point. Why? Because after such appliances are on a network, they can be monitored for breakdowns, software upgrades, and so on without your having to manually monitor them.

Network infrastructure

Workstations must be electronically interconnected in order to communicate. The equipment over which the *network traffic* (electronic signals) travels between computers on the network is the *network infrastructure*.

Network hubs

In a typical office network, a strand of wiring similar to phone cable is run from each computer to a central location, such as a phone closet, where each wire is connected to a network hub. The *network hub,* similar conceptually to the hub of a wheel, receives signals transmitted by each computer on the network and sends the signals out to all other computers on the network.

Figure 2-1 illustrates a network with a star-shaped *topology* (the physical design of a network). Other network topologies include *ring* and *bus*. Home networks typically use a star topology because it's the simplest to install and troubleshoot.

Figure 2-1:
It's all in the stars — a typical network star-shaped topology.

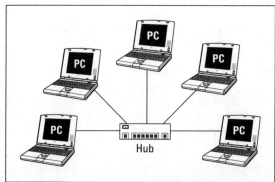

Bridges

A network *bridge* provides a pathway for network traffic between networks or segments of networks. A device that connects a wireless network segment to a wired network segment is a type of network bridge. In larger networks, network bridges are sometimes used to connect networks on different floors in the same building or in different buildings. In a wireless home network, the device that manages the wireless network, an *access point*, often acts as a bridge between a wireless segment of the network and a wired segment.

Hubs and switches

Networks transmit data in bundles called *packets*. Along with the raw information being transmitted, each packet also contains the network address of the computer that sent it and the network address of the recipient computer. Network hubs send packets indiscriminately to all ports of all computers connected to the hub — which is why you don't see them much any longer.

A special type of hub called a *switched hub* examines each packet, determines the addressee and port, and forwards the packet only to the computer and port to which it is addressed. Most often, switched hubs are just called *switches*. A *switch* reads the addressee information in each packet and sends the packet directly to the segment of the network to which the addressee is connected. Packets that aren't addressed to a particular network segment are never transmitted over that segment, and the switch acts as a filter to eliminate unnecessary network traffic. Switches make more efficient use of the available transmission bandwidth than standard hubs and therefore offer higher aggregate throughput to the devices on the switched network.

Routers

Over a large network and on the Internet, a *router* is analogous to a supereffi-cient postal service — it reads the addressee information in each data packet and communicates with other routers over the network or Internet to determine the best route for each packet to take. Routers can be a stand-alone device, but more often, home networks use a device known as a *cable/DSL (digital subscriber line) router.* This type of router — which marries a cable or DSL modem and a router — uses a capability called *Network Address Translation* (NAT) to enable all the computers on a home network to share a single Internet address on the cable or DSL network. Such routers also exist for satellite and dial-up connections. These are called *WAN routers* generically because they have access to your *wide-area network* connection, whether it's broadband or dial-up.

So, your local-area network, or LAN, in your home connects to your wide-area network, or WAN, which takes signals out of the home.

Transmission Control Protocol/Internet Protocol (TCP/IP) is the most common protocol for transmitting packets around a network. Every computer on a TCP/IP network must have its own *IP address*, which is a 32-bit numeric address that's written as four numbers separated by periods (for example, 192.168.1.100). Each number of these four numbers is known as an *octet,* which can have a value from 0 (zero) to 255. The Internet transmits packets by using the TCP/IP protocol. When you use the Internet, the Internet service provider (ISP) — such as AOL, EarthLink, or your cable or DSL provider — assigns a unique TCP/IP number to your computer. For the period that your computer is connected, your computer "leases" this unique address and uses it like a postal address to send and receive information over the Internet to and from other computers.

A WAN router with the Network Address Translation (NAT) feature also helps to protect the data on your computers from intruders. The NAT feature acts as a protection because it hides the real network addresses of networked computers from computers outside the network. (For more details on NAT, see Chapter 9.) Many WAN routers also have additional security features that more actively prevent intruders from gaining unauthorized access to your network through the Internet. This type of protection is sometimes described generically as a *firewall.* Good firewall software usually offers a suite of tools that not only block unauthorized access but also help you to detect and monitor suspicious computer activity. In addition, these tools also provide you with ways to safely permit computers on your network to access the Internet.

Internet gateways

These days, you can get a device that really does it all: a *wireless Internet gateway.* These devices combine all the features of an access point, a router, and a broadband modem (typically, cable or DSL). Some wireless Internet gateways even include a print server (that enables you to connect a printer directly to the gateway and use it from any networked PC), a dial-up modem, and even some Ethernet ports for computers and devices that connect to your network by using wires.

For example, the MiAVo Series Gateways (www.netopia.com) include a built-in DSL modem, a router, a wireless access point, and other networking features, such as a firewall and an easy-to-use graphical user interface (GUI) for configuring and setting up the gateway.

Not many of these devices are on the market; you can't buy many of them off-the-shelf, but you can get them directly from your broadband service provider.

The term *gateway* gets used lots by different folks with different ideas about what such a device is. Although our definition is the most common (and, in our opinion, correct), you may see some vendors selling devices that they call Internet gateways that don't have all the functions we describe. For example, some access points and routers that don't have built-in broadband modems are also called gateways. We don't consider them to be Internet gateways, because they link to the WAN modem. They're more of a modem gateway, but no one uses that term — it just isn't as catchy as an Internet gateway. We call them *wireless gateways* to keep everyone honest. Keep these subtle differences in mind when you're shopping.

Network interface adapters

Wireless networking is based on radio signals. Each computer, or *station,* on a wireless network has its own radio that sends and receives data over the network. As in wired networks, a station can be a *client* or a *server.* Most stations on a wireless home network are desktop personal computers with a wireless network adapter, but they could also be a portable device, such as a laptop or a PDA.

Each workstation on the network has a network interface card or adapter that links the workstation to the network (we discuss these in Chapter 1). This is true for wireless and *wireline* (wired) networks. In some instances, such as where the wireless functionality is embedded in the device, the network interface adapter is merely internal and preinstalled in the machine. In other instances, these internal and external adapters are either ordered with your workstation or device, or you add them during the installation process. We describe these options in the following subsections.

Figure 2-2 shows an external wireless networking adapter designed for attachment to a computer's Universal Serial Bus (USB) port, and Figure 2-3 shows an internal wireless networking adapter designed for installation in a desktop computer.

Figure 2-2:
A wireless network adapter that attaches to a computer's USB port.

Figure 2-3:
A wireless network adapter for installation inside a desktop computer.

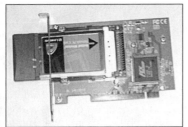

PC Cards

When you want to add wireless networking capability to a laptop computer, your first choice for a wireless network interface should probably be a Personal Computer Memory Card International Association (PCMCIA) card (also called a PC Card; shown in Figure 2-4). Nearly all Windows and some Mac notebooks and laptops have PCMCIA ports that are compatible with these cards. (An AirPort card is a special type of PC Card. In Chapter 8, we tell you more about the AirPort card and how to set up a wireless Mac network.)

Figure 2-4:
A PC Card wireless network adapter.

All wireless PC Cards must have an antenna so that the built-in radio can communicate with an access point. Most have a built-in patch antenna that's enclosed in a plastic casing that protrudes from the PC while the card is fully inserted. You should always take care when using this type of card because it's likely to get damaged if it's not stored properly when not in use (or if your dog knocks your laptop off the coffee table — don't ask!).

PCI adapters

Nearly all desktop PCs have at least one Peripheral Component Interconnect (PCI) slot. This PCI slot is used to install all sorts of add-in cards, including network connectivity. Most wireless NIC manufacturers offer a wireless PCI adapter — a version of their product that can be installed in a PCI slot (see Figure 2-5).

Some wireless PCI adapters are cards that adapt a PC Card for use in a PCI slot. The newest designs, however, mount the electronics from the PC Card on a full-size PCI Card with a removable dipole antenna attached to the back of the card.

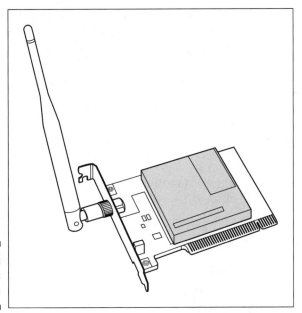

Figure 2-5:
A wireless
PCI adapter.

USB adapters

The USB standard has, over the past several years, become the most widely used method of connecting peripherals to a personal computer. First popularized in the Apple iMac, USB supports a data transfer rate many times faster than a typical network connection and is, therefore, a good candidate for connecting an external wireless network adapter to either a laptop or a desktop computer. Several wireless networking hardware vendors offer USB wireless network adapters. They're easy to connect, transport, and reposition in order to get better reception.

Most computers built in the past two or three years have at least two (and many times as many as eight) USB ports. If your computer has a USB port and you purchased a wireless USB network interface adapter, see Chapter 7 for more on setting up that adapter.

USB wireless NICs are sometimes a better choice than PC Cards or PCI cards because you can more easily move the device around to get a better signal, kinda like adjusting the rabbit ears on an old TV. If a computer doesn't have a PC Card slot — which most don't — but does have a USB port, you either need to install a PCI adapter or select a USB wireless network adapter.

Note that there are two forms of USB adapters: ones that have cables and ones that don't. The cabled USB adapters allow for positioning of the antenna; the noncabled ones connect directly in a fixed way into the back of your computer, and are designed for economy of size. You may hear either of these form factors referred to as *dongles*. (See Chapter 5 for more about form factors.)

CF and SDIO cards

Many popular handheld personal digital assistant (PDA) computers now come with wireless built right into them. If you still have an older PDA, you may consider a Compact Flash (CF) interface to enable a connection with your PDA. With a Compact Flash card, such as the one from Linksys shown in Figure 2-6, you can connect a Pocket PC to a wireless home network. (For more about PDAs and how they can enhance your wireless home network experience, check out Chapter 1.)

Figure 2-6:
A Compact Flash card wireless network interface card.

CF cards are small, 1½-inch-wide electronic modules that you insert into a CF card slot. The CF card slot where you insert the card is a 1½-inch slot in the top edge of the Pocket PC. Compact Flash refers to the technology used to store software or other data on the device. Many users employ CF cards to expand the memory in their Pocket PCs and for many other PDA add-ons.

Other manufacturers now use the similarly sized and shaped SDIO (Secure Digital Input Output) card for expansion. SD cards are simply a different form of flash memory (there are dozens — if you've ever investigated digital cameras, you know this!), and SDIO cards are simply Input/Output (communications) cards that use that flash memory slot.

Most Pocket PC manufacturers provide either standard or optional support for add-on cards built to the Compact Flash or SDIO form factor. Linksys, for example, makes the WCF12 model (www.linksys.com; $34.99), which works

Wi-Fi network adapters and the Palm OS

Over the past couple of years, Palm has split its handheld product line into four distinct categories. The Zire line, considered the basic organizer, supports Bluetooth only with the Zire 72 Special Edition model. None of the other Zire models has any options for wireless connectivity. The Tungsten line provides integrated Bluetooth connectivity in all versions. The Life Drive line is the new high-end product for home users, with 4 gigabytes of drive (enough space to hold lots of MP3 files and camera photos as well as other features, like Bluetooth, a voice recorder, and everything else you've come to expect from a Palm PDA). Finally, the top of the line is the Treo fully integrated cell phone PDA. This completely integrated handheld device can use Bluetooth, Wi-Fi, and the cellular network to make a connection. It is the ultimate in wireless "techno" toys.

At this point, Bluetooth technology seems to be the dominant method of connecting PDAs and other small devices to local-area networks. The list of potential applications of wireless technology to handheld electronic devices is virtually limitless.

with most PDAs that still use CF cards. Most PDAs these days include integrated support for IEEE 802.11b/g wireless networking, as well as for Bluetooth, for example.

Although Pocket PCs are typically more expensive than Palm PDAs (see the nearby sidebar, "Wi-Fi network adapters and the Palm OS"), they boast software applications more akin to a full-size PC, and they're perfect candidates for wireless network connectivity. You can use them for data synchronization, Internet access, and connecting with other Pocket PCs.

Get the (Access) Point?

Let's talk some more about the central pivot point in your wireless network: the access point. Somewhat similar in function to a network hub, an *access point* in a wireless network is a special type of wireless station that receives radio transmissions from other stations on the wireless and forwards them to the rest of the network. An access point can be a stand-alone device or a computer that contains a wireless network adapter along with special access-point management software. Most home networks use a stand-alone AP, such as shown in Figure 2-7.

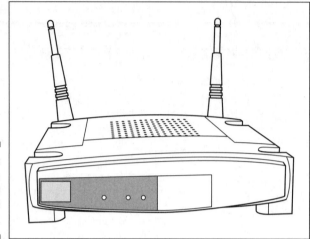

Figure 2-7:
A stand-alone access point.

Because many homes and businesses use wireless networking, a method is needed to distinguish one wireless network from another. Otherwise, your neighbor may accidentally send a page to the printer on your network. (That could be fun, or that could be a little scary.) Three parameters can be used to uniquely identify each segment of a wireless network:

✔ **Network name:** When you set up your wireless network, you should assign a unique name to the network. Some manufacturers refer to the network name by one of its technical monikers — *service set identifier* (SSID) or perhaps *extended service set identifier* (ESSID). This can be confusing and comes up most often if you're using equipment from different manufacturers. Rest assured, however, that network name, SSID, and ESSID all mean the same thing.

If the AP manufacturer assigns a network name at the factory, it assigns the same name to every AP it manufactures. Consequently, you should assign a different network name to avoid confusion with other APs that may be nearby (like your neighbor's). *Note:* All stations and the AP on a given wireless network must have the same network name to ensure that they can communicate.

Assigning a unique network name is good practice, but don't think of the network name as a security feature. Most APs broadcast their network name, so it's easy for a hacker to change the network name on his computer to match yours. Changing the network name from the factory setting to a new name just reduces the chance that you and your neighbor accidentally have wireless networks with the same network name.

✔ **Channel:** When you set up your wireless network, you have the option of selecting a radio channel. All stations and the access point must broadcast on the same radio channel in order to communicate. Multiple radio channels are available for use by wireless networks and some of the newer wireless APs use multiple channels to increase the speed of the network. The number of channels available varies according to the type of wireless network you're using and the country in which you install the wireless network. Wireless stations normally scan all available channels to look for a signal from an AP. When a station detects an AP signal, the station negotiates a connection to the AP.

✔ **Encryption key:** Because it's relatively easy for a hacker to determine a wireless network's name and the channel on which it's broadcasting, every wireless network should be protected by a secret encryption key unless the network is intended for use by the general public. Only someone who knows the secret key code can connect to the wireless network.

The most popular wireless network technology, *Wi-Fi,* comes with two types of security: Wired Equivalent Privacy (WEP) and *Wi-Fi Protected Access* (WPA). WEP uses the RC4 encryption algorithm and a private key phrase or series of characters to encrypt all data transmitted over the wireless network. For this type of security to work, all stations must have the private key. Any station without this key cannot get on the network. WPA, which is now built in to all new Wi-Fi equipment and comes as a free upgrade on most older Wi-Fi equipment, is far more secure than WEP, and we recommend that you use it. WPA uses Temporal Key Integrity Protocol (TKIP) encryption, which dynamically changes the security key as the connection is used. We talk about using both these types of systems in Chapter 10, with our primary emphasis on WPA.

You commonly find AP functionality bundled into the same device as several separate but related functions. For example, some APs perform the functions of a router, a switched hub, and a DHCP server as well as normal AP functions. Similar devices may even throw in a print server. This Swiss army knife-like approach is often a real bargain for use in a wireless home network.

Wireless networking devices can operate in one of two modes: infrastructure mode or ad hoc mode. The next two subsections describe the difference between these two modes.

Infrastructure mode

When a wireless station (such as a PC or a Mac) communicates with other computers or devices through an AP, the wireless station is operating in *infrastructure mode.* The station uses the network infrastructure to reach another computer or a device rather than communicate directly with the other computer or device. Figure 2-8 shows a network that consists of a wireless network segment with two wireless personal computers, and a wired network segment with three computers. These five computers communicate through the AP and the network infrastructure. The wireless computers in this network are communicating in infrastructure mode.

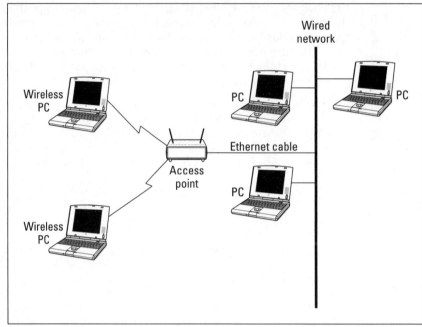

Ad hoc mode

Whenever two wireless stations are close enough to communicate with each other, they're capable of establishing an *ad hoc network:* that is, a wireless network that doesn't use an AP. Theoretically, you could create a home network out of wireless stations without the need for an AP. It's more practical, however, to use an AP; an AP is more effective because it facilitates communication between many stations at once (as many as 30 stations simultaneously in a single wireless network segment). In addition, an AP can create a connection, or *bridge,* between a wireless network segment and a wired segment.

Ad hoc mode isn't often used in wireless home networks, but it could be used on occasion to connect two computers to transfer files where no AP is in the vicinity to create a wireless infrastructure.

Your Wireless Network's Power Station: The Antenna

The main interface between your access point or network interface card and the network is the antenna. Signals generated and received by your wireless gear are dependent on a high-quality antenna interface. To be smart in wireless networking, you need to know the basics about antennas. If you know how they work, you can better optimize your network.

Access point antennas vary from manufacturer to manufacturer. Many APs have a single external antenna about five inches long. This type of antenna is a *dipole* antenna. Some APs have two external dipole antennas. Dual external antenna models should provide better signal coverage throughout the house. APs with dual antennas may transmit from only one of the antennas but receive through both antennas by sampling the signal and using whichever antenna is getting the strongest signal — a *diversity antenna system*.

Typical omnidirectional dipole antennas attach to the AP with a connector that enables you to position the antenna at many different angles; however, omnidirectional dipole radio antennas send and receive best in the vertical position.

The range and coverage of a Wi-Fi wireless AP used indoors is determined by these factors:

- ✔ **AP transmission output power:** This is the power output of the AP's radio, usually referred to as *transmission power* or *TX power*. Higher power output produces a longer range. Wi-Fi APs transmit at a power output of less than 30 dBm (one watt). Government agencies around the world regulate the maximum power output allowed. APs for home use generally have power outputs in the range 13 dBm (20 mW) to 15 dBm (31.6 mW). The higher the power rating, the stronger the signal and the better range your wireless network will have. Some wireless networking equipment manufacturers offer add-on amplifiers that boost the standard signal of the AP to achieve a longer range. We talk about boosters in Chapter 18. (For more on TX power, see the nearby sidebar, "TX power output and antenna gain.")

- ✔ **Antenna gain:** The AP's antenna and the antennas on the other devices on the network improve the capability of the devices to send and receive radio signals. This type of signal improvement is *gain*. Antenna specifications vary depending on vendor, type, and materials. Adding a higher-gain antenna at either end of the connection can increase the effective range.

- ✔ **Antenna type:** Radio antennas both send and receive signals. Different types of antennas transmit signals in different patterns or shapes. The most common type of antenna used in wireless home networks, the dipole antenna, is described as *omnidirectional* because it transmits its signal in all directions equally. In fact, the signal from a dipole antenna radiates 360 degrees in the horizontal plane and 75 degrees in the vertical plane, to create a doughnut-shaped pattern. Consequently, the area directly above or below the antenna gets a very weak signal.

Some types of antenna focus the signal in a particular direction and are referred to as *directional antennas*. In special applications where you want an AP to send its signal only in a specific direction, you could replace the omnidirectional antenna with a directional antenna. In a home, omnidirectional is usually the best choice, but that also depends on the shape of the home; some antennas are better for brownstones and multifloor buildings because they have a more spherical signal footprint rather than the standard flat-ish one.

✔ **Receive sensitivity:** The *receive sensitivity* of an AP or other wireless networking device is a measurement of how strong a signal is required from another radio before the device can make a reliable connection and receive data.

✔ **Signal attenuation:** A radio signal can get weaker as a result of interference caused by other radio signals because of objects that lie in the radio wave path between radios and because of the distance between the radios. The reduction in signal is *attenuation*. Read through Chapter 6 for a discussion of how to plan the installation of your wireless network to deal with signal attenuation.

To replace or add an antenna to an AP or other wireless device, you need to have a place to plug it in — as obvious a statement as that is, many antennas aren't detachable, and you can't add another antenna. Some access points use reverse TNC connectors that let optional antennas be used in 802.11b/g

---

TX power output and antenna gain

TX power output is measured in milliwatts (mW), but is also often expressed by using dBm units of measurement. (*dBm* measures, in decibels, a radio's amount of power.) The Federal Communication Commission (FCC) permits an AP to have a maximum power output of 1,000 mW (1 watt), which is the same as 30 dBm. Wi-Fi APs typically have maximum output power of 100 mW (20 dBm) or less. APs for home use generally have power outputs in the range 13 dBm (20 mW) to 15 dBm (31.6 mW). The higher the power rating, the stronger the signal and the better range your wireless network will have.

Antenna gain is usually expressed in dBi units (which indicate, also in decibels, the amount of

gain an antenna has). An antenna with a 4 dBi gain increases the output power (the effective isotropic radiated power, or EIRP) of the radio by 4 dBm. The FCC permits IEEE 802.11 radios a maximum EIRP of 36 dBm when the device is using an omnidirectional antenna. The antennas included with wireless home networking equipment are typically omnidirectional detachable dipole antennas with gains of from 2 dBi to 5 dBi. Some manufacturers offer optional high-gain antennas. (*Note:* The maximum EIRP output permitted in Japan is 100 mW; and the maximum output in Europe is only 10 mW.)

products, but there's a minor trend away from using detachable antennas in 802.11a products because of potential conflict in the frequency channels allocated to 802.11a. This situation potentially thwarts misuse, but also robs those deploying access points of their ability to choose optimal antennas.

Industry Standards

One of the most significant factors that has led to the explosive growth of personal computers and their impact on our daily lives has been the emergence of industry standards. Although many millions of personal computers are in use now around the world, only three families of operating system software run virtually all these computers: Windows, Mac OS, and Unix (including Linux). Most personal computers used in the home employ one of the Microsoft Windows operating systems or one of the Apple Macintosh operating systems. The existence of this huge installed base of potential customers has enabled hundreds of hardware and software companies to thrive by producing products that interoperate with one or more of these industry standard operating systems.

Computer hardware manufacturers recognize the benefits of building their products to industry standards. To encourage the adoption and growth of wireless networking, many companies that are otherwise competitors have worked together to develop a family of wireless networking industry standards that build on and interoperate with existing networking standards. As a result, reasonably priced wireless networking equipment is widely available from many manufacturers. Feel safe buying equipment from any of these manufacturers because they're all designed to work together, with one important caveat. The current three major flavors of this wireless networking technology for LAN applications are IEEE 802.11a, 802.11b, and 802.11g. You just have to pick the flavor that best fits your needs and budget. (**Note:** There are other wireless standards for other applications in the home, like Bluetooth for short-range communications. We talk about these standards later in Chapter 3 and elsewhere wherever their discussion is appropriate.)

The Institute of Electrical and Electronics Engineers

The *Institute of Electrical and Electronics Engineers* (IEEE) is a standards-making industry group that has for many years been developing industry standards that affect the electrical products we use in our homes and businesses every day. At present, the IEEE 802.11b/g standard is the overwhelming market leader in terms of deployed wireless networking products. Products that comply with this standard weren't the first wireless networking technology on the market — but they are now, by far, the dominant market installed base. As you will soon see, the new MIMO–enabled and 802.11 Pre-N products are coming on strong.

The Wi-Fi Alliance

In 1999, several leading wireless networking companies formed the Wireless Ethernet Compatibility Alliance (WECA), a nonprofit organization (www.weca. net). This group has recently renamed itself the Wi-Fi Alliance and is now a voluntary organization of more than 200 companies that make or support wireless networking products. The Wi-Fi Alliances' primary purpose is to certify that IEEE 802.11 products from different vendors will *interoperate* (work together). These companies recognize the value of building a high level of consumer confidence in the interoperability of wireless networking products.

The Wi-Fi Alliance organization has established a test suite that defines how member products will be tested by an independent test lab. Products that pass these tests are entitled to display the Wi-Fi trademark, which is a seal of interoperability. Although no technical requirement in the IEEE specifications states that a product must pass these tests, Wi-Fi certification encourages consumer confidence that products from different vendors will work together.

The Wi-Fi interoperability tests are designed to ensure that hardware from different vendors can successfully establish a communication session with an acceptable level of functionality. The test plan includes a list of necessary features. The features themselves are defined in detail in the IEEE 802.11 standards, but the test plan specifies an expected implementation.

IEEE 802.11b

In 1990, the IEEE adopted the document "IEEE Standards for Local and Metropolitan Area Networks," which provides an overview of the networking technology standards used in virtually all computer networks now in prevalent use. The great majority of computer networks use one or more of the standards included in IEEE 802; the most widely adopted is IEEE 802.3, which covers Ethernet.

IEEE 802.11 is the section that defines wireless networking standards and is often called *wireless Ethernet*. The first edition of the IEEE 802.11 standard, adopted in 1997, specified two wireless networking protocols that can transmit at either one or two megabits per second (Mbps) using the 2.4 GHz radio frequency band, broken into 14 5-MHz channels (11 in the United States). IEEE 802.11b-1999 is a supplement to IEEE 802.11 that added subsections to IEEE 802.11 that specify the protocol used by Wi-Fi-certified wireless networking devices.

The IEEE 802.11b protocol is backward compatible with the IEEE 802.11 protocols adopted in 1997, using the same 2.4 GHz band and channels as the slower protocol. The primary improvement of the IEEE 802.11b protocol is a technique that enables data transmission at either 5.5 Mbps or 11 Mbps.

802.11b is the *old* standard. Most vendors no longer sell 802.11b equipment (or they sell one single line of products for customers who want to replace old gear). You shouldn't consider buying 802.11b if you're buying new Wi-Fi gear. 802.11g, which we discuss in a moment, is compatible with 802.11b but much faster and not a penny more expensive.

IEEE 802.11a: Fast, faster, and fastest

IEEE adopted 802.11a-1999 at the same time it adopted 802.11b. IEEE 802.11a specifies a wireless protocol that operates at higher frequencies than the IEEE 802.11b protocol and uses a variety of techniques to provide data transmission rates of 6, 9, 12, 18, 24, 36, 48, and 54 Mbps. 802.11a has 12 non-overlapping channels in the United States and Canada, but most deployed products use only 8 of these channels.

Some wireless networking vendors offer proprietary enhancements to IEEE 802.11a-compliant products that double the top speed to more than 100 Mbps.

An increasing number of products based on the IEEE 802.11a standard have reached the market. In addition to the higher transmission speeds, IEEE 802.11a offers these advantages over IEEE 802.11b:

- **Capacity:** 802.11a has about four times as many available channels, resulting in about eight times the network capacity: that is, the number of wireless stations that can be connected to the AP at one time and still be able to communicate. This isn't a significant advantage for a wireless home network because you almost certainly will never use all the network capacity available with a single access point (approximately 30 stations simultaneously).

- **Less competition:** Portable phones, Bluetooth, and residential microwave ovens use portions of the same 2.4 GHz radio frequency band used by 802.11b, which sometimes results in interference. By contrast, few devices other than IEEE 802.11a devices use the 5 GHz radio frequency band. *Note:* A growing number of cordless phones are starting to use this same frequency range, so the relative uncrowdedness of the 5 GHz spectrum isn't likely to last forever.

✔ **Improved throughput:** Tests show as much as four to five times the data link rate and throughput of 802.11b in a typical office environment. *Throughput* is the amount of data that can be transferred over the connection in a given period. (See the nearby sidebar, "Gauging your network's throughput.")

When does a + b = g?

The last of the IEEE standards-based products to hit the street is 802.11g, and these products are selling like hotcakes. The g standard was finalized in June 2003. The appeal of 802.11g is so great that many vendors didn't wait for the final standard to be adopted before they released their first products based on this technology.

IEEE 802.11g is backward compatible with 802.11b wireless networking technology but delivers the same transmission speeds as 802.11a — up to 54 Mbps — thus effectively combining the best of both worlds. The 802.11g products are outselling a and b products these days and have become the new standard for Wi-Fi networking.

Gauging your network's throughput

Wi-Fi standards call for different speeds, up to 11 Mbps for 802.11b and up to 54 Mbps for 802.11a and g — newer devices try to communicate at up to 110 Mbps. Radios attempt to communicate at the highest speed. If they encounter too many errors (dropped bits), the radios steps down to the next fastest speed and repeats the process until a strong connection is achieved. So, although we talk about 802.11g, for example, being 54–110 Mbps in speed, the reality is that unless you're very close to the AP, you're not likely to get that maximum rate. Signal fade and interference cut into your speeds, and the negotiated rate between the two devices drops.

That discussion represents just the speed. The actual throughput is another, related, matter. *Throughput* represents the rate at which the validated data flows from one point to another. It may take some retransmissions for that to occur, so your throughput is less than the negotiated speed of the connection. It may not be unusual for you to get only 40 to 50 percent of your maximum connection speed. In fact, that's rather normal.

IEEE 802.11g equipment offers a nice upgrade path to people who have already invested in IEEE 802.11b equipment. When the first products were released, they carried prices that were only marginally more expensive than plain-old IEEE 802.11b. Older products had some interoperability problems with IEEE 802.11b equipment, but those problems have all been ironed out. Now, you're more likely to find a combined product that supports both 802.11g and 802.11b — and many times you can find products that support a/b/and g.

If you plan to do streaming video over your network, you should seriously consider purchasing an access point that supports multiple standards — dual-mode, tri-standard a/b/g products — and doesn't default to the slowest speed when it sees an older wireless device. Many low-end APs slow down all the wireless connections they're supporting when they communicate with any older wireless device that works only at a slower speed.

The ISM bands

This section talks in detail about frequency bands used by the various standards. In 1985, the Federal Communication Commission (FCC) made changes to the radio spectrum regulation and assigned three bands designated as the *i*ndustrial, *s*cientific, and *m*edical (ISM) bands. These frequency bands are

- ✔ **902 MHz–928 MHz:** A 26 MHz bandwidth
- ✔ **2.4 GHz–2.4835 GHz:** An 83.5 MHz bandwidth
- ✔ **5.15–5.35 GHz and 5.725 GHz–5.825 GHz:** A 300 MHz bandwidth

The FCC also opened some additional frequencies, known as Unlicensed National Information Infrastructure (U-NII), in the lower reaches of the five GHz frequencies.

The purpose of the FCC change was to encourage the development and use of wireless networking technology. The new regulation permits a user to operate, within certain guidelines, radio equipment that transmits a signal within each of these three ISM bands without obtaining an FCC license.

Wireless networks use radio waves to send data around the network. IEEE 802.11a uses part of the U-NII frequencies, and IEEE 802.11b and g use the ISM 2.4 GHz band.

An important concept when talking about frequencies is the idea of overlapping and non-overlapping channels. As we discuss in Chapter 18, signals from other APs can cause interference and poor performance of your wireless network. This happens specifically when the APs' signals are transmitting on the same (or sometimes nearby) channels. Recall that the standards call for a number of channels within a specified frequency range.

The frequency range of 802.11b, for example, is between 2.4 GHz and 2.4835 GHz, and it's broken up into 14 equally sized channels. (Only 11 can be used in the United States — any equipment sold for use here allows you to access only these 11 channels.) The problem is that these channels are defined in such a way that many of the channels overlap with one another — and with 802.11b, there are only three non-overlapping channels. Thus, you wouldn't want to have channels 10 and 11 operating side by side because you would get signal degradation. You want non-interfering, non-overlapping channels. So you find that people tend to use Channels 1, 6, and 11, or something similar. 802.11a doesn't have this problem because its eight channels, in the 5 GHz frequency band, don't overlap; therefore, you can use contiguous channels. As with 802.11b and g, however, you don't want to be on the same channel.

Chapter 3

Bluetooth, HPNA, and HomePlug

- -

- -

Getting the most from computer technology is all about selecting the best and most dominant technology standards. The most dominant technology for wireless home networks is now clearly the Wireless Fidelity (Wi-Fi) family of technologies defined by the IEEE 802.11a, 802.11b, and 802.11g standards (which we describe in Chapter 2). Wi-Fi is, simply, the reason that you're reading this book (we're guessing) and the technology that has made "wireless networks" such a huge hit.

But, Wi-Fi isn't the only game in town. You run into other home networking standards when you buy and install your Wi-Fi gear — standards that will make it easier to get Wi-Fi where you want it.

Another popular wireless technology is Bluetooth, a short-range wireless networking system that's built into many cellular phones. Even if you intend to purchase and use only Wi-Fi wireless networking equipment, you should still be aware of Bluetooth. Who knows? — it may even come in handy for you.

We also talk about a few other key wired home networking standards (oops, did we say a dreaded word: *wired?*): Home Phone Networking Alliance (HPNA), the standard for networking over your installed phone wiring in your home; and HomePlug, the standard for networking over your electrical power cables in your home. As surprising as it may seem, you can actually connect your computers, access points, and other devices over these in-wall cables. What's more, many APs come with these interfaces onboard to make it easier for you to install that AP wherever you want it. Isn't that nice? You betcha.

Who or What Is Bluetooth?

One of the most often talked about wireless standards, besides Wi-Fi, is *Bluetooth*. The Bluetooth wireless technology, named for the tenth-century Danish King Harald Blatand "Bluetooth," was invented by the L.M. Ericsson company of Sweden in 1994. King Harald helped unite his part of the world during a conflict around A.D. 960. Ericsson intended for Bluetooth technology to unite the mobile world. In 1998, Ericsson, IBM, Intel, Nokia, and Toshiba founded the Bluetooth Special Interest Group (SIG), Inc., to develop an open specification for always-on, short-range wireless connectivity based on the Ericsson Bluetooth technology. Its specification was publicly released on July 26, 1999. The Bluetooth SIG now includes 3Com, Agere, Ericsson, IBM, Intel, Microsoft, Motorola, Nokia, Toshiba, and nearly 2,000 other companies. Dozens of Bluetooth-enabled products are already on the market, with many more on the way.

Sometimes a network of devices communicating via Bluetooth is described as a *personal-area network* (PAN) to distinguish it from a network of computers often called a local-area network (LAN). In March 2002, the Institute of Electrical and Electronics Engineers (IEEE) approved IEEE 802.15.1, a standard for wireless PANs (WPANs), which was adapted from portions of the Bluetooth wireless specification. IEEE 802.15.1 is fully compliant with the v1.1 specification. As IEEE worked toward the 802.15 standard, the Bluetooth SIG simultaneously has been working on Bluetooth Version 3.0. Any new Bluetooth standard will likely also become an updated IEEE 802.15 standard. (Read more at the Bluetooth Web site, at `www.bluetooth.com`.)

The following list is a small sampling of existing Bluetooth products:

- Microsoft Wireless IntelliMouse Explorer for Bluetooth (a wireless mouse)
- Apple Wireless Keyboard and Mouse
- IOGEAR Bluetooth wireless stereo hcadphone kit
- HP Deskjet 450 printer
- Palm Tungsten T-5 handheld computer
- Motorola V3 RAZR mobile phone
- Motorola Bluetooth Handsfree Car Kit
- Belkin Bluetooth Universal Serial Bus (USB) Adapter

Although originally intended as a wireless replacement for cables, Bluetooth is being applied to make it possible for a wide range of devices to communicate with each other wirelessly with minimal user intervention. The technology is designed to be low-cost and low-power to appeal to a broad audience and to conserve a device's battery life.

The projected growth plans for Bluetooth are phenomenal. The number of devices enabled with Bluetooth is expected to jump from nearly nothing in 2000 to more than 300 million in 2005, growing to nearly a billion units (yup, *billion* with a *b*) in 2009, according to industry analyst firm In-Stat/MDR.

Wi-Fi versus Bluetooth

Wi-Fi and Bluetooth are designed to coexist in the network, and although they certainly have overlapping applications, each has its distinct zones of advantage.

The biggest differences between Wi-Fi and Bluetooth are

✔ **Distance:** Bluetooth is lower powered, which means that its signal can go only short distances (up to 10 meters, or a bit more than 30 feet). 802.11 technologies can cover your home, and in some cases more, depending on the antenna you use. Some Bluetooth devices on the market operate under a high-powered scheme (called Class 1 Bluetooth devices), which can reach up to 100 meters. Most home Bluetooth devices don't have this kind of range, mainly because they're designed to be battery powered, and the shorter *Class 2* range of 10 meters provides a better trade-off between battery life and range.

✔ **Application:** Bluetooth is designed as a replacement of cables: that is, trying to get rid of that huge tangle of cables that link your mouse, printer, monitor, scanner, and other devices on your desk and around your home. In fact, the first Bluetooth device was a Bluetooth headset, which eliminated that annoying cable to the telephone that got in the way of typing. New cars are also becoming outfitted with Bluetooth so that you can use your cell phone in your car, with your car's stereo speakers and an onboard microphone serving as your hands-free capability. Pretty neat, huh?

Wi-Fi (802.11a, 802.11b, and 802.11g) and Bluetooth are similar in certain respects: They both enable wireless communication between electronic devices but are more complementary than direct competitors. Wi-Fi technology is most often used to create a wireless network of personal computers that can be located anywhere in a home or business. Bluetooth devices usually communicate with other Bluetooth devices in relatively close proximity.

The easiest way to distinguish Wi-Fi from Bluetooth is to focus on what each one replaces:

✔ **Wi-Fi is wireless Ethernet:** Wi-Fi is a wireless version of the Ethernet communication protocol and is intended to replace networking cable that would otherwise be run through walls and ceilings to connect computers in multiple rooms or even multiple floors of a building.

✔ **Bluetooth replaces peripheral cables:** Bluetooth wireless technology operates at short distances — usually about 10 meters — and most often replaces cables that connect peripheral devices, such as a printer, keyboard, mouse, or personal digital assistant (PDA) to your computer.

✔ **Bluetooth replaces IrDA:** Bluetooth can also be used to replace another wireless technology — Infrared Data Association (IrDA) wireless technology — that's already found in most laptop computers, PDAs, and even many printers. Although IR signals are very secure and aren't bothered with radio frequency (RF) interference, IrDA's usefulness is hindered by infrared's requirement for line-of-sight proximity of devices. Just like the way your TV's remote control must be pointed directly at your TV to work, the infrared ports on two PDAs must be lined up to trade data, and your laptop has to be "pointing" at the printer to print over the infrared connection. Because Bluetooth uses radio waves rather than light waves, line-of-sight proximity isn't required.

Like Wi-Fi, Bluetooth offers wireless access to LANs, including Internet access. Bluetooth devices can potentially access the Public Switched Telephone Network (PSTN: you know, the phone system) and mobile telephone networks. Bluetooth should be able to thrive alongside Wi-Fi by making possible such innovative solutions as a hands-free mobile phone headset, print-to-fax, and automatic PDA, laptop, and cell phone/address book synchronization.

Piconets, Masters, and Slaves

Communication between Bluetooth devices is similar in concept to the ad hoc mode of Wi-Fi wireless networks (which we describe in Chapter 2). A Bluetooth device automatically and spontaneously forms informal WPANs, called *piconets,* with from one to seven other Bluetooth devices that have the same Bluetooth profile. Piconets get their name from merging the prefix *pico* (probably from the Italian word *piccolo* [small]) and *net*work. A capability called *unconscious connectivity* enables these devices to connect and disconnect almost without any user intervention.

A particular Bluetooth device can be a member of any number of piconets at any moment in time (see Figure 3-1). Each piconet has one *master,* the device that first initiates the connection. Other participants in a piconet are *slaves*.

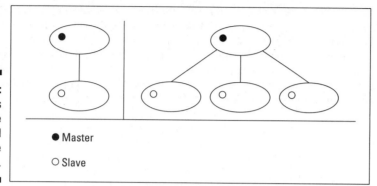

Figure 3-1:
Piconets
have one
master and
at least one
slave.

The three types of Bluetooth connections are

- ✔ **Data-only:** When communicating data, a master can manage connections with as many as seven slaves.

- ✔ **Voice-only:** When the Bluetooth piconet is used for voice communication (for example, a wireless phone connection), the master can handle no more than three slaves.

- ✔ **Data and voice:** A piconet transmitting both data and voice can exist between only two Bluetooth devices at a time.

Each Bluetooth device can, in full compliance with the Bluetooth standard, join more than one piconet at a time. A group of more than one piconet with one or more devices in common is a *scatternet*. Figure 3-2 depicts a scatternet made up of several piconets.

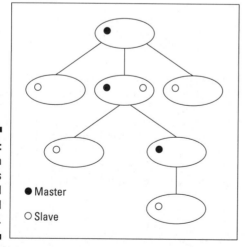

Figure 3-2:
A Bluetooth
scatternet is
composed
of several
piconets.

The amount of information sent in each packet over a Bluetooth connection and the type of error correction that is used determine the data rate a connection can deliver. Bluetooth devices can send data over a piconet by using 16 different types of packets. Sending more information in each packet (that is, sending longer packets) causes a faster data rate. Conversely, more robust error correction causes a slower data rate. Any application that uses a Bluetooth connection determines the type of packet used and, therefore, the data rate.

Bluetooth isn't nearly as fast as Wi-Fi — most Bluetooth devices reach a maximum data rate of 723 Kbps (compare that to 54 Mbps for 802.11g and a), but that's not usually a huge deal because Bluetooth is typically not used for transferring huge files and the like. The newest version of Bluetooth (Bluetooth 2.0) includes something called *EDR* (Enhanced Data Rate) that allows data transfers at speeds of up to 2.1 Mbps.

To maintain the security of the data you send over a Bluetooth link, the Bluetooth standard includes several layers of security. First, the two Bluetooth devices that are connecting use *authentication* to identify each other. After the authentication process is done (sometimes called *pairing,* in the Bluetooth world), the devices can begin sharing information. The data being sent across the radio link is *encrypted* (scrambled) so that only other authenticated devices have the key that can *decrypt* (unscramble) the data.

Both Wi-Fi (the 802.11b and g versions) and Bluetooth use the 2.4 GHz frequency radio band, but note the significant differences in how these technologies use the band. Bluetooth radios transmit a signal strength that complies with transmission regulations in most countries and is designed to connect at distances from 10 centimeters to 10 meters through walls and other obstacles — although like any radio wave, Bluetooth transmissions can be weakened by certain kinds of construction material, such as steel or heavy concrete. Although Bluetooth devices can employ a transmission power that produces a range in excess of 100 meters, you can assume that most Bluetooth devices are designed for use within 10 meters of other compatible devices, which is fine for the applications for which Bluetooth is intended, such as replacing short-run cables.

To make full use of the 2.4 GHz frequency radio band and to reduce the likelihood of interference, Bluetooth uses a transmission protocol that hops 1,600 times per second between 79 discrete 1 MHz-wide channels from 2.402 GHz to 2.484 GHz. Each piconet establishes its own random hopping pattern so that you can have many piconets in the same vicinity without mutual interference. If interference does occur, each piconet switches to a different channel and tries again. Even though Wi-Fi (802.11b/g) and Bluetooth both use the 2.4 GHz band, both protocols use hopping schemes that should result in little, if any, mutual interference.

Understanding Bluetooth versions

Bluetooth has been around for a few years now and, like most technologies, has undergone some growing pains and revisions over time. In fact, multiple versions of Bluetooth-certified equipment are available, as newer and more capable variants of Bluetooth arrive on the market.

The most common variant of Bluetooth these days is known as Bluetooth 1.2. This is basically a version of Bluetooth that has just all the bugs ironed out. Bluetooth 1.2 devices (most currently available devices, in other words), are *backward compatible* with earlier Bluetooth 1.0 and 1.1 devices. So, they work the same way, at the same speeds — just better. (Some technical advances in 1.2 allow most devices to have better "real world" speeds, but functionally they're identical.)

The big news in the Bluetooth world is the Bluetooth 2.0 standard. You can think of Bluetooth 2.0 in comparison with the 1.x variants as being sort of like 802.11g compared to 802.11b. It's faster (with a maximum speed three times as high — 2.1 Mbps vs. around 700 Kbps for the EDR or enhanced data rate), and it's better at resisting interference and just basically works better all around). Not many Bluetooth 2.0 devices are on the market yet — and not all support the EDR speeds. If you're shopping for something that may be sending larger files, like a Bluetooth-equipped laptop, you should consider insisting on Bluetooth 2.0 and EDR.

Coming down the pike is an even faster Bluetooth 3.0 standard — and the Bluetooth folks are looking at new technologies like UWB (see the sidebar "Ultra cool ultra wideband (UWB) coming soon" for more on this technology) to make Bluetooth even faster in the future.

Integrating Bluetooth into Your Wireless Network

Products that are the first to take advantage of Bluetooth technology include the following:

- Mobile phones
- Cordless phones
- PDAs
- Bluetooth adapters for PCs
- Bluetooth hands-free car kits
- Videocameras

✔ Refrigerators

✔ Microwaves

✔ Data projectors

✔ Scanners

✔ Printers

You can get a great idea of all the various ways that Bluetooth can be used in your network by going to the official Bluetooth products Web site, at www.bluetooth.com/products/. We also go into great detail in Chapter 15 about some of the more common ways you use Bluetooth.

One of the more interesting and most widely used applications of Bluetooth technology is for cell phones. Bring your Bluetooth-enabled phone home and dock it in a power station near your PC, and it instantly logs on to your wireless home network via a Bluetooth connection to a nearby PC or Bluetooth access point. Phones that function as PDAs can update their address books and sync data from the PC. All your events, to-do lists, grocery lists, and birthday reminders can be kept current just by bringing your Bluetooth-enabled product in range. You can even get Bluetooth headsets for your Bluetooth phones — getting rid of that wireless headset hassle.

Bluetooth technology is advancing into the arena of autos, too. The Bluetooth SIG formed the Car Profile Working Group in December 1999, in response to interest by the automotive industry. This working group has defined how Bluetooth wireless technology will enable hands-free use of mobile phones in automobiles. Car manufacturers have begun to embrace Bluetooth in a big way over the past year or two. Acura was perhaps the first car maker to offer Bluetooth (at least in the U.S. market) with the Acura TL. Using the Bluetooth in this car, you can "pair" your mobile phone and then use the steering wheel controls, navigation system screen and controller, and the car's audio system to control and make phone calls. Very cool. Other manufacturers like BMW, MINI, Toyota, and Lexus have followed suit. We talk about this topic more in Chapter 15.

The current versions of Microsoft Windows Mobile and Windows XP (Service Pack 2) offer built-in support for Bluetooth devices. All versions of Mac OS (from v. 10.2 Jaguar on) also have integrated support for Bluetooth.

Wirelessly synching your PDAs

Bluetooth is onboard inside PDAs, like the Dell Axim X51v (www.dell.com/axim; $449), which has both 802.11b and Bluetooth inside. That's really cool. Running Windows Mobile 5.0 (the latest and greatest version), the Axim can go anywhere you go and keep you connected — using Wi-Fi in offices or hot spots or pairing up with a Bluetooth device, like a laptop or even an

EVDO-enabled wireless phone (see Chapter 16 for more on EVDO) when you're out in the middle of nowhere.

If you have an older PDA, without built-in Bluetooth, you can buy an adapter that fits into the CF (compact flash) or SDIO (Secure Digital Input/Output) slots of these devices (where you may also slip an extra memory card into them. For example, the IOGEAR CF Bluetooth adapter (`www.iogear.com`), works with most Windows Mobile-powered handheld computers. An example of a CF Bluetooth adapter is shown in Figure 3-3. For example, if you have your Bluetooth-enabled PDA in your pocket and walk into the room where your Bluetooth-enabled PC is located, the two automatically synchronize your calendar, your e-mail, and your to-do list — with *no* intervention on your part. Or, if your cell phone is Bluetooth enabled, you can transfer your contact list wirelessly from your Bluetooth-enabled PC to the phone's address list. (That would cut down on those expensive directory assistance calls, wouldn't it?)

Figure 3-3:
Use a Bluetooth Compact-Flash card in some PDAs.

Toshiba and other manufacturers have released Bluetooth PC Cards that add the Bluetooth wireless technology to any PC with a PC Card slot. Other adapters are available that plug into a USB port, which makes it possible to easily add Bluetooth capability to any desktop or laptop PC (see Figure 3-4). Prices for these adapters range widely — from as low as about $50 to as much as $170.

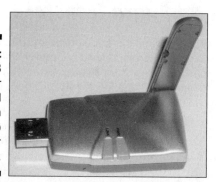

Figure 3-4:
Use a USB adapter to add Bluetooth capability to a desktop or laptop PC.

Ultracool ultra wideband (UWB) is coming

With all the innovation happening in the Wi-Fi and Bluetooth area, more neat stuff is on its way. *Ultra wideband* (UWB) is a revolutionary wireless technology for transmitting digital data over a wide spectrum of frequency bands with very low power. It can transmit data at very high rates (for wireless LAN applications in the home). Within the power limit allowed under current FCC regulations, Ultra wideband also has the ability to carry signals through doors and other obstacles that tend to reflect signals at more limited bandwidths and a higher power. At higher power levels, UWB signals can travel to significantly greater ranges.

Ultra wideband radio broadcasts digital pulses (rather than traditional sine waves) that are timed precisely on a signal across a very wide spectrum at the same time. Transmitter and receiver are coordinated to send and receive pulses with an accuracy of trillionths of a second! Not only does UWB enable high data rates, but it also does so without suffering the effects of multipath interference. *Multipath* is the propagation phenomenon that results in signals reaching the receiving antenna by two or more paths, usually because of reflections of the transmitted signal off walls or mirrors or the like. Because UWB has the ability to *time-gate* (that is, prescribe the precise time when it's

supposed to receive the data), the receiver allows it to ignore signals arriving outside a prescribed time interval, such as signals caused by multipath reflections.

UWB is still in the early stages, but it's coming on strong. UWB is simpler, cheaper, less power-hungry, and 100 times faster than Bluetooth. What more could you want? UWB communication devices could be used to wirelessly distribute services such as phone, cable, and computer networking throughout a building or home.

One big — no, make that *huge* — issue holding up the development of UWB is the fact that multiple companies and groups are trying to create UWB products, and none of them is compatible with the others. So, we're facing a bit of a VHS-versus-Betamax situation as products become closer to market.

The good news here is that two big groups supporting UWB — the Wireless USB and Wireless 1394 (FireWire) groups — have begun to support a single UWB standard known as WiMedia (`www.wimedia.org`). If more and more players (like consumer electronics vendors) begin to support the WiMedia Alliance, we may *finally* begin to see UWB in everyday products like DVD players and TVs — we sure hope it happens soon!

Wireless printing and data transfer

Hewlett-Packard and other printer companies manufacture printers that have built-in Bluetooth wireless capability, which enables a computer that also has Bluetooth wireless capability to print sans printer cables. Other examples are a wireless keyboard and a wireless mouse from Microsoft that both use Bluetooth technology to replace their traditional cables.

Another great use of Bluetooth wireless technology is to wirelessly transfer your digital photographs from your Bluetooth-enabled digital camera to your Bluetooth-enabled PC or Bluetooth-enabled printer — or even directly to your Bluetooth-enabled PDA. The newest wave of PDAs from several manufacturers includes wireless-enhanced models that include both Bluetooth and Wi-Fi built in. Wouldn't it be cool to carry your family photo album around on your Palm or iPAQ to show off at the office?

Extending Your Wireless Home Network with "No New Wires" Solutions

Wireless networking is great — so great that we wrote a book about it. But, in many instances, wireless is just one way to do what you want; and often, wireless solutions need a hand from *wireline* (that is, wired) solutions to give you a solid, reliable connection into your home network.

A common application of wireline and wireless networking is a remote AP that you want to link back into your home network. Suppose that your cable modem is in your office in the basement, and that's where you have your AP. Now suppose that you want wireless access to your PC for your TV, stereo, and laptop surfing in the master bedroom on the third floor. Chances are that your AP's signal isn't strong enough for that application up there. How do you link one AP to the other?

You could install a wired Ethernet solution, which would entail running new Cat 5e cables through your walls up to your bedroom. It's pretty messy if you ask us, but this approach certainly provides as much as 100 Mbps if you need it.

If you *can* run CAT-5e cable and create an Ethernet network in your walls, you should, by all means *do so*! But most folks can't do this, so these other solutions are the way to go.

A more practical way to get your cable modem up to the third floor is to run an HPNA or HomePlug link between the two points. Think of this as one long extension cord between your router or AP in the basement and your AP in your bedroom. HPNA, as we discuss shortly, does this over your standard phone lines; HomePlug does it over electrical lines. Although the effective throughput doesn't match 54 Mbps today (it may in the near future — read on!), it will likely exceed the speed of your Internet connection. If that's your primary goal, these are great, clean, and very easy options for you. Check out the next two sections for more.

Network Power (line)!

Companies have been talking about powerline networking for some time, but only recently have they really gotten it right. For several years now, networking companies like D-Link have been selling products based on the *HomePlug* powerline networking standard.

The powerline networking concept takes a little getting used to. Most of us are used to plugging an AC adapter or electrical cable into the wall and then another Ethernet cable into some other networking outlet for the power and data connections. With HomePlug, those two cables are reduced to one — the power cable! That electrical cord *is* your LAN connection, — along with all the rest of the electrical cabling in your house. Cool, huh? To connect to your computer, you run an Ethernet cable from the HomePlug device (router, AP, and so on) to your computer, hub, or switch.

Networking on powerlines is no easy task. Powerlines are noisy, electrically speaking, with surges in voltage level and electrical interferences introduced by all sorts of devices both within and external to the home. The state of the electrical network in a home is constantly changing as well when devices are plugged in and turned on. Because of this, the HomePlug standard adopts a sophisticated and adaptive *signal processing algorithm,* which is a technique used to convert data into electrical signals on the power wiring. Because HomePlug uses higher-frequency signals, the technology can avoid some of the most common sources of noise on the powerline.

The current version of HomePlug (called HomePlug 1.0) can offer up to 14 Mbps networking over the powerline — faster than 802.11b or HomePNA but slower than 802.11g or a and the higher-speed, wired Ethernet solutions. Besides the speed, HomePlug offers other benefits:

✔ **Ubiquity:** Power outlets are all over your house and are more plentiful than phone jacks and Ethernet outlets. With HomePlug, every one of the dozens (or even hundreds) of power outlets in the house becomes a data-networking jack.

✔ **Integrated:** HomePlug can be built right into many networked appliances. The almost legendary Internet refrigerator that we discuss in several places in this book is a great concept, but even we don't have a Cat 5e outlet in the dark nook behind our fridges. However, we do have a power outlet, and so do you.

✔ **Encrypted:** HomePlug has a built-in encryption system. Because power signals can bleed back into the local power network and because you

Taking powerline faster

In August 2005, the folks at the HomePlug Powerline Alliance (www.homeplug.org — the folks who develop the standards and certify HomePlug gear) approved the forthcoming next generation of HomePlug, known as *HomePlug AV.* This standard provides faster HomePlug connections — as fast as 200 Mbps is the promise — which means that HomePlug will be fast enough to support carrying full speed Wi-Fi connections and other data-intensive home networking needs. like HDTV (high-definition TV).

In the meantime, some vendors are offering their own HomePlug *Turbo* products based on a chip from Intellon (one of the primary HomePlug chip makers). The Turbo variant can handle raw data speeds of up to 85 Mbps, which makes it suitable for extending 802.11g Wi-Fi networks. Expect to see APs with built-in HomePlug Turbo capabilities by the end of 2006.

may not want to share your LAN with your neighbors, you can turn on HomePlug's encryption. In that way, only devices that have your password can be on the network.

Like the wireless systems we describe throughout this book, most HomePlug systems come with encryption turned off by default. We recommend that you get your network up and running first — and then turn on encryption after you've proven to yourself that your network is working.

The most common application for HomePlug is as an Ethernet or a USB bridge. These devices look and act much like the external USB Wi-Fi NICs that we discuss in Chapter 2. You need two of them: one to connect to an Ethernet port on your router (or any LAN jack in your home) and another to plug into the wall outlet wherever you need LAN access.

The bridge typically has a power cord on one side of the box and an Ethernet or USB connector on the other. Plug the power cord into any wall outlet and plug the Ethernet or USB into the computer or other networked devices, and you have a connection. Pat has been using a NETGEAR Powerline Ethernet bridge like this for a spot in his house that has neither Ethernet nor good wireless coverage, and he loves it. Danny has a Belkin Powerline Ethernet Adapter connecting his office (where the cable modem is) to another adapter in the kids' computing area (where all the screaming is). Figure 3-5 shows a typical use of HomePlug bridges.

Powerline networking through HomePlug is a great complement to a wireless network, but we probably would never use it to replace our wireless LANs. Use it where you need it. HomePlug is quick, cheap (bridges cost about $80 each, with prices dropping rapidly), and perfect for networking on demand.

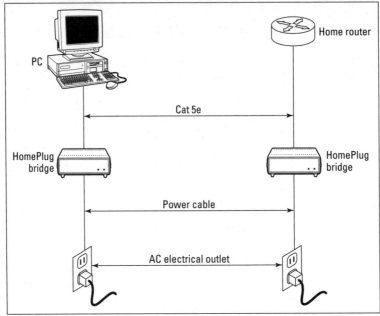

Figure 3-5:
Plug your
computer
into the
wall — and
that's all.

Another possible use of HomePlug Ethernet adapters is to connect remote APs to your network. Simply use a pair of Ethernet adapters — one plugged directly into a wired Ethernet port on your main router or AP, and the other plugged into the wall in a remote location. Now plug an inexpensive access point into that remote location and you're ready to go wireless!

Using your TV cables to extend your Wi-Fi network

An interesting approach to expanding your 802.11b or g wireless network's reach has recently been launched on the market by AuraOne Systems. The AuraGrid Wireless Extension system (which costs $89 for a 4-room kit) is designed to use your home's coaxial cable wiring — the wires used to connect your TVs to the cable TV network — as an antenna extension system that brings your wireless network signal to all the nooks and crannies in your home.

To use the system, you simply need to install the AuraGrid duplexer in your garage (or wherever

your cable TV lines enter the house), and then simply connect antenna devices to each outlet where you want to improve your wireless signal. Finally, connect the antenna port on your access point to an AuraGrid splitter. That's s it! If you can hook up your VCR and TV, you can handle this process. The AuraGrid works with only cable TV systems and interferes with a satellite TV signal, so if you have DirecTV or DISH Network, you can't use those wires for this purpose.

Another way to use phone lines

Although HPNA is perhaps the most common and well-known technology that uses phone lines to carry data around the home, it's not the only one. An Israeli company named SercoNet (www.serconet.co.il) has created a technology designed specifically to extend wireless (Wi-Fi) networks throughout the home by using phone lines.

The SercoNet system (it's working with multiple partners to bring it to market) uses phone lines as essentially long antenna cables for Wi-Fi signals. A SercoNet-powered solution would pick up the output of your AP at one

location (a phone jack near your AP) and then carry that radio signal over the phone lines. At the remote location (like Danny's infamous third floor in the brick-and-stone house), you plug another SercoNet-powered device into a phone jack. The signal is regenerated and transmitted anew — which gives you a clean, high-powered, and full-speed Wi-Fi signal. (There's no scaling down on the speed like today's HPNA or HomePlug solutions — SercoNet can carry full 802.11g or a speeds.)

Keep your eyes open for this one if you have a big house and want to extend your Wi-Fi.

Home Phoning (ET Got It Backward!)

Using your home phone lines to network devices is called (you guessed it) *phone line networking*. This fairly mature technology grew up at about the same time as the digital subscriber line (DSL) industry, around the mid-1990s. Phone line networking standards have been developed by an industry group named HomePNA, or sometimes just HPNA (Home Phoneline Networking Association; www.homepna.org).

HPNA equipment is getting hard to find. The technology is still alive, but has been not particularly successful as folks flocked to Wi-Fi and HomePlug and skipped HPNA entirely. However, some companies are still making HPNA gear, and the faster HPNA 3.0 standard (which we discuss later in this chapter) is being explored by some broadband service providers and may be included in forthcoming broadband modem-router combinations. All in all, however, HPNA isn't necessarily a great long-term bet — we won't *not* recommend it if you find a good deal on some equipment, but we also don't think that we would spend much money on HPNA these days because we wouldn't be sure that replacement equipment would ever be available.

Several types of HPNA are available:

- ✔ **HPNA 1.0:** The first HPNA standard operates at a slower speed (1.3 Mbps) and is disappearing from the shelves.

- ✔ **HPNA 2.0:** Much faster than 1.0, this version can reach speeds similar to those of an Ethernet LAN. It's advertised as 10 Mbps, but the maximum speed is 16 Mbps. This version is backward compatible with HPNA 1.0.

✔ **HPNA 3.0:** A 3.0 version of the standard that allows much higher speeds is in the works. The goal is to reach speeds of up to 128 Mbps initially, with later versions reaching 240 Mbps — enough speed to carry even high-definition video signals. These are coming soon, so check stores for which version is available when.

Although the newer 2.0 products can talk to older 1.0 ones, having even one HPNA 1.0 device connected to your phone lines slows down *all* the HPNA 2.0 devices to 1.3 Mbps. Make sure that all yours are 2.0 if you want that technology. The new 3.0 version will have improved backward compatibility so that HPNA 3.0 devices (when they show up) aren't slowed down just because older HPNA endpoints are connected to the phone lines.

HomePNA products are available in several different form factors. You're likely to encounter them in two major ways:

✔ **Built into the AP, router, or other device:** These are installed in peripheral or entertainment devices (such as Internet-enabled stereos) right from the factory.

✔ **A stand-alone adapter:** Some HomePNA Ethernet and USB adapters are external devices that connect to a computer's Ethernet or USB ports by using a cable. You can also get internal Network Interface Card (NIC) adapters in PC Card and Peripheral Component Interconnect (PCI) Card formats for laptop and desktop machines.

The typical HomePNA interface has a regular RJ-11 phone jack that you plug into your nearest outlet. The HomePNA system operates on different frequencies than analog or DSL telephone services, so you can simultaneously use a single phone line for your computer LAN and for all the other things you now use it for (making phone calls, sending and receiving faxes, or connecting to the Internet).

To connect your HomePNA endpoints (the computers or audio systems or other devices using HomePNA in your home) back onto your Internet connection, you need to connect the HomePNA network through your router to your Internet connection. The main source of such routers is the company 2Wire (www.2wire.com), which sells broadband modem-router devices through phone companies for DSL service.

Typically, getting HPNA delivered by your DSL provider is the *only* way most folks get involved in HPNA these days.

Part II
Making Plans

The 5th Wave   By Rich Tennant

"You the guy having trouble staying connected to the network?"

In this part . . .

This part of the book helps you plan for installing your wireless home network — from deciding what you will connect to the network to making buying decisions and planning the installation of wireless networking equipment in your home.

Chapter 4

Planning a Wireless Home Network

*W*e're sure that you have heard this sage advice: "One who doesn't plan is doomed to failure." On the other hand, management guru and author Peter Drucker says, "Plans are only good intentions unless they immediately degenerate into hard work." Because you're going to be spending your hard-earned money to buy the equipment necessary for your wireless network, we assume that you want to do a little planning before you start building your network. But, if you prefer to shoot first and aim later, feel free to skip this chapter and Chapter 5.

In this chapter, we show you how to plan a wireless home network — from selecting a wireless technology (you can choose from several variants) to deciding what things to connect and where to connect them to the all-important act of budgeting. You also find out about other issues you should consider when planning your home network, including connecting to the Internet; sharing printers, other peripherals, and fun, noncomputer devices; and security. When you're ready to begin buying the wireless home networking parts (if you haven't done so already), head to Chapter 5, where we give some detailed advice about buying exactly the equipment you need. In Part III, we show you how to set up and install your wireless home network.

Deciding What to Connect to the Network

Believe it or not, some technogeeks have a computer in every room of their houses. We have some close friends who fit into that category (including, well, ourselves). You may not own as many computers as we do (Danny has more than 10 in his house), but you probably own more than one, and we're guessing that you have at least one printer and some other peripherals. You're wirelessly networking your home for a reason, no matter whether it's to share that cool, new color ink jet printer (or scanner or digital video recorder) or to play your computer-based video files on your new wide-screen TV or to give every computer in the house always-on access to the Internet. Whatever your reason, the first thing you must do when planning a wireless home network is to determine what you want connected to the network.

Counting network devices

The first step to take in planning a network is to count the number of devices you want to attach to the network — that means any computer or device that you want attached to your broadband Internet connection, to your file servers, or to shared resources, like printers. Bottom line: You almost certainly will connect to your network each of the computers you use regularly.

Next, consider devices that aren't necessarily computers in the traditional sense, but that can benefit from a network connection — for example, the printers we mention in the preceding paragraph. You don't need to connect a printer directly to a single PC in a networked environment — you can connect it to a device known as a *print server* and let all your networked PCs access it. Similarly, you can connect devices, like *NAS* (Network Attached Storage), that let you store big files in a centralized location (or even do PC backups over the network). In Chapter 14, we talk about a whole big bunch of networkable devices that can go on your wireless LAN.

If you're an audiophile or just enjoy digital media, you should consider adding your home entertainment system to your network so that you can share MP3 files, play video games, and watch DVDs from anywhere in your house, wirelessly! (These cool gadgets are covered in Chapters 11 through 13.)

You can even make your phone calls over your wireless network with one of the Wi-Fi phones we talk about in Chapter 15.

"PDA? Smart phone? What's what?"

The value of a PDA is a hotly debated subject. "Experts" agree that the value of any device is measured by its use. If you use it and are comfortable with it, it has value. If it sits in its case most of the time, you should think about listing it on eBay and getting some of your money back.

Most people these days already own a PDA and don't even know it. Cell phones are now packed with power, and most contain many, if not all, of the functions of a PDA in both full and limited forms. But having it and using it are two different things, and most consumer cell phones — though they contain all the features — aren't designed to share data outside of the device. Yes, you can carry the coolest games, but at some point you will probably want to get some work done and that can't happen if you can't

share any of the information from one device to another. Most integrated PDAs and cell phones these days have the ability to link directly to many types of wireless networks. They can store and transfer all types of data from Word documents, contacts, e-mails, instant messaging, JPEG pictures, and MPEG video files. These integrated devices can use the cellular network as well as your wireless home network and Bluetooth, for example, to connect to other computers, your network, and the Internet directly. When you're considering one of these devices, consider compatibility with the applications you already use. If the device doesn't work with what you have or expect to get, you have paid a good chunk of cash for a device you probably won't use.

Don't forget about your personal digital assistant (PDA), if you're lucky enough to own one of those little gems and it's wireless enabled — which most are these days — you can add it to your total number of devices. If you happen to have an older PDA that has wireless embedded into it, wireless adapters are available that fit into the Compact Flash, or specialty, slot in most typical PDAs. These adapters enable you to connect your PDA wirelessly to a computer, the Internet in the case of a cell phone PDA, or to your home network. (Hop to Chapters 2 and 3 for the lowdown on different types of wireless connectivity.)

As you plan out your network and count devices, consider that some devices already have built-in all the wireless network capabilities they need. For example, most laptop computers now sold already support at least 802.11g wireless networking — so you should count them on your list, but you don't need to spend any money to add them to your network.

Choosing wired or wireless

After you know *what* you're networking, you need to choose *how* to network it. By that, we mean that you have to decide what to connect to your home's network with wires and what you should use wireless networking for. At first glance, this decision may seem obvious. You would expect us to always recommend using *wireless* because this book talks about *wireless* networks; however, using both wired and wireless connections can sometimes make the most sense.

Wireless network devices and wired network devices can be used on the same network. Both talk to the network and to each other using a protocol known as Ethernet. (You should be getting used to that term by now if you have been reading from the beginning of the book. If not, read through Chapters 1 and 2 for more information about networking technology.)

The obvious and primary benefit of connecting to a network wirelessly is that you eliminate wires running all over the place. But, if two devices are sitting on the same desk or table — or are within a few feet of each other — connecting them wirelessly may be pointless. You can get Ethernet cables for $5 or less; an equivalent wireless capability for two devices may top $100 when everything is said and done. Keep in mind, however, that your computer must have a wired network adapter installed to be able to make a wired connection to the network. Fortunately, wired network adapters are dirt cheap these days. Virtually all new computers come with one installed as a standard feature (at no additional charge).

Figure 4-1 shows a simple drawing of a network that connects a wireless PC to a wired PC through two network devices: an access point (AP) and a hub or switch. (Recall that your *AP* connects wireless devices to the rest of the wired network. A network *hub* or *switch* is often used to connect PCs to the network by a wired connection. In Chapter 1, we describe the purpose of and differences between APs and hubs and switches.) If you think that it seems absurd to need two network devices to connect two computers, you're not alone. Hardware manufacturers have addressed this issue by creating APs that have a built-in switch — in fact, it's hard to buy an AP that doesn't have a switch (as well as a broadband *router*) built into it. See the section "Choosing an access point," later in this chapter, for more information about these multifunction APs.

Figure 4-1:
A network
can use
both
wireless
and wired
connections.

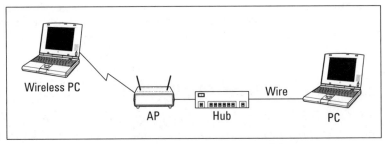

Choosing a wireless technology

After you know what you're networking *and* what will be on your wireless network, you have to decide *how to network wirelessly.* As we discuss extensively in Chapter 2, three main variants of wireless networking technologies exist: 802.11a, 802.11b, and 802.11g.

Collectively, all these technologies are usually referred to as *Wi-Fi,* which isn't a generic term but, rather, refers to a certification of *interoperability.* The folks at the Wi-Fi Alliance (`www.wi-fi.org`) do extensive testing of new wireless gear, to make sure that it works seamlessly with wireless equipment from different manufacturers. When it works, it gets the Wi-Fi logo on the box and you can rest assured that it works in your network.

Wi-Fi-certified gear works together — as long as it's of a *compatible* type. That means that any 802.11b or 802.11g Wi-Fi-certified gear works with any other equipment of that type; similarly, any 802.11a Wi-Fi-certified gear works with any other 802.11a gear that has been certified. 802.11b/g gear *does not* work with 802.11a gear, even if it has all been certified.

The discussion of wireless technology quickly degenerates into a sea of acronyms and technospeak. If you need a refresher on all this alphabet soup — or to begin from square one — Chapter 2 is a primer on jargon, abbreviations, and other nuts-and-bolts issues.

For home users, the three most important practical differences between 802.11a, 802.11b, and 802.11g networks are speed, price, and compatibility:

- ✔ **802.11b** is an older standard that is only used on a few pieces of equipment these days. You typically find only 802.11b in your network if you have *legacy* equipment that's been around for a few years.

- ✔ **802.11g** equipment is only slightly more expensive than similar 802.11b equipment but is at least four times faster.

- ✔ **802.11a** is as fast as 802.11g but is costs a bit more (typically) and has a shorter range.

- ✔ **802.11a and 802.11b/802.11g** are *not* compatible.

- ✔ **802.11b and 802.11g** *are* compatible.

Because 802.11g is compatible with 802.11b, an AP that includes 802.11g should work with any 802.11b device as well (though not always at the higher 54 Mbps speed of 802.11g). Thus, you don't have to look for a dual-mode 802.11b-and-802.11g AP.

Going even faster

In Chapter 2, we discuss all the faster variants of 802.11g — the proprietary Super G products, the *MIMO* products, and those labeled as *Pre-N* (meaning that they're designed for the forthcoming but not-yet-approved 802.11n standard). All these systems can go faster and further than plain old 802.11g systems (meaning higher throughput speeds and greater range).

The good thing about all these systems (at least all the systems we have seen on the market) is that they're backward compatible with 802.11g. So, you can buy them and safely feel that they

will work with whatever gear you bring into the network. You may even get a speed and range benefit *without* having matching gear on both ends.

To get the maximum benefit (speed, range, or both), however, you need to buy all your Wi-Fi gear (the AP or router and the network adapters, for example) from the same vendor, or from vendors supporting the same standards. You *will* pay more for this privilege. Check out Chapter 2 for our recommendations.

If your primary reason for networking the computers in your house is to enable Internet sharing, 802.11b is theoretically more than fast enough because your Internet connection probably won't exceed the 11 Mbps of the 802.11b connection any time soon — unless you're one of the lucky few who lives where fiber optic Internet services (like Verizon's FiOS service) are being installed.

Despite that fact, we don't recommend that you buy 802.11b gear. 802.11b is basically a dead technology, superseded by 802.11g. In fact, you would save only a few bucks by buying 802.11b gear new, and it's increasingly hard to even find.

The 802.11g standard is the baseline you should build your network around.

If you want to hedge your bets, look for an AP that can handle both 802.11a and 802.11b/g technology standards. Linksys, NETGEAR, D-Link, and several other leading manufacturers of wireless home networking equipment already offer a/b/g dual-mode, tri-standard wireless devices.

If you feel the real need for speed, consider a Super G, MIMO, or Pre-N product (discussed in the nearby sidebar, "Going even faster").

Choosing an access point

The most important and typically most expensive device in a wireless network is the access point (AP; also sometimes called a base station). An AP acts like a wireless switchboard that connects wireless devices on the network to each other and to the rest of the wired network; it's required to create a wireless home network. Figure 4-2 depicts three PCs connected wirelessly to each other through an AP.

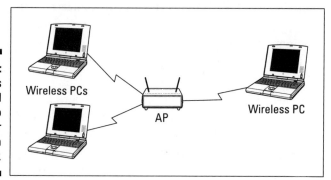

Wireless PCs

AP

Wireless PC

The vast majority of APs now available aren't *just* access points. Instead, most incorporate the functionality of a *broadband router* (which connects multiple computers to an Internet connection), a *network switch* (which connects multiple wired computers together) and even a *firewall* (which helps keep "bad guys" off your network).

The most popular APs for use in home networks are those that can do one or more of the following:

- ✔ **Connect wired PCs:** A *switch* is an enhanced version of a network hub that operates more efficiently and quickly than a simple hub. By building a switch inside the AP, you can use the one device to connect PCs to your network by using either wired network adapters or wireless adapters. We cover hubs and switches in more detail in Chapter 1.

- ✔ **Assign network addresses:** Every computer on a network or on the Internet has its own address: its Internet Protocol (IP) address. Computers on the Internet communicate — they forward e-mail, Web pages, and the like — by sending data back and forth from IP address to IP address. A *Dynamic Host Configuration Protocol* (DHCP) server dynamically assigns private IP addresses to the computers on your home network so that they can communicate. You could use a software utility in Windows (or Mac OS) to manually assign an IP address to each computer, but that process is tedious and much less flexible than automatic address assignment.

- ✔ **Connect to the Internet:** With a *cable/digital subscriber line (DSL) router* between a broadband modem and your home network, all computers on the network can access the Internet directly. An AP combined with a DHCP and a cable or DSL router is sometimes called a *wireless Internet gateway*. (See the "Connecting to the Internet" section, later in this chapter, for more about the Network Address Translation [NAT] feature that makes Internet sharing possible and for more on Internet connectivity.)

✔ **Add a print server:** A *print server* enables you to connect a printer directly to the network rather than connect it to one of the computers on the network. See the "Adding printers" section, later in this chapter.

✔ **Connect in many ways:** The most common method of connecting an AP to your computer or to the wired portion of your network is through an Ethernet port, but other options may be much easier to install if your house isn't wired with Ethernet cable. If you have created a HomePNA wired network by using the phone lines in your home, look for an AP that has a HomePNA port. Similarly, if you have set up a HomePlug wired network using the power lines in your home, shop for an AP with HomePlug connectivity. (For more on HomePNA and HomePlug, skip to Chapter 3.)

Access points with HomePlug built into them are very handy when you want to add a second AP to your network in a remote part of the house (somewhere that doesn't get good coverage from your main AP). With HomePlug, you can plug a small device (like the Belkin Powerline Ethernet Adapter [www.belkin.com]) into the wall and have an instant extra network connection with no special connections. (You need to have two HomePlug devices, one in — or near — your main AP or router and one in the location you want to extend the network to, of course.)

✔ **Provide firewall security:** A *firewall* is a device that basically keeps the bad guys off your network and out of your computers. We talk much more about firewalls in Chapter 10, but basically, a firewall is typically included in your access point to provide network security.

✔ **Be combined with a modem:** If you're a cable Internet or DSL subscriber, you may be able to use your own modem rather than lease one from your Internet service provider (ISP). In that case, consider purchasing a modem that's also a wireless AP. A cable or DSL modem combined with a wireless Internet gateway is the ultimate solution in terms of installation convenience and equipment cost savings.

You typically can't buy a modem/AP/router combination off the shelf (or at most Internet retailers) like you can buy a nonmodem AP/router. You get these all-in-one devices directly from your broadband service provider in almost all cases.

Deciding where to install the access point

If you have ever experienced that dreaded dead zone while talking on a cellular phone, you know how frustrating poor wireless coverage can be. To avoid this situation within your wireless home network, you should strive to install your wireless network equipment in a way that eliminates dead wireless network zones in your house. Ideally, you determine the best placement of your AP so that no spot in your house is left uncovered; but, if that isn't possible for some reason, you should at least find out where, if anywhere, the dead zones in your house are in order to optimize your signal coverage.

To achieve optimum signal coverage, the best place to install an AP is near the center of your home. Think about where you will place the AP when you make your buying decision. All APs can sit on a shelf or table, but some APs can also be mounted to a wall or ceiling. When making your AP selection, ensure that it can be installed where it works best for the configuration of your house as well as keeps the AP out of reach of your little ones or curious pets.

The position of the access point is critical because your entire signal footprint emanates from the AP in a known way, centered from the AP's antennas. Sometimes, not enough consideration is given to the positioning of the access point because they so often work pretty well out of the box, just sitting on a table.

Other people install the AP wrong in the first place. For example, probably one of the worst manufacturing decisions ever done to access points was to put mounting brackets on them. People get the impression that you should then — duh — mount them on the wall. That's great except for the fact that, depending on the antenna you have, you may just kill most of your throughput. You see, when an antenna is flush up against a wall, as is typical in a wall mount situation, the signals of the antenna reflect off the wall back at the antenna, causing interference, and driving down throughput precipitously. Yech. (But you see, customers *want* their wall mount brackets, so product managers at wireless LAN companies decided that they had to give it to them.) The best mounting is six or more inches off the wall.

The vertical positioning of the mounting point is important as well. Generally, you have more interference lower to the ground. If you did a cross section of your house in one-foot intervals, when you get higher and higher, you would see less on your map. Thus, signals from an access point located on a shelf low to the ground will find more to run into than the ones that are mounted higher. Although this may sound like common sense, consider that most DSL and cable modems are installed by technicians who are used to installing phone and cable TV lines. How many of these are generally located 5 feet off the floor? They're not; they tend to be along the floorboards and low to the ground or in the basement. It's not surprising that a combined DSL access point router would be plugged in low to the ground, too.

See where we're going with this? You don't care where your cable modem is, but you should care where your AP functionality is located. And, if you have an integrated product, you're probably tempted to swap out the cable modem for the cable modem access point. Simply moving that unit higher almost always does a world of good.

Moving an AP out of the line of sight of microwaves, cordless phones, refrigerators, and other devices is a good idea, too. Mounting the AP in the laundry room off the kitchen doesn't make a great deal of sense if you plan to use the

Wireless interference in the home

Probably the single biggest performance killer in your wireless home network is interference in the home. The Federal Communications Commission (FCC) set aside certain unlicensed frequencies that could be used for low-power wireless applications. In specific frequency bands, manufacturers can make (and you can use) equipment that doesn't require a license from the FCC for the user to operate. This is different from, for example, buying a 50,000-watt radio transmitter and blasting it over your favorite FM radio frequency band, which would be a major no-no because those bands are licensed for certain power levels.

As a result, all sorts of companies have created products (including cordless phones, wireless radio frequency [RF] remote controls, wireless speakers, TV set extenders, and walkie-talkies) that make use of these frequency bands. If you have lots of wireless devices already in your home, there is a good chance that they may use some of the same frequency bands that your wireless home network uses.

Another form of wireless interference comes from devices that emit energy in the same bands, such as microwave ovens. If you have a cordless phone with its base station near a microwave and you notice that the voice quality degrades every time you use the microwave, that's because the micro (radio) waves are in the same radiation band as your cordless phone. Motors, refrigerators, and other home consumer devices do the same thing.

What's the answer? The good news is that you can deal with almost all these by knowing what to look for and being smart about where you place your equipment. If your access point is in the back office and you want to frequently work in the living room with your laptop — but your kitchen is in the middle — you may want to look at adding a second access point in the living room and link it with the office via any of a number of alternative connections options (which we talk about in Chapter 3) that are immune to the microwave problems we mention earlier.

Remember these specific things to look for when shopping. You see cordless phones operating primarily in the 900 MHz, 2.4 GHz, and 5 GHz frequencies. The 900 MHz phones pose no problems — but are also almost impossible to find these days — and the 2.4 GHz and 5 GHz phones interfere with your wireless network signals (in the 802.11b/g and 802.11a frequency ranges, respectively). Just know that cordless phones and wireless home networks really don't like each other much. In Chapter 19, we talk about cordless phones, which carry your voice *over* your wireless network, and are part of the network instead of interfering with it.

AP primarily in rooms on the other side of the kitchen. Passing through commonly used interferers (all those metal appliances) like that generally isn't a smart move.

Factors that affect signal strength

Many variables affect whether you get an adequate signal at any given point in your house, including these factors:

✓ **Distance from the AP:** The farther away from the AP, the weaker the signal. Wi-Fi 802.11g networks, for example, promise a maximum operating range of 100 feet at 54 Mbps to 300 feet at 1 Mbps. Indoors, a realistic range at 54 Mbps is about 60 feet. 802.11a networks have an even shorter range. Range differs from vendor to vendor as well.

Many of the proprietary (non-standards-based) 802.11g networks we discuss in Chapter 2 (using Super G or MIMO systems) have significantly longer ranges than standards-based 802.11g systems. You need to have the proprietary equipment on both ends of the connection to gain the maximum-range gain with these systems. If you have a particularly large home (or one that is difficult to cover wirelessly), you may want to seriously consider paying a few extra bucks for a MIMO-based system.

✔ **The power of the transmitter:** Wi-Fi APs transmit at a power output of less than 30 dBm (one watt).

✔ **The directivity or gain of the antennas attached to the AP and to wireless network adapters:** Different antennas are designed to provide different radiation patterns. That's a fancy way of saying that some are designed to send radio waves in all directions equally, yet others concentrate their strength in certain directions. We talk more about this in Chapter 6, but the thing to keep in mind here is that different brands and models of access points have different kinds of antennas designed for different applications. Check out the specifications of the ones you're looking at before you buy them.

✔ **The construction materials used in the walls, floors, and ceilings:** Some construction materials are relatively transparent to radio signals, but other materials — such as marble, brick, water, paper, bulletproof glass, concrete, and especially metal — tend to reflect some of the signal, thus reducing signal strength.

✔ **Your house plan:** The physical layout of your house may not only determine where it's practical to position an AP, but also affect signal strength because the position of walls and the number of floors, brick fireplaces, basements, and so on can partially or even completely block the wireless network's radio signal.

✔ **Client locations:** Reception is affected by the distance from the AP to the rooms in your house where someone will need wireless network access.

✔ **Stationary physical objects:** Objects permanently installed in your home — such as metal doors, heating ducts, and brick fireplaces — can block some or all of the signal to particular spots in your house.

✔ **Movable physical objects:** Other types of objects, including furniture, appliances, plants, and even people can also block enough of the signal to cause the network to slow down or even to lose a good connection.

✔ **APs:** Interference can also be caused by the presence of other APs. In other words, if you have a big house (too big for a single AP to cover), you have to keep in mind that in parts of the house — like in the area that's pretty much directly between the two APs — you find that the radio waves from each AP can interfere with the other. Check out the following subsection for more information regarding this phenomenon.

You should attempt to keep a direct line between APs, residential gateways, and the wireless devices on your network. A wall that is 1.5 feet thick, at a 45° angle, appears to be almost 3 feet thick. At a 2° angle, it looks more than 42 feet thick. Try to make sure that the AP and wireless adapters are positioned so that the signal travels straight through a wall or ceiling for better reception.

RF interference

Nowadays, many devices that once required wires are now wireless, and this situation is becoming more prevalent all the time. Some wireless devices use infrared technology, but many wireless devices, including your wireless network, communicate by using radio frequency (RF) waves. As a consequence, the network can be disrupted by RF interference from other devices sharing the same frequencies used by your wireless network.

Among the devices most likely to interfere with 802.11b and 802.11g networks are microwave ovens and cordless telephones that use the 2.4 GHz band. The best way to avoid this interference is to place APs and computers with wireless adapters at least 6 feet away from the microwave and the base station of any portable phone that uses the 2.4 GHz band.

Bluetooth devices also use the 2.4 GHz band, but the hop pattern of the Bluetooth modulation protocol all but ensures that any interference is short enough in duration to be negligible.

Because relatively few devices are trying to share the 5 GHz frequencies used by 802.11a, your network is less likely to experience RF interference if it's using 802.11a.

You should also try to keep all electric motors and electrical devices that generate RF noise through their normal operation, such as monitors, refrigerators, electric motors, and Universal Power Supply (UPS) units at least 3 and preferably 6 feet away from a wireless network device.

Signal obstacles

Wireless technologies are susceptible to physical obstacles. When you decide where best to place your APs, look at Table 4-1, which lists obstacles that can affect the strength of your wireless signals. The table lists common household obstacles (although often overlooked) as well as the degree to which the obstacle is a hindrance to your wireless network signals.

Table 4-1   How Common Household Items Affect a Wi-Fi Signal

Obstruction	Degree of Attenuation	Example
Open space	Low	Backyard
Wood	Low	Inner wall; door; floor
Plaster	Low	Inner wall (older plaster is lower than newer plaster)
Synthetic materials	Low	Partitions; home theater treatments
Cinder block	Low	Inner wall; outer wall
Asbestos	Low	Ceiling (older buildings)
Glass	Low	Nontinted window
Wire mesh in glass	Medium	Door; window
Metal tinted glass	Medium	Tinted window
Human body	Medium	Groupings of people (dinner table)
Water	Medium	Damp wood; aquarium; in-home water treatments
Bricks	Medium	Inner wall; outer wall; floor
Marble	Medium	Inner wall; outer wall; floor
Ceramic (metal content or backing)	High	Ceramic tile; ceiling; floor
Paper	High	Stack of paper stock, such as newspaper piles
Concrete	High	Floor; outer wall; support pillar
Bulletproof glass	High	Windows; door
Silvering	Very high	Mirror
Metal	Very high	Inner wall; air conditioning; filing cabinets; reinforced concrete walls and floors

Source: Intel (http://www.intel.com/business/bss/infrastructure/wireless/deployment/ considerations.htm#relative; www.intel.com/network/connectivity/solutions/wireless/ deploy_site.htm); TeleChoice

The RF doughnut

The shape of the radio signal that is transmitted to the rooms in your home is determined by the type of antenna you have attached to the AP. The standard antenna on any AP is an *omnidirectional* antenna, which broadcasts its signal in a spherical shape. The signal pattern that radiates from a typical omnidirectional dipole antenna is shaped like a fat doughnut with a tiny hole in the middle. The hole is directly above and below the antenna.

The signal goes from the antenna to the floor above and the floor below as well as to the floor on which the AP is located. If your house has multiple floors, try the second floor first. Most AP manufacturers claim a range of 100 feet indoors (at 11 Mbps for 802.11b or at 54 Mbps for 802.11a and 802.11g). To be conservative, assume a range of 60 feet laterally and one floor above and below the AP. Keep in mind that the signal at the edges of the "doughnut" and on the floors below or above the AP are weaker than the signal nearer the center and on the same floor as the AP.

Because of this signal pattern, you should try to place the AP as close to the center of your house as is practically possible. Use a drawing of your house plan to locate the center of the house. This spot is your first trial AP location.

Draw a circle with a 60-foot radius on your house plan, using the trial AP location as the center of the circle. If your entire house falls inside the circle, one AP will probably do the job. Conversely, if some portion of the house is outside the circle, coverage may be weaker in that area. You need to experiment to determine whether you get an adequate signal there.

If you determine that one AP will not cover your house, you need to decide how best to place two APs (or even three, as necessary). The design of your house determines the best placement. For a one-level design, start at one end of the house and determine the best location for a 60-foot radius circle that covers all the way to the walls. The center of this circle is the location of the first AP. Then move toward the other end of the house, drawing 60-foot radius circles until the house is covered. The center of each circle is a trial location of an AP. If possible, don't leave any area in the house uncovered. Don't forget your garage: With the right gear (like the Rockford Fosgate OmniFi), you can synchronize your wireless network with your car, including sending digital movies and MP3 files. (See Chapter 14 for more about connecting to your car.)

 You may want to consider reading Chapter 18 on troubleshooting before you finish your planning. Some good tips in that chapter talk about setting up and tweaking your network.

Adding printers

In addition to connecting your computers, you may want to connect your printers to the network. Next to sharing an Internet connection, printer sharing is perhaps the biggest cost-savings reason for building a network of home computers. Rather than buy a printer for every PC, everyone in the house can share one printer. Or, maybe you have one color ink jet printer and one black-and-white laser printer. If both printers are connected to the network, all computers on the network can potentially print to either printer. Or, perhaps you just want to sit by the pool with your wireless laptop and still be able to print to the printer up in your bedroom; it's easy with a network-attached printer.

You can also share other peripherals, such as network-aware scanners and fax machines. Leading manufacturers of digital imaging equipment (like Hewlett-Packard) offer feature-rich, multiple-function peripherals that combine an ink jet or laser printer with a scanner, copier, telephone, answering machine, and fax machine all-in-one device. If you want to share such a device over your network, make sure that you buy one that comes with network server software.

Here are two ways to share printers over a wired or wireless network:

- ✔ **Connect to a computer:** The easiest and cheapest way to connect a printer to the network is to connect a printer to one of the computers on the network. Windows enables you to share any printer connected to any Windows computer on the network. (For more on this topic, read Chapter 11.) The computer to which the printer is connected has to be running for any other computers on the network to use the printer. Similarly, if you're using Apple computers, any computer connected to the network can print to a printer that's connected to one of the computers on the network.

- ✔ **Print server:** Another way to add a printer is through a print server. Several hardware manufacturers produce print server devices that enable you to connect one or more printers directly to the network. Some of these devices connect via a network cable, and others are wireless. Many high-end printers even have print server options that are installed inside the printer cabinet. For home use, stand-alone network print servers are a bit pricey. Surprisingly, some manufacturers bundle a print server with their cable or DSL router at little or no additional cost. If you shop around, you can probably find a wireless AP, cable or DSL router, and print server bundled in one device for less than the cost of some stand-alone print servers.

You should be able to get your home network printer connections for free. Obviously, it doesn't cost anything to connect a printer to a computer that's already connected to the network. Several manufacturers also include a print server for free with other network devices. If you don't need one of those devices, just connect the printer you want to share to one of the computers on your home network.

Figure 4-3 depicts a home network with one printer connected to one of the PCs on the network and another printer connected to a wireless Internet *gateway,* which is a device that bundles a wireless AP and a cable/DSL router into a single unit. In this case, the wireless Internet gateway also has a connection for a printer and acts as a print server. Read through Chapters 1 and 5 for more information about these devices, what they do, and how to choose between them.

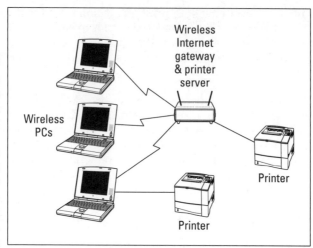

Figure 4-3:
A wireless home network with a wireless Internet gateway and a bundled print server.

Connecting your printer to the wireless Internet gateway device is advantageous because a print server permits the printer to stand alone on the network, untethered from any specific computer. When you want to print to a printer that's connected directly to a computer on the network, that computer must be present and turned on; and, in many cases, you must have a user account and appropriate permission to access the shared printer. A print server makes its printers always available to any computer on the network — even from poolside.

Most folks don't mind having their printer connected to a computer or to a gateway device in their home — meaning that the computer is connected via peripheral cables to one of these devices. You may, however, want to make your printer *itself* wireless — so you can stick it *anywhere* in your house, even if that means that it's far away from any PCs or gateway devices. In this case, you may consider buying a *wireless print server* that can either be an internal part of your printer (it is an optional module from the printer manufacturer) or that sits next to your printer. In this case, your printer is completely decoupled from your wired network — the server is a wireless network *client* as well as the hardware and software to run the printer itself.

Why would you spring for the extra money (about $80 to $100)? Here's an example. Pat had a spot (a closet) right in the middle of his house (literally!) where he wanted to hide a printer — but no wires and no PCs nearby. A wireless print server solved the problem and got his printer out of the way (and still in a convenient location).

Adding entertainment and more

When you're planning your wireless network, don't forget to plan to add a few gadgets for fun and relaxation. The wildly popular video-game consoles from Sony, Microsoft, and Nintendo all offer network connectivity and Internet connectively. Don't forget to consult with the gamers in your household when planning where you need network coverage in your home. And, don't forget to take a look at Chapter 12 for the skinny about connecting your favorite console to your wireless network, as well as info on network-based, multiuser PC gaming.

An increasing number of consumer electronics devices, such as digital home entertainment systems, are network aware. Feature-packed home media servers can store thousands of your favorite MP3s and digital videos and make them available over the network to all the computers in your house. Several even include optional wireless networking connectivity. Connecting the sound and video from your PC to your home theater is even possible — really. Imagine surfing the Internet on a wide-screen TV! Jump to Chapter 13 for the details about connecting your A/V gear to your wireless home network.

Some of the coolest home electronic technology in recent years enables you to control the lights, heating, cooling, security system, home entertainment system, and pool right from your computer. Equally exciting technology enables you to use a home network to set up a highly affordable home video monitoring system. By hooking these systems to your wireless network and hooking the network to the Internet, you can make it possible to monitor and control your home's utilities and systems, even while away from home. Check out Chapter 14 for more about these smart home technologies as well as additional cool things you can network, such as connecting to your car or using your network to connect to the world.

Connecting to the Internet

When you get right down to it, the reason that most people build wireless networks in their homes is to share their Internet connection with multiple computers or devices that they have around the house. That's why we did it — and we bet that's why you're doing it. We have reached the point in our lives where a computer that's not constantly connected to a network and to the Internet is just about useless. We're not really even exaggerating much here. Even things you do locally (use a spreadsheet program, for example) can be enhanced by an Internet connection; in that spreadsheet program, you can link to the Internet to do real-time currency conversions.

What a wireless network brings to the table is true whole-home Internet access. Particularly when combined with an always-on Internet connection (which we discuss in just a second) — but even with a regular dial-up modem connection — a wireless network lets you access the Internet from just about every nook and cranny of the house. Take the laptop out to the back patio, let a visitor connect from the guest room, or do some work in bed. Whatever you want to do and wherever you want to do it, a wireless network can support you.

A wireless home network — or any home network, for that matter — provides one key element. It uses a *NAT router* (we describe this item later in this section) to provide Internet access to multiple devices over a single Internet connection coming into the home. With a NAT router (which typically is built into your access point or in a separate home network router), you can not only connect more than one computer to the Internet, but also simultaneously connect multiple computers (and other devices, like game consoles) to the Internet over a single connection. The NAT router has the brains to figure out which Web page or e-mail or online gaming information is going to which *client* (PC or device) on the network.

Not surprisingly, to take advantage of this Internet-from-anywhere access in your home, you need some sort of Internet service and modem. We don't get into great detail about this topic, but we do want to make sure that you keep it in mind when you plan your network.

Most people access the Internet from a home computer in these ways:

- ✔ Dial-up telephone connection
- ✔ Digital subscriber line (DSL)
- ✔ Cable Internet
- ✔ Satellite broadband

DSL, cable, and satellite Internet service are often called *broadband* Internet service, which is a term that gets defined differently by just about everyone in the industry. For our purposes, we define it as a connection that's faster than a dial-up modem connection (sometimes called *narrowband*) and that's always on. That is, you don't have to use a dialer to get connected, but instead you have a persistent connection that's available immediately without any setup steps necessary for the users (at least after the first time you have set up your connection).

Broadband Internet service providers are busily wiring neighborhoods all over the United States, but none of the services is available everywhere. (Satellite is available almost everywhere, but, as with satellite TV, you need to meet certain criteria, such as having a view to the south: that is, facing the satellites, which orbit over the equator.) Where it's available, however, growing numbers of families are experiencing the benefits of always-on and very fast Internet connectivity.

In some areas of the country, wireless systems are beginning to become available as a means of connecting to the Internet. Most of these systems use special radio systems that are proprietary to their manufacturers. That is, you buy a transceiver and an antenna and hook it up on your roof or in a window. But a few are using modified versions of Wi-Fi to provide Internet access to people's homes. In either case, you have some sort of modem device that connects to your AP via a standard Ethernet cable, just like you would use for a DSL or cable modem connection.

For the purpose of this discussion of wireless home networks, DSL and cable Internet are equivalent. If you can get both at your house, shop around for price and talk to your neighbors about their experiences. You may also check out www.broadbandreports.com, which is a Web site where customers of a variety of broadband services discuss and compare their experiences. As soon as you splurge for a DSL or cable Internet connection, the PC that happens to be situated nearest the spot where the installer placed the DSL or cable modem is at a distinct advantage because it is the easiest computer to connect to the modem — and therefore to the Internet. Most DSL and cable modems connect to the PC through a wired network adapter card. The best way, therefore, to connect any computer in the home to the Internet is through a home network.

You have two ways to share an Internet connection over a home network:

- **Software-based Internet connection sharing:** Windows 2000, Windows XP, and Mac OS X enable sharing of an Internet connection. Each computer in the network must be set up to connect to the Internet through the computer that's connected to the broadband modem. The disadvantage with this system is that you can't turn off or remove the computer that's connected to the modem without disconnecting all computers from the Internet. In other words, the computer that's connected to the modem must be on for other networked computers to access the Internet through it.

- **Cable or DSL router:** When you connect a cable or DSL router between the broadband modem and your home network, all computers on the network can access the Internet without going through another computer. The Internet connection no longer depends on any computer on the network. Cable and DSL routers are also DHCP servers and typically include switches. In fact, the AP and the modem can also include a built-in router that provides instant Internet sharing all in one device.

As we mention earlier in the chapter, nearly all APs now available for home networks have a cable or DSL router built-in.

Read through Chapter 9 for the details on how to set up Internet sharing.

Given the fact that you can buy a router (either as part of an access point or a separate router) for well under $60 these days (and prices continue to plummet), we think that it's really false economy to skip the router and use a software-based Internet connection sharing setup. In our minds, at least, the advantage of the software-based approach (*very* slightly less money up front) is outweighed by the disadvantages (requiring the PC to always be on, lower reliability, lower performance, and much bigger electric bill each month).

Both software-based Internet connection sharing and cable or DSL routers enable all the computers in your home network to share the same network (IP) address on the Internet. This capability uses *network address translation* (NAT). A device that uses the NAT feature is often called a *NAT router*. The NAT feature communicates with each computer on the network by using a private IP address assigned to that local computer, but the router uses a single public IP address in data it sends to computers on the Internet. In other words, no matter how many computers you have in your house sharing the Internet, they look like only one computer to all the other computers on the Internet.

Whenever your computer is connected to the Internet, beware the potential that some malicious hacker may try to attack your computer with a virus or try to break into your computer to trash your hard drive or steal your personal information. Because NAT technology hides your computer behind the NAT server, it adds a measure of protection against hackers, but you shouldn't rely on it solely for protection against malicious users. You should also consider purchasing full-featured firewall software that actively looks for and blocks hacking attempts, unless the AP or router you purchase provides that added protection. We talk about these items in more detail in Chapter 10.

As we recommend in the section "Choosing an access point," earlier in this chapter, try to choose an AP that also performs several other network-oriented services. Figure 4-4 depicts a wireless home network using an AP that also provides DHCP, NAT, a printer server, and switched hub functions in a single stand-alone unit. This wireless Internet gateway device then connects to the DSL or cable modem, which in turn connects to the Internet. Such a configuration provides you with connectivity, sharing, and a little peace of mind, too.

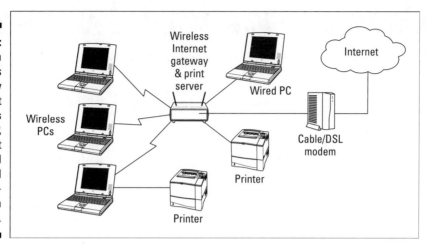

Figure 4-4:
Go for a
wireless
gateway
that
combines
AP, DHCP,
NAT, print
server, and
switched
hub func-
tions in
one unit.

If you already have a wired network and have purchased a cable or DSL router Internet gateway device without the AP function, you don't have to replace the existing device. Just purchase a wireless access point. Figure 4-5 depicts the network design of a typical wired home network with an AP and wireless stations added. Each PC in the wired network is connected to the cable or DSL router, which is also a switch. By connecting the AP to the router, the AP acts as a bridge between the wireless network segment and the existing wired network.

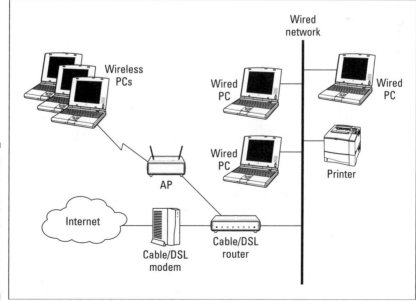

Figure 4-5:
A wired
home
network
with an
AP and
wireless
stations
added.

Budgeting for Your Wireless Network

Assuming that you already own at least one computer (and probably more) and one or more printers that you intend to add to the network, we don't include the cost of computers and printers in this section. In addition, the cost of subscribing to an ISP isn't included in the following networking cost estimates.

Wireless networking hardware — essentially APs and wireless network adapters — is available at a wide range of prices. With a little planning, you won't be tempted to bite on the first product you see. You can use the following guidelines when budgeting for an AP and wireless network adapters. Keep in mind, however, that the prices for this equipment will certainly change over time, perhaps rapidly. Don't use this information as a substitute for due diligence and market research on your part.

Pricing access points

At the time this chapter was written, wireless access points for home use ranged in price from about $35 (street price) to around $100.

Street price is the price at which you can purchase the product from a retail outlet, such as a computer-electronics retail store or an online retailer. The dreaded *suggested retail price* is often higher.

Multifunction access points that facilitate connecting multiple computers to the Internet — *wireless Internet gateways* if they contain modem functionality, and *wireless gateways* or *routers* if they don't — range in price from about $50 to $150.

You need to budget roughly $60 for an 802.11b/g AP and about $160 for an 802.11 Pre-N (draft) AP. An 802.11a AP is harder to find and you will most likely see a combination a/b/g AP for about $350.

The price differentials between the cheapest APs and the more expensive models generally correspond to differences in features. For example, APs that support multiple wireless standards are more expensive than similar APs that support only one standard. Similarly, an AP that is also a cable or DSL router costs more than an AP from the same manufacturer that doesn't include the router feature. You can also expect to pay a little more for the most popular brand names, such as Linksys. You don't need to buy the most expensive AP to get adequate performance.

You may run across APs from well-known companies, such as Cisco and 3COM, that are significantly more expensive than the devices typically purchased for home use. These "industrial-strength" products include advanced features and come with management software that enables corporate IT departments to efficiently and securely deploy enterprise-level wireless networks. The underlying technology, including the speed and the range of the wireless radios used, are essentially the same as those used in the economically priced APs used in most wireless home networks; but the additional features and capabilities of these enterprise-level products save IT personnel countless hours and headaches rolling out dozens of APs in a large wireless network.

Pricing wireless network adapters

Wireless network adapters range from $25 to $125, depending on whether you purchase 802.11a, b, g, or Pre-N technology and whether you purchase a PC Card, USB, or internal variety.

Like APs, wireless network adapters that support multiple standards are somewhat more expensive than their counterparts. An 802.11a/b/g card costs between $25 and $100. The NETGEAR WAG511 tri-standard card had a street price of $75 as this book went to press. Wow!

Looking at a sample budget

If your plan involves a cable Internet connection, a laptop computer, and a home desktop computer that you want to connect via an 802.11b wireless home network, Table 4-2 shows a reasonable hardware budget.

Table 4-2   A Hypothetical 802.11g Wireless Home Network Budget

Item	Price Range	Quantity Needed
Access point	$35–$100	1
Wireless network adapters	$25–$100	2
Network cable	$10–$20	1
Cable or DSL modem (optional)	$75–$100	1

Planning Security

Any network can be attacked by a persistent hacker, but a well-defended network discourages most hackers sufficiently to keep your data safe. However, it's easier for a hacker to gain access to a wireless network through the air than to gain physical access to a wired network, making wireless networks, and even home networks, more vulnerable to attack. Because a Wi-Fi signal is a radio signal, it keeps going and going and going, like ripples in a pond in a weaker and weaker form, until it hits something solid enough to stop it. Anyone with a portable PC, wireless network adapter, and an external antenna in a van driving by your house or even in your neighbor's house next door has a reasonable chance of accessing your wireless network. (Such skullduggery is known as *war driving*.) So, you must plan for security. We give you all the down-and-dirty details in Chapter 10, but here are some key things to keep in mind:

✔ **Internet security:** Any Internet connection — especially always-on broadband connections, but dial-up connections, too — can be vulnerable to attacks arriving from the Internet. To keep your PCs safe from the bad folks (who may be thousands of miles away), you should turn on any firewall features available in your AP or router. Some fancier APs or routers include a highly effective kind of firewall (a stateful packet inspection [SPI] firewall), but even just the basic firewall provided by any NAT router can be quite effective. You should also consider installing antivirus software as well as personal firewall software on each PC or Mac on your network for an extra level of protection.

✔ **Airlink security:** This is a special need of a wireless home network. Wired networks can be made secure by what's known as *physical security*. That is, you literally lock your doors and windows, and no one can plug into your wired network. In the wireless world, physical security is impossible (you can't wrangle those radio waves and keep them in the house), so you need to implement airlink security. You can't keep the radio waves from getting out of the house, but you can make it very hard for someone to do anything with them (like read the data they contain). Similarly, you can use airlink security to keep others from getting onto your access point and freeloading on your Internet connection. The primary means of providing airlink security now — and new advances are on the way — is called WPA (Wi-Fi Protected Access). You absolutely should use WPA (and do a few other tricks that we discuss in Chapter 10) to preserve the integrity of your wireless home network.

Chapter 5

Choosing Wireless Home Networking Equipment

In This Chapter

▶ Picking out your access point

▶ Getting certified and sticking with standards

▶ Being compatible is *very* important!

▶ Finding out about bundled networking features

▶ Understanding the rest of the "options list"

▶ Locking down your network with security features

▶ Covering the whole house with wireless

▶ Keeping your network managed

▶ Staying within budget

▶ Protecting your investment

*W*hen you're building something — in this case, a wireless home network — the time comes when you have to make up your mind what building supplies to buy. To set up a wireless home network, you need, at minimum, an access point (AP) and a wireless networking adapter for each computer or other network-enabled device you want to have on the network. This chapter helps you evaluate and choose from among the growing number of APs and wireless networking adapters on the market.

The advice in this chapter applies equally to PCs and Macs. You can use any access point for a Mac as long as it has a Web interface (that is, it doesn't require a PC program to configure it). Despite that statement, if you have a Mac, you may want to consider using the Apple AirPort Extreme system because it's easier to set up and use. On the network adapter/client side of the link, AirPort Extreme cards are definitely easier for a Mac owner — it's somewhere between difficult and impossible to get many third-party Wi-Fi cards to work with a Mac.

Access Point Selection

The heart of each wireless home network is the access point (AP), also known as a base station. Depending on an AP's manufacturer and included features, the price of an AP suitable for home use ranges from about $35 to $100. Differences exist from model to model, but even the lowest-price units are surprisingly capable.

For most wireless home networks, the most important requirements for a wireless access point are as follows (sort of in order of importance):

- ✔ Certification and standards support (Wi-Fi certification)
- ✔ Compatibility and form factor
- ✔ Bundled server and router functionality
- ✔ Operational features
- ✔ Security
- ✔ Performance (range and coverage) issues
- ✔ Manageability
- ✔ Price
- ✔ Warranties
- ✔ Customer and technical support

With the exception of pricing (which we cover in Chapter 4), we explore the selection of access point products in depth in terms of these requirements throughout the following sections.

In Chapter 4, we describe how to plan the installation of a wireless home network, including how to use your AP to determine the best location in your house as well as the number of APs you need. If you can determine a location that gives an adequate signal throughout your entire house, your single AP obviously is adequate. If some areas of your home aren't covered, you either need one or more additional APs or a more powerful AP (and we tell you how to do that in Chapter 18). Fortunately, most residences can be covered by the signal from a single AP.

Certification and Standards Support

We talk in Chapter 2 about the Wi-Fi Alliance and its certification process for devices. You should ensure, at minimum, that your devices are Wi-Fi certified.

This certification provides you with the assurance that your wireless LAN equipment has been through the wringer of interoperability and compliance testing and meets all the standards of 802.11b, g, or a.

In fact, there's even more to Wi-Fi certification than just meeting the 802.11b/g/a standards. Wi-Fi certification means that a particular piece of equipment has been thoroughly tested to work with other similar Wi-Fi equipment, regardless of brand. This is the interoperability part of the certification, and it means that you can plug a D-Link adapter into your desktop computer, use a built-in Intel Centrino adapter in your notebook, and a NETGEAR AP as the hub of your network, and everything will just work.

Back in the early days of wireless networking, this interoperability was *not* assured, and you really needed to buy all your equipment from the same vendor — and then you were "locked in" to that vendor. Wi-Fi certification frees you from this concern.

The Wi-Fi Alliance certifies a bunch of different things:

- ✓ **General Wi-Fi certification:** For 802.11b, g, and a equipment (as well as *multimode* equipment that supports more than one standard at a time — like 802.11g and dual-mode network adapters), this certification simply lets you know that a given piece of Wi-Fi-certified gear will connect to another piece of gear using the same standard.

  This certification is the bottom line "must have" that you should look for when you buy a wireless LAN system.

- ✓ **Security certification:** Equipment that has been certified to work with the WPA (Wi-Fi Protected Access) security system (see Chapter 10 for more on this topic). WPA-certified equipment can be certified by the Wi-Fi Alliance for any of these types of WPA:

  - • **WPA Personal:** This is the minimum you should look for — equipment which has been certified to work with the WPA Personal (or WPA-PSK) system described in Chapter 10.

    If you can help it, don't buy any Wi-Fi gear that isn't certified for at least WPA Personal. We think that this is the minimum level of security you should insist on with a Wi-Fi network.

  - • **WPA Enterprise:** This business-oriented variant of WPA provides the ability to use a special *802.1X* or *RADIUS* server (explained in Chapter 10) to manage users on the network. For the vast majority of wireless home networkers, this capability is overkill, but it doesn't hurt to have it (any WPA Enterprise-certified system also supports WPA Personal).

  - • **WPA2 Personal:** The latest and greatest version of WPA is WPA2 — it adds a more secure encryption system called *AES* to make WPA even more secure.

- **WPA2 Enterprise:** This is the latest variant of the business-oriented WPA Enterprise standard.

✔ Other certifications: The Wi-Fi Alliance provides a number of other specialized certifications, like the following:

- **WMM:** *Wi-Fi MultiMedia* certification can be found on a growing number of audio/video and voice Wi-Fi equipment (these items are discussed in Chapters 13 and 14, respectively). WMM-certified equipment can provide on your wireless LAN some *Quality of Service (QoS),* which can give your voice, video, or audio data priority over other data being sent across your network. We talk about WMM where appropriate in those chapters.

- **EAP:** EAP (or *Extensible Authentication Protocol*) is part of the WPA Enterprise/802.1X system used in business wireless LANs — EAP provides the mechanism for authenticating users (or confirming that they are who they say they are). A number of different EAP types can be used with WPA Enterprise — each type can be certified by the Wi-Fi Alliance. You don't need to worry about this unless you're building a WPA Enterprise security system for your network.

A number of *prestandard* wireless LAN devices are available on the market now, as vendors begin to sell equipment before the forthcoming 802.11n standard (discussed in Chapter 2) is finalized and ratified. Some of these products are sold as 802.11g products enhanced with MIMO, but other vendors have begun selling their products as Pre-N — which implies that these products are supposed to be "close to," if not compatible with, the eventual 802.11n gear that's expected to hit the market in late 2006 (or later).

Don't believe it! Back when 802.11g was a new standard, lots of Pre-G gear hit the streets, and vendors guaranteed that it would be compatible with the final standard. That will probably happen eventually with 802.11n, but as we write in late 2005, the 802.11n standard is so far up in the air that *no one* has enough knowledge of what it will encompass to truly create Pre-N gear that will be interoperable with the final standard.

Having said that, there's nothing wrong with the MIMO/Pre-N gear on the market now. In fact, it's faster than regular 802.11g gear (with which it is fully compatible) *and* it has a longer range. Just don't think that you will be able use this equipment with 802.11n gear (when it finally arrives) — chances are overwhelmingly high that you won't.

Compatibility and Form Factor

When choosing an AP, make sure that it (and its setup program) is compatible with your existing components, check its form factor, and determine whether wall-mountability and outdoor use are important to you.

Hardware and software platform: Make sure that the device you're buying supports the hardware and software platform you have. Certain wireless devices support only Macs or support only PCs. And some devices support only certain versions of software.

Setup program and your operating system: Make sure that the setup program for the AP you plan to buy runs on your computer's operating system and the next version of that operating system (if it's available). Setup programs run only on the type of computer for which they were written. A setup program designed to run on Windows, for example, doesn't run on the Mac OS, and vice versa. Luckily, as we note later in this chapter, most vendors are moving toward browser-based configuration programs, which are much easier to support than stand-alone configuration utilities.

As a general rule, if you're using Windows 98 or 2000 (or Mac OS 9), make sure that the devices you buy works up through Windows XP (and Mac OS X). This ensures your ability to use this wireless equipment in the future if you upgrade parts of your network and also helps you get the most value from your investment.

Form factor: Also, make sure that the *form factor* (that is, the shape and form of the device, like whether it's external or a card) is what you're looking for. For example, don't assume that if you have a tower PC, you should install a PCI card. It's nice to have the more external and portable form factors, such as a Universal Serial Bus (USB) adapter, because you can take it off if you need to borrow it for something or someone else.

USB comes in two versions: USB 1.1 and USB 2.0. If your computer has a USB 1.1 port, it has a maximum data-transfer speed of 12 Mbps. USB 2.0 ports can transfer data at 480 Mbps, which is 40 times faster than USB 1.1. If you plan to connect an 802.11a or 802.11g device to a USB port, it must be USB 2.0.

Many brands of PC Cards include antennas that are enclosed in a casing that is thicker than the rest of the card. The card still fits in the PC Card slot, but the antenna can block the other slot. For most users, this shouldn't pose a serious problem; however, several manufacturers offer wireless PC Cards that have antenna casings no thicker than the rest of the card. If you actively use both your PC Card slots (perhaps you use one for a FireWire or USB 2.0 card), make sure that the form of the PC Card you're buying doesn't impede using your other card slot.

Even better, all cards should come from the same company that manufactured the AP you select, to ensure maximum interoperability and to take full advantage of any extended features the AP offers.

Wall-mountability: If you plan to wall-mount your device, make sure that the unit is wall mountable because many are not.

Outdoor versus indoor use: Finally, some devices are designed for outdoor — not indoor — use. If you're thinking about installing it outside, look for devices hardened for environmental extremes.

Bundled Functionality: Servers, Gateways, Routers, and Switches

Wireless APs are readily available that perform only the AP function; but for home use, APs that bundle additional features are much more popular, for good reason. In most cases, you should shop for an AP that's also a network router and a network switch — a wireless gateway like the one we define in Chapter 2. To efficiently connect multiple computers and to easily share an Internet connection, you need devices to perform all these functions, and purchasing one multipurpose device is the most economical way to accomplish that.

DHCP servers

To create an easy-to-use home network, your network should have a Dynamic Host Configuration Protocol (DHCP) server. A *DHCP server* dynamically assigns an IP address to each computer or other device in your network. This function relieves you from having to keep track of all the devices on the network and assign addresses to each one manually.

Network addresses are necessary for the computers and other devices on your network to communicate. Because most networks now use a set of protocols (Transmission Control Protocol/Internet Protocol, or TCP/IP) with network addresses (Internet Protocol [IP] addresses), we refer to network addresses as *IP addresses* in this book. In fact, the Internet uses the TCP/IP protocols, and every computer connected to the Internet must be identified by an IP address.

When your computer is connected to the Internet, your Internet service provider (ISP), such as America Online (AOL) or EarthLink, has assigned your computer an IP address. However, even when your computer isn't connected to the Internet, it needs an IP address to communicate with other computers on your home network.

The DHCP server can be a stand-alone device, but it's typically a service provided by either a computer on the network or a network router. The DHCP server maintains a database of all the current DHCP clients — the computers and other devices to which it has assigned IP addresses — issuing new addresses as each device's software requests an address.

Windows, Macintosh, and most other types of computers — as well as network devices — can automatically communicate over the network with a DHCP server to request the server to issue an IP address.

When your wireless network needs some order

Your home network is composed of many parts. If you're smart, you've consolidated them as much as possible because having fewer devices means easier installation and troubleshooting. But suppose that you have a cable modem, a router, a switch, and an access point — not an unusual situation if you grew your network over time. Now suppose that the power goes out. Each of these devices resets at different rates. The switch will probably come back fairly quickly because it's a simple device. The cable modem will probably take the longest to resync with the network, and the AP and router will come back up probably somewhere in-between.

The problem that you, as a client of the DHCP server (which is likely in the router in this instance), have is that not all the elements are in place for a clean IP assignment to flow back to your system. For example, the router needs to know the WAN IP address in order for you to have a good connection to the Internet. If the cable modem hasn't renegotiated its connection, it cannot provide that to the router. If the AP comes back online before the router, it cannot get its DHCP from the router to provide connectivity to the client. Different devices react differently when something isn't as it should be on startup.

Our advice: If you have a problem with your connectivity that you didn't have before the electricity went out and came back on, follow these simple steps. Turn everything off, start at the farthest point from the client, and work back toward the client, to let each device get its full start-up cycle complete before moving to the next device in line — ending with rebooting your PC or other wirelessly enabled device.

Gateways, NAT, and cable or DSL routers

A *wireless gateway* is a wireless AP that enables multiple computers to share the same IP address on the Internet. This fact would seem to be a contradiction because every computer on the Internet needs its own IP address. The magic that makes an Internet gateway possible is Network Address Translation (NAT). Most access points you buy now are wireless gateways.

Most vendors call these wireless gateways something like *wireless routers* or *wireless broadband routers* or perhaps *wireless cable/DSL routers*. They tend to emphasize the wireless and the router parts of the wireless gateway's functionality.

A device that typically provides the NAT service to a home network is called a cable/digital subscriber line (DSL) router or broadband router. (Note that you can also purchase a broadband modem that doubles as a router, but the typical modem isn't a router.) Cable/DSL routers used in home networks also provide the DHCP service. The router communicates with each computer or other device on your home network via private IP addresses — the IP addresses assigned by the DHCP server. (See the section "DHCP servers," earlier in this chapter.) However, the router uses a single IP address — the one assigned by your ISP's DHCP server — in packets of data intended for the Internet.

In addition to providing a method of sharing an Internet connection, the NAT service provided by a broadband router also adds a measure of security because the computers on your network aren't directly exposed to the Internet. The only computer visible to the Internet is the broadband router. This protection can also be a disadvantage for certain types of Internet gaming and computer-to-computer file transfer applications. If you find that you need to use one of these applications, look for a router with features called *DMZ* (for *demilitarized zone*) and *port forwarding* that expose just enough of your system to the Internet to play Internet games and transfer files. (Read more about this topic in Chapter 12.)

A *wireless Internet gateway* is an AP that's bundled with a cable or DSL modem or router. By hooking this single device to a cable connection or DSL line, you can share an Internet connection with all the computers connected to the network, wirelessly. By definition, all wireless Internet gateway devices also include several wired Ethernet ports that enable you to add wired devices to your network as well as wireless devices.

Switches

Wireless gateway devices available from nearly any manufacturer include from one to eight Ethernet ports with which you can connect computers or other devices via Ethernet cables. These gateway devices are not only wireless APs but are also wired switches that efficiently enable all the computers on your network to communicate either wirelessly or over Ethernet cables.

As we discuss in Chapter 2, there is a huge difference in performance between a switch and a hub. Just because a device says that it has four ports or eight ports doesn't mean that it's one or the other — it could be either. Look for words like *switched LAN ports* for an embedded switch in the device.

Make sure that the switch ports support at least *100BaseT* Ethernet — this is the 100 Mbps variant of Ethernet. You should also ensure that the switch supports the *full duplex* variant of 100BaseT — meaning that it supports 100 Mbps of data in both directions at the same time.

Even though you may intend to create a wireless home network, sometimes you may want to attach a device to the network through a more traditional network cable. For example, we highly recommend that you configure an AP for the first time with the AP attached by a network cable directly to your computer. At times, it may also be convenient to connect one of the other computers in your home directly to your AP.

Print servers

A few multifunction Internet gateways add a feature that enables you to add a printer to the network: a print server. Next to sharing an Internet connection, printer sharing is the most cost-effective reason to network home computers because everyone in the house can share one printer. Wireless print servers have become much more economical in the past few years. However, when the print server is included with the Internet gateway device, it's suddenly very cost effective.

The disadvantage of using the print server bundled with the AP, however, is apparent if you locate your AP in a room or location other than where you would like to place your printer. Consider a stand-alone print server device (discussed in Chapter 14) if you want to have your printer wirelessly enabled but not near your AP.

When you choose an AP with a print server, make sure that you have the right interface to your printer — most printers these days use USB connections, but a few still use the parallel port connection. We recommend that you choose an AP print server that supports USB 2.0 for faster printing of big graphically intensive files.

Operational Features

Most APs share a common listing of features, and most of them don't vary from one device to the next. Here are some unique, onboard features that we look for when buying wireless devices — and you should, too. Among them are

- ✔ **Wired Ethernet port:** Okay, this one seems basic, but having a port like this saves you time. We tell you time and again to install your AP first on your wired network (as opposed to trying to configure the AP via a wireless client card connection) and then add on the wireless layer (like the aforementioned client card). You can save yourself lots of grief if you can get your AP configured on a direct connection to your PC because you reduce the things that can go wrong when you add the wireless clients.

- ✔ **Auto channel select:** Some access points, typically more expensive models designed for office use, offer an automatic channel-selection feature, which is cool. For example, the NETGEAR ProSafe 802.11g Access Point selects its own frequency channel, based on interference situation, bandwidth usage, and adjacent channel use, by using its Auto Channel Select feature. It's beneficial when you're first deploying your ProSafe AP or adding a ProSafe unit in an existing environment. The ProSafe AP uses a special bit of software, known as AutoCell, that evaluates the existing radio usage (from other APs nearby) and automatically adjusts channel selection, power level, and more to minimize the effects of interference. And, if you have more than one ProSafe AP installed, they can work together using AutoCell to complement rather than compete with each other. That's pretty nice because as you can read in Chapter 6 and in the troubleshooting areas of Chapter 18, channel selection can try your patience. (You may wonder why it's necessary to pay more for more business-class access points — this is a good reason.)

- ✔ **Power over Ethernet (PoE):** Because every AP is powered by electricity (where's Mr. Obvious when you need him?), you should also consider whether the location you choose for an AP is located near an electrical outlet. High-end access points, intended for use in large enterprises and institutions, offer a feature known as Power over Ethernet (PoE). PoE enables electrical power to be sent to the AP over an Ethernet networking cable so that the AP doesn't have to be plugged into an electrical outlet. Modern residential electrical codes in most cities, however, require outlets every eight feet along walls, so unless you live in an older home, power outlets shouldn't be a real issue. But, if you're putting the cable on the ceiling, running one cable sure is easier than two!

There's an IEEE standard for POE; it's IEEE 802.3af.

✔ **Detachable antennas:** In most cases, the antenna or antennas that come installed on an AP are adequate to give you good signal coverage throughout your house. However, your house may be large enough or be configured in such a way that signal coverage of a particular AP could be significantly improved by replacing a stock antenna with an upgraded version. Also, if your AP has an internal antenna and you decide that the signal strength and coverage in your house are inadequate, an external antenna jack allows you to add one or two external antennas. Several manufacturers sell optional antennas that extend the range of the standard antennas; they attach to the AP to supplement or replace the existing antennas.

The FCC requires that antenna and radio be certified as a system. Adding a third-party, non-FCC-certified antenna to your AP violates the FCC regulations and runs the risk of causing interference with other radio devices, such as certain portable telephones.

✔ **Uplink port:** APs equipped with internal three- and four-port hub and switch devices are also coming with a built-in, extra uplink port. The *uplink port* — also called the crossover port, output, X, or bridge — is used to add even more wired ports to your network by uplinking the AP with another hub or switch. This special port is normally an extra connection next to the last available wired port on the device, but it can look like a regular Ethernet jack (with a little toggle switch next to it). You want an uplink port — especially if you have an integral router or DSL or cable modem — so that you can add more ports to your network while it grows. (And it will grow.)

Security

Unless you work for the government or handle sensitive data on your computer, you probably aren't overly concerned about the privacy of the information stored on your home network. Usually, it's not an issue anyway because someone would have to break into your house to access your network. But, if you have a wireless network, the radio signals transmitted by your wireless network don't automatically stop at the outside walls of your house. In fact, a neighbor or even someone driving by on the street in front of your house can use a computer and a wireless networking adapter to grab information right off your computer, including deleting your files, inserting viruses, and using your computer to send spam — unless you take steps to protect your network.

The security technology that comes standard with all Wi-Fi equipment is Wired Equivalent Privacy (WEP). Perhaps the most well-publicized aspect of Wi-Fi wireless networking is the fact that the WEP security feature of Wi-Fi networks can be *hacked* (broken into electronically). Hackers have successfully retrieved secret WEP keys used to encrypt data on Wi-Fi networks. With these keys, the hacker can decrypt the packets of data transmitted over a wireless network. The significance of this problem may have been overblown in the media because changing keys regularly greatly reduces the risk of a successful WEP attack. Nonetheless, many business and government agencies have prohibited the implementation of wireless networks that rely only on WEP to protect the privacy of data.

Since 2003, the Wi-Fi Alliance has been certifying and promoting a replacement security technology for WEP: Wi-Fi Protected Access (WPA). WPA is based on an IEEE standards effort known as 802.11i (so many 802.11's huh?). This technology, which makes cracking a network's encryption key much more difficult, is standard in most Wi-Fi access points and network adapters available now. As discussed earlier in this chapter, in the section "Certification and Standards Support," look for Wi-Fi Alliance certifications for WPA equipment.

See Chapter 10 for a full discussion of how to set up basic security for your wireless home network.

Many AP manufacturers have added, in addition to encryption features such as WEP (or WPA), a variety of security features often described loosely as *firewall protection.* One of the most common security features is typically described as a *MAC filter* because it enables you to set up a list of Media Access Control (MAC) addresses that are permitted to access the network. (The manufacturer of each networking device assigns a unique MAC address to the device at the factory.) A MAC filter can prevent network access by devices not on a predetermined list of MAC addresses.

Don't depend on the MAC filter feature as the sole form of security for your wireless home network. A determined hacker can discover the MAC address of one of your computers and then use software to masquerade as that MAC address. The AP would permit the hacker to join the network. This is a *spoof attack.*

Other useful firewall features to look for when buying an AP include

- **Network Address Translation** (NAT), which we discuss earlier in this chapter
- **Virtual Private Network** (VPN) pass-through that allows wireless network users secure access to corporate networks

> ✔ **Monitoring software** that logs and alerts you to computers from the Internet attempting to access your network
>
> ✔ **Utilities** that enable you to log content that's transmitted over the network as well as to block access to given Web sites

We talk much more about security in Chapter 10. We encourage you to read that chapter so that you can be well prepared for the process when you're ready to install your equipment.

Range and Coverage Issues

An AP's functional *range* (the maximum distance from the access point at which a device on the wireless network can receive a useable signal) and *coverage* (the breadth of areas in your home where you have an adequate radio signal) are important criteria when selecting an AP. Wi-Fi equipment is designed to have a range of up to 100 meters when used outdoors without any obstructions between the two radios. Coverage depends on the type of antenna used.

Just like it's hard to know how good a book is until you read it, it's hard to know how good an AP is until you install it. Buying an AP is definitely the type of thing for which you do your research ahead of time and hope that you make the right choice. Buying ten APs and returning the nine you don't want is simply impractical. (Well, maybe not impractical, but rather rude.) The key range and coverage issues, such as power output, antenna gain, or receive sensitivity (which we cover in Chapter 2) aren't well labeled on retail boxes. Nor are these issues truly comparable among devices, either, because of the same lack of consistent information. Because many of these devices are manufactured by using the same chipsets, performance usually doesn't vary extensively from one AP to another. However, that is a broad generalization, and some APs do perform badly. Our advice: Read the reviews and be forewarned!

In Chapter 2, we tell you about the differences in range between 802.11b/g systems and 802.11a systems, with the latter having slightly less range, if all other things are equal. Of the many good reasons to go for 802.11a systems, a big one is the lack of interference in the 5 GHz frequency range. And, if you have range issues, we help you figure out in Chapter 18 how to boost that range (and your throughput).

The new Pre-N and MIMO systems on the market use multiple antennas and special techniques to boost, or "focus," the antenna power and greatly increase the range of the AP over a standard 802.11g model. These systems work best when mated to Pre-N or MIMO network adapters from the same manufacturer, and many provide a range increase even with plain old 802.11g network adapters as well.

Manageability

When it comes to installing, setting up, and maintaining your wireless network, you rely a great deal on your device's user interface, so check reviews for this aspect of the product. In this section, we discuss the many different ways to control and manage your devices.

Web-based configuration

APs, wireless clients, and other wireless devices from all vendors ship with several utility software programs that help you set up and configure the device. An important selling feature of any wireless device is its setup process. The ideal setup procedure can be accomplished quickly and efficiently. Most available APs and devices can be configured through either the wired Ethernet port or a USB port.

The best setup program varieties enable you to configure the device by connecting through the Ethernet port and accessing an embedded set of Web (HyperText Markup Language; HTML) pages. Look for an AP with one of these. This type of setup program — often described as *Web-based* — can be run from any computer that's connected to the device's Ethernet port and that has a Web browser. Whether you're using Windows, the Mac OS, or Linux, you can access any device that uses a Web-based configuration program.

Software programming

When shopping for an AP, look for one with an automated setup process. Several AP manufacturers provide setup software that walks you step by step through the entire process of setting up the AP and connecting to your network. The Windows variety of automated setup programs are typically called *wizards*. If you're new to wireless technology, a setup wizard or other variety of automated setup program can help you get up and running with minimum effort.

Versions of Windows starting with Windows XP and versions of the Mac OS starting with Mac OS 9 are more wireless aware than earlier versions of these operating systems. Automated setup programs are typically quick and easy to use when written to run on either Windows XP or Mac OS 9 or later.

Even if an AP comes with a setup wizard, it also ships with configuration software that permits you to manually configure all the available AP settings. For maximum flexibility, this configuration software should be Web based (refer to the preceding section).

Telnetting to your device

When all else fails, you can rely on some good old, stand-by back doors in computing. With your computer, it's the command prompt interface. With your wireless device, it's telnetting, which sounds very Scandinavian but isn't even close. *Telnet* is a terminal emulation program for TCP/IP networks such as the Internet; a *terminal emulation program* emulates what you would see if you were sitting at a terminal attached to the device you want to manage. The Telnet program runs on your computer and links your PC to a device on the network: in this case, your AP. You can then enter commands through the Telnet program, and they're executed as though you were entering them directly into the AP or through the manufacturer's Web-based program.

To start a Telnet session, you enter the IP address of the device and log in by entering a valid username and password. You're then presented with a screen that is decidedly old-fashioned, but you can get the job done here. To telnet to a device, you may have to connect with it via a serial interface cable or a null modem cable like a crossover Ethernet cable (an Ethernet cable with certain wires reversed). Danny recently had to use Telnet to manage a dial-up router that he had just purchased on eBay because the software provided with the router wouldn't support XP — but he could get in via telnetting.

Windows ships with a free Telnet program: HyperTerminal. If you find that your software doesn't work and you need to get to the device, ask technical support whether you can telnet to the device (and leave the skis at home).

Upgradeable firmware

Wireless networking technology is still evolving. As a result, many features of Wi-Fi access points are implemented in updateable chips known as *firmware*. Before you decide which AP to buy, determine whether you can get feature updates and fixes from the vendor and whether you can perform the updates by upgrading the firmware (see the nearby sidebar, "Performing firmware updates," for some pointers). Check also for updated management software to match up with the new or improved features included in the updated firmware.

You may feel that frequent firmware updates are evidence of faulty product design. Acknowledging that wireless technology will continue to be improved, buying a product that can be upgraded to keep pace with these changes without the need to purchase new equipment can save you money in the long run.

Performing firmware updates

Most firmware updates come in the form of a downloadable program you run on a computer connected to the AP (or other device) by a cable (usually Ethernet, but sometimes USB). Make sure that you carefully read and follow the instructions that accompany the downloadable file. Updating the firmware incorrectly can lead to real headaches. Here are a few tips:

✔ Make sure that you make a backup of your current firmware before performing the update.

✔ Never turn off the computer or the AP while the firmware update is in progress.

✔ If something goes wrong, look through the AP documentation for instructions on how to reset the modem to its factory settings.

Price

Although we can't say much directly about price (except that the least expensive item is rarely the one you want), we should mention other things that can add to the price of an item. Check out which cables are provided (yes, wireless devices need cables, too!). In an effort to trim costs, some (not many) companies don't provide an Ethernet cable for your AP (which you need for initial setup).

Also, before you buy, check out some of the online price comparison sites, like CNET (`shopper.cnet.com`) or Yahoo! Shopping (`shopping.yahoo.com`). Internet specials pop up all the time.

Warranties

There's nothing worse than a device that dies one day after the warranty expires. The good news is that because most of these devices are solid state, they work for a long time unless you abuse them by dropping them on the floor or something drastic. In our experience, if your device is going to fail for build reasons, it does so within the first 30 days or so.

You encounter a rather large variance of warranty schedules among vendors. Some warranties are for only one year, and some are lifetime in length. Most are limited in some fashion, like covering parts and labor but not shipping.

When purchasing from a store, be sure to ask about its return policy for the first month or so. Many stores give you 14 days to return items, and after that, purchases have to be returned to the manufacturer directly, which is a huge pain in the rumpus, as Pat would say. If you only have 14 days, get the device installed quickly so that you can find any problems right away.

Extended service warranties are also often available through computer retailers. (We never buy these because by the time the period of the extended warranty expires, they're simply not worth their price given the plummeting cost of the items.) If you purchase one of these warranties, however, make sure that you have a clear understanding of the types of problems covered as well as how and when you can contact the service provider if problems arise. As we mention earlier in this chapter, if you don't purchase a warranty, you probably need to contact the product manufacturer for support and warranty service rather than the store or online outlet where you purchased the product.

Customer and Technical Support

Good technical support is one of those things you don't appreciate until you can't get it. For support, check whether the manufacturer has toll-free or direct-dial numbers for support as well as its hours of availability. Ticklish technical problems seem to occur at the most inopportune times — nights, weekends, holidays. If you're like us, you usually install this stuff late at night and on weekends. (We refuse to buy anything from anyone with only 9 a.m.–5 p.m., M–F hours for technical support.) Traditionally, only the high-end (that is to say, expensive) hardware products came with 24/7 technical support; however, an increasing number of consumer-priced computer products, including wireless home networking products, offer toll-free, around-the-clock, technical phone support.

Part III
Installing a Wireless Network

The 5th Wave   By Rich Tennant

"... and Bobby here found a way to extend our data transmission an additional 3000 meters using coax cable. How'd you do that, Bobby—repeaters?"

In this part . . .

*N*ow comes the work: installing a wireless network in your home and getting it up and running. Whether you're a Mac user or have PCs running a Windows operating system — or both — this part of the book explains how to install and configure your wireless networking equipment. No doubt you're also interested in sharing a single Internet connection and, of course, making your home network as secure as possible. This part covers these topics as well.

Chapter 6

Installing Wireless Access Points in Windows

. . . .

In This Chapter

▶ Doing your proper planning

▶ Installing a wireless network access point (AP)

▶ Modifying AP configuration

. . . .

*I*n this chapter, we describe the installation and configuration of your wireless home network's access point. We explain how to set up and configure the access point so that it's ready to communicate with any and all wireless devices in your home network. In Chapter 7, we describe the process for installing and configuring wireless network adapters.

Chapters 6 and 7 deal solely with Windows-based PCs. For specifics on setting up and installing wireless home networking devices on a Mac, see Chapter 8.

Before Getting Started, Get Prepared

Setting up an AP does have some complicated steps where things can go wrong. You want to reduce the variables to as few as possible to make debugging any problems as easy as possible. Don't try to do lots of different things all at once, like buy a new PC, install Windows XP, add a router, add an AP, and wireless clients — all at the same time. (Go ahead and laugh, but lots of people try this.) We recommend that you follow these steps:

1. **Get your PC set up first on a stand-alone basis.**

   If you have a new computer system, it probably shouldn't need much setup because it should be preconfigured when you buy it. If you have an older system, make sure that no major software problems exist before you begin. If you have to install a new operating system (OS), do it now. Bottom line: Get the PC working fine on its own so that you have no problems when you add functionality.

2. **Add in your dial-up or broadband Internet connection for that one PC.**

   Ensure that everything is working on your wired connection first. If you have a broadband modem, get it working on a direct connection to your PC first. If you're using a dial-up connection, again — get that tested from your PC so that you know that the account is active and works. Make sure that you can surf the Web (go to a number of sites that you know work) to ascertain that the information is current (as opposed to coming from your cache memory storage from earlier visits to the site).

3. **Choose (and do) which of the following makes sense for your configuration.**

   a. **If you're sharing a broadband or dial-up connection with a router, add in your home network routing option.**

      This step entails shifting your connection from your PC to your router, and your router will have instructions for doing that. After that's working, make sure that you can add another PC or other device, if you have one. Make sure that it can connect to the Internet and that the two devices can see each other on the local-area network. This action establishes that your logical connectivity among all your devices and the Internet is working. Because you may be installing an AP on an existing broadband or dial-up network, we're covering the AP installation first; we cover the installation of the router and your Internet sharing in Chapter 9.

   b. **If you plan to use this machine as the gateway to the Internet (as opposed to a router), turn on Internet sharing on your host PC.**

      Get that going and working, and test it with other connected devices. Again, check out Chapter 9 for info on this topic.

4. **Try adding wireless to the equation: Install your wireless AP and wireless NICs and disconnect the wired cable from each to see whether they work — one at a time is always simpler.**

   By now, any problems that occur can be isolated to your wireless connection. If you need to fall back on dialing into or logging on to your manufacturer's Web site, you can always plug the wired connection in and do so.

If your AP is in an all-in-one cable modem/router/AP combo, that's okay. Think about turning on the elements one at a time. If a wizard forces you to do it all at once, go ahead and follow the wizard's steps; just recognize that if all goes wrong, you can reset the device to the factory settings and start over (it's extreme, but usually saves time).

Setting Up the Access Point

Before you install and set up a wireless network interface adapter in one of your computers, you should first set up the wireless access point (also sometimes called a *base station*) that will facilitate communication between the various wireless devices in your network. In this section, we describe how to set up a typical AP.

Preparing to install a wireless AP

The procedure for installing and configuring most wireless APs is similar from one manufacturer to the next — but not exactly the same. You're most likely to be successful if you locate the documentation for the AP you have chosen and follow its installation and configuration instructions carefully.

Because having a network makes it easy to share an Internet connection, the best time to set up the AP for that purpose is during initial setup (but we give you the details for setting up Internet sharing in Chapter 9). In terms of setting up a shared Internet connection, you will already have a wired computer on your broadband (cable or digital subscriber line [DSL]) or dial-up Internet connection. This is very helpful as a starting place for most AP installations because most of the information you need to set up your AP is already available on your computer. If you don't have a wired computer on your Internet connection — that is, this is the first computer you're connecting — first collect any information (special login information, such as username or password) that your Internet service provider (ISP) has given you regarding using its services.

Before you begin plugging things in, make sure that you've done your research and gathered the following data:

✔ **Ensure that your computer has a standard wired Ethernet connection.** Most AP configurations require wired access for their initial setup. An Ethernet port is normally found on the back of your computer; this port looks like a typical telephone jack, only a little bit wider. If you don't have an Ethernet adapter, you should buy one and install it in your computer. Alternatively, if your computer has a Universal Serial Bus (USB) port (preferably USB 2.0, also known as USB High Speed), you can purchase an AP that connects to the USB port.

Very few APs have this USB interface, and almost all PCs now have an Ethernet port — so using USB to connect to your AP is extremely rare these days. We mention it just to cover all bases.

✔ **Collect your ISP's network information.** You need to know the following information; if you don't already know this stuff, ask the tech support folks at your ISP or check the support pages of the ISP's Web site:

- **Your Internet protocol (IP) address:** This is the equivalent of your network's phone number. Your IP address identifies your network on the Internet and enables communications. It's always four 1- to 3-digit numbers separated by periods (125.65.24.129, for example).

- **Your Domain Name System (DNS) server:** This special computer within your ISP's network translates IP addresses into host names. *Host names* are the (relatively) plain English names for computers attached to the Internet. For example, the *wiley.com* part of www. wiley.com is the host name of the Web server computers of our publisher.

- **Whether your ISP is delivering all this to you via Dynamic Host Configuration Protocol (DHCP):** In almost all cases, the Internet service you get at home uses DHCP, which means that a *server* (or computer) at your ISP's network center automatically provides all the information listed in the preceding above, without you needing to enter anything manually. It's a great thing!

In the vast majority of cases, your ISP *does* use DHCP, and you don't have to worry about any of this information.

✔ **Collect the physical address of the network card used in your computer** *only if you're already connected.* Many ISPs use the physical address as a security check to ensure that the computer connecting to its network is the one paying for the service. Many AP and Internet access devices available today permit you to change their physical addresses (Media Access Control [MAC] addresses) to match the physical address of your existing network card, which eliminates the need for you to get your Internet service provider to adjust your account — or in many cases, charge you more. This feature is typically called *MAC address cloning.*

Installing the AP

If you're connecting your first computer with your ISP, the ISP should have supplied you with all the information we list in the preceding section except for the physical address of the network card (which isn't needed if you aren't already connected).

Before you install your wireless gear, buy a 100-foot Ethernet cable. If you're installing your AP at a distance farther than that away from your router or Internet-sharing PC, you may get a longer cable. Trust us: This is one of those things that comes with having done this a lot. You need a wired backup to your system to test devices and debug problems. To do that (unless you want to keep moving your gear around, which we don't recommend), you need a long cable. Or two. Anyone with a home network should have extra cables, just like you have electrical extension cords around the house. You can get good-quality 100-foot CAT 5e patch cables online at places like Deep Surplus (www.deepsurplus.com) or a host of other online retailers for around $15.

When you're ready to do the AP installation, follow these steps.

1. **Gather the necessary information for installing the AP (see the preceding bulleted list) by following these steps:**

    a. **Choose Start⇨Programs⇨Accessories⇨Command Prompt.**

    This step brings up the command prompt window, which is a DOS screen.

    b. **Type** IPCONFIG /ALL **and then press Enter.**

    The information you receive scrolls down the screen. Use the scroll bar to slide up to the top and write down the networking information we list earlier in this chapter (physical address, IP address, default gateway, subnet mask, DNS servers) and whether DHCP is enabled). You use this information to configure the AP in Step 4.

2. **Run the setup software that accompanies the AP or device containing your AP, like a wireless or Internet gateway.**

    The software probably starts when you insert its CD-ROM into the CD drive. In many cases, this software detects your Internet settings, which makes it much easier to configure the AP for Internet sharing and to configure the first computer on the network. For example, Figure 6-1 shows the Linksys Wireless-G Setup utility that accompanies the Linksys WAP54G Wireless-G Access Point, which is a wireless gateway from Linksys, a division of Cisco Systems, Inc.

Figure 6-1:
The Linksys
Wireless-G
Access
Point Setup.

3. **When you're prompted by the setup software to connect the AP (see Figure 6-2), unplug the network cable that connects the broadband modem to your computer from the computer's Ethernet port and plug this cable into the Ethernet port that's marked *WAN* or *Modem* on your network's cable or DSL router or Internet gateway.**

If you're using an Internet or wireless gateway, run a Cat 5e cable from one of its Ethernet ports to the computer on which you're running the setup software. (*Cat 5e cable* is a standard Ethernet cable or patch cord with what look like oversized phone jacks on each end. You can pick one up at any computer store or Radio Shack.)

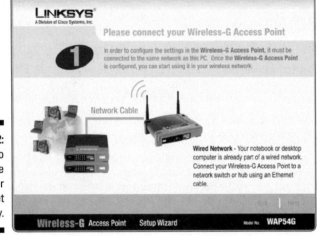

Figure 6-2:
It's time to connect the AP or Internet gateway.

If you're using a separate AP and router (in other words, if your AP *is not* your router, you need to connect a Cat 5e cable between the AP and one of the router's Ethernet ports. Then, connect another cable from another one of the router's Ethernet ports to the computer on which you're running the setup software.

Most newer APs try to obtain an IP address automatically and configure themselves for you by picking the channel and setting default parameters for everything else (see Figure 6-3). In most cases, you need to manually configure the security and some of the other information you collected in Step 1 (so have that information handy).

4. **Record the following access point parameters.**

The following list covers the AP parameters you most often encounter and need to configure, but the list isn't comprehensive. (Read more about them in the following subsection.) You need this information if you plan to follow the steps for modifying AP configuration, which we cover in the later section "Changing the AP Configuration." (What did you expect that section to be called?) Other settings you probably don't need to change include the transmission rate (which normally adjusts automatically to give the best throughput), RTS/CTS protocol settings, the beacon interval, and the fragmentation threshold.

- Service set identifier (SSID)

- Channel

- WEP or WPA keys (see Chapter 10 for more details on this subject)

- Password

- MAC address

- Dynamic or static wide-area network (WAN) IP address

- Local IP address

- Subnet mask

- PPPoE (Point-to-Point Protocol over Ethernet) — usually found on DSL connections, and rarely for cable modems

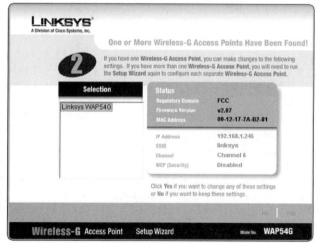

Figure 6-3:
What the AP can find on its own.

5. Complete the installation software and you're finished.

After you complete the AP setup process, you should now have a working access point ready to communicate with another wireless device.

Configuring AP parameters

Here's a little more meat on each of the access point parameters you captured in Step 4 of the preceding section.

✔ **Service set identifier (SSID):** The SSID (sometimes called the *network name, network ID,* or *service area*) can be any alphanumeric string, including upper- and lowercase letters, up to 30 characters long. The AP manufacturer may set a default SSID at the factory, but you should change this setting. Assigning a unique SSID doesn't really add much security; nonetheless, establishing an identifier that's different from the factory-supplied SSID makes it a little more difficult for intruders to access your wireless network. And, if you have a nearby neighbor with a wireless AP of the same type, you don't get the two networks confused. When you configure wireless stations, you need to use the same SSID or network name that's assigned to the AP.

✔ **Channel:** This is the radio channel over which the AP communicates. If you plan to use more than one AP in your home, you should assign a different channel (over which the AP communicates) for each AP to avoid signal interference. If your network uses the IEEE 802.11b or IEEE 802.11g protocols, 11 channels, which are set at 5 MHz intervals, are available in the United States. However, because the radio signals used by the IEEE 802.11b/g standard spread across a 22 MHz-wide spectrum, you can only use as many as three channels (typically 1, 6, and 11) in a given wireless network.

You can use other channels besides 1, 6, and 11 in an 802.11b or g network, but those three channels are the ones that are *non-interfering.* In other words, you could set up three APs near each other using these channels and they wouldn't cause any interference with each other.

If you're setting up an 802.11a AP, you have 11 channels from which to choose. But because these channels are 20 MHz wide and don't overlap, you really have 11 channels with which to work, compared with only 3 with IEEE 802.11b or 802.11g. If you operate only one AP, all that really matters is that all wireless devices on your network must be set to the same channel. If you operate several APs, give them as much frequency separation as possible to reduce the likelihood of mutual interference.

Table 6-1 contains the channel frequencies for the different wireless standards.

Table 6-1	Channel Frequencies for Wireless Standards
2.4 GHz (802.11b/g)	*5 GHz (802.11a)*
Channel 1–2.412 GHz	Channel 36–5.180 GHz
Channel 2–2.417 GHz	Channel 40–5.200 GHz

2.4 GHz (802.11b/g)	5 GHz (802.11a)
Channel 3–2.422 GHz	Channel 44–5.220 GHz
Channel 4–2.427 GHz	Channel 48–5.240 GHz
Channel 5–2.432 GHz	Channel 52–5.260 GHz
Channel 6–2.437 GHz	Channel 56–5.280 GHz
Channel 7–2.422 GHz	Channel 60–5.300 GHz
Channel 8–2.447 GHz	Channel 64–5.320 GHz
Channel 9–2.452 GHz	
Channel 10–2.457 GHz	
Channel 11–2.462 GHz	
Channel 12–2.467 GHz	
Channel 13–2.472 GHz	
Channel 14–2.477 GHz (Japan only)	

Notes
802.11b/g:
Channel 3 is default FCC, ETSI, Japan.
Channel 12 is for ETSI countries only.
For France, Channels 10–13 are applicable only.
802.11a:
These channels are only valid in US/Canada and Japan at this time.
Source: ORiNOCO

Most access points, such as some from Linksys, default to Channel 6 as a starting point and detect other access points in the area so that you can determine which channel to use, which is cool.

When you have multiple access points and set your 802.11a, b, or g access points all to the same channel, sometimes roaming doesn't work when users move about the house, and the transmission of a single access point blocks all others that are within range. As a result, performance degrades significantly. (You notice this when your *throughput,* or speed of file and data transfers, decreases noticeably.) Use different, widely separated channels for b and g; you have to use different channels for a only because 802.11a channels are all non-overlapping.

✔ **WPA:** Wi-Fi Protected Access (WPA) is the newest and best available solution in Wi-Fi security. Two versions of this are available for home users: WPA Pre-Shared Key and WPA Radius.

- **Pre-Shared Key (PSK)** gives you a choice of two encryption methods: TKIP (Temporal Key Integrity Protocol), which utilizes a stronger encryption method and incorporates Message Integrity Code (MIC) to provide protection against hackers, and AES (Advanced Encryption System), which utilizes a symmetric 128-bit block data encryption.

- **RADIUS** (Remote Authentication Dial-In User Service) utilizes a RADIUS server for authentication and the use of dynamic TKIP, AES, or WEP. RADIUS servers are specialized computer devices that do nothing but authenticate users and provide them with access to networks (or deny unauthorized users access). If you don't know what a RADIUS server is all about, chances are good that you don't have one.

WPA Pre-Shared Key is often called WPA Home, and WPA with RADIUS is often referred to as WPA Enterprise (enterprise in this case means business, not the starship!). The names are telling because the gear sold for home networks usually supports WPA Home and rarely supports WPA Enterprise (because most home users don't have a RADIUS server). We talk about both types of WPA in much greater detail in Chapter 10.

✔ **WEP keys:** You should always use some security on your wireless network and if your network cannot support WPA, you should use, at minimum, Wired Equivalent Privacy (WEP) encryption. Only a determined hacker with the proper equipment and software can crack the key. If you don't use WEP or some other form of security, any nosy neighbor with a laptop, wireless PC card, and range-extender antenna may be able to see and access your wireless home network. Whenever you use encryption, all wireless stations in your house attached to the wireless home network must use the same key. Sometimes the AP manufacturer assigns a default WEP key. Always assign a new key to avoid a security breach.

Read Chapter 10 for great background info on WEP and WPA.

✔ **Password:** Configuration software may require that you enter a password to make changes to the AP setup. The manufacturer may provide a default password (see the user documentation). Use the default password when you first open the configuration pages, and then immediately change the password to avoid a security breach. (*Note:* This isn't the same as the WEP key, which is also called a *password* by some user interfaces [UIs].) Make sure that you use a password you can remember and that you don't have to write down. Writing down a password is the same as putting a sign on the equipment that says "Here's how you hack into me." If you ever lose the password, you can always reset a device to its factory configuration and get back to the point where you took it out of the box — but you can avoid that situation by using a password you can remember.

✔ **MAC address:** The *Media Access Control (MAC) address* is the physical address of the radio in the AP. You should find this number printed on a label attached to the device. You may need to know this value for troubleshooting, so write it down. The AP's Ethernet (RJ-45) connection to the wired network also has a MAC address that's different from the MAC address of the AP's radio.

✔ **Dynamic or static wide-area network (WAN) IP address:** If your network is connected to the Internet, it must have an IP address assigned by your ISP. Most often, your ISP dynamically assigns this address. Your router or Internet gateway should be configured to accept an IP address dynamically assigned by a DHCP server. It's possible, but unlikely, that your ISP will require a *set* (static) IP address.

✔ **Local IP address:** In addition to a physical address (the MAC address), the AP also has its own network (IP) address. You need to know this IP address to access the configuration pages by using a Web browser. Refer to the product documentation to determine this IP address. In most cases, the IP address is 192.168.*xxx.xxx*, where *xxx* is between 1 and 254. It's also possible that an AP could choose a default IP that's in use by your cable or DSL router (or a computer that got its IP from the cable or DSL router's DHCP server). Either way, if an IP conflict arises, you may have to keep the AP and cable or DSL routers on separate networks while configuring the AP.

✔ **Subnet mask:** In most cases, this value is set at the factory to 255.255. 255.0. If you're using an IP addressing scheme of the type described in the preceding paragraph, 255.255.255.0 is the correct number to use. This number, together with the IP address, establishes the subnet on which this AP will reside. Network devices with addresses on the same subnet can communicate directly without the aid of a router. You really don't need to understand how the numbering scheme works except to know that the AP and all the wireless devices that will access your wireless network must have the same subnet mask.

✔ **PPPoE:** Many DSL ISPs still use Point-to-Point Protocol over Ethernet (PPPoE). The values you need to record are the user name (or user ID) and password. PPPoE is used by the DSL provider as a means of identifying and authorizing users.

Changing the AP Configuration

Each brand of AP has its own configuration software you can use to modify the AP's settings. Some products provide several methods of configuration. The most common types of configuration tools for home and small-office APs are

✔ **Software-based:** Some APs come with access point setup software you run on a workstation to set up the AP over a wireless connection, a USB cable, or an Ethernet cable.

✔ **Web-based:** Many of the newer lines of APs intended for home and small-office use have a series of HyperText Markup Language (HTML; Web) forms stored in firmware. You can access these forms by using a Web browser over a wireless connection or over a network cable in order to configure each AP.

To access your AP's management pages with a Web browser, you need to know the local IP address for the AP. If you didn't make note of the IP address when you initially set up the AP, refer to the AP's user guide to find this address. It's a number similar to 192.168.2.1. If you're using an Internet gateway, you can also run ipconfig (Windows 2000 and Windows XP), as we describe in Chapter 7. The Internet gateway's IP address is the same as the default gateway.

Many APs and wireless routers have their administrative and configuration Web page IP addresses printed on labels on the backs or bottoms of the APs. If you can't remember your AP's IP address, check there. In a worst-case scenario, go to the manufacturer's Web site and download the support documents or manual for your AP.

When you know the AP's IP address, run your Web browser software, type the IP address on the Address line, and then press Enter or click the Go button. You probably see a screen that requests a password. This password is the one you established during initial setup for the purpose of preventing unauthorized individuals from making changes to your wireless AP's configuration. After you enter this password, the AP utility displays an AP management screen. If you're not using a Web-based tool, you need to open the application that you initially installed to make any changes.

Within the AP's management utility, you can modify all the AP's settings, such as the SSID, channel, and WEP encryption key. The details of how to make these changes vary from manufacturer to manufacturer. Typically, the AP management utility also enables you to perform other AP management operations, such as resetting the AP, upgrading its firmware, and configuring any built-in firewall settings.

AP manufacturers periodically post software on their Web sites that you can use to update the AP's firmware that's stored in the circuitry inside the device. If you decide to install a firmware upgrade, follow the provided instructions very carefully. *Note:* Do *not* turn off the AP or your computer while the update is taking place.

The best practice is to modify AP settings only from a computer that's directly connected to the network or the AP by a network cable. If you must make changes over a wireless connection, think through the order that you will make changes, or you could orphan the client computer. For example, if you want to change the wireless network's WEP key, change the key on the AP first and make sure that you write it down. As soon as you save the change to the AP, the wireless connection is effectively lost. No data passes between the client and the AP, so you no longer can access the AP over the wireless connection. To reestablish a useful connection, you must change the key on the client computer to the same key you entered on the AP.

Chapter 7

Setting Up Your Windows PCs for Wireless Networking

In This Chapter

▶ Installing wireless network interface adapters

▶ Modifying your adapter's settings

▶ Windows XP's Wireless Zero Configuration

▶ Going wireless with Windows Merlin, Ozone, and Magneto

*I*n this chapter, we describe the installation and configuration of wireless devices on Windows computers. To that end, we explain how to set up and configure the wireless network interface adapter in each of your computers (and other wireless devices) so that they can communicate with the access point (AP) and with one another. Finally, we also include special coverage for installing and configuring wireless network adapters in computers running Windows XP (it's amazingly easy) and in handheld computers running one of the Microsoft mobile operating systems (or OSs).

Read through Chapter 6 for information about physically installing APs, and see Chapter 8 for a discussion of setting up a Mac-based wireless network. If you find yourself lost in acronyms, check out Chapter 2 for the background on this equipment.

Setting Up Wireless Network Interface Adapters

After you have the AP successfully installed and configured (see Chapter 6), you're ready to install and set up a wireless network interface adapter in each client device. Wireless network adapters all require the same information to be installed, although the installation on different platforms may differ to some degree. From most manufacturers, the initial setup procedure differs somewhat depending on the operating system that's running your computer.

In this section, we walk you through installing device drivers and client software before addressing the typical setup procedure for various wireless network interface adapters.

If you're using Windows XP, you can also set up your wireless network interface adapter by using the built-in Windows XP support for wireless networking. See the section "Wireless Zero Configuration with Windows XP," later in this chapter, for more information.

The installation procedure for most types of PC devices consists of installing the hardware (the device) in your computer and then letting Windows detect the device and prompt you to supply a driver disc or CD. With most wireless network adapters, however, you should install the software provided with the wireless networking hardware *before* installing the hardware. This strategy ensures that the setup software can examine your computer's hardware, software, network, and Internet settings *before* you have installed any wireless hardware.

Installing device drivers and client software

Whenever you install an electronic device in your Windows PC, including a wireless network interface adapter, Windows needs to know certain information about how to communicate with the device. This information is a *device driver*. When you install a wireless network adapter, depending on which version of Windows you're using, you may be prompted to provide the necessary device driver. Device driver files typically accompany each wireless networking device on an accompanying CD-ROM. Most wireless device manufacturers also make the most up-to-date device driver files available for free download from their technical support Web sites.

When you install the wireless adapter into your computer, Windows uses the device driver files to add the adapter to your computer's hardware configuration. The new network adapter's driver also must be configured properly in order for it to communicate with other computers over the Windows network.

Even if you receive a driver CD with your wireless network interface adapter, we still recommend checking the manufacturer's Web site for the most recent software. Wireless networking technology is still evolving, so keeping up with the changes is paramount. For example, to address the security flaws in WEP (which we talk about in Chapter 10), different security (or encryption) protocols are becoming available or will soon be available. For example, as we discuss in Chapter 10, a new system, WPA, will soon be available. To take advantage of this system, you need to download the newest driver software as well as the newest *firmware,* which is the special software that resides in the flash memory on your network adapter and which enables it to do its job.

The exact procedure for installing the drivers and software for the wireless network adapters varies from manufacturer to manufacturer, so read the documentation that accompanies the product you're installing *before* you begin. Although the details may differ from the instructions that accompany your product, the general procedure is in the following set of steps.

Because some antivirus programs often mistake installation activity for virus activity, shut down any antivirus programs you may have running on your PC *before* you begin any installation of software or hardware. (Remember to turn it back on when you're done!)

1. **Insert into the CD-ROM drive the CD that accompanies the wireless network adapter.**

   If the CD's startup program doesn't automatically begin, choose Start⇨ Run or use Windows Explorer to run the Setup.exe program on the CD.

2. **Install the software for configuring the network adapter by following the instructions on your screen.**

   Typically, you follow along with an installation wizard program.

Don't insert the network adapter until prompted to do so by the installation software (see Figure 7-1). In some cases, you may be prompted to restart the computer before inserting the adapter. For some older versions of Windows, you're prompted to insert your Windows CD in order for the setup program to copy needed networking files.

Because you installed the wireless network adapter's drivers and configuration software before inserting the adapter, the operating system should be able to automatically locate the driver and enable the new adapter.

Figure 7-1:
Don't
connect
your
wireless
network
adapter until
prompted by
the setup
software.

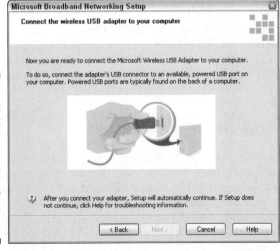

If Windows can't find the driver, it may start the Found New Hardware Wizard (or Add/Remove Hardware Wizard or even New Hardware Wizard — it depends on which OS you're using). If this does happen, don't panic. You can direct Windows to search the CD-ROM for the drivers it needs, and they should be installed without issues (although you may have to reboot again).

After you insert or install your wireless network adapter (and restart the computer, if prompted to do so), you're prompted to configure the new adapter.

3. **You need to make sure that the following settings, at minimum, match those of your network's wireless AP:**

- **SSID (network name or network ID):** Most wireless network adapter configuration programs display a list of wireless networks that are in range of your adapter. In most instances, you see only one SSID listed. If you see more than one, it means that one (or more) of your neighbors also has a wireless network that's close enough for your wireless adapter to "see." Of course, it also means that your neighbor's wireless adapter can see your network too. This is one good reason to give your wireless network a unique SSID (network name), and it's also a compelling reason to use encryption.

- **WPA Passphrase (or WEP Key):** Enter the same key or passphrase you entered in the AP's configuration. We discuss this concept in greater detail in Chapter 10.

After you configure the wireless network adapter, the setup program may announce that it needs to reboot the computer. Newer versions of Windows, such as Windows XP, don't have to reboot.

One of the common applications installed with a wireless adapter is a bandwidth monitor. This handy tool is used to debug problems and inform you of connection issues. Almost all these tools are graphical in nature and can help you determine the strength of the signal to your AP device as well as the distance you can travel away from the device before the signal becomes too weak to maintain a connection.

PC Cards and mini-PCI cards

Most wireless network adapters are PC Cards. Nearly all Windows laptops and some Mac laptop computers have PC Card ports that are compatible with these cards. The hottest new wireless (draft) standard, 802.11g, however, is available on some platforms (notably, the Apple Macintosh) only on mini-PCI cards capable of transmitting data at speeds faster than the PC Cards are capable of handling. The 802.11g interfaces come on mini-PCI cards or standard-size

PC Cards. The Apple AirPort Extreme 802.11g wireless adapter, for example, comes only in a mini-PCI version that doesn't install in most older Macs. Nevertheless, Linksys, NETGEAR, D-Link, and others offer an 802.11g PC Card wireless network interface adapter. Most such devices already come preinstalled in portable computers and in some desktop computers.

Except for PC Cards specifically labeled "Made for Windows XP," the installation procedure for most types of PC Cards, peripherals (such as modems), and wired network cards consists of plugging the card into the PC Card slot and supplying a driver disc or CD when prompted to do so. With most PC Card wireless network adapters, however, installing the software drivers *before* inserting the PC Card for the first time is important. Doing so ensures that the correct driver is present on the computer when the operating system recognizes that you have inserted a PC Card. Installing the drivers first also ensures that you can configure the software when you install the device.

If you're installing a PC Card in a Windows-based computer with a PC Card slot, use the following general guidelines and don't forget to refer to the documentation that comes with the card for detailed instructions. (See Chapter 8 if you're a Mac user.)

Even if you received a CD with the PC Card, checking the manufacturer's Web site for the most recent drivers and client station software is a good idea. Wireless networking technology is continually evolving, so we recommend that you keep up with the changes.

To install a wireless PC card in your computer, follow these steps:

1. **Insert the CD that accompanies the PC Card into the CD-ROM drive.**

   If the setup program doesn't automatically start, choose Start⇨Run (in Windows) or open Windows Explorer to run the Setup.exe program on the CD.

2. **Install the wireless client software.**

   During this installation, you may be asked to indicate the following:

   - Whether you want the PC Card set to infrastructure (AP) mode or to ad hoc (peer-to-peer) mode. Choose infrastructure mode to communicate through the AP. We talk about the difference between infrastructure and ad hoc modes in Chapter 2.

   - The SSID (network name).

   - Whether you will use a network password (which is the same as WPA or WEP encryption).

3. **After the wireless station software is installed, restart the computer.**

4. **While the computer restarts, insert the PC Card wireless network adapter into the available PC Card slot.**

   Windows 2000 is Plug and Play–compliant, so it should recognize that you have inserted a new device in the PC Card slot and automatically search the hard disk for the driver.

   Windows XP comes with generic drivers for many wireless PC cards, to make installation much simpler than ever. Some newer PC Cards, which are made specifically for XP, have no software included and rely on XP to take care of it. Even so, we recommend that you follow the directions that come with your PC Card and check whether your card is compatible with XP. Later in this chapter, we discuss the Windows XP Net Zero configuration tools, which provide software for many Windows XP-compliant and -noncompliant cards.

   When Windows finds the driver, it enables the driver for the card and you're finished.

Wireless network interface adapter manufacturers periodically post on their Web sites software you can use to update the *firmware* (software that's stored in the circuitry and chips inside the card). In most cases, firmware updates address specific hardware or software issues. If you aren't aware of a problem with the card or an important new feature you need, you should probably leave well enough alone. However, if you like to stay on the cutting edge, we suggest that you regularly check the manufacturer's Web site for updates.

Compact Flash cards

Some Pocket PCs have optional attachments that make it possible to add PC Card devices. Most Pocket PC manufacturers provide either standard or optional support for add-on cards built to the Compact Flash (CF) or SDIO form factor. We cover CF and SDIO cards in more detail in Chapter 2.

Installing a wireless network interface adapter in a Pocket PC is about as easy as it gets (we show you how in a moment), but configuring the device so that you can synchronize with your PC *and* use your Pocket PC to access the Internet can be a little tricky (and we show you that procedure later in this chapter).

The installation procedure varies in precise detail from manufacturer to manufacturer, but you can follow these general steps:

1. **Install the software that came with the Compact Flash (CF) or SDIO card and then insert the card into the CF or SDIO slot in your Pocket PC when prompted to do so.**

2. **Connect the Pocket PC to the desktop or laptop PC that you plan to use to configure your Pocket PC.**

   This step usually involves placing the Pocket PC in the cradle that's attached by a cable to your desktop or laptop computer, just like you do when you're synchronizing your calendar.

3. **Insert the setup CD that came with the wireless network interface CF card into your computer's CD-ROM drive.**

   If the setup software doesn't run automatically, choose Start⇨Run (in Windows) or open Windows Explorer to start it.

4. **Install the software by following the onscreen instructions.**

   If prompted to choose between infrastructure mode and ad hoc mode, choose infrastructure mode (which is the mode that causes your CF card to talk to the AP) rather than directly to other wireless devices (ad hoc mode).

5. **When prompted to enter the network name or SSID, enter the name you used when you set up the AP.**

   Refer to the discussion of Pocket PC 2002 (later in this chapter) for more information about configuring wireless client software on your Pocket PC.

6. **On the Pocket PC, run the wireless network adapter's configuration program.**

   To run the configuration utility for the Linksys WCF11 wireless adapter, for example (as shown in Figure 7-2), you choose Start⇨Programs and then click the WCF11 Config icon. You may have to unplug the card and reinsert it for the configuration utility to be able to "see" the card the first time.

Figure 7-2:
The configuration utility for the Linksys WCF11 wireless adapter.

7. **Using the wireless adapter's configuration utility on the Pocket PC, turn on the encryption feature and enter the same encryption key you entered in the AP's configuration software.**

At this point, you should have a valid link between the wireless network adapter in the Pocket PC and the AP. (The Linksys utility, for example, has a Link button you can click to display a screen showing link quality and signal strength.) You aren't quite ready to use the wireless card to synchronize your Pocket PC with your PC, however. You must follow the steps in the later section, "Synchronizing and Internet Access," to do just that.

PCI and PCIx cards

If you purchase a wireless networking adapter that fits inside your PC, you must make sure that you have the right type for your computer. Most desktop computers built in the past five years contain PCI slots. The type of slot your computer has is most likely standard PCI. If you have a newer computer that uses PCIx, you're all set because PCIx is fully backward compatible. That means that you can use standard PCI cards in PCIx slots. The only difference you see is that the card doesn't fill the slot — the PCIx card slot is almost twice the length of the older standard PCI slot. Refer to your computer's documentation to determine which type of slot is inside your computer and then purchase a wireless network interface adapter to match.

Most manufacturers choose to mount a PC Card on a standard PCI adapter. Some of the newest PCI adapters consist of a mini-PCI adapter mounted to a full-size PCI adapter. In either of these configurations, a black rubber dipole-type antenna, or another type of range-extender antenna, is attached to the back of the PCI adapter.

Most PCI cards come with specific software and instructions for installing and configuring the card. We can't tell you exactly what steps you need to take with the card you buy, but we can give you some generic steps. Don't forget to read the manual and follow the onscreen instructions on the CD that comes with your particular card.

Follow these general guidelines for installing a PCI adapter card:

1. **Insert into the CD-ROM drive the CD that accompanied the adapter.**

If necessary, choose Start⇨Run (in Windows) or open Windows Explorer to run the `Setup.exe` program on the CD.

2. **Select the option for installing the PCI card driver software.**

At this point, the driver is only copied to the computer's hard drive. The driver is added to the operating system in Step 4.

3. **If you're prompted to restart the computer, select No, I Will Restart My Computer Later and then click the Next (or Finish) button.**

During the install process, many Windows-based computers prompt you to restart the computer by displaying a pop-up box with a question similar to "New drivers have been installed, do you want to restart for the changes to take effect?" The normal reaction may be to do what it asks and click the OK button — but *don't do it!* The software installation needs to be fully completed before the computer can be restarted. You know that it's completed because the installation wizard (not a Windows pop-up) prompts you for your next step. After the software has completed its installation process, *it* prompts you in its own software window to restart your computer, or it informs you that you need to restart to complete the installation.

4. **After the computer restarts, install the PC Card wireless station (client) software in accordance with the instructions that came with it.**

In some cases, Steps 2 and 4 are accomplished in a single software-installation step. In other cases, you install only the wireless station software at this point.

While the wireless station software is being installed, you may need to indicate whether you want the PC Card to be set to infrastructure (AP) mode or to ad hoc (peer-to-peer) mode. Choose infrastructure mode to cause the wireless network adapter to use the AP to communicate with other network devices. You may also need to provide the SSID (network name) and to indicate whether you will use WEP encryption.

5. **After both the PCI card driver and the wireless station software are installed, shut down the computer.**

6. **Unplug the computer and install the PCI card in an available slot.**

7. **Plug in the computer and restart it.**

Windows recognizes that you have installed new hardware and automatically searches the hard drive for the driver. When Windows finds the driver, it enables the driver for the adapter, and you're done.

USB adapters

If you purchased a USB adapter, it's easy to install in your USB port. All new PCs and laptops come with at least one USB port (and usually two). Most USB adapters attach to the USB port via a USB cable. Some new devices are so lightweight and compact that you can plug them directly into the USB port. (See Chapter 8 if you're a Mac user.)

Here are the general guidelines for installing a USB wireless NIC:

1. **Insert into the CD-ROM drive the CD that accompanied the USB adapter.**

   If the CD's AutoRun feature doesn't cause the setup program to start, use the Run command from the Start button (in Windows) or open Windows Explorer to run the Setup.exe program on the CD.

2. **Install the wireless station (client) software.**

   During the installation of the wireless station software, you may be asked to indicate whether you want the USB wireless adapter to be set to infrastructure (access point) mode or to ad hoc (peer-to-peer) mode. Choose infrastructure mode to cause the wireless network adapter to use the AP to communicate with other network devices. You may also be asked for the SSID (network name) and to indicate whether you will use WEP encryption.

3. **After the wireless station software is installed, restart the computer.**

4. **After the computer restarts, attach the USB adapter to one of the computer's USB ports by running a USB cable from the network adapter to the USB port.**

   Windows should recognize that you have installed new hardware and automatically search the hard disk for the driver. When Windows finds the driver, it enables the driver for the adapter. That's it — you're all finished.

Modifying Wireless Network Adapters

Some occasions may warrant modifying one or more of the adapters' parameters. For example, you may need to change the adapter's WEP key or SSID to match changes you have made to the AP. The wireless network adapter's manufacturer has provided utility software for this purpose. For example, Figure 7-3 shows the NETGEAR (www.netgear.com) Client Manager program you can use to select a different wireless network SSID or to change the WPA passphrase or WEP key. (For more about SSIDs, WPA passphrases, and WEP keys, see the steps in the first section of this chapter.)

If you use Windows XP, however, you can use the operating system's utilities to change settings in your wireless network interface adapter. Windows XP is the first Windows operating system that has support for wireless networking built in. We talk about this built-in support in the later section "Wireless Zero Configuration with XP."

Figure 7-3:
The
NETGEAR
Client
Manager.

Synchronizing and Internet Access

To get your Pocket PC to synchronize with your PC through the wireless adapter — and to enable wireless access to the Internet — follow these general steps:

1. **On the Pocket PC, choose Start➪Settings➪Connections➪Network Adapters. Then select the wireless network adapter from the list of installed adapters on the Network Adapters screen and click Properties.**

   A screen similar to what's shown in Figure 7-4 appears. Click the IP Address tab. Marking the default setting (the Use Server-Assigned IP Address radio button) is easiest. The DHCP server on your network that assigns the IP addresses for all the other devices on the network also assigns the IP address for your Pocket PC.

2. **Determine the IP address of the PC with which the Pocket PC will synchronize.**

   Choose Start➪(All) Programs➪Accessories➪Command Prompt. In the command prompt window that appears, type **ipconfig**, and then press Enter. Copy the IP address for the PC's network adapter and then close the command prompt window.

3. **On the Pocket PC, go to the Name Servers tab of the wireless network adapter's Properties screen.**

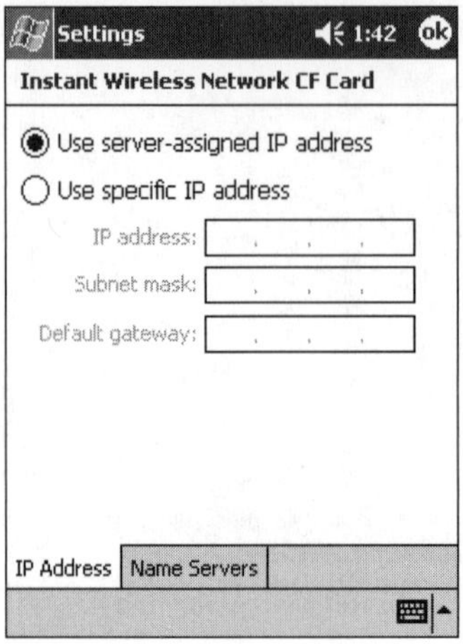

Figure 7-4:
Assigning
an IP
address
for your
Pocket PC.

You accessed the Properties screen in Step 1; it should still be visible on the Pocket PC.

4. In the WINS text box, enter the PC's IP address you copied in Step 4.

Figure 7-5 shows the Name Servers tab with the WINS address filled in.

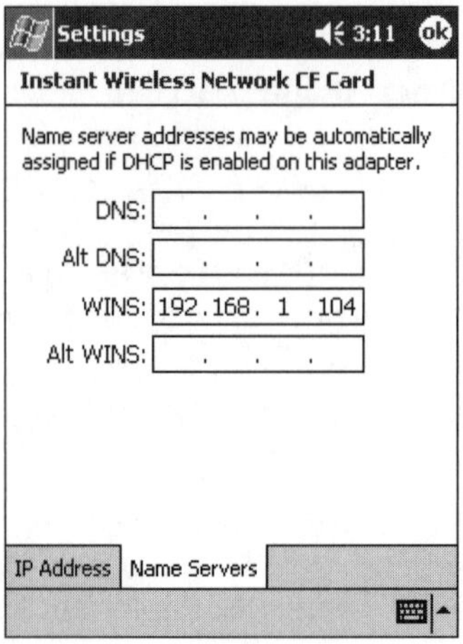

Figure 7-5:
Supplying
a WINS
address.

You should now be able to wirelessly synchronize the Pocket PC with the PC. If your wireless network is connected to the Internet, you should be able to wirelessly access the Internet on your Pocket PC. To check for the functionality of these two features, proceed to Steps 5 and 6.

5. **While the Pocket PC is not in its cradle, choose Start⇨ActiveSync and then click the Sync button (on the ActiveSync screen that appears).**

   You should see the ActiveSync pop-up window on the PC and a message on the Pocket PC telling you that the two computers are synchronizing.

6. **Launch Internet Explorer and browse the Internet to find out whether you have wireless access to the Internet.**

Wireless Zero Configuration with XP

Windows XP makes connecting to new wireless networks easier through a service that Microsoft has dubbed *Wireless Zero Configuration*. Although the Microsoft claim of zero configuration is a bit of an exaggeration, configuration is pretty easy. When you're installing or configuring a wireless adapter that's supported by Windows XP, you don't need to use software provided by the manufacturer. Instead, Windows XP itself recognizes the adapter and provides the necessary driver and configuration software.

Easy installation

As an alternative to the manufacturer's installation and configuration software, follow these steps to install and configure a supported wireless network adapter. (*Note:* We recommend that you check the documentation that accompanies your wireless adapter to determine whether it's supported by Windows XP Zero Configuration before continuing with these steps.)

1. **If you plan to use a wireless network interface adapter that you have to install inside the case of the computer, turn off the computer and install the PCI or ISA adapter.**

2. **Log on to Windows XP as a user with administrator rights.**

   If you installed Windows XP, you probably have administrator rights. To check, choose Start⇨Settings⇨Control Panel⇨User Accounts to display the User Accounts screen that shows the accounts on your computer. If you're not listed as Computer Administrator, you need to find out who is the administrator and get that person to change your account.

3. **Insert the PC Card or attach the USB adapter.**

   Windows XP displays a message that your new hardware is installed and ready to use.

   Because your computer is within range of your network's wireless AP (they have to be close enough to talk to each other), Windows XP announces that at least one wireless network is available and suggests that you click the Network icon to see a list of available networks.

4. **Click the Network icon in the notification area of the task bar in the lower-right corner of the screen.**

Windows XP displays the Wireless Network Connection dialog box, as shown in Figure 7-6.

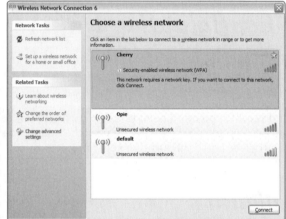

Figure 7-6:
The
Wireless
Network
Connection
dialog box.

5. **In the Network Key text box, type the WPA passphrase or WEP key you used in the AP configuration, enter the key again in the Confirm Network Key text box, and then click the Connect button.**

The dialog box disappears, and Windows XP displays a balloon message that announces a wireless network connection and indicates the connection's speed and signal strength (poor, good, or excellent). The Network icon on the status bar flashes green occasionally to indicate network traffic on the wireless connection.

In a matter of minutes, you have installed and configured a wireless network connection. If you have trouble connecting, you can access more configuration information by clicking the Advanced button in the Wireless Network Connection dialog box (refer to Figure 7-6) to display the Wireless Network Connection Properties dialog box (shown in Figure 7-7).

Automatic network connections

Easy installation and configuration is only half the Windows XP wireless networking story. If you know that you will use your computer to connect to several different wireless networks — perhaps one at home and another at work — Windows XP enables you to configure the wireless adapter to automatically detect and connect to each network on the fly, without further configuration.

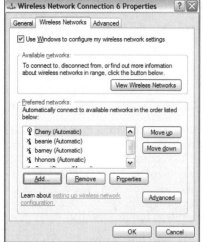

Figure 7-7:
The
Wireless
Network
Connection
Properties
dialog box.

To configure one or more wireless networks for automatic connection, follow these steps:

1. **In the notification area of the status bar at the bottom of the screen, click the Network icon to display the Wireless Network Connection dialog box and then click the Properties button.**

2. **In the Wireless Network Connection Properties dialog box that appears (refer to Figure 7-7), click the Wireless Networks tab.**

   Notice that your wireless home network is already listed. If your computer is in range of the second wireless network, its SSID is also listed.

3. **To add another network to the list, click the Add button on the Wireless Networks tab.**

4. **In the Wireless Network Properties dialog box that appears, type in the Network Name text box the network name (SSID) of the other wireless network to which you will connect your computer.**

   You may want to enter the network name (SSID) for the wireless network at your office, for example.

5. **If you're connecting to a wireless network at your office, make sure that you have appropriate authorization and check with the network**

administrator for encryption keys and authorization procedures that she has implemented.

If the network administrator has implemented a system for automatically providing users with WEP keys, click OK.

If the wireless network to which you plan to connect doesn't have an automatic key distribution system in place, do this:

    a. Deselect the check box labeled The Key Is Provided for Me Automatically.

    b. Enter the WEP key.

    c. Click OK to save this network SSID.

6. **Move on to the next network (if any) that you want to configure.**

Notice the Key Index scroll box near the bottom of the dialog box. By default, the key index is set to 1. Your office network administrator knows whether you need to use the key index. This feature is used if the system administrator has implemented a *rotating key system,* which is a security system used in some office settings. You don't need to mess with this feature unless you're setting up your computer to use at work — it's not something you use in your wireless home network.

7. **After adding all the necessary wireless networks, click OK on the Wireless Networks tab of the Wireless Network Connection Properties dialog box.**

Windows XP now has the information it needs to automatically connect the computer to each wireless network whenever the wireless station comes into range.

Tracking Your Network's Performance

After you have your network adapters and APs installed and up and running, you may think that you have reached the end of the game — wireless network nirvana! And, in some ways, you have, at least after you go through the steps in Chapter 9 and get your network and all its devices connected to the Internet. But, part of the nature of wireless networks is the fact that they rely on the transmission of radio waves throughout your home. If you have ever tried to tune in a station on your radio or TV but had a hard time getting a signal (who hasn't had this problem — besides kids who have grown up on cable TV and Internet radio, we suppose), you probably realize that radio waves can run into interference or just plain peter out at longer distances.

Obviously, the transmitters used in Wi-Fi systems use very low power levels — at least compared with commercial radio and television transmitters — so the issues of interference and range that are inherent to any radio-based system are even more important for a wireless home network.

Luckily, the client software that comes with just about any wireless network adapter includes a tool that enables you to take a look at the performance of your network — usually in the form of a signal strength meter and perhaps a link test program. With most systems (and client software), you can view this performance-monitoring equipment in two places:

- **In your system tray:** Most wireless network adapters install a small signal-strength meter on the Windows system tray (usually found in the lower-right corner of your screen, although you may have moved it elsewhere on your screen). This signal-strength meter usually has a series of bars that light up in response to the strength of your wireless network's radio signal. It's different with each manufacturer, but most that we have seen light up the bars in green to indicate signal strength. The more bars that light up, the stronger your signal.

- **Within the client software itself:** The client software you installed along with your network adapter usually has some more elaborate signal-strength system that graphically (or using a numerical readout) displays several measures of the quality of your radio signal. This is often called a *link test* function, although different manufacturers call it different things. (Look in your manual or in the online help system to find it in your network adapter's client software.) The link test usually measures several things:

  - **Signal strength:** Also called *signal level* in some systems, this is a measure of the signal's strength in dBm. The higher this number, the better, and the more likely that you can get a full-speed connection from your access point to your PC.

  - **Noise level:** This is a measure of the interference that's affecting the wireless network in your home. Remember that electronics in your home (such as cordless phones and microwaves) can put out their own radio waves that interfere with the radio waves used by your home network. Noise level is also measured in dBm, but in this case, lower is better.

  - **Signal to Noise Ratio (SNR):** This is really the key determinant to how good the performance of your wireless network is. This ratio is a comparison of the signal (the good radio waves) with the noise (the bad ones). SNR is measured in dB, and a higher number is better.

Network "sniffer" software, like NetStumbler (discussed in Chapter 16), includes even more powerful network test functionality. If you want to get involved in a detailed survey of your wireless environment, choose one of these programs.

Many link test programs not only provide an instantaneous snapshot of your network performance but also give you a moving graph of your performance over time. This snapshot can be really helpful in two ways. First, if you have a laptop PC, you can move it around the house to see how your network performance looks. Second, it can let you watch the performance while you turn various devices on and off. For example, if you suspect that a 2.4 GHz cordless phone is killing your wireless LAN, turn on your link test and keep an eye on it while you make a phone call.

When you grow more comfortable with your wireless LAN — and start using it more and more — you can leverage these tools to tweak your network. For example, you can have your spouse or a friend sit in the living room watching the link test results while you move the access point to different spots in the home office. Or, you can use the link test with a laptop to find portions of your house that have weak signals and then use these results to decide where to install a second access point.

Chapter 8

Setting Up a Wireless Mac Network

*I*f you're an Apple Macintosh user and you've just decided to try wireless networking, this chapter is for you. This chapter covers installing and setting up the AirPort Extreme Card in an Apple computer as well as setting up an AirPort Extreme Base Station. We focus on Mac OS X (v. 10.4 Tiger) because that is the most current version of the Mac operating system at the time of this writing, but the advice we offer in this chapter gets you up and running with *any* version of OS X.

Note: Apple has phased out OS 9 support for its recent computers. If you have an older Mac that still runs only OS 9, you're not out of luck — OS 9 PCs can support and connect to AirPort networks, but not all the features we are discussing here apply.

Understanding AirPort Hardware

Back in 1999, Apple Computer had a (typically flamboyant) product launch for the iBook notebook PC, and part of that big dog-and-pony show (*all* Apple product launches are extravaganzas!) was the introduction of the AirPort Wi-Fi wireless networking system. AirPort was the first real mainstream, consumer-friendly and consumer-focused wireless networking system. Over the years, AirPort (it's gone through a few name changes and design upgrades over time, as we discuss) has become an integral part of the Apple product lineup, and is installed (or available) in *all* of Apple's PCs and notebook computers.

The AirPort product line includes both *client adapters* (known as AirPort cards) which are installed inside Apple computers, and also *access points* or *wireless routers* (known as AirPort base stations) that act as the base station for a Wi-Fi network.

The Apple AirPort products use the same Wi-Fi 802.11g technology that has become popular throughout the wireless LAN world. Apple computers equipped with AirPort Extreme Cards can connect to any Wi-Fi–compatible 2.4 GHz 802.11b or 802.11g wireless network — regardless of whether the network uses Apple equipment — including Windows wireless networks.

The current generation of AirPort products (dubbed AirPort Extreme) is compatible with the 802.11g standard. You may also run into some older generations of AirPort equipment (just plain *AirPort* by name) that is compatible with the older 802.11b standards.

Getting to know the AirPort Card

Apple computer models were the first on the market to feature a special wireless adapter — known as the AirPort Card — as an option. The original AirPort card was similar in form to a PC Card (a Personal Computer Memory Card International Association [PCMCIA] Card) but was designed to be installed in a special AirPort slot inside an Apple computer. If you get your hands on one of the original AirPort cards, you should not try to use it in a PC Card slot found on most laptop computers. As we mention in the nearby sidebar, "The amazing disappearing AirPort Card," the original 802.11b AirPort card is no longer being produced and supplies are limited — luckily, all Macs built in the past two years support the newer AirPort Extreme card.

The current AirPort Extreme Card is a mini-PCI card (well, it's the same size and shape, but designed to fit *only* in AirPort slots in Macs). It's designed to fit inside an Apple computer, such as several of the newest PowerBook G4s, iBooks, and iMacs, but doesn't fit in the original AirPort slot in older Macs. The AirPort Extreme card has a retail price of $79. The AirPort Extreme card is Wi-Fi certified to be compliant with 802.11g, so it connects to any Wi-Fi-certified 802.11b or 802.11g access point, including (but not limited to) the Apple AirPort base stations.

Apple AirPort Extreme–ready computers

The Apple computer models that are compatible with the AirPort Extreme Card are

- Power Mac G5
- Power Mac G4 (FW 800)

✔ PowerBook G4 (12-inch)

✔ PowerBook G4 (12-inch DVI)

✔ PowerBook G4 (15-inch FW800)

✔ PowerBook G4 (17-inch)

✔ iMac (the 17-inch version, the USB 2.0 version, and all G5 versions)

✔ iBook G4

✔ eMac (ATI Graphics)

✔ eMac (USB 2.0)

Apple computers that are equipped for installation of an AirPort Extreme Card have an antenna built into the body of the computer. When you install the AirPort Card, you attach the AirPort Extreme Card to the built-in antenna. (All radios need an antenna to be able to send and receive radio signals, and wireless networking cards are no exception.)

If your older Mac doesn't support AirPort Extreme, you can try using a standard Wi-Fi network adapter with the drivers found at `www.ioxperts.com/devices/devices_80211b.html`.

The amazing disappearing AirPort Card

The original AirPort card — the one that fits into all the older G3 and Titanium G4 PowerBooks, the original iBooks, and original iMacs has been discontinued by Apple. Not because they aren't good guys and not because they don't want to sell such cards to their customers. The problem is that the 802.11b chips inside these cards are no longer available (the chip vendors are spending all their time building 802.11g chips like those found in the AirPort Extreme card).

The result is that cards for these Macs are extremely rare — the only real source of these cards is the small number that have been stockpiled by folks who repair Macs as "service parts." Think back to Economics 101, and you can see how this situation may drive up prices, and indeed it has, as we've seen these older cards (which originally cost about $100) for more than $150 on eBay and on various reseller Web sites (they're nowhere to be found on Apple's own site).

The only other alternative is to find a third-party Wi-Fi adapter that can work with your older Mac. For notebook computers like the PowerBook, it's a PC card adapter (see Chapter 2 for more on this), and for desktop Macs (like Power Macs), it's a PCI card. The AirPort software built into Mac OS X doesn't work with these devices (and almost none of them has a set of Mac *driver* software). The solution is to mate a card with some specialized software that works with a Macintosh.

The most popular solution here is to find an 802.11b PC or PCI card that works with the IOXpert 802.11b Driver for Mac OS X ($19.95 after a free trial period). This software works with a large number of 802.11b cards and all versions of OS X (including the current Tiger version). Go to `www.ioxperts.com/devices/devices_80211b.html` to find out more, to see a list of compatible (and *incompatible*) cards, and to download the trial version.

"Come in, AirPort Base Station — over. . . ."

The Apple access point (AP) is the AirPort Extreme Base Station. In addition to serving as a wireless AP, it can act as a cable or digital subscriber line (DSL) router and Dynamic Host Configuration Protocol (DHCP) server, which automatically assigns a network address to every computer on a network. It even has a built-in dial-up modem in case you connect to the Internet that way.

The Airport Extreme Base Station can be used to connect to America Online (AOL) — most access points don't even have dial-up modems any more. And, very few can connect to AOL. If you don't have broadband and use AOL, consider buying an ABS as your access point for a Mac network (or even a Windows network) to get this capability. If you *can* get broadband, however, we recommend that you use AOL for Broadband (`http://discover.aol.com/price_plans/bfsbroadband.adp`) rather than dial into the AOL service!

The AirPort Extreme Base Station has a few pretty cool features (which may or may not justify its rather substantial $199 selling price), including the following:

- ✒ **That built-in modem:** For most of us, this is no longer worth all that much, but for two groups of people, it is a big deal. The first, obviously, are those who can't get any broadband service where they live (though satellite service is available *almost* everywhere). The second is folks who work at home or otherwise feel the need for a backup service — having a dial-up account that you can use when the cable modem is down is a great thing to be able to rely on.

- ✒ **An antenna port and a line of external antennas:** The AirPort Extreme Base Station includes an external antenna port, and Apple sells a range of special antennas through its partner Dr. Bott (`www.drbott.com`), with designs that can boost the signal omnidirectionally or in a specific direction.

  If you *really* need to boost the output of an AirPort Extreme Base Station, check out QuickerTek (`www.quickertek.com`). Its 27dBm Transceiver can extend the range of this Base Station out to a half a mile!

- ✒ **A USB printer port:** The AirPort Extreme Base Station includes a USB port and print server functionality (refer to Chapter 5 for more on this topic), so you can hook any USB printer into your Base Station and access it from any computer (Mac or PC) on your network. If you have an Ethernet printer (like those big, fancy laser printers found in many offices), you can also connect that to the AirPort Extreme Base Station and access it from throughout your network.

✔ **A bridging feature:** You can use more than one Airport Extreme Base Station (or another cool Apple product called the Airport Express — which we discuss in the next section) to create a *bridged* network using a system called *WDS* (Wireless Distribution System). Using WDS, you can have a single base station (connected to your broadband connection) be the hub of your network and use other base stations in different locations to retransmit your signals so that your network can cover a considerably larger area.

The real advantage of the AirPort Extreme Base Station is that it has what we find to be the best, most well-integrated, and easiest to use software of any wireless AP out there — as long as you're using an OS X Macintosh to set things up and operate your network. Like most things Mac, you pay more and you don't necessarily have freedom of choice (though any 802.11g or b Wi-Fi compliant system works), but you gain in ease of use and elegance.

In particular, the ease of use of the WDS bridging mode in AirPort is light years ahead of other WDS systems we've used from other vendors. If you're a Mac person and think that you may need to use WDS to reach your entire network, definitely consider paying a bit more to go with Apple base stations.

Despite that, going with the AirPort Extreme has a few disadvantages:

✔ **Price, price, price:** At nearly $200, the AirPort Extreme costs more than twice what even the fanciest name-brand APs from NETGEAR, Linksys, and D-Link cost.

✔ **Not the fastest or longest range:** Many vendors sell APs that support MIMO/Pre-N (see Chapter 2) or other extended 802.11g modes that provide faster or longer-range connections, or both — the AirPort Extreme offers only the 54 Mbps of the 802.11g standard.

✔ **Only one Ethernet port:** Most APs have at least four *wired* Ethernet ports on their built-in Ethernet switch, allowing connections to your nonwireless PCs and devices. The AirPort Extreme has only one Ethernet port, so you need to spend $30 or more on a separate Ethernet switch if you have more than one wired client on your network.

✔ **Windows configuration is so-so:** Although you *can* configure an AirPort Extreme using Windows, the experience isn't nearly as well integrated as it is in Macintosh OS X.

✔ **Price:** Did we mention this one already? You can buy *three* APs with similar functionality for the price of one AirPort Extreme, if you shop around.

Figure 8-1 shows the AirPort Extreme Base Station.

Figure 8-1:
Apple gets
you unwired
with the
AirPort
Extreme
Base
Station.

Getting aboard the Express

The AirPort Extreme isn't the only Apple entry into the AP space (and, in fact, it's not even the most interesting!). Apple also has a small form factor (about the size of a deck of cards) access point known as the AirPort Express (see Figure 8-2).

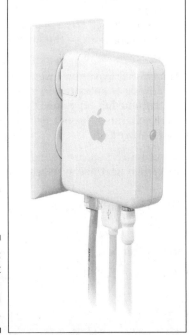

Figure 8-2:
The AirPort
Express is a
jack of all
trades.

This $129 device can fulfill a *bunch* of different roles in your wireless life, including the following:

- ✔ **It can be a full-fledged AP and router:** The AirPort Express can do pretty much everything any full-size AP can do — you can build your entire wireless LAN around an AirPort Express.

- ✔ **It can be a *travel router*:** A cool new category of APs are those designed for use on the road — travel routers that you can pack up and plug into any broadband access (like that available in most hotels), and provide yourself with an instant Wi-Fi hot spot. The small size of the AirPort Express lets you stick it in your laptop bag and bring it wherever you go.

- ✔ **It can be a WDS repeater:** As we mention in the earlier section about the AirPort Extreme base station, the Apple AirPort system supports the WDS standard, which allows you to extend your network throughout even a *huge* house by having your wireless signals hop from AP to AP until they reach your distant clients.

- ✔ **It can be a USB print server:** You can plug a USB printer into the AirPort Express and get printer access from the entire network.

- ✔ **It can play *AirTunes*:** Perhaps our favorite feature of the AirPort Express is its support for AirTunes. AirTunes is the Apple software system, which lets you listen to the music in your iTunes collection (and from your iPod) throughout your entire network. The AirPort Express has analog and digital audio connectors that let you plug it into a stereo or home theater.

We talk about AirTunes more in Chapter 13.

Like the AirPort Extreme Base Station, the AirPort Express uses the 802.11g standard and can work with any type of Wi-Fi certified 802.11g or 802.11b client.

Using AirPort with OS X Macs

Apple makes it exceptionally easy to configure an AirPort Extreme Base Station or an AirPort Express. All Mac OS X computers that are capable of working with an AirPort system will have two bits of software installed inside the Utilities folder (found within your Applications folder):

- ✔ AirPort Setup Assistant
- ✔ AirPort Admin Utility

The Setup Assistant is a "follow along with the steps" program (like the Wizard programs often used on Windows computers) that guides you step-by-step through the setup of an AirPort system by asking you simple questions. The Admin Utility is used for tweaking and updating your settings later on, after you already have everything set up. Most people can just use the Setup Assistant for all their configuration needs — though we recommend that you occasionally run the Admin Utility program to upgrade the *firmware* (the underlying software inside your AirPort), as we discuss later, in the section "Upgrading AirPort Base Station firmware on OS X."

Configuring the AirPort Base Station on OS X

When you've purchased a new AirPort Extreme Base Station or AirPort Express (that you will use as a base station), the easiest way to set it up for use in your wireless home network is to use the AirPort Setup Assistant. The AirPort Setup Assistant reads the Internet settings from your computer and transfers them to the Base Station so that you can access the Internet over your wireless network. To use the AirPort Setup Assistant, follow these steps:

1. **Before running the AirPort Setup Assistant, set up your computer to connect to the Internet by dial-up modem or by broadband (cable or DSL) modem.**

   Check with your ISP for instructions on getting connected:

   If you connect to the Internet by dial-up modem: Connect the telephone line to the phone line port on the Base Station.

   If you connect to the Internet by DSL or cable modem: Use an Ethernet cable to connect the modem to the Base Station's WAN port.

2. **Click the Applications Folder in your Dock.**

3. **When the Applications folder opens, double-click on the Utilities folder icon.**

4. **In the Utilities folder, double-click the AirPort Setup Assistant icon to display the AirPort Setup Assistant window, as shown in Figure 8-3.**

5. **Select the Set Up a New AirPort Base Station button and then click the Continue button in the lower-right corner of the window.**

   If your computer is in range of only your one wireless network, the Setup Assistant automatically configures your AirPort Card to select that network and proceeds to the America Online Access panel. However, if you happen to be in range of more than one wireless network, you see the Select an AirPort Network panel, which asks you to select your network from a pop-up list. Your network will have its name assigned at the factory, similar to *Apple Network xxxxxx,* where *xxxxxx* is a six-digit hexadecimal number. After selecting your network, click the Continue button to go to the next panel.

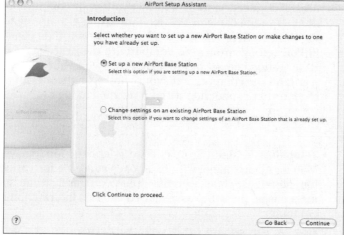

Figure 8-3:
The OS X
AirPort
Setup
Assistant
window.

6. **In the America Online Access panel:**

   • **If you connect to the Internet via AOL:** Select the I Am Using America Online button and then click the Continue button.

   • **If you're not using AOL:** Select the I Am Using Another Internet Service Provider button and then click the Continue button to display the Internet Access panel.

7. **In the Internet Access panel, choose one of the following options and then click the Continue button:**

   • **Telephone Modem:** Select this button if you connect to the Internet through a dial-up modem. The AirPort Base Station is one of the few wireless access points that includes a 56 Kbps modem. When you select this option, all the computers connected to your wireless network may be able to share a single dial-up connection.

   If you have one of the new Airport Extreme Base Stations, you may not have a built-in version. There are two versions, and the less expensive one doesn't have a modem.

- **Local Area Network:** You should select this button if your computer is connected to a high-speed LAN.

- **Cable Modem or DSL Using Static IP or DHCP:** Select this button if you connect to the Internet by cable modem or by DSL, but only if your ISP doesn't use the PPP over Ethernet (PPPoE) protocol.

- **Cable Modem or DSL Using PPPoE:** If your ISP uses the PPPoE protocol, select this button. It's important that you make a successful connection to the Internet with your computer connected directly to the cable or DSL modem before attempting to configure the Base Station. The AirPort Setup Assistant then can copy the PPPoE settings from your computer to the Base Station so that the Base Station can log on to the Internet with your user ID and password. All the computers on your wireless network can then share the Internet connection without needing to log on.

The next panel you see at this step depends on the choice you make in Step 7:

- **Telephone Modem:** If you choose Telephone Modem, you see the Modem Access panel with text boxes available for various dial-up parameters, such as username, password, and phone number. In most cases, the setup assistant copies this information from your computer.

- **LAN, or Broadband Using Static IP or DHCP:** If you choose either a LAN or a broadband (cable modem or DSL) connection that doesn't use PPPoE, the Ethernet Access panel presents the option to use DHCP or to assign a static IP address. If your ISP has assigned you a static IP address — along with other values, such as subnet mask, router address, domain name, and DHCP client name — you have to enter this data if it isn't automatically copied from your computer.

- **Broadband Using PPPoE:** If you select the Cable Modem or DSL Using PPPoE option, the PPPoE Access panel presents text boxes for entering an account name, password, and other account information sometimes required by PPPoE providers. Again, in most cases, this information is automatically copied from your computer.

After you enter the appropriate information, click the Continue button to display the Network Name and Password panel.

8. **In the Network Name and Password panel that appears, enter the name and password you want to use for your wireless network and then click the Continue button to display the Base Station Password panel.**

The Base Station Password panel gives you the options to use the network password as your Base Station password or to assign a different password for changing the settings on your Base Station. If you're the only person who will configure the computers on the network, using the same one in both places is probably the easiest. However, if you plan to share the network password with other users, assign a different password to the Base Station so that only you can change the Base Station's settings.

9. **Click the Continue button to display the Conclusion panel.**

   The Conclusion panel informs you that the Setup Assistant is ready to set up your Base Station.

10. **Click the Continue button.**

    After the Setup Assistant downloads the new settings to the Base Station, it displays a message that it's waiting for the Base Station to reset. As soon as the Base Station resets, the Setup Assistant displays a panel announcing that it's finished and that it has been able to configure this computer to connect to the Internet.

11. **Click the Done button to close the AirPort Setup Assistant.**

Upgrading AirPort Base Station firmware on OS X

In this section, we explain how to upgrade the firmware of a new AirPort Extreme Base Station. Upgrading the firmware on your AirPort Extreme Base Station through a direct Ethernet cable connection is easiest. Use an Ethernet cable (either a straight-through cable or a crossover cable; the Base Station automatically detects the type of cable you're using) to connect your computer's Ethernet port to the Base Station's LAN port. You can also do the upgrade over a wireless connection.

To upgrade the firmware of a new AirPort Base Station that you're setting up for the first time, follow these steps:

1. **In the Dock, click on the Applications folder.**

2. **When the Applications folder opens, double-click to open the Utilities folder.**

3. **Double-click the AirPort Admin Utility icon to display the Select Base Station window, as shown in Figure 8-4.**

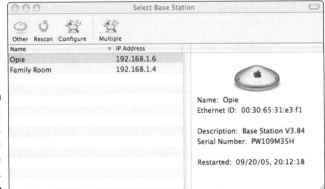

Figure 8-4:
The OS X
Select Base
Station
window.

4. **Highlight the Base Station name and then click the Configure button.**

5. **After a message pops up requesting a password, enter** public **as the password and then click OK.**

   • If the firmware installed in the Base Station is older than the firmware that was supplied with your updated software, you see a message prompting you that a newer version of the Base Station software is available. Click the Upload button to install it.

   • If a message pops up stating that uploading the software will cause the wireless network to be disconnected, click OK. The new firmware is copied to the Base Station.

   If the Base Station window is displayed when you click the Configure button — rather than a message that a newer version of the Base Station software is available — your Base Station already contains the most recent firmware. Close the Base Station window and then close the AirPort Admin Utility.

6. **After a message says that the system is waiting for the Base Station to restart and that the Base Station has been successfully updated, click OK.**

7. **When the Select Base Station window returns, close it.**

8. **Disconnect the Ethernet cable between your computer and the Base Station, if you're using one.**

Connecting another computer to your AirPort network on OS X

When you set up your AirPort Base Station by following the directions in the preceding section, you also set up the AirPort Card in the computer you used to configure the Base Station. However, you need to configure the AirPort

Cards in the other Mac computers in your house to enable them to connect to the AirPort network. Follow these steps:

1. **Click and hold the Applications folder in the Dock, and select the Internet Connect application.**

2. **When the Internet Connect opens, select the AirPort tab, as shown in Figure 8-5.**

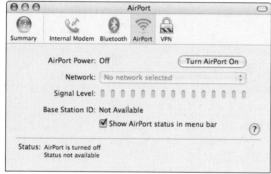

Figure 8-5:
Start making
your
connection
here.

3. **Make sure that the AirPort Power is on — if it's not, click the button labeled Turn AirPort On.**

4. **Use the Network pull-down menu to select the AirPort network you created.**

5. **Select the Show AirPort Status in menu bar check box while you're at it. This step streamlines the process the next time you want to get connected to this network.**

   If you've turned on Encryption for your AirPort network, you're prompted to enter a password.

6. **Select the appropriate type of encryption (see Chapter 10 for more on this topic; we recommend that you use WPA Personal), and then type your password in the Password text box, as shown in Figure 8-6. Select the Remember password in the My Keychain check box to retain the password for future use.**

7. **Click the OK button.**

8. **When the Internet Connect window indicates that you're connected to the AirPort network, you can close the window. You're all done.**

   Figure 8-7 shows the Pat's PowerBook connected to his network, Cherry.

After you've gone through these steps, you have an AirPort icon on your menu bar. The next time you want to connect to this AirPort network, simply go up to the menu bar, click on the AirPort icon, and select the network name. That's it!

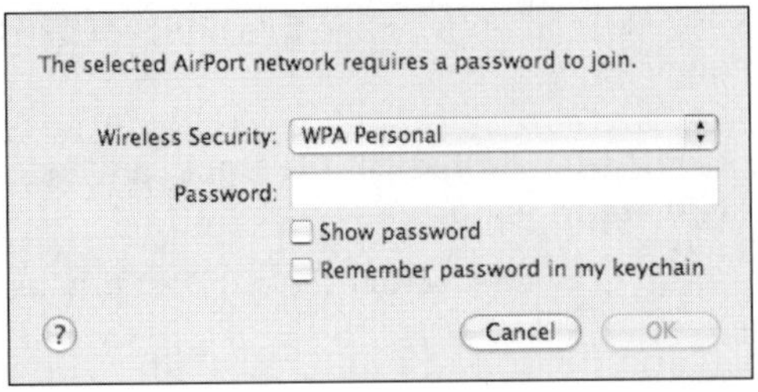

Figure 8-6:
Enter your
password
here.

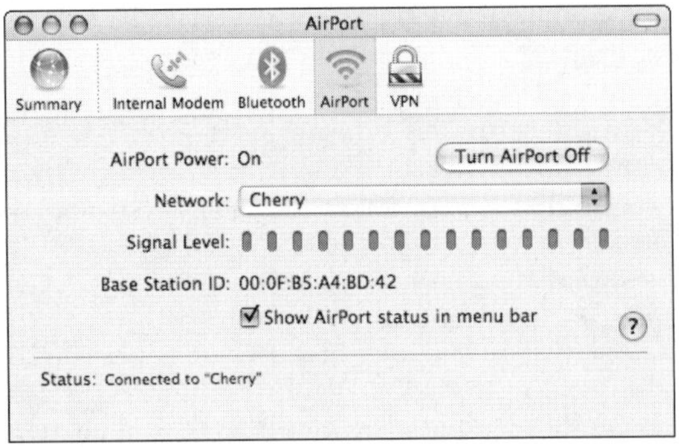

Figure 8-7:
All done!

Adding a Non-Apple Computer to Your AirPort Network

One reason that wireless home networking has become so popular is the interoperability between wireless networking equipment from different vendors. Because it adheres to the standards and is Wi-Fi-certified, Apple wireless networking equipment is no exception. You can even use a Windows or Linux computer to connect to an Apple AirPort Base Station.

The procedure for entering the wireless network parameters in non-Apple wireless software for configuring a wireless network adapter varies by manufacturer. Follow these general steps to add your non-Apple computer (or even Apple computer with non-Apple wireless hardware and software) to your AirPort Network:

1. **Select the network name of the AirPort Base Station.**

   The wireless network adapter configuration software usually presents a list of available wireless networks in range of the adapter. Select from the list the network name you assigned to the AirPort Base Station.

   For example, in Windows XP, right-click the Network icon in the notification area of the taskbar and then select View Available Wireless Networks from the pop-up menu that appears. Then select the AirPort Base Stations network name from the list presented in the Wireless Network Connection dialog box.

2. Enter the network password (your WEP key or WPA Passphrase).

If you're using WEP, the password you entered in the AirPort Base Station setup probably doesn't work. Here's how to find the password — the WEP key — that works. Apple uses a different password naming convention than other wireless manufacturers. Fortunately, Apple has provided a function in the AirPort Admin Utility that does the conversion for you:

  a. Using the computer you used to configure the AirPort, open the AirPort Admin Utility.

  b. Select your Base Station from the list and then click the Configure icon.

  c. When presented with a pop-up window, enter the password for configuring the base station and then click OK to display the main AirPort Admin Utility window.

  d. From the Base Station menu, choose Equivalent Network Password.

   Note: If the toolbar isn't visible, click the View menu and choose Show Toolbar.

   The utility opens a drop-down window that displays the equivalent network password (WEP key) that you should enter in the configuration software for your non-Apple wireless network adapter.

3. Make sure that you set the adapter to obtain an IP address automatically.

How you do this depends on what kind of PC and which PC operating system you're using.

4. Close the configuration software, and you should be connected to the AirPort network.

If you're not connected, go through the steps again and pay particular attention to enter the equivalent network password correctly.

If you're really having a hard time, try turning WEP off on your AirPort Base Station (deselect the Use Encryption check box in the Airport Setup Program) and see whether you can connect without any encryption. If this works, double-check your Equivalent Network Password and look in the manual for your network adapter. You may need to enter a special code before the Equivalent Network Password — we discuss this topic in Chapter 10.

If you're using Windows XP and have Wireless Zero Configuration enabled, just follow the steps we discuss in Chapter 7 for that software — you can connect to an AirPort network really simply and quickly that way.

Connecting to Non-Apple-Based Wireless Networks

One scenario you may encounter in a home network is the need to connect a Macintosh computer to a non-Apple-based network. Follow the procedures outlined in this chapter for adding a computer to a wireless network — using the Internet Connect AirPort pane, the procedure should be identical. If you have any trouble, it almost certainly relates to the network password. Here are a few troubleshooting tips to resolve password issues:

✔ **Try turning off encryption on the wireless network.** If you can successfully connect your Mac to the network without the need of a password, you can be sure that the password was the problem. Don't leave the network unprotected, however. Read on.

✔ **Check the password configuration.** When you turn on the access point's encryption, determine whether the password is an alphanumeric value or a hexadecimal number. Some hardware vendors provide configuration software that has you enter a pass phrase, but the software then generates a hexadecimal number. You have to enter the hexadecimal number, not the pass phrase, in the AirPort software.

✔ **Watch for case-sensitivity.** If the Windows-based access point configuration software enables you to enter an alphanumeric password, keep in mind that the password is case sensitive. For WEP, the password should be either exactly 5 characters (letters and numbers) for 64-bit encryption or 13 characters for 128-bit encryption. You should then enter exactly the same characters in the Password text box in the AirPort pane of Internet Connect.

✔ **Use current software.** Make sure that you're using the most current version of AirPort software. The most up-to-date software makes it easier to enter passwords connecting to a Windows-based wireless network. The new software automatically distinguishes between alphanumeric and hexadecimal passwords. With earlier versions of the software, to connect to a WEP-encrypted Windows-based network, you have to type quotation marks around alphanumeric values and type a dollar sign ($) in front of hexadecimal numbers.

These guidelines should help you get your Mac connected to a Windows wireless network, including the capability to share the Internet. Keep in mind, however, that other factors determine whether you can also share files, printers, and other resources over the wireless network.

Chapter 9

Setting Up Internet Sharing

- -

In This Chapter

▶ Using an Internet gateway or router

▶ Deciding how to share your Internet access

▶ Obtaining an IP address automatically

▶ Enabling Internet connection sharing

▶ Configuring your Windows XP firewall

- -

*O*ne of the most popular uses of personal computers is to access the Internet. In this chapter, we describe how you can use a network, including a wireless network, to share a single Internet connection among all the computers on the network. We also describe how to obtain an Internet Protocol (IP) address automatically in Windows 2000 and Windows XP and Mac OS X. In addition, the chapter explains how to set up sharing of Internet connections without the need to buy a router in Windows 2000 and Windows XP and Mac OS X.

In Chapter 7, we describe how to set up and configure wireless network interface adapters by using the installation software that accompanies the adapters. When you set up wireless adapters that way, the installation software (in most cases) properly configures the adapter to make it possible for computers on the network to communicate and to take advantage of the Internet-sharing capabilities of Internet gateways, Dynamic Host Configuration Protocol (DHCP) servers, and cable and digital subscriber line (DSL) routers. Occasionally, however, you may need to change network settings of a wireless network adapter.

Deciding How to Share Your Internet Connection

Whether you've installed a wireless network or are using some other type of network devices to create a home network, you no doubt want all your networked computers to have access to an Internet connection. Here are two ways to share an Internet connection over the network:

- ✔ **Connection sharing:** All network users access the Internet via one computer that's specifically set up for doing just that.

- ✔ **A router or an Internet gateway:** A router handles the traffic management to enable all network users access to the Internet. An Internet gateway is a broadband modem with a bundled-in router. A wireless Internet gateway adds an access point (AP) to the mix.

Connection sharing

Windows 2000 and Windows XP enable Internet connection sharing, as does Mac OS X. When using this method to share an Internet connection, each computer in a wired or wireless network is set up to connect to the Internet through the computer that's connected to the modem that's connected to the Internet. The disadvantage with this system is that you can't turn off or remove the computer that's connected to the modem without also disconnecting all computers from the Internet. In addition, simultaneous usage (several people on the network using the Internet at one time) can slow down the computer providing the connection.

Mac OS X v. 10.2 (called Jaguar) or later (meaning 10.3 Panther and 10.4 Tiger) include a program for the Apple AirPort system, called AirPort Software Base Station. The Base Station enables you to share an Internet connection by creating a software-based wireless Base Station in one of the computers on your network. Other computers on the network with wireless network adapters can access the Internet through the Base Station software. Again, the computer that's running this Base Station software has to be turned on for the other computers in the wireless network to gain access to the Internet, and this Base Station computer is affected by the same performance degradation as in the preceding scenario.

Routers and gateways

By connecting a router between the broadband modem and your home network, all computers on the network can access the Internet without going through another computer. The Internet connection no longer depends on any computer on the network.

The types of routers used in homes are often cable or DSL routers. These devices are also DHCP servers and include Network Address Translation (NAT) services. The most popular type of device for sharing an Internet connection over a home network, often described as a *wireless gateway,* combines the features of a router, a DHCP server, a NAT server, a proxy server, a firewall, and the capabilities of a wireless AP. In addition to wireless connectivity, most of these devices also have several Ethernet ports for connecting computers with network cable, which gives you the flexibility of adding wired devices and expanding your network connections. Each computer connects to the wireless gateway; the wireless gateway device connects to the broadband (usually DSL or cable) modem; and the modem connects to the Internet.

The nature of the Internet and Transmission Control Protocol/Internet Protocol (TCP/IP) networking requires that every connecting machine or device has to have a unique IP address. For information to get to its proper destination, every piece of information has to contain the IP address it came from and the IP address it's going to for it to get from one point to another.

A NAT server allows for the conversion of one IP address to one or many other IP addresses. This means that a whole group of computers can look like just one computer to the rest of the Internet. This situation is becoming more the norm in both home and corporate networks these days because we have many more computers and devices using the Internet now than we have IP addresses to give them. Connecting to an Internet service provider (ISP) typically delivers one IP address to the device performing the connection. This is true for dial-up, cable, and satellite modems as well DSL. That IP address is used by the computer or Internet gateway that the modem connects to.

If you have one computer, getting an IP address assigned to your computer is very simple because the modem device delivers the IP address to the computer, and the computer uses that address as its own and connects to the Internet. If you have more than one computer or device to connect, you have to share the one IP address that the modem receives among those machines. NAT creates an internal addressing scheme using one of the reserved IP address ranges that the Internet doesn't use. (192.168.*x.x* is the most commonly used Class B network for home or office networks using NAT.) Many companies and almost all cable and DSL routers use this address range on the networks behind them. In many cases, it's a given that the IP address of the cable or DSL router is 192.168.0.1, 192.168.1.1 or 192.168.2.1. These addresses are the most common (others could possibly be used) and are used as the default address range in most devices on which NAT is configured for use.

In case your neighborhood IT guru is discussing your network with you, you can tell her that you've used a class C address range derived from one of the reserved class B networks. Or not — it's up to you! We personally wouldn't want to start that conversation unless we had *lots* of time to spend on it. Well, Ed might, but he's *our* IT guru, so it's expected.

After the address translation is in place, a DHCP server then assigns the local IP addresses for all the devices connected inside your home network. The Internet gateway's NAT function enables all computers connected to the Internet through the Internet gateway device to share the same IP address on the Internet. Figure 9-1 depicts a wireless home network that uses an Internet gateway providing NAT and DHCP to share Internet access to three computers over wireless connections and to two more over wired connections.

Sharing dial-up Internet connections

You can use connection sharing and a home network to share a single dial-up connection. This would be especially practical if you have a dedicated telephone line for Internet access. You can use a dial-up modem to connect to the Internet on the dedicated line, leave the connection running, and then share this connection with all the computers on your home network so that they can access the Internet.

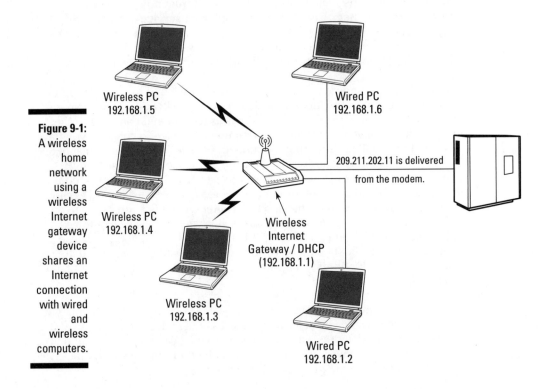

Figure 9-1: A wireless home network using a wireless Internet gateway device shares an Internet connection with wired and wireless computers.

Wireless PC
192.168.1.5

Wired PC
192.168.1.6

Wireless PC
192.168.1.4

209.211.202.11 is delivered from the modem.

Wireless Internet Gateway / DHCP
(192.168.1.1)

Wireless PC
192.168.1.3

Wired PC
192.168.1.2

Similarly, if you purchase an Internet gateway that includes a dial-up modem, you can use the gateway to share a dial-up connection (these are very hard to find — your best bet is to look for a used one on eBay if you need dial-up). You can connect the gateway to the Internet by using the dial-up modem and then use the gateway's router feature to share this connection with all the networked computers. Some Internet gateways (usually those designed for small businesses) combine both a broadband (DSL, usually) modem and a dial-up modem in one box. You can use the dial-up modem as a backup system if your broadband connection ever goes down or as a dial-in method for connecting to your network when you're away from the home or office.

The Apple AirPort Extreme includes a dial-up modem (standard on older AirPort Base Stations and optional on the AirPort Extreme Base Station) and also includes ISP logon features that can successfully connect to AOL, but you still need multiple AOL accounts for multiple users to access the Internet simultaneously through AOL.

Obtaining an IP Address Automatically

For the computers in your home network to communicate effectively with one another, whether they're connected to the network by wire or wirelessly, all computers must have IP (network) addresses that can route (talk to) each other, on the same network. For example, the local IP addresses 192.168.*0*.1 and 192.168.*0*.55 are in the same address range, but the IP addresses 192.168.*0*.1 and 192.168.*1*.55 are not. Note that the number after the second dot (referred to by computer geeks as the *third octet*) must be the same for the address to be in the same local network. This arrangement assumes that the two devices holding these addresses share the same physical space. In addition, all must have the same subnet mask, which is typically 255.255.255.0.

A *subnet* (or subnetwork) is simply a portion of a network (like your wireless home network) that has been portioned off and grouped as a single unit. When you use a wireless Internet gateway, all your computers are placed in the same subnet. The single IP address assigned to your modem can provide Internet access to all the computers on the subnet. The numbers used to identify the subnet are also referred to as the *subnet mask*. As we mention previously, you typically use 255.255.255.0 as your subnet mask. The important thing is to ensure that all computers and devices connected to your wireless home network are within the same address range — otherwise, they don't connect to the Internet. Most of the time, you don't have to do anything here because your computer should have its IP address and subnet mask set up by the DHCP of your AP device.

You can manually assign the IP address of each device connected to the network, but (luckily) you usually don't have to worry about using this feature. For some applications, such as gaming or videoconferencing — and for some noncomputer devices on your network, such as game consoles — you may have to enter a static IP address into your router's configuration. In the majority of cases, however — that is, for most normal PC Internet connections — the DHCP server built into cable and DSL routers and wireless Internet gateways takes care of IP address assignments for you.

One of the most common errors when setting up a home network comes from using a router providing DHCP and NAT and combining it with a wireless access point that also provides DHCP and NAT. If you're using two devices rather than a combined one, you need to be sure that you enable the DHCP and NAT services only on the router that's connected to the modem device. The AP should have an option when it's configured to be set up as a bridge device. This turns off its services and allows the device to be a wireless conduit to the network created by the DHCP and NAT services of the Internet gateway. Failing to do this can result in a segmented home network in which the wired devices cannot share with the wireless devices or the wireless devices cannot share with anything but themselves and are unable to access the Internet through your ISP.

Suppose that you install a network adapter (refer to Chapter 7), launch your Web browser, and try to reach the Internet. If you then have problems (assuming that everything else is connected and other computers on the network can successfully access the Internet), perhaps the IP address wasn't properly assigned to the adapter. Before you start panicking, try shutting down and restarting the computer. Often, restarting the computer causes the network adapter to properly obtain an IP address from the network's DHCP server. If you still can't reach the Internet, follow the instructions in this section to configure the network adapter to automatically obtain an IP address. (Also check out Chapter 18, where we cover some basic troubleshooting techniques for wireless home networks.)

Configuring a device on the network (wired or wireless) to automatically obtain an IP address from a DHCP server is very easy. Throughout the rest of this section, we outline the steps necessary for automatically obtaining an IP address from a DHCP server for various operating systems: Windows 2000 and Windows XP and Mac OS X. After you complete the applicable procedure, the DHCP server leases a local IP address to the device you're configuring, which enables it to communicate with other IP devices on the network.

Sometimes you have to restart your computer to successfully achieve the desired result.

When a DHCP server *leases* an IP address, the server doesn't assign that IP address to another device until the lease runs out or the device that is leasing the address releases it. Each time when you restart your computer — or periodically, if you leave your computer on all the time — the DHCP server renews the lease, which allows the computer to keep the IP address it has been given.

Domain Name System (DNS) servers

When the DHCP server assigns an IP address, it also specifies the IP addresses for Domain Name System (DNS) servers and for a default gateway. *Domain names* are text-based names that represent one or more registered IP addresses used on the Internet. When you type a Uniform Resource Locator (URL) in your Web browser, DNS servers translate the text-based domain names in the URL into the equivalent IP addresses. You don't have to know the IP addresses, just the domain names. The DNS server addresses are supplied by your ISP's DHCP server and are passed on by your home network's DHCP server to each workstation. The *default gateway* takes care of sending network traffic to devices that have IP addresses outside the local subnet. The wireless Internet gateway device or the cable or DSL router you installed in your wireless network is the default gateway for each of the computers on your network.

Windows 2000

If the computer is running the Widows 2000 operating system, follow these steps to set the network adapter to obtain its IP address automatically from a DHCP server:

1. **Choose Start⇨Settings⇨Network and Dial-up Connections.**

   The Network and Dial-up Connections window appears, as shown in Figure 9-2.

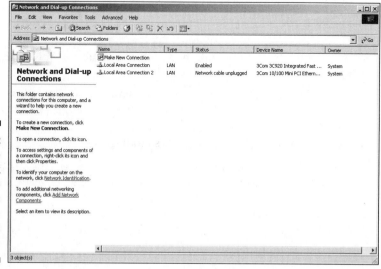

Figure 9-2: The Network and Dial-up Connections window in Windows 2000.

2. **Highlight the Local Area Connection item for the network adapter you want to configure.**

3. **Choose File⇨Properties.**

   The Local Area Connection Properties dialog box appears, as shown in Figure 9-3.

Figure 9-3:
The
Properties
dialog box
for the
network
adapter in
Windows
2000.

4. **Highlight the Internet Protocol (TCP/IP) option and then click the Properties button.**

   The Internet Protocol (TCP/IP) Properties dialog box appears, as shown in Figure 9-4.

5. **On the General tab, select both the Obtain an IP Address Automatically and the Obtain DNS Server Address Automatically options.**

6. **Click OK to return to the Local Area Connections dialog box and then click OK again to return to the Network and Dial-up Connections window.**

7. **Close the Network and Dial-up Connections window.**

   Windows 2000 applies the change to the network settings and obtains an IP address for the network adapter from your network's DHCP server.

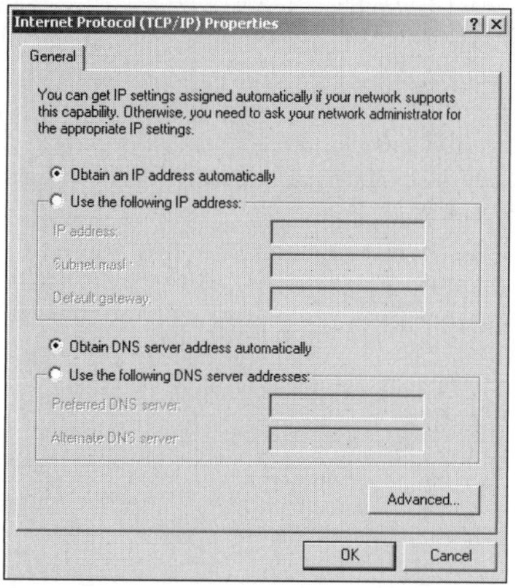

Figure 9-4:
The Internet
Protocol
(TCP/IP)
Properties
dialog box in
Windows
2000.

Windows XP

If your computer is running the Windows XP operating system, follow these steps to set the network adapter to obtain its IP address automatically from a DHCP server:

1. **Choose Start➪Network Connections.**

   If Network Connections doesn't appear on the Start menu, choose Control Panel and then double-click the Network Connections icon on the Control Panel.

   The Network Connections window appears, as shown in Figure 9-5.

2. **In the LAN or High-Speed Internet section of the Network Connections window, highlight the Wireless Network Connection item for the network adapter you want to configure.**

   For example, in Figure 9-5, the wireless network interface adapter device is listed as Linksys Wireless-B USB in the Network Connections window.

3. **Choose File➪Properties.**

   The Wireless Network Connection Properties dialog box appears, as shown in Figure 9-6.

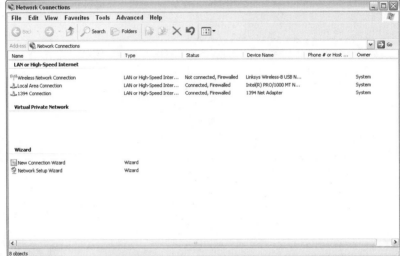

Figure 9-5:
The
Network
Connections
window in
Windows XP.

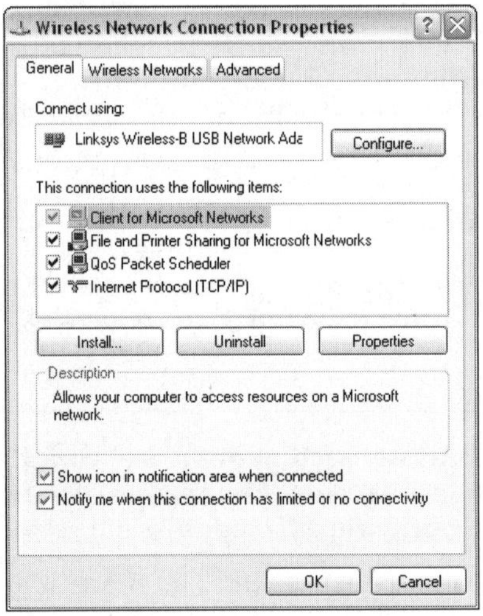

Figure 9-6:
The
Properties
dialog box
for the
network
adapter in
Windows XP.

4. **On the General tab, highlight the Internet Protocol (TCP/IP) option, and then click the Properties button.**

   The Internet Protocol (TCP/IP) Properties dialog box appears, as shown in Figure 9-7.

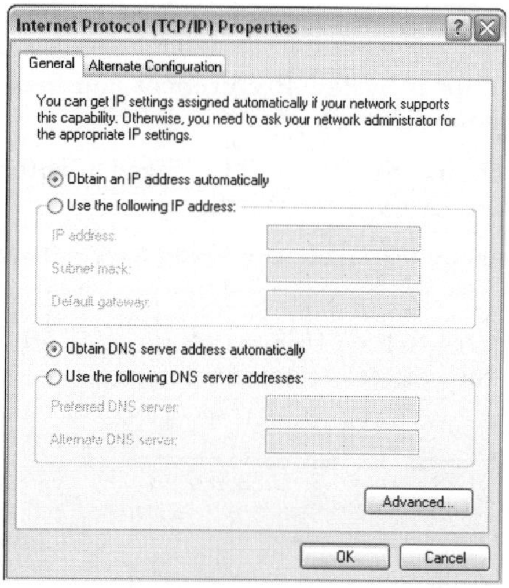

Figure 9-7:
The Internet
Protocol
(TCP/IP)
Properties
dialog box in
Windows XP.

5. **On the General tab, select both the Obtain an IP Address Automatically and the Obtain DNS Server Address Automatically options and then click OK.**

   You return to the Wireless Network Connection Properties dialog box.

6. **Click OK again to return to the Network Connections window and then close that window.**

   Windows XP applies the change to the network settings and obtains an IP address for the network adapter from your network's DHCP server.

Mac OS

If the computer is running the Mac OS 9.*x* operating system, follow these steps to set the network adapter to obtain its IP address automatically from a DHCP server:

1. **From the Apple menu, display the Control Panels list, select TCP/IP, and then click OK to display the TCP/IP window.**

2. **From the Connect Via drop-down menu, choose the network device you want to configure.**

3. **From the Configure drop-down menu, choose Using DHCP Server.**

4. **Close the TCP/IP window, and save changes when you're prompted.**

   Mac OS sends a request to the DHCP server for an IP address and assigns that address to the network device.

If the computer is running the Mac OS X operating system:

1. **From the Apple menu, choose System Preferences and then click the Network icon to display the Network pane.**

2. **From the Show menu, choose the network interface adapter you want to configure. In almost all cases, it's AirPort.**

3. **On the TCP/IP tab (see Figure 9-8), choose Using DHCP from the Configure menu.**

   The Mac OS sends a request to the DHCP server for an IP address and assigns that address to the network adapter.

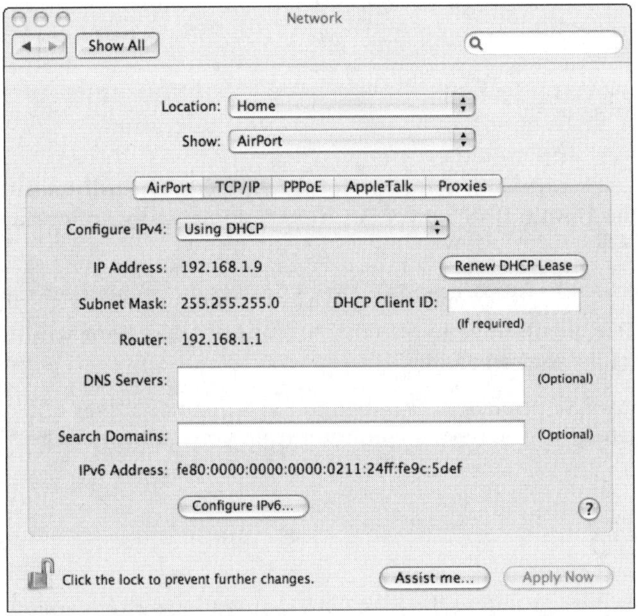

Figure 9-8:
The TCP/IP tab of the Mac OS X Network pane.

Setting Up Internet Connection Sharing

Internet gateways and cable and DSL routers are certainly the easiest way to accomplish Internet connection sharing, but we know of a more economical method — software-based sharing using an attached PC. We should say, right up front, that we think that the *hardware* approach — that is, using a wireless Internet gateway or a cable or DSL router — is the best way to go. But, if you really need to save a few bucks (and we mean only a few because you can get a good 802.11g router for $50 these days), try this approach. It works, but it's not as good as the hardware approach because it can affect the performance of both your network overall as well as the particular computer you use for Internet connection sharing. Windows 2000 and later versions of Windows provide a software-based solution for sharing an Internet connection over a local-area network (LAN). This option is available whether you're using a wired network, a wireless network, or a combination of the two.

Software-based Internet connection sharing isn't efficient if you have more than four computers trying to share an Internet connection simultaneously. The cost of a broadband router is far less than the cost of a dedicated computer in most cases. And broadband routers usually contain other features that this software connection sharing doesn't offer, such as port forwarding (Port Address Translation; PAT) to forward incoming requests to specific machines based on port, as well as offering a demilitarized zone (DMZ). (A *DMZ*, in the network world, is a network zone that has no firewall protection — we discuss this topic more in Chapter 10.) On the other hand, if you have an extra computer lying around and have time on your hands to maintain it, software-based Internet connection sharing could be your best option. (We're still not convinced.)

When you set up a Windows software-based shared Internet connection, you select one computer to be the *Internet connection host* — the computer (running Windows 2000 or later) that is always turned on and always connected to the Internet so that any other networked computer can access the Internet through it. This Internet connection host computer also must have two network adapters: one that connects to the Internet and another that communicates with the local-area network. The connection to the Internet could be through a dial-up modem, a broadband modem, or a connection to another larger network that connects to the Internet. After you complete the setup wizard, Windows turns the Internet connection server computer into both a DHCP server and your gateway to your broadband connection and the Internet.

You need to understand what Windows Internet Connection Sharing does *not* do: It doesn't convert the Internet connection host into a wireless access point. By contrast, software included with Mac OS 9 and Mac OS X v. 10.2 or later *is* capable of turning your AirPort-enabled Mac into an AP.

Using Windows Internet Connection Sharing software is equivalent to adding a cable or DSL router to your network. You could, for example, purchase a *stand-alone* AP — one that's not also a router and DHCP server — and attach it to your PC via an Ethernet port. All wireless PCs in your house can then connect to the AP, which in turn connects to your host PC. You then connect a dial-up modem to your computer (or perhaps installed inside your computer) or connect the modem to a second Ethernet port. You can then share your Internet connection (through the dial-up modem or through a broadband modem) with the computers that connect wirelessly to the AP. Figure 9-9 depicts a wireless home network that uses Windows Internet Connection Sharing to provide an Internet connection to all wireless PCs on the network.

When using Windows Internet Connection Sharing, the host computer must always be on, with Windows running, so that the other computers in the home network can access the Internet. In addition, each of the other computers on the network must be set up to obtain an IP address automatically, which we describe in the earlier section "Obtaining an IP Address Automatically."

Windows 2000

To set up Internet connection sharing in Windows 2000:

1. **Choose Start⇨Settings and then click the Network and Dial-up Connections menu item to display the Network and Dial-up Connections window.**

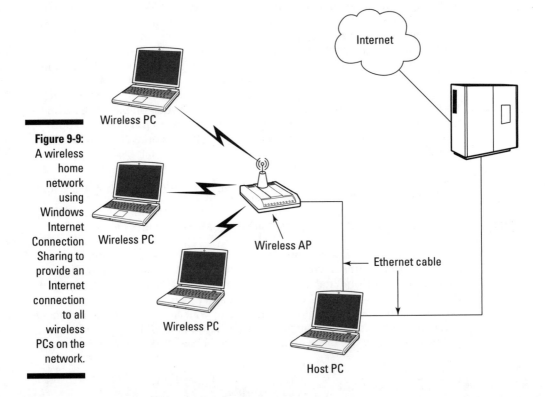

Figure 9-9:
A wireless home network using Windows Internet Connection Sharing to provide an Internet connection to all wireless PCs on the network.

2. **Highlight the Local Area Connection item for the network connection device that will be connected to the Internet.**

3. **Choose File⇨Properties to display the Local Area Connection Properties dialog box.**

4. **On the Sharing tab, select the Enable Internet Connection Sharing for This Connection check box, as shown in Figure 9-10, and then click OK.**

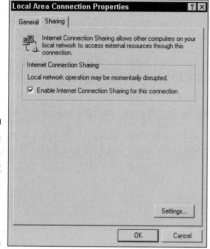

Figure 9-10:
Enable
Internet
connection
sharing in
Windows
2000.

A pop-up message informs you of the local IP address to be assigned to the host computer (192.168.0.1) when it restarts. The message also instructs you to set each of the client computer's TCP/IP settings to obtain an IP address automatically (which we discuss earlier in this chapter).

5. **If you're that sure that you want to enable Internet Sharing, click the Yes button.**

You're returned to the Network and Dial-up Connections window.

6. **Close the Network and Dial-up Connections window.**

After completing these steps, this Windows 2000 PC is now both a DHCP server and a NAT server, equivalent to a broadband router. You may need to restart any PC or AP that is connected to the PC for the IP addresses to be reassigned.

To remove Internet connection sharing, display the Sharing tab of the Local Area Connection Properties dialog box and then clear the Enable Internet Connection Sharing for This Connection check box.

Windows XP

To set up Internet connection sharing in Windows XP:

1. **Choose Start⇨Control Panel.**

2. **Double-click the Network Connections icon in the Control Panel to display the Network Connections window.**

3. **Highlight the Network Connection item for the network device you want to use to connect to the Internet and then choose File⇨ Properties.**

   The Local Area Connection Properties dialog box appears.

4. **On the Advanced tab, select the Allow Other Network Users to Connect through This Computer's Internet Connection check box, as shown in Figure 9-11.**

Figure 9-11:
Enable
Internet
connection
sharing in
Windows XP.

By default, the Allow Other Network Users to Control or Disable the Shared Internet Connection check box is selected. Unless you want other users on the network to be able to enable and disable the shared connection, clear this check box. For dial-up modems, you can also cause the modem to dial automatically when another computer on the network attempts to access the Internet.

Using the same process as just mentioned on your dial-up networking connection, select the Establish a Dial-up Connection Whenever a Computer on My Network Attempts to Access the Internet check box. Then click OK (refer to Figure 9-11).

You're returned to the Network Connections window.

5. **Close the Network Connections window.**

When you complete these steps, this Windows XP PC is now both a DHCP server and a NAT server, equivalent to a broadband router. You may need to restart any PC or AP that is connected to the PC for the IP addresses to be reassigned.

 To remove Internet connection sharing, display the Advanced tab of the Local Area Connection Properties dialog box and clear the Allow Other Network Users To Connect through This Computer's Internet Connection check box.

Mac OS X

To set up Internet connection sharing in Mac OS X v. 10.2 or later:

1. **From the Apple menu, click System Preferences to display the System Preferences pane.**

2. **Click the Sharing icon in the System Preferences panel to display the Sharing panel.**

   If you don't see the Sharing icon, click the Show All button on top of the System Preferences pane, and it appears.

3. **Click the Internet tab, as shown in Figure 9-12.**

   Mac OS X senses which adapter is now connected to the Internet and offers an option to share that connection with other computers on your local network.

4. **Click the Start button to start sharing.**

5. **Close the Sharing panel and the System Preferences panel.**

   After you complete these steps, this Mac OS X computer is now both a DHCP server and a NAT server, equivalent to a broadband router. You may need to restart any computer or AP that is connected to the PC for the IP addresses to be reassigned.

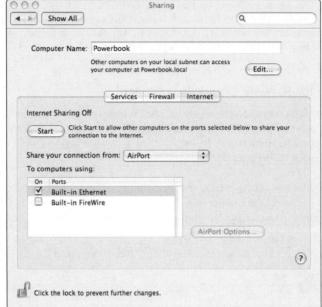

Figure 9-12:
The Internet
tab in the
Sharing
pane of
Mac OS X.

To remove Internet connection sharing, display the Internet tab of the Sharing pane in System Preferences and click the Stop button.

The host PC has to be turned on for the other computers sharing its connection to be able to access the Internet.

Setting Up Your Windows XP Firewall

In August 2004, Microsoft released Service Pack 2 for Windows XP. This was a significant upgrade to the operating system for both Windows XP Home and Windows XP Professional users. The whole point of the service pack was security, and it delivered!

Service Pack 2 was by no means a small upgrade to the OS. At more than 250 megabytes, this service pack was more of an OS replacement than an upgrade. Although to outward appearances, not much had changed, under the hood a great deal was going on. The service pack makes many changes to Windows XP to better protect computers against hackers, viruses, and other security risks. Probably the biggest change to Windows XP was the inclusion — and automatic enablement — of the Windows Security Center and Firewall built into the operating system.

Getting SP2

If you have not installed Service Pack 2, we recommend that you do it. The small problems you have with the configuration are well worth it to save you from much of the bad stuff that is coming down your Internet connection. If you still need to get Service Pack 2, you can install it in one of three ways:

- ✔ You can use Windows Update to get it. You can find it by going to the Start menu and choosing Start⇨All Programs⇨Windows Update.

- ✔ You can download it from the Microsoft Web site: `www.microsoft.com/windowsxp/sp2/default.mspx`.

- ✔ Or, you can Order a CD for it from the Microsoft Web site: `www.microsoft.com/windowsxp/downloads/updates/sp2/cdorder/en_us/default.mspx`. If you're using an IDSL (144K) Internet connection or slower, we recommend that you order the CD. The download is very large, and you would be lucky to get it to complete if you try it on a slow connection.

In April 2005, Microsoft began forcing the download of SP2 by making it a requirement for using the Microsoft Automatic Updates. Automatic Updates is one of the methods Microsoft uses to ensure that your operating system is working and secure — it's also the best way you can get all the software updates you need to be compatible with all the latest hardware and software that comes out on the market. We recommend that you turn on Automatic Updates if you've not already done so (it's part of Security Center — Windows XP Service Pack 2 prompts you to do so if you've not already!)

Setting the firewall on your shared connection

As we mention earlier in this chapter, the Windows Firewall is turned on by default on a SP2 computer. It can limit your ability to share your Internet connection and, in some cases, other things, like files and printers, across your network.

If you already have a third-party software firewall installed on your computer (like Zone Alarm — `www.zonealarm.com`), you need to consult the documentation for that software. Most manufacturers have updates on their Web sites for the software and also have helpful configuration information. If you happen to be running both the Windows Firewall and another software firewall, you should turn one of them off. Having both of them helps with security, but it makes using Internet connection sharing almost impossible to set up because one of them always blocks something you want to do and determining which one of them is doing the blocking can be lots of trouble. Which one you decide to turn off depends on how that firewall works with multiple network connections and configurations.

If you happen to decide to turn off the Windows firewall, all you need to do is go into the windows Control Panel and double-click on Security Center. Click on the Windows Firewall link under the Manage Security Settings For section and then select Off from the General tab, as shown in Figure 9-13. This action turns off the firewall on all your network connections.

Figure 9-13:
The
Windows
Firewall
General
Settings tab.

Don't turn off the Windows Firewall unless you have some other firewall software and virus-protection software running on your computer. Doing so is an open invitation to hackers and loose viruses to come in and do lots of damage to all the computers on your network.

Most firewalls — Windows included — allows you to set different settings per network connection. You should consider two things when you're using a shared connection. First, "Will the computer doing the sharing need to share anything else?" and, second, "Will the computers using the shared connection need any special type of connectivity?" — such as a secure VPN connection to your office or an unrestricted connection to your favorite gaming site.

If you're using the Windows Firewall and you need to make adjustments to the connection you're sharing, you can do so by going to the Control Panel, as just described. In the Windows Firewall dialog box, go to the Exceptions tab and check off the application that you want to allow an open connection from the Internet. As you can see in Figure 9-14, we're allowing our instant messaging client and some software free access in both directions — this way, we can taunt our friends as we destroy the army of Orcs they attacked us with.

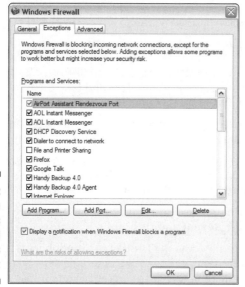

Figure 9-14:
The
Windows
Firewall
Exceptions
tab.

If you don't see the application you need — or selecting it from the Exceptions list doesn't work — most likely, the application itself isn't compatible with the Windows Firewall and you need to create a special exception for it. Many software vendors have updated their Web sites with the specific information you need to adjust this. We strongly recommend that you check the software vendor's sites to ensure that you're opening up only what you need and not opening up too much.

For every exception you make, you're opening an electronic hole in the firewall that is protecting your computers from the ne'er-do-wells of the outside world. Our recommendation is to open only what you really need and nothing more. If you're not sure, check with your vendors to ensure that you're not opening a hole that causes more trouble than it's worth.

If you need to create a custom exception, you can do that from the Advanced tab of the Windows Firewall dialog box. As we mention earlier in this chapter, sometimes you want to share files and folders from the machine you're using to share the Internet connection. In these cases, the firewall can sometimes get in the way of doing this by blocking the traffic that supports file sharing.

To set up an exception, just follow these steps:

1. **On the Advanced tab of the Windows Firewall dialog box, in the Network Connection Settings section, select the network connection that is connected internally to your other computers.**

   Be sure that you have the right one (your wireless network adapter) because you don't want to open up your files to the outside world by sharing by mistake the Internet side of your connection rather than the home network side (which usually is your Ethernet adapter).

You don't ever want to allow file sharing externally to the Internet. It opens up your computer to an almost uncountable number of viruses that scan the Net for Windows computers with file sharing "open" so that they can easily infect those computers and take them over to find and infect other computers on the Internet.

2. **After you have selected the correct connection, click on the Settings button to bring up the Advance Settings dialog box.**

   Use the Add button to bring up the Service Settings dialog box to add the specific service you need. In this case, we're adding file sharing, so we can share files with the rest of our internal network.

3. **Type** Local File Sharing **for the description,** 127.0.0.1 **for the IP address, and** 445 **for both the external and internal port fields.**

   TCP should be selected by default. The 127.0.0.1 loopback address refers back to the same computer — it's a standard networking shortcut for an IP address that means this machine (see Figure 9-15).

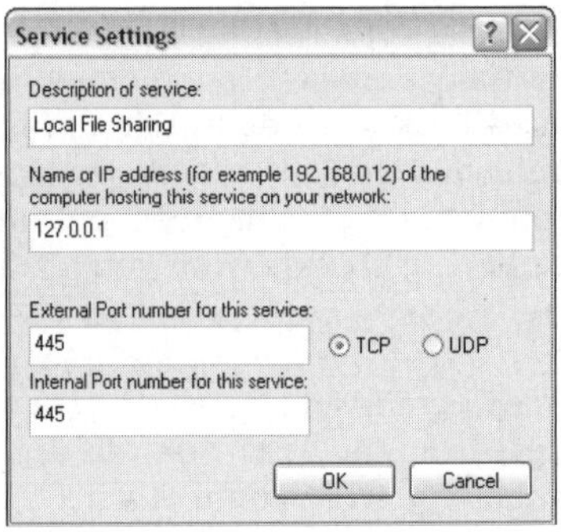

Figure 9-15:
Setting up
local file
sharing in
the Service
Settings
dialog box.

4. **Click OK when you're done, and then place a check mark next to the newly added service.**

5. **Click OK two more times to close the remaining windows; the change takes effect immediately.**

If you have troubles with your file sharing after following these steps, you need to return to the Service Settings window, as described earlier. Repeat Steps 5–7 four times to add four additional services. Rather than 445, however, the services use ports 135, 136, 137, and 138, respectively.

After you get it working, you may want to experiment by removing the new services (or ports), one by one, until it stops working again — and then add again the one that caused everything to break. That way, you can eliminate the open ports you don't need.

Chapter 10

Securing Your Wireless Home Network

*I*f you read the news — well, at least if you read the same networking news sources that we do — you've probably seen and heard a thing or two (or a hundred) about wireless local-area network (LAN) security. In fact, you really don't need to read specialized industry news to hear about this topic. Many major newspapers and media outlets — *The New York Times*, the *San Jose Mercury News*, and *USA Today*, among others — have run feature articles documenting the insecurity of wireless LANs. Most of these stories have focused on *wardrivers*, those folks who park in the lots in front of office buildings, pull out their laptops, and easily get onto corporate networks.

In this chapter, we talk a bit about these security threats and how they may affect you and your wireless home network. We also (helpful types that we are) give you some good advice on how you can make your wireless home network more secure. We talk about a system called *WPA (Wi-Fi Protected Access)* that can make your network secure to most attacks, and also an older system called *WEP (Wired Equivalent Privacy)* which doesn't do such a good job, but may be the best you can do in many cases.

The advice we give in this chapter applies equally to your wireless network, whether it uses 802.11b, a, or g (or even pre-N, as discussed in Chapter 2). We're not specific to any particular 802.11 technology in this chapter because the steps you take to batten down the hatches on your network are virtually identical, regardless of which version of 802.11 you choose. (If you missed our discussion on 802.11 basics, jump over to Chapter 2.)

No network security system is absolutely secure and foolproof. And, as we discuss in this chapter, Wi-Fi networks have some inherent flaws in their security systems, which means that even if you fully implement the security system in Wi-Fi (WPA or especially WEP), a determined individual could still get into your network.

We're not trying to scare you off here. In a typical residential setting, chances are good that your network won't be subjected to some sort of determined attacker like this. Follow our tips, and you should be just fine.

Assessing the Risks

The biggest advantage of wireless networks — the fact that you can connect to the network just about anywhere within range of the base station (up to 300 feet) — is also the biggest potential liability. Because the signal is carried over the air via radio waves, anyone else within range can pick up your network's signals, too. It's sort of like putting an extra RJ-45 jack for a wired LAN out on the sidewalk in front of your house: You're no longer in control of who can access it.

One thing to keep in mind is that the bad guys who are trying to get into your network probably have bigger antennas than you do. Although you may not pick up a usable signal beyond a few hundred feet with that PC card with a built-in antenna in your laptop PC, someone with a big directional antenna that has much more *gain* than your PC's antenna (gain is a measure) may be able to pick up your signals and you would never know that it was happening.

General Internet security

Before we get into the security of your wireless LAN, we need to talk for a moment about Internet security in general. Regardless of what type of LAN you have — wireless or wired or using power lines or phone lines or even none — when you connect a computer to the Internet, some security risks are involved. Malicious *crackers* (the bad guys of the hacker community) can use all sorts of tools and techniques to get into your computers and wreak havoc.

For example, someone with malicious intent could get into your computer and steal personal files (such as your bank statements you've downloaded using Quicken) or mess with your computer's settings — or even erase your hard drive. Your computer can even be hijacked (without your knowing it) as a jumping off point for other people's nefarious deeds; as a source of an attack on another computer (the bad guys can launch these attacks remotely using your computer, which makes them that much harder to track down); or even as source for spam e-mailing.

What we're getting at here is that you need to take a few steps to secure *any* computer attached to the Internet. If you have a broadband (digital subscriber line [DSL], satellite, or cable modem) connection, you *really* need to secure your computers. The high-speed, always-on connections that these services offer make it easier for a cracker to get into your computer. We recommend that you take three steps to secure your computers from Internet-based security risks:

- **Use and maintain antivirus software.** Many attacks on computers don't come from someone sitting in a dark room, in front of a computer screen, and actively cracking into your computer. They come from viruses (often scripts embedded in e-mails or other downloaded files) that take over parts of your computer's operating system and do things you don't want your computer doing (like sending a copy of the virus to everyone in your e-mail address book and then deleting your hard drive). Pick out your favorite antivirus program and use it. Keep the *virus definition files* (the data files that tell your antivirus software what's a virus and what's not) up to date. And, for heaven's sake, use your antivirus program!

- **Install a personal firewall on each computer.** *Personal firewalls* are programs that basically take a look at every Internet connection entering or leaving your computer and check it against a set of rules to see whether the connection should be allowed. After you've installed a personal firewall program, wait about a day and then look at the log. You may be shocked and amazed at the sheer number of attempted connections to your computer that have been blocked. Most of these attempts are relatively innocuous, but not all are. If you have broadband, your firewall may block hundreds of these attempts every day.

  We like ZoneAlarm (www.zonelabs.com) for Windows computers as well as the firewall built into Windows XP Service Pack 2 (which is very good, but doesn't have as many features as ZoneAlarm), and we use the built-in firewall on our Mac OS X computers.

- **Turn on the firewall functionality in your router.** Whether you use a separate router or one integrated into your wireless access point, it will have at least some level of firewall functionality built in. Turn this function on when you set up your router or access point. (It's an obvious option in the configuration program and may well be turned on by default.) We like to have both the router firewall and the personal firewall software running on our PCs. It's the belt-and-suspenders approach, but it makes our networks more secure.

In Chapter 12, we talk about some situations (particularly when you're playing online games over your network) where you need to disable some of this firewall functionality. We suggest that you do this only when you must. Otherwise, turn on that firewall — and leave it on.

Some routers use a technology called *stateful packet inspection* (SPI) firewalls, which examine each packet (or individual group) of data coming into the router to make sure that it was truly something requested by a computer on the network. If your router has this function, we recommend that you try using it because it's a more thorough way of performing firewall functions. Others simply use Network Address Translation (NAT, which we introduce in Chapter 2 and further discuss in Chapter 16) to perform firewall functions. This strategy isn't quite as effective as stateful packet inspection, but it works quite well.

There's much more to Internet security — like securing your file sharing (if you've enabled it) — that we just don't have the space to get into. Check out Chapter 9 for a quick overview on this subject. To get really detailed about these subjects, we recommend that you take a look at *Home Networking For Dummies*, by Kathy Ivens (Wiley Publishing, Inc.) for coverage of those issues in greater detail.

Airlink security

The area we really want to focus on in this chapter is the aspect of network security that's unique to wireless networks: the airlink security. In other words, these security concerns have to do with the radio frequencies being beamed around your wireless home network.

Traditionally, computer networks use wires that go from point to point in your home (or in an office). When you have a wired network, you have physical control over these wires. You install them, and you know where they go. The physical connections to a wired LAN are inside your house. You can lock the doors and windows and keep someone else from gaining access to the network. Of course, you have to keep people from accessing the network over the Internet, as we mention in the preceding subsection, but locally it would take an act of breaking and entering by a bad guy to get on your network. (It's sort of like on *Alias* where they always seem to have to go deep into the enemy's facility to tap into anything.)

No security!

The vast majority of wireless LAN gear (access points and network cards, for example) is shipped to customers with all the security features turned off. That's right: zip, nada, zilch, no security. A wide-open access point sits there waiting for anybody who passes by (with a Wi-Fi–equipped computer, at least) to associate with the access point and get on your network.

This isn't a bad thing in and of itself; initially configuring your network with security features turned off and then enabling the security features after things are up and running is easier than doing it the other way 'round. Unfortunately, many people never take that extra step and activate their security settings. So, a huge number of access points out there are completely open to the public (when they're within range, at least).

Folks who have spent some time wardriving (which we describe in this chapter's introduction) say that as much as 60 percent of all access points they encounter have no security methods in place.

We should add that some people *purposely* leave their access point security turned off in order to provide free access to their neighborhoods. (We talk about this topic in Chapter 16.) But, we find that many people don't intend to do so and have done so unknowingly. We're all for sharing, but keep in mind that it could get you in trouble with your broadband provider (who may cancel your line if you're sharing with neighbors). If you don't want other people on your network, take the few extra minutes it takes to set up your network security.

Wireless LANs turn this premise on its head because you have absolutely no way of physically securing your network. Of course, you can do things like go outside with a laptop computer and have someone move the access point around to reduce the amount of signal leaving the house. But that's really not 100 percent effective, and it can reduce your coverage within the house. Or, you could join the tinfoil hat brigade ("The CIA is reading my mind!") and surround your entire house with a Faraday cage. (Remember those from physics class? We don't either, but they have something to do with attenuating electromagnetic fields.)

Some access points have controls that let you limit the amount of power used to send radio waves over the air. This solution isn't perfect (and it can dramatically reduce your reception in distant parts of the house), but if you live in a small apartment and are worried about beaming your Wi-Fi signals to the apartment next door, you may try this. It doesn't keep a determined cracker with a supersize antenna from grabbing your signal, but it may keep honest folks from accidentally picking up your signal and associating with your access point.

Basically, what we're saying here is that the radio waves sent by your wireless LAN gear will leave your house, and there's not a darned thing you can do about it. Nothing. What you can do, however, is make it difficult for other people to tune into those radio signals, thus (and more importantly) making it difficult for those who can tune into them to decode them and use them to get onto your network (without your authorization) or to scrutinize your e-mail, Web surfing habits, and so on.

You can take several steps to make your wireless network more secure and to provide some airlink security on your network. We talk about these topics in the following sections, where we discuss both easy and more complex methods of securing your network.

Getting into Encryption and Authentication

Two primary (and related) security functions enable you to secure your network: encryption and authentication.

- **Encryption:** Uses a cryptographic *cipher* to scramble your data before transmitting it across the network. Only users with the appropriate *key* can unscramble (or decipher) this data.

- **Authentication:** Simply the act of verifying that a person connecting to your wireless LAN is indeed someone you want to have on your network. With authentication in place, only authorized users can connect with your APs and gain access to your network and to your Internet connection.

With most wireless network systems, you take care of both these functions with a single step — the assignment of a network *key* or *pass phrase* (we explain later in this chapter, in the section "Enabling Encryption," where each of these is used). This key or pass phrase is a secret set of characters (or a word) that only you and those you share it with know.

The key or pass phrase is often known as a *shared secret* — you keep it secret, but share it with that select group of friends and family whom you want to allow to access your network. With a shared secret (key or pass phrase), you perform both of these security functions:

- You authenticate users because only those who have been given your supersecret shared secret have the right "code word" to get into the network. Unauthenticated users (those who don't have the shared secret) cannot connect to your wireless network.

✔ Your shared secret provides the mechanism to encrypt (or scramble) all data being sent over your network so that anybody who picks up your radio transmissions sees nonsensical gibberish, not data that they can easily read.

The two primary methods of providing this authentication and encryption are

✔ Wired Equivalent Privacy *(WEP)*

✔ Wireless Protected Access *(WPA)*

We talk about both these security systems in more detail in the remaining parts of this chapter. WEP, an older system, provides only a limited amount of security because certain flaws in the encryption system used within WEP make it easy for *crackers* to figure out your shared secret (the *WEP Key*) and therefore gain access to your network and your data.

WPA is the current, up-to-date, security system for Wi-Fi networks (there are several variants, which we discuss later in this chapter), and it provides you with much greater security than does WEP. If you have the choice, *always* use WPA in your network rather than WEP.

The "shared secret" method of securing a network is by far the most common and the easiest method. But it doesn't really provide truly "bulletproof" user authentication, simply because the fact that you have to share the same secret pass phrase or key with multiple people makes it a bit more likely that somehow that secret will get into the wrong hands. (In fact, some experts would probably hesitate to even call it an authentication system.)

For most home users, this *isn't* a problem (we don't think that you have to worry about giving Nana the pass phrase for your network when she's in town visiting her grandkids), but in a busy network (like in an office), where people come and go (employees, clients, customers, and partners, for example), you can end up in a situation where just too many people have your shared secret.

When this happens, you're stuck with the onerous task of changing the shared secret and then making sure that everyone who needs to be on the network has been updated. It's a real pain.

These kinds of busy networks have authentication systems that control the encryption keys for your network and authorize users on an individual basis (so that you can allow or disallow anyone without having to start from scratch for *everyone,* like you do with a shared secret).

If you have this kind of busy network, you may want to consider securing your network with a system called *WPA-Enterprise* and *802.1x*. See the sidebar "802.1x, the corporate solution," later in this chapter, for more information on this topic.

Introducing Wired Equivalent Privacy (WEP)

The original system for securing a wireless Wi-Fi network is known as *WEP*, or *Wired Equivalent Privacy.* The name comes from the admirable (but, as we discuss, not reached) goal of making a wireless network as secure as a wired one.

In a WEP security system, you enter a *key* in the Wi-Fi client software on each device connecting to your network. This key must match the key you establish when you do the initial setup of your access point or wireless router (which we describe in Chapter 6).

WEP uses an encryption protocol called *RC4* to secure your data. Although this protocol (or *cipher*) isn't inherently bad, the way that it's implemented in WEP makes it relatively easy for a person to snoop on your network and figure out what your key is. And, after the bad guys have your key, they can access your network (getting into PCs and other devices attached to the network or using your Internet connection for their own purposes), or even stealthily intercept everything sent across the wireless portion of your network and decode it without your ever knowing!

It doesn't even take some sort of superhacker skills to do this either — anyone with a Windows or Linux or Mac PC with wireless capabilities can download free and readily available software from the Web and, in a matter of days (potentially just hours or even minutes!), figure out your key. It's not paranoia if they really are out to get you.

How about a bit more about WEP?

WEP encrypts your data so that no one can read it unless they have the key. That's the theory behind WEP, anyway. WEP has been a part of Wi-Fi networks from the beginning. (The developers of Wi-Fi were initially focused on the business market, where data security has always been a big priority.) The name itself belies the intentions of the system's developers; they wanted to make wireless networks as secure as wired networks.

WEP key length: Do the math

If you're being picky, you may notice that WEP keys aren't really as long as their names say they are. The first 24 bits of the key are called an *initialization vector,* and the remaining bits comprise the key itself. Therefore, 128-bit keys are really only 104 bits long, and 64-bit keys are really only 40 bits long. When you enter a 128-bit key (and you do the math), you see that there are only 26 alphanumeric characters (or digits) for you to enter in the key (4 bits per digit × 26 = 104 bits). This isn't something you really need to know because everyone adds the 24 initialization vector bits to the WEP key length number, but just in case you were curious, we just thought we would mention it.

To make WEP work, you must activate it on all the Wi-Fi devices in your network via the client software or configuration program that came with the hardware. And, every device on your network must use the same WEP key to gain access to the network. (We talk a bit more about how to turn on WEP in the later section "Clamping Down on Your Wireless Home Network's Security.")

For the most part, WEP is WEP is WEP. In other words, it doesn't matter which vendor made your access point or which vendor made your laptop's PC card network adapter — the implementation of WEP is standardized across vendors. Keep this one difference in mind, however: WEP key length. Encryption keys are categorized by the number of bits (1s or 0s) used to create the key. Most Wi-Fi equipment these days uses *128-bit* WEP keys, but some early gear (like the first generation of the Apple AirPort equipment) supported only a *64-bit* WEP key.

Many access points and network adapters on the market even support longer keys — for example, many vendors support a 256-bit key. Keep in mind that the longest standard (and common) key is 128 bits. Most equipment enables you to decide how long to make your WEP key; you can often choose between 64 and 128 bits. Generally, for security purposes, you should pick the longest key available. If, however, you have some older gear that can't support longer WEP key lengths, you can use a shorter key. If you have one network adapter that can handle only 64-bit keys but you have an access point that can handle 128-bit keys, you need to set up the access point to use the shorter, 64-bit key length.

You can almost always use a shorter-than-maximum key length (like using a 64-bit key in a 128-bit-capable system), but you can't go the other way. So, if you set up your access point to use a 128-bit key, your older 64-bit network adapter cannot connect to it.

Should you use WEP?

WEP sounds like a pretty good deal, doesn't it? It keeps your data safe while it's floating through the ether by encrypting it, and it keeps others off your access point by not authenticating them. But, as we mention earlier in this chapter, WEP isn't really all that secure because some flaws in the protocol's design make it not all that hard for someone to "crack" your WEP code and gain access to your network and your data. For a typical home network, a bad guy with the right tools could capture enough data flowing across your network to "crack" WEP in a matter of hours.

Almost all APs, wireless routers or gateways, and network adapters now being sold support the newer (and much more secure) WPA protocol. And, almost any PC with Windows XP or Macintosh OS X will also have built-in support for WPA. So, there are a many good reasons to skip over WEP entirely and just go with WPA.

But (there's often a "but" to be found in these situations), at times you may need to consider using WEP encryption. You run into this situation with certain pieces of Wi-Fi gear because you can't have "mixed" encryption methods on the same network. In other words, you can't have laptop A connected to the Wi-Fi AP using WPA and laptop B connected using WEP. It's one security system or the other.

We say earlier in this chapter that almost all PCs support WPA, but the dirty little secret of the Wi-Fi business is that not all Wi-Fi peripheral devices — like wireless print servers, media adapters, and other "non-PC" devices — support WPA yet.

If any device on your network doesn't support WPA, you need to use WEP on that network. Similarly, if you have a device that doesn't even support WEP (an exceedingly rare situation that we've *only rarely* run across — and it happens less and less often over time), you can't even use WEP on that network.

A better way: WPA

If you can use it — meaning if your access point or wireless gateway and *all* the wireless clients on your network support it — you should enable and use WPA as the airlink security system on your network.

WPA is significantly more secure than WEP and keeps the bad guys off your network much more effectively than any implementation of WEP.

Two variants of WPA are now available: WPA and WPA2. The major difference between these two is the *cipher,* or *encryption,* system used to encode the data being sent across the wireless network. WPA2 — which is the latest and greatest most powerful wireless security system — uses a system called AES *(Advanced Encryption Standard),* which is pretty much uncrackable by mere mortals. But, even the original WPA version (that's just WPA to you and me) is much more secure than WEP.

WPA2 is also known as 802.11i. 802.11i is simply the IEEE (the folks who make the standards for wireless LANs) standard for advanced Wi-Fi security. WPA was a step toward 802.11i, set by the Wi-Fi Alliance only. WPA2 incorporates all the security measures included in 802.11i.

What's better about WPA?

- ✔ **More random encryption techniques:** WPA has basically been designed as an answer for all the current weaknesses of WEP, with significantly increased encryption techniques. One of WEP's fatal flaws is that because its encryption isn't sufficiently random, an observer can more easily find patterns and break the encryption. WPA's encryption techniques are basically more random — and thus harder to break.

- ✔ **Automatic key changes:** WPA also has a huge security advantage in the fact that it automatically changes the key (although you, as a user, get to keep using the same password to access the system). So, by the time a bad guy has figured out your key, your system would have already moved on to a new one.

It's possible to use an 802.1x system, as described in the sidebar "802.1x: The corporate solution," later in this chapter, to provide automatic key changes for WEP systems. This is *not* something you would find in anyone's home network, but some business do it, and it does indeed minimize the impact of WEP's fixed keys.

- ✔ **More user-friendly:** WPA is easier for consumers to use because there's no hexadecimal stuff to deal with — just a plain text password. The idea is to make WPA much easier to deal with than WEP, which takes a bit of effort to get up and running (depending on how good your access point's configuration software is).

Clamping Down on Your Wireless Home Network's Security

Well, that's enough of the theory and background, if you've read from the beginning of this chapter. It's time to get down to business. In this section, we discuss some of the key steps you should take to secure your wireless network from intruders. None of these steps is difficult, will drive you crazy, or make your network hard to use. All that's really required is the motivation to spend a few extra minutes (after you have everything up and working) battening down the hatches and getting ready for sea. (Can you tell that Pat used to be in the Navy?)

The key steps in securing your wireless network, as we see them, are the following:

1. Change all the default values on your network.

2. Enable WPA.

3. Close your network to outsiders (if your access point supports this).

Hundreds of different access points and network adapters are available on the market. Each has its own, unique configuration software. (At least each vendor does; and often, different models from the same vendor have different configuration systems.) You need to RTFM (Read the Fine Manual!). We give you some generic advice on what to do here, but you really, really, really need to pick up the manual and read it before you do this to your network. Every vendor has slightly different terminology and different ways of doing things. If you mess up, you may temporarily lose wireless access to your access point. (You should still be able to plug a computer in with an Ethernet cable to gain access to the configuration system.) You may even have to reset your access point and start over from scratch. Follow the vendor's directions (as painful at that may be — there's a reason that people buy *For Dummies* books). We tell you the main steps you need to take to secure your network; your manual gives you the exact line-by-line directions on how to implement these steps on your equipment.

Most access points also have some wired connections available — Ethernet ports you can use to connect your computer to the access point. You can almost always use this wired connection to run the access point configuration software. When you're setting up security, we recommend making a wired connection and doing all your access point configuration in this manner. That way, you can avoid accidentally blocking yourself from the access point when your settings begin to take effect.

Getting rid of the defaults

It's incredibly common to go to a Web site like Netstumbler.com, look at the results of someone's Wi-Fi reconnoitering trip around their neighborhood, and see dozens of access points with the same exact service set identifier (SSID, or network name; refer to Chapter 2). And, it's usually *Linksys* because Linksys is the most popular vendor out there (though NETGEAR, D-Link, and others are also well represented). Many folks bring home an access point, plug it in, turn it on, and then do nothing. They leave everything as it was set up from the factory. They don't change any of the default settings.

Well, if you want people to be able to find your access point, there's nothing better (short of a sign on the front door; check out our discussion in Chapter 16 of *warchalking* — the practice of leaving marks on sidewalks to point out open APs) than leaving your default SSID broadcasting out there for the world to see. In some cities, you could probably drive all the way across town with a laptop set to Linksys as an SSID and stay connected the entire time. (We don't mean to just pick on Linksys here. You could probably do the same thing with an SSID set to default, the D-Link default, or any of the top vendor's default settings.)

When you begin your security crusade, the first thing you should do is to change all the defaults on your access point. You should change, at minimum, the following:

- ✔ Your default SSID
- ✔ Your default administrative password

You want to change this password because if you don't, someone who gains access to your network can guess at your password and end up changing all the settings in your access point without your knowing. Heck, if they want to teach you a security lesson — the tough love approach, we guess — they could even block you out of the network until you reset the access point. These default passwords are well known and well publicized. Just look on the Web page of your vendor, and we bet that you can find a copy of the user's guide for your access point available for download. Anyone who wants to know them does know them.

When you change the default SSID on your access point to one of your own making, you also need to change the SSID setting of any computers (or other devices) you want to connect to your LAN. To do this, follow the steps we discuss in this part's earlier chapters.

Dealing with the WEP hex and ASCII issues

One area that is consistently confusing when setting up a WEP key — and often a real pain in the rear end — is the tendency of different vendors to use different formats for the keys. The most common way to format a key is to use *hexadecimal* (hex) characters. This format represents numbers and letters by using combinations of the numbers 0–9 and the letters A–F. (For example, the name of Pat's dog, Opie, would be represented in hexadecimal as *4f 70 69 65*.) A few other vendors use *ASCII*, which is simply the letters and numbers on your keyboard.

Although ASCII is an easier-to-understand system for entering WEP codes (it's really just plain text), most systems make you use hexadecimal: It's the standard. The easiest way to

enter hex keys on your computers connecting to your access point is to use the pass phrase we discuss in the section "Enabling encryption," elsewhere in this chapter. If your network adapter client software lets you do this, do it! If it doesn't, try entering the WEP key you wrote down when you generated it (it's probably hexadecimal). If that doesn't work either, you may have to dig into the user's manual and see whether you need to add any special codes before or after the WEP key to make it work. Some software requires you to put the WEP key inside quotation marks; others may require you to put an *0h* or *0x* (that's a zero and an h or an x character) before the key or an *h* after it (both without quotation marks).

This tip really falls under the category of Internet security (rather than airlink security), but here goes: Make sure that you turn off the Allow/Enable Remote Management function (it may not be called this exactly, but it's something like that). This function is designed to allow people to connect to your access point over the Internet (if they know your IP address) and do any or all the configuration stuff from a distant location. If you need this turned on (perhaps you have a home office and your IT gal wants to be able to configure your access point remotely), you know it. Otherwise, it's just a security flaw waiting to happen, particularly if you haven't changed your default password. Luckily, most access points have this function set to Off by default, but take the time to make sure that yours does.

Enabling encryption

After you eliminate the security threats caused by leaving all the defaults in place (see the preceding section), it's time to get some encryption going. Get your WPA (or WEP) on, as the kids say.

We've already warned you once, but we do it again, just for kicks: Every access point has its own system for setting up WPA or WEP, and you need to follow those directions. We can give only generic advice because we have no idea which access point you're using.

To enable encryption on your wireless network, we suggest that you perform these generic steps:

1. **Open your access point's configuration screen.**

2. **Go to the Wireless, Security, or Encryption tab or section.**

   We're being purposely vague here; bear with us.

3. **Select the radio button or check box labeled Enable WPA or WPA PSK (or, if you're using WEP, the one that says Enable WEP or Enable Encryption or Configure WEP).**

   You should see a menu similar to the one shown in Figure 10-1. (It's for a NETGEAR access point or router.)

4. **If you're using WEP, select the check box or the pull-down menu to the appropriate WPA key length for your network. If you're using WPA, skip this step.**

   We recommend 128-bit keys if all the gear on your network can support it. (See the earlier section "How about a bit more about WEP?" for the lowdown on WEP keys.)

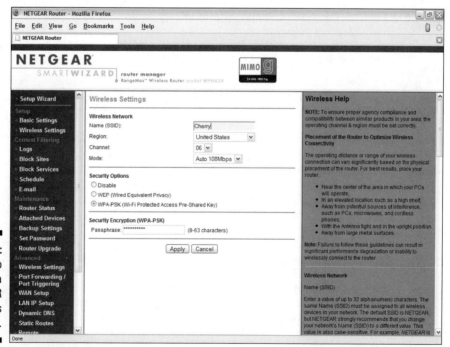

Figure 10-1: Setting up WPA on a NETGEAR access point.

5. **For WPA, create a pass phrase that will be your network's *shared secret*. For WEP, create your own key if you prefer (we prefer to let the program create one for us):**

   a. **Type a pass phrase in the Passphrase text box.**

   b. **Click the Generate Keys button.**

Remember the pass phrase. Write it down somewhere, and put it someplace where you won't accidentally throw it away or forget where you put it. Danny likes to tape his pass phrase note to the box that his Wi-Fi gear came in so that he can always track it down.

Whether you create your own key or let the program do it for you, a key should now have magically appeared in the key text box. *Note:* Some systems allow you to set more than one key (usually as many as four keys), such as the system shown in Figure 10-1. In this case, use Key 1 and set it as your default key by using the pull-down menu.

Remember this key! Write it down. You need it again when you configure your computers to connect to this access point.

Some access point's configuration software doesn't necessarily show you the WEP key you've generated — just the pass phrase you've used to generate it. You need to dig around in the manual and menus to find a command to display the WEP key itself. (For example, the Apple AirPort software shows just the pass phrase; you need to find the *Network Equivalent Password* in the Airport Admin Utility to display the WEP key — in OS X, this is in the Base Station Menu.)

For WEP, the built-in wireless LAN client software in Windows XP numbers its four keys from 0–3 rather than 1–4. So, if you're using Key 1 on your access point, select Key 0 in Windows XP.

6. **Click OK to close the WPA or WEP configuration window.**

   You're done turning on WPA or WEP. Congratulations.

Can we repeat ourselves again? Will you indulge us? The preceding steps are *very* generic. Yours may vary slightly (or, in rare cases, significantly). Read your user's guide. It tells you what to do.

After you configure WPA or WEP on the access point, you must go to each computer on your network, get into the network adapter's client software (as we describe in Chapters 7 and 8), turn on WEP, and enter either the pass phrase or the WEP key. Typically, you find an Enable Security dialog box containing a check box to turn on security and one to four text boxes for entering the key. Simply select the check box to enable WEP, enter your key in the appropriate text box, and then click OK. Figure 10-2 shows this process using Windows XP and its built-in Wireless Zero Configuration client.

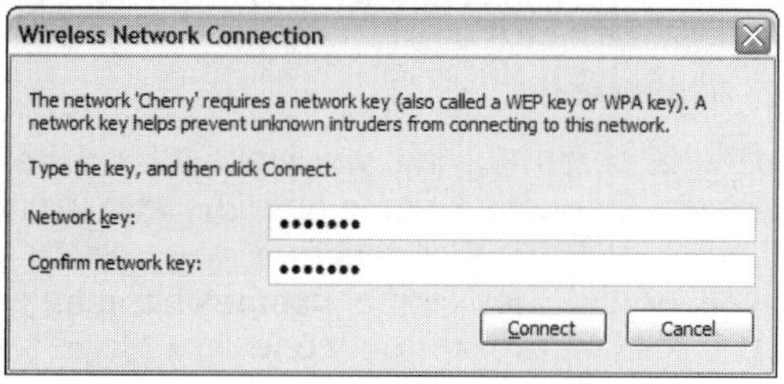

Figure 10-2:
Setting
up WPA
using the
Windows
XP Wireless
Zero Config.

Wireless Network Connection ☒

The network 'Cherry' requires a network key (also called a WEP key or WPA key). A
network key helps prevent unknown intruders from connecting to this network.

Type the key, and then click Connect.

Network key: ••••••••

Confirm network key: ••••••••

[Connect] [Cancel]

Closing your network

The last step we recommend that you take in the process of securing your
wireless home network (if your access point allows it) is to create a *closed
network* — a network that allows only specific, predesignated computers and
devices onto it. You can do two things to close down your network, which
makes it harder for strangers to find your network and gain access to it:

✔ **Turn off SSID broadcast:** By default, most access points broadcast their
   SSID out onto the airwaves. This makes it easier for users to find the network and associate with it. If the SSID is being broadcast and you're in
   range, you should see the SSID on your computer's network adapter
   client software and be able to select it and connect to it. That is, assuming that you have the right WEP key, if WEP is configured on that access
   point. When you create a closed network, you turn off this broadcast so
   that only people who know the exact name of the access point can connect to it.

You can find access points even if they're not broadcasting their SSIDs
(by observing other traffic on the network with a network *sniffer* program), so this security measure is an imperfect one — and no substitute
for enabling WPA. But, it's another layer of security for your network.
Also, if you're in an area where you will have lots of people coming into
your home and wanting to share your connection, you may not want to
close off the network, thus balancing convenience for your friends
against the small exposure of a more open network.

✔ **Set access control at the MAC layer:** Every network adapter in the
   world has assigned to it a unique number known as a Media Access
   Controller (MAC) address. You can find the MAC address of your network adapter by either looking at it (it's usually physically printed on
   the device) or using software on your computer:

   • **Open a DOS window and use the `winipcnfg` command in
     Windows 95/98/Me or the `ipconfig/all` command on Windows
     NT/2000/XP.**

   • **Look in the Network Control Panel/System Preference on a Mac.**

With some access points, you can type the MAC addresses of all the devices you want to connect to your access point and block connections from any other MAC addresses.

Again, if you support MAC layer filtering, you make it harder for friends to log on to when visiting. If you have some buddies who like to come over and mooch off your broadband connection, you need to add their MAC addresses as well, or else they cannot get on your network. Luckily, you need to enter their MAC addresses only one time to get them "on the list," so to speak, so you don't need to do it every time they show up — at least until you have to reset the access point (which shouldn't be that often).

Neither of these "closed" network approaches is absolutely secure. MAC addresses can be *spoofed* (imitated by a device with a different MAC address, for example), but both are ways to add to your overall security strategy.

Going for the Ultimate in Security

Setting up your network with WPA security keeps all but the most determined and capable crackers out of your network and prevents them from doing anything with the data you sent across the airwaves (because this data is securely encrypted and appears to be just gibberish).

But, WPA has a weakness, at least the way it's most often used in the home: the preshared key (your shared secret or pass phrase) that allows users to connect to your network and that unlocks your WPA encryption.

Your preshared key can be vulnerable in two ways:

- ✔ **If it's not sufficiently difficult to guess (perhaps you used the same word for your pass phrase as you used for your network's ESSID):** You would be shocked by how many people do that! Always try to use a pass phrase that combines letters and numbers (upper- and lowercase is best) and doesn't use simple words from the dictionary.

- ✔ **If you've given it to somebody to access your network and then they give it out to someone else:** For most home users, this isn't a big deal, but if you're providing access to a large number of people (maybe you have a hot spot set up), it's hard to put the genie back in the bottle when you've given out the pass phrase.

Neither of these two circumstances is usually a problem for the typical home — WPA-PSK (WPA Home) is more than sufficient for most users. But, if you want to batten down the hatches, you may consider using an AP (and wireless clients) that supports *WPA Enterprise*.

802.1x: The corporate solution

Another new standard that's being slowly rolled out into the Wi-Fi world is 802.1x. This isn't an encryption system but, rather, an authentication system. An 802.1x system, when built into an access point, would allow users to connect to the access point and give them only extremely limited access (at least initially). In an 802.1x system, the user could connect to only a single network port (or service). Specifically, the only traffic the user could send over the network is an authentication server, which would exchange information (such as passwords and encrypted keys) with the user to establish that he was allowed on the network. After this authentication process has been satisfactorily completed, the user is given full (or partial, depending on what policies the authentication server has recorded for the user) access to the network.

WPA Enterprise uses a special server, known as a *RADIUS* server and a proto- col called 802.1x (see the nearby sidebar, "802.1x: The corporate solution"), which provide authentication and authorization of users using special cryp- tographic keys. When a RADIUS server is involved in the picture, you get a more secure authorization process than the simple shared secret used in WPA Home. You also get a new encryption key created by the RADIUS server on an ongoing basis — which means that even if your key got figured out by a bad guy, it would change before any damage could be done.

Now you *can* create and operate your own RADIUS server on a spare com- puter in your home (see the commercial software available at `www.lucid link.com`, or the free software at `www.freeradius.org`), but that topic is really beyond the scope of *Wireless Home Networking For Dummies*, 2nd Edition. (We do tell you more about this subject in our *other* wireless book, *Wireless Network Hacks & Mods For Dummies*, also published by Wiley.)

You *can* use a *hosted RADIUS* service on the Internet. Such services charge you a small monthly fee (about $5 per month) and let you use a RADIUS server that's hosted and maintained in someone's data center. All you need to do is pay your monthly bill and follow a few simple steps on your access point and PCs to set up RADIUS authentication and WPA Enterprise.

You need to have an AP that supports WPA Enterprise — check the documen- tation that came with yours because not all do.

Several services out there provide WPA Enterprise RADIUS support. Here are a couple of our favorites:

✔ **SecureMyWiFi**: Offered by WiTopia (`www.witopia.net`), SecureMyWiFi provides security for one AP and as many as five users for free, and charges for additional users.

✔ **McAfee Wireless Security**: The folks at McAfee (the big antivirus and security software company) recently bought a company known as Wireless Security Corp, and have begun offering their hosted Wi-Fi RADIUS service. This service is also available for users of certain Linksys routers, under the Linksys brand name.

802.1x is *not* something we expect to see in any wireless home LAN any time soon. It's really a business-class kind of thing that requires lots of fancy servers and professional installation and configuration. We just thought we would mention it because you no doubt will hear about it when you search the Web for wireless LAN security information.

Part IV
Using a Wireless Network

In this part . . .

Here's where things get fun: After you get your wireless home network installed and running, you probably can't wait to use it, in both practical and fun ways. In this part, we cover the basics on what you can do with your network, such as share printers, files, folders, and even hard drives. But, you can do many other cool things over a wireless network, too, such as play multiuser computer games, connect your audiovisual equipment, and operate various types of smart-home conveniences. We cover all these great topics here. One chapter in this part talks about using Bluetooth-enabled devices, and another chapter describes how to find and use wireless hot spots so that you can access the Internet in public locations.

Chapter 11

Putting Your Wireless Home Network to Work

*R*emember that old Cracker Jack commercial of the guy sitting in the bed when the kid comes home from school? "What did you learn in school today?" he asks. "Sharing," says the kid. And then, out of either guilt or good manners, the old guy shares his sole box of caramel popcorn with the kid.

You shouldn't hog your caramel popcorn, and you shouldn't hog your network resources, either. We're going to help you share your Cracker Jacks now! (After all, that's kinda the purpose of the network, right?) You have a wireless network installed. It's secure. It's connected. Now you can share all sorts of stuff with others in your family — not just your Internet connection, but also printers, faxes, extra disk space, Telephony Application Programming Interface (TAPI) devices (telephone-to-computer interfaces and vice versa for everybody else), games, A/V controls — oodles and oodles of devices.

In this chapter, we give you a taste of how you can put your wireless network to work. We talk about accessing shared network resources, setting up user profiles, accessing peripheral devices across the network (such as network printing), checking out your Network Neighborhood, and other such goodies.

Entire books have been written about sharing your network, such as *Home Networking For Dummies* (by Kathy Ivens); and other books, such as *Mac OS X All-in-One Desk Reference For Dummies* (by Mark L. Chambers, Erick Tejkowski, and Michael L. Williams) and *Windows XP For Dummies* (by Andy Rathbone); all from Wiley Publishing, Inc., include some details about networking. These books are all good. In fact, some smart bookstore should bundle them together with *Wireless Home Networking For Dummies* because they're complementary. In this chapter, we expose you to the network and what's inside it (and there's probably a free prize among those Cracker Jacks somewhere, too!), and that should get you started. But, if you want to know more, we urge you to grab one of these more detailed books.

It's one thing to attach a device to the network — either directly or as an attachment — but it's another to share it with others. Sharing your computer and devices is a big step. You not only open yourself up to lots of potential unwanted visitors (like bad folks sneaking in over your Internet connection), but you also make it easier for friendly folks (like your kids) to erase stuff and use things in unnatural ways. That's why you can (and should!) control access by using passwords or by allowing users to only read (open and copy) files on your devices (rather than change them). In Windows 2000 and Windows XP, security is paramount, and you must plan how, what, and with whom you share. Definitely take the extra time to configure your system for these extra security layers. We tell you in this chapter about some of these mechanisms (see the later section "Setting permissions"); the books we mention previously go into these topics in more detail.

A Networking Review

Before we get too far into the concept of file sharing, we review the basic networking concepts (which we touch on in earlier chapters of this book): that is, what a network is and how it works.

Basic networking terminology

Simply defined, a *network* is something that links computers, printers, and other devices. These days, the standard protocol used for most networking is Ethernet. A *protocol* is the language that devices use to communicate with each other on a network.

For one device to communicate with another under the Ethernet protocol, the transmitting device needs to accomplish a few things. First, it must announce itself on the network and declare which device it's trying to talk to. Then it must authenticate itself with that destination device — by confirming that the sending device is who it says it is. This is done by sending a proper name, such as a domain or workgroup name, and also a password that the receiving device accepts.

For our purposes, when we talk about networking, we're talking about sharing devices on a Windows-based network. Windows 95/98/Me start the network tour with *Network Neighborhood.* In Windows XP (both Professional and Home) and Windows 2000 Professional, it's called *My Network Places.* Although both show the same information and serve the same function, My Network Places has more layers. In Network Neighborhood, you see all the computers and other network devices that are on your network. Your computer knows this because it has been monitoring your Ethernet network and has seen each device announce itself and what it has to offer to the entire network when each one first powered up.

With the release of Windows XP Professional and Home, Microsoft introduced a new look and feel to the desktop. The differences in the new look were drastic enough that during the beta testing of XP, Microsoft decided to offer people a choice about to which look and feel they want by implementing *themes.* When we reference the XP desktop in this chapter, we're referencing what's known as the *Windows Classic Theme* in XP. If, at any point, you're having trouble following any of our steps, do this:

1. **Right-click the desktop and then choose Properties from the pop-up menu that appears.**

2. **On the Themes tab of the Display Properties dialog box, choose Windows Classic from the Themes pull-down menu.**

   You can always change the theme back without doing any damage to any personal preferences you set up for yourself.

Setting up a workgroup

To set up networking on any Windows-based computer, you need to decide on a few basic networking options. Many of these are decided for you, based on the equipment you happen to be using on your network. As an example, if you have a server on your wireless network, you have many more options concerning the type of network you may create. With a server on your network, you gain the ability to centralize your security policies and to use domains to control devices. In Windows, a *domain* is a set of network resources (applications, printers, and so on) for a group of users. The user only has to log on to the domain to gain access to the resources, which may be located on one or a number of different servers in the network.

If you don't have a server (which most of us don't on our home networks), you end up using the most common type of network: a *workgroup*.

The distinction between a workgroup and a domain can best be summed up in one word: security. Domains make managing, maintaining, and modifying security much simpler. In many cases, the *domain controller* — the server that controls the domain — can set up security on each device on the network remotely, and security can be managed in groups so that you don't have to add every family member to every machine or device on the network. Of course, all this great management comes at a price. Servers tend to be expensive and require a much higher skill level to maintain. The initial setup of a domain can take lots of planning and time to implement. We don't take you through setting up your own domain because you can find more detailed books already written on the subject. If you do happen to choose some type of domain for networking, keep in mind that the security of your domain is only as strong as the security on each individual piece of equipment attached to your network — and that includes *all* your wireless devices.

On the other hand, setting up a workgroup is relatively simple. All that's really required is to decide on the name of your workgroup. Many people use family names or something similar. Microsoft has a default of *Workgroup* MSHome for workgroups in Windows, for example.

To set up a workgroup in Windows 2000 or Windows XP, start by right-clicking the My Computer icon (in the upper-left corner of your desktop) or by choosing Start⇨Settings⇨Control Panel and then double-clicking the System icon. On the Network Identification tab of the System Properties window that opens, you can click the Network ID button to have a wizard walk you through the process of setting up your networking options. A simpler method is to click the Properties button and just enter the computer name, description, and workgroup name (and a handy way to quickly check — and rename if necessary — workgroup names on the computers on your network).

Will You Be My Neighbor?

"Hello! I'm here!" When a computer attached to a network is turned on, it broadcasts its name to every other device on the network and asks every device to broadcast as well. If that computer is sharing something, such as a folder or a printer, the other devices can see it. By asking the other devices to broadcast, it can then see all of them. This process is repeated (on average) every 15 minutes in most networks with Windows computers attached to them.

The "Hello, I'm here" process is a great way to add devices to a network. Unfortunately, it's not too great at detecting whether a device falls off or is disconnected from that network. If a machine or shared device seems to be visible on your network but doesn't respond when you try to access it, the problem may not be on your computer. Devices that get disconnected from your network don't immediately appear to be disconnected on some of your other computers. They usually get removed from the list of available networked computers only if they fail to answer the every-15-minute "Hello" calls from the other machines.

The My Network Places icon is your ticket to the network and seeing what shared resources are available, like a printer. (The risk versus reward of sharing these types of items just makes sense. The chances of a bad guy getting into your printer and printing documents are rather low — there's not much reward for doing that.)

You can see what's shared on your network by checking out your PC's My Network Places.

Double-click the My Network Places icon (also usually found on your desktop) to see options such as Entire Network and Computers Near Me. Microsoft added a layer to the old Network Neighborhood icon and consolidated the devices in the same workgroup or domain to the Computers Near Me folder. The Entire Network folder still shows all available devices on your physical network. The root of the My Network Places folder is now reserved for shortcuts to network resources that you tend to use regularly.

My Network Places (see Figure 11-1) serves a similar (but enhanced) purpose. My Network Places gives you access to your entire network resources and also enables you to add shortcuts to your favorite places. To check out everything that's on your home network, click the Entire Network icon. This action shows you your workgroup.

Regardless of the operating system, you always see devices that are set up to share represented by small computer icons. If you double-click one of these icons, you can see any shared printers, folders, or other devices represented by appropriate icons. Sometimes you have to *drill down* (continue to double-click icons) a little to find all the shared items on your network.

In general, you see two types of devices on your network:

✔ **Stand-alone network devices:** These are computers, storage devices, gaming devices, and so on that have a network port and are on the network in their own right.

✔ **Attached devices:** These are peripherals, drives, or other devices that are on the network because they're attached to something else, like a PC.

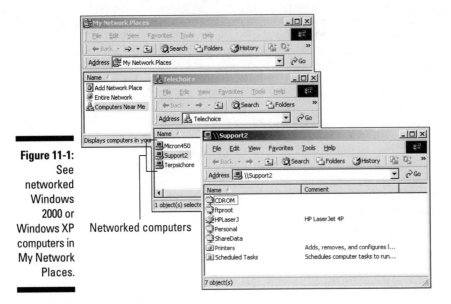

Figure 11-1:
See networked Windows 2000 or Windows XP computers in My Network Places.

Networked computers

Just double-click your workgroup to see all your home computers and other networked devices. Click any to see what you can share within them.

All this mouse clicking can be a pain. Save your wrist and create a shortcut to your shared resources by clicking the Add Network Place icon within My Network Places. Shortcuts are especially handy for people who have networked devices out on the Internet that they visit often, such as File Transfer Protocol (FTP) sites.

If you find a computer that you expect to be on the network but it's not, make sure that its workgroup name is the same as the other machines — this is a common mistake. (See the earlier section "Setting up a workgroup.")

We find using Windows Explorer to be the best way to visualize what's on your computer and your network. You can get to Windows Explorer in all Windows operating systems in the same two ways. Either right-click the Start button and choose Explore, or choose Start⇨Programs⇨Windows Explorer. Figure 11-2 shows Windows Explorer looking at available network resources.

Just because you see a device in My Network Places doesn't mean that you can *share* with that device — where *share* means that you can view, use, copy, and otherwise work on files and resources on that device. The devices need to be set up for sharing for that to happen. (Think of it like your regular neighborhood, where you can see many of the houses, but you can't go in some of them because they're locked.) To set up sharing, see the next section.

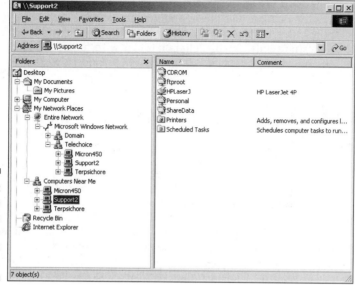

Figure 11-2:
Use
Windows
Explorer to
see network
resources.

Sharing — I Can Do That!

File sharing is a basic feature of any home network. Whether sharing MP3 files on a computer with other devices (including your stereo, as we discuss in Chapter 13) or giving access to financial files for Mom and Dad to access on each other's computers, sharing files is a way to maintain one copy of something and not have a zillion versions all over the network.

You can share your whole computer, you may want to share only certain things (documents or folders), or you may want to share some stuff only in certain ways. Here's an idea of what you can share in your network:

✔ **The whole computer:** You can choose to make the whole computer or device accessible from the network. (We really don't advise sharing your whole computer because it exposes your entire PC to anyone who accesses your network.)

✔ **Specific internal drives:** You can share a specific hard drive, such as one where all your MP3s are stored or your computer games.

✔ **Specific peripheral drives:** You can share PC-connected or network-enabled peripheral drives, like an extra Universal Serial Bus (USB)-attached hard drive, a Zip or Jaz backup drive, or an external CD/DVD read/write drive.

✔ **Files:** You can set up particular folders or just a specific file to share across your network. *Note:* File storage schemes on devices are *hierarchical:* If you share a folder, all files and folders within that folder will be shared. If you want to share only one file, share a folder with only the one file in it (but if you add an additional file to that folder, it too will be shared).

Enabling sharing on Windows 2000 or Windows XP

In Windows 2000 or Windows XP, sharing is enabled by default on each network connection on your machine. If you have a wired network card and a wireless card, you can have sharing enabled On on one card and Off on the other. This is very helpful if you only want to share files on one of the networks you connect to. (See our description in Chapter 9 for setting your Windows Firewall connection.) For example, if you want to share files when connected to your wireless home network and turn off sharing when you plug your laptop in at work, turn sharing on for your wireless card and off for your wired Ethernet card. When you first install a new network card, or wireless network card, for our purposes, the default is to have sharing turned on.

You can never be too protected

The number of ways that someone can get on your network multiplies with each new technology you add to your network. We note in Chapter 10 that wireless local-area networks (LANs) seep out of your home and make it easy for others to log in and sniff around. If someone does manage to break into your network, the most obvious places to snoop around and do damage are the shared resources. Sharing your C: drive (which is usually your main hard drive), your Windows directory, or your My Documents directory makes it easier for people to get into your machine and do something you would rather they not.

You see, sharing broadcasts to the rest of the network the fact that something is shared, telling everyone who has access your computer's name on the network and how to find it. Sharing can broadcast that availability across firewalls, proxies, and servers. Certain types of viruses and less-than-friendly hackers look for these specific areas (like your shared C: drive) in broadcast messages and follow them back to your machine.

If you're going to share these parts of your system on your network, run a personal firewall or, in the case of Windows XP, the Windows Firewall on your machines for an added layer of security, or it's likely to be compromised at some point. Get virus software. Protect your machine, and limit your exposure to risk. (And, by all means, be sure to follow our advice in Chapter 10 for securing your wireless network.)

To enable sharing on a Windows 2000 or Windows XP machine, follow these steps, which are quite similar to those in the preceding section:

1. **Choose Start⇨Settings⇨Network and Dial-up Connections.**

2. **Right-click the icon of the network connection over which you want to enable File and Printer Sharing and then choose Properties from the pop-up menu that appears.**

3. **On the General tab for network cards and on the Network tab for dial-up connections, select the check box for File and Printer Sharing for Microsoft Networks.**

This step enables your PC to share files and also printers.

Use Windows Explorer to find and move shared files.

When you right-click any folder or file and then select Sharing from the pop-up menu that appears, you can control the sharing of that file.

Setting permissions

In Windows 2000 or Windows XP, controlling the sharing of files is a bit more complex in previous versions because of the enhanced security that comes with those operating systems. To share folders and drives, you must be logged on as a member of the Server Operators, Administrators, Power Users, or Users groups. Throughout the rest of this section, we describe these user types and then show you how to add users to your 2000 or Windows XP network.

Determining user types

The *Server Operators* group is really used only on large networks that incorporate the Microsoft Active Directory technology; if you're trying to set up your office computer at home, you may run into this (but it's not very likely). The groups you need to concern yourself with are the Administrators, Power Users, and Users groups:

- ✔ **Administrators** are system gods. Anyone set up as an administrator can do anything he wants — no restrictions.

- ✔ **Power Users** can't do as much as administrators, but they can do a lot — as long as what they're doing doesn't change any of the files that make Windows operate. In other words, Power Users can add and remove software, users, hardware, and so on to a system as long as their actions don't affect any files keeping the system running the way it's running.

✔ **Users** are just that: Users simply use what the system has to offer and aren't able to do anything else. The Users group provides the most secure environment in which to run programs, and it's by far the best way to give access to your resources *without* compromising the security of your computer and network.

How do you know what kind of access you have? Unfortunately, that's not an easy thing to find out unless you're an administrator. If you know that you're not an administrator, the only way to find out what you *can* do is by trying to do it. If you don't have the proper access to do something, you see a warning message telling you exactly that — sometimes the message may tell you what access you need to have in order to do what you want.

Adding users

For others to get access to what you have shared, you need to give them permission. You do that by giving them a logon on your computer and assigning them to a group — essentially adding them to the network as a user. The group is then given certain rights within the folder you have shared; every user in the group has access only to what the group has access to. For more details on this process, we strongly recommend that you use the Windows Help file to discover how to set up new users and groups on your system.

In Windows 2000 or Windows XP, creating users and adding them to groups is best done by using the administrator logon. If you're using an office computer and you're not the administrator or a member of the Power Users group, you can't create users. Talk to your system administrator to get permission and help in setting up your machine.

We're guessing that you're the administrator of your home-networked computer (it's your network, right?), and so you have access to the administrator logon. Thus, you can set up new users by logging on to the machine as administrator. As with the hierarchical folder permissions, user permissions are hierarchal as well. If you're a Power User, you can only create users who have less access than yourself. By using the administrator logon, you can create any type of user account you may need.

Unless you're very comfortable with the security settings of Windows 2000 or Windows XP, you should never give new user accounts more access than the Users group provides. (For a description of user types, see the preceding section.) Keep in mind that by creating these accounts, you're also creating a logon that can be used to turn on and access your computer directly. For the purposes of sharing files and peripherals, the standard Users group provides all the access that any individual on the network would normally need.

To add users to your network, follow these steps:

1. **Choose Start➪Settings➪Control Panel and double-click the Users and Passwords icon.**

   This step brings up the Users and Passwords dialog box.

2. **Click the Add button to launch the New User Wizard and add users to your machine.**

3. **Follow the wizard's onscreen prompts to enter a name, logon name, description, password, and then which group the user will be part of.**

   New users should always start as part of the Users group (also referred to as the Restricted Access group), which is the lowest possible access level. Starting users at the lowest possible access level is the best way for you to share your files without compromising your network's security.

Accessing shared files

Whether drives, folders, or single files are set up for sharing on your wireless home network, you access the shared thing in pretty much the same way. On any networked PC, you simply log on to the network, head for Network Neighborhood (or My Network Places, as the case may be), and navigate to the file (or folder or drive) you want to access. It's really as easy as that.

Just because you can *see* a drive, folder, or file in Network Neighborhood, however, doesn't necessarily mean that you have *access* to that drive, folder, or file. It all depends on set permissions.

Be Economical: Share Those Peripherals

Outside of the fact that there's only so much space on your desk or your kitchen countertop, you simply don't need a complete set of peripherals at each device on your network. For example, digital cameras are becoming quite popular, and you can view pictures on your PC, on your TV, and even in wireless picture frames around the house. But you probably need only one color printer geared toward printing high-quality photos for someone to take home (after admiring your wireless picture frames!).

The same is true about many peripherals: business card scanners, backup drives (such as Zip and Jaz drives), and even cameras. If you have one device and it's network enabled, anyone on the wireless network should be able to access that for the task at hand.

Setting up a print server

The most common shared peripheral is a printer. Setting up a printer for sharing is really easy, and using it is even easier.

You may have several printers in your house, and different devices may have different printers — but they all can be shared. You may have the color laser printer on your machine, a less expensive one (with less expensive consumables like printer cartridges, too) for the kid's computer, and a high-quality photo printer maybe near the TV set plugged into a USB port of a networkable A/V device. Each of these can be used by a local device — if it's properly set up.

Here are the steps you need to take to share a printer:

1. Enable printer sharing within the operating system of the computer to which the printer is attached.

2. Set up sharing for the installed printer.

   We say *installed* printer because we assume that you've already installed the printer locally on your computer or other device.

3. Remotely install the printer on every other computer on the network.

   We describe remote installation in the aptly named section "Remotely installing the printer on all network PCs," later in this chapter.

4. Access the printer from any PC on the network!

Throughout the rest of this section, we go through these four general steps in much more detail.

Sharing your printer in Windows 2000 or Windows XP

Windows 2000 and Windows XP are more sophisticated than previous Windows operating systems and subsequently have a *server type* of print sharing. In other words, they offer all the features of a big network with servers on your local machine. These features include the ability to assign users to manage the print queue remotely, embed printer software for easier installation, and manage when the printer is available based on a schedule you define.

To share a printer on Windows 2000 or Windows XP, follow these steps:

1. **Choose Start⇨Settings⇨Printers and Faxes (or simply choose Start⇨ Printers and Faxes, depending on how your Start menu is configured).**

2. **Right-click the printer in the Printers folder and choose Properties from the pop-up menu that appears.**

3. **On the Sharing tab of the dialog box that appears, click the Additional Drivers button.**

4. **Select which operating systems you want to support to use this shared printer and also select the other types of drivers needed for your other computer systems and devices; then click OK.**

5. **When prompted, insert a floppy disk or CD-ROM and direct the subsequent dialog boxes to the right places on those devices to get the driver for each operating system you chose.**

   Windows finds those drivers and downloads them to the Windows 2000 or Windows XP's hard drive. Then, when you go to install the printer on your other computers (see the next section), the Windows 2000 or Windows XP machine, which is sharing the printer, automatically transfers the proper printer drivers and finishes the installation for you. It's darned sweet, if you ask us!

Before you go out and start to put your newly shared printer on all your computers, you may want to create a shared folder on the computer you're using to host your printer. In the folder, copy the driver software that came with the printer. If, in the process of installing the printer on other workstations, you need a driver that isn't automatically available — such as an OS X driver for the printer — it's ready and available on your network so that you don't have to go looking for installation CDs to bring to the computer you're trying to set up. Trust us, this one can save you a *ton* of frustration.

Remotely installing the printer on all network PCs

The third step is done at every other PC in the house. Basically, you install the printer on each of these computers, but in a logical way — *logically* as opposed to *physically* installing and connecting the printer to each computer. You install the printer just like any other printer except that you're installing a *network* printer, and the printer installation wizard searches the network for the printers you want to install.

The process you use will vary depending on the operating system you use and the type of printer you're trying to install. In every case, read the printer documentation before you start because some printers require their software to be partially installed before you try to add the printer. We've seen this often with multifunction printers that support scanning, copying, and faxing.

With Windows, the easiest way to start the installation of a printer is to look inside My Network Places, find the computer sharing the printer, and double-click the shared printer. This action starts the Add Printer Wizard, which takes you through the process of adding the printer. This wizard works like any good wizard — you make a few selections and click Next a lot. If you didn't add the drivers to the shared printer already, you may be asked for the printer drivers. Just use the Browse button to direct the wizard to look in the shared folder or CD-ROM drive where you put the printer software on the computer that the printer is attached to.

You have two options for installing a network printer:

- **From your Printers folder:** In Windows 2000 or Windows XP, choose Start⇨Settings⇨Printers and Faxes (or simply Start⇨Printers and Faxes, depending on how your Start menu is configured).

- **From My Network Places:** Double-click the computer that has the printer attached. An icon appears, showing the shared printer. Right-click it and then choose Install from the pop-up menu that appears.

Either route leads you to the Add Printer Wizard, which guides you through the process of adding the network printer.

Don't start the Add Printer Wizard unless you have installed the proper drivers to the shared printer or you have the installation CDs for your printer handy. The Add Printer Wizard installs the printer *drivers* (software files that contain the info required for Windows to talk to your printers and exchange data for printing). The wizard gets these from the CD that comes with your printer. If you don't have the CD, go to the Web site of your printer manufacturer and download the driver to your desktop and install from there. Don't forget to delete the downloaded files from your desktop when you're done installing them on the computer.

Note also that the wizard allows you to browse your network to find the printer you want to install. Simply click the plus sign next to the computer that has the printer attached, and you should see the printer below the computer. (If not, recheck that printer sharing is enabled on that computer.)

At the end of the wizard screens, you have the option to print a test page. We recommend that you do this. You don't want to wait until your child has to have a color printout for her science experiment (naturally, she waits until 10 minutes before the bus arrives to tell you!) to find out that the printer doesn't work.

Accessing your shared printers

After you have the printers installed, how do you access them? Whenever your Print window comes up (by pressing Ctrl+P in most applications), you see a field labeled Name for the name of the printer accompanied by a pulldown menu of printer options. Use your mouse to select any printer — local or networked — and the rest of the printing process remains the same as though you had a printer directly plugged into your PC.

You can even make a networked printer the default printer by right-clicking the printer and then choosing Set As Default Printer from the pop-up menu that appears.

Sharing other peripherals

Sharing any other peripheral is quite similar to sharing printers. You need to make sure that you're sharing the device on the computer it's attached to. Then you need to install that device on another PC by using that device's installation procedures. Obviously, we can't be specific about such an installation because of the widely varying processes that companies use to install devices. Most of the time — like with a printer — you need to install the drivers for the device you're sharing on your other computers.

Note that some of the devices you attach to your network have integrated Web servers in them. This is getting more and more common. Danny's AudioReQuest (www.request.com) music server, for example, is visible on his home network and is addressable by any of his PCs. Thus, he can download music to and from the AudioReQuest server and sync it to his other devices he wants music on. Anyone else in the home can do the same — even remotely, over the Internet. We talk more about the AudioReQuest system in Chapter 13.

Danny has also set up a virtual CD server in his home to manage all the CDs his kids have for their games. This server is shared on the home network. By using Virtual CD software from H+H Zentrum fuer Rechnerkommunikation GmbH (www.virtualcd-online.com; $85 for a five-user license), Danny has loaded all his CDs and DVDs onto a single machine so that his kids (he has four) can access those CDs from any of their individual PCs (he has four *spoiled* kids). Rather than look to the local hard drive for the CD, any of the kids' PCs looks to the server to find the CD — hence, the name *virtual CD*. Now those stacks of CDs (and moans over a scratched CD!) are gone.

Sharing between Macs and Windows-based PCs

If you have an OS X (versions 10.2, 10.3 or 10.4) you don't need to do anything special to get your Mac connected to a PC network for file-sharing purposes. All these versions of OS X support Windows networking protocols right out of the box, with no add-ons or extra software required.

Getting on a Windows network

To connect to your Windows PCs or file servers, simply go the OS X Finder and then select Go⇨Connect to Server (⌘+K). In the dialog box that appears, you can type the IP address or host name of the server you're connecting to and then click the Connect button. Alternatively, click the Browse button in the dialog box to search your local network for available servers and shares.

Bonjour, Madam!

One cool feature that Apple has added to its newest version of Mac OS — Mac OS v. 10.2, often called Jaguar — is a networking system named Bonjour. Bonjour, previously known as Rendezvous, is based on an open Internet standard (IETF, or Internet Engineering Task Force, Zeroconf) and is being adopted by a number of manufacturers outside of Apple.

Basically, Bonjour (and Zeroconf) is a lot like Bluetooth (which we discuss in Chapter 15) in that it allows devices on a network to discover each other without any user intervention or special configuration. Bonjour is being slowly incorporated into many products, such as printers, storage devices (basically, networkable hard drives), and even household electronics like TiVos (hard-drive-based television personal video recorders [PVRs]).

Here's one great feature about Bonjour: On Macs equipped with Apple AirPort network adapter cards, it lets two (or more) Macs in range of each other — in other words, within Wi-Fi range — *automatically* connect to each other for file sharing, Instant Messaging, and other tasks without going through any extra steps of setting up a peer-to-peer network.

Bonjour is enabled automatically in Mac OS v. 10.2/3/4 computers if you enable Personal Fire Sharing (found in the System Preferences; look for the Sharing Icon) or use the Apple iChat Instant Messaging Program, the Apple Safari Web browsers, or any Bonjour-capable printer connected to your Airport network.

Letting Windows users on your network

To let Windows users access your Mac, you must simply "turn on" file sharing in your Mac's System Preferences. To do so, follow these steps:

1. **Open up System Preferences (click on the System Preferences icon on your Mac's dock).**

2. **Click on the Sharing tab to view your file-sharing options. Make sure that the Services tab is opened.**

3. **Select Windows Sharing in the services listing, and then click the Start button to activate it. Close the Sharing dialog box.**

That's it! Your Mac automatically turns on Windows sharing and opens the appropriate holes (ports) in your firewall. If you haven't already enabled accounts on your Mac for sharing, you're prompted by OS X to do so now. Simply click the Enable Accounts button, and in the dialog box that opens, select the accounts (or users) of your Mac that you want to allow access to. To do this, just select the check box to each name you want to enable, and then click Done. That's all there is to it. If you want to connect to your LAN from a Windows computer, simply browse your Neighborhood Network in Windows XP or enter your network's address on an Explorer address bar (it's something like the following:

```
\192.168.1.3\username
```

(Substitute *your* Mac OS X username for *username,* of course!)

Chapter 12

Gaming Over a Wireless Home Network

*I*n case you missed it, gaming is huge. We mean *huge*. The video gaming industry is, believe it or not, bigger than the entertainment industry generated by Hollywood. Billions of dollars per year are spent on PC game software and hardware and on gaming consoles such as PlayStation and Xbox. You probably know a bit about gaming — we bet that you have at least played *Minesweeper* on your PC or *Pong* on an Atari when you were a kid. What you may not know is that video gaming has moved online in a big way. For that, you need a network.

All three of the big gaming console vendors — Sony (www.us.playstation. com), Microsoft (www.xbox.com), and Nintendo (www.gamecube.com) — have created for their latest consoles inexpensive networking kits that let you connect your console to a broadband Internet connection (such as a cable or digital subscriber line [DSL]) to play against people anywhere in the world. Online PC gaming has also become a huge phenomenon, with games such as *EverQuest Online* attracting millions of users.

A big challenge for anyone getting into online gaming is finding a way to get consoles and PCs in different parts of the house connected to your Internet connection. For example, if you have an Xbox, it's probably in your living room or home theater, and we're willing to bet that your cable or DSL modem is in the home office. Lots of folks string a Cat 5e Ethernet cable down the hall and hook it into their game machine — a great approach if you don't mind tripping over that cable at 2 a.m. when you let the dogs out. Enter your wireless home network, a much better approach to getting these gaming devices online.

In this chapter, we talk about some of the hardware requirements for getting a gaming PC or game console online. In the case of gaming consoles, you need to pick up some extra gear because none of the current online kits contains wireless gear. We also talk about some steps you need to take to configure your router (or the router in your access point [AP], if they're the same box in your wireless local-area network [LAN]) to get your online gaming up and running.

We're approaching this chapter with the assumption that your wireless gaming network will be connecting to the Internet using some sort of always-on, broadband connection, such as DSL or a cable modem, using a home router (either the one built into your access point or a separate one). We have two reasons for this assumption: First, we think that online gaming works much, much better on a broadband connection; second, because with some console systems (particularly the Xbox), you're *required* to have a broadband connection to use online gaming. And, even if the console (like the PS2) doesn't *require* broadband, many of the games *do*.

One of the biggest things broadband brings to your gaming experience is speed. A big part of online gaming isn't so much how quickly you can kill your opponent or cross over your dribble but, rather, how quickly the central gaming host computer in the middle of it all knows that you performed a certain action (and recognizes it). How frustrating to fire a missile at a helicopter only to find out that the helicopter blew you up first because the system registered its firing before yours. The time it takes for your gaming commands to cross the Internet — in gaming, at least — is often a matter of virtual life or death.

Get your online game on!

The biggest trend in PC gaming (besides the ever-improving quality of graphics enabled by the newest hardware) is the development of online gaming. Broadband Internet connectivity has become widespread — more than half of Americans who access the Internet at home use broadband, according to the Pew Internet Life Survey. This has allowed online PC gaming to grow beyond simplistic (and low-speed) Java games (which still can be fun — check out `games.yahoo.com`) and move toward high-speed, graphics-intensive, multiplayer games like Quake III.

If you have not yet checked out online gaming, you may not realize what a big deal it is. In parts of the world where broadband is ubiquitous — like South Korea, where almost every home is wired with DSL or cable — broadband online games boast tens of millions of users. Here in the United States, this trend has not quite reached those proportions, but millions of users are still playing various multiplayer online games. Face it: It's just plain fun to reach out and blow up your buddy's tank from 1,000 miles away.

You can find out how fast your connection is by pinging the other machines or the central server. (*Pinging* is a process in which you use an application on your computer — usually just called *ping*, accessible from the DOS or CMD window — to send a signal to another computer and see how long it takes to get there and back, like a sonar beam on a submarine pinging another sub.)

PC Gaming Hardware Requirements

We should preface this section of the book by saying that this book isn't entitled *Gaming PCs For Dummies*. Thus, we don't spend any time talking about PC gaming hardware requirements in any kind of detail. Our gamer pals will probably be aghast at our brief coverage here, but we really just want to give you a taste of what you may want to think about if you decide to outfit a PC for online gaming. In fact, if you're buying a PC for this purpose, check out the classes of computers called *gaming PCs,* optimized just for this application. Throughout this chapter, we use the term *gaming PC* generically to mean any PC in your home that you're using for gaming — not just special-purpose gaming PCs.

Your best resource, we think, is to check out an online gaming Web site that has a team of experts who review and torture-test all the latest hardware for a living. We like CNET's `www.gamespot.com` and `www.gamespy.com`.

At the most basic level, you really just need any modern multimedia PC (or Macintosh, for that matter) to get started with PC gaming. Just about any PC or Mac purchased since 2002 or so will have a fast processor and a decent graphics or video card. (You hear both terms used.) If you start getting into online gaming, start thinking about upgrading your PC with high-end gaming hardware or even consider building a dedicated gaming machine. Some key hardware components to keep in mind are the following:

- **Fast processor:** Much of the hard work in gaming is done by the video card, but a fast Pentium 4 or AMD Athlon (or PowerPC G4, for Macs) central processing unit (CPU) is always a nice thing to have.

- **Powerful video card:** The latest cards from ATI and nVIDIA (`www.nvidia.com`) contain incredibly sophisticated computer chips dedicated to cranking out the video part of your games. If you get to the point where you know what frames per second (fps) is all about and you start worrying that yours are too low, it's time to start investigating faster video cards.

  We're big fans of the ATI (`www.ati.com`) Radeon X1800 XL card, but then we're suckers for fast hardware that can crank out the polygons (the building blocks of your game video) at mind-boggling speeds.

✔ **Fancy gaming controllers:** Many games can be played by using a standard mouse and keyboard, but you may want to look into some cool specialized game controllers that connect through your PC's Universal Serial Bus (USB) ports. For example, you can get a joystick for flying games or a steering wheel for driving games. Check out Creative Technologies (www.creative.com) for some cool options.

✔ **Quality sound card:** Many games include a *Surround sound* soundtrack, just like DVDs provide in your home theater. If you have the appropriate number of speakers and the right sound card, you hear the bad guys creeping up behind you before you see them on the screen. Très fun.

Networking Requirements for PC Gaming

Gaming PCs may (but don't have to) have some different innards than regular PCs, but their networking requirements don't differ in any appreciable way from the PC you use for Web browsing, e-mail, or anything else. You shouldn't be surprised to hear that connecting a gaming PC to your wireless network is no different from connecting any PC.

You need some sort of wireless network adapter connected to your gaming PC to get it up and running on your home network (just like you need a wireless network adapter connected to *any* PC running on your network, as we discuss in Chapter 5). These adapters can fit in the PC Card slot (of a laptop computer, for example) or connect to a USB or Ethernet port of a desktop computer. If you have a Mac that you're using for gaming, you probably will use one of the Apple AirPort or AirPort Extreme cards (which we discuss in Chapter 8). There's nothing special you need to do, hardware-wise, with a gaming PC.

When it comes to *playing* online games, you may need to do some tweaking to your home network's router — which may be a stand-alone device or part of your access point. In the upcoming sections "Dealing with Router Configurations" and "Setting Up a Demilitarized Zone (DMZ)," we discuss these steps in further detail.

Depending on which games you're playing, you may not need to do any special configuring. Some games play just fine without any special router configurations — particularly if your PC isn't acting as the *server* (which means that other people aren't connecting to your PC from remote locations on the Internet).

Getting Your Gaming Console on Your Wireless Home Network

Although PC gaming can be really cool, we find that many people prefer to use a dedicated game console device — such as a PlayStation 2 (PS2) or an Xbox — to do their gaming. And, although hard-core gamers may lean toward PC platforms for their gaming (often spending thousands of dollars on ultra-high-end gaming PCs with the latest video cards, fastest processor and memory, and the like), we think that for regular gamers, consoles offer some compelling advantages:

- ✓ **They're inexpensive.** Price points are always dropping, but as we write, you can buy a PS2 or Xbox for $149 or a Nintendo GameCube for even less ($99). Even if you dedicate an inexpensive PC for gaming, you probably will spend closer to $1,000 — and even more if you buy the fancy video cards and other equipment that gives the PC the same gaming performance as a console.

- ✓ **They're simple to set up.** Although it's not all that hard to get games running on a PC, you're dealing with a more complicated operating system on a PC. You have to install games and get them up and running. On a game console, you simply shove a disc into the drawer and you're playing.

- ✓ **They're in the right room.** Most folks don't want PCs in their living rooms or home theaters, although some really cool models are designed just for that purpose. A game console, on the other hand, is relatively small and inconspicuous and can fit neatly on a shelf next to your TV.

- ✓ **They work with your biggest screen.** Of course, you can connect a PC to a big-screen TV system (using a special video card), and it's getting easier. But consoles are designed to plug right in to your TV or home theater system, using the same cables you use to hook up a VCR or DVD player. You can even use the Xbox or PS2 as a DVD player!

Today's game consoles can offer some awesome gaming experiences. Try playing the Xbox game *Halo 2* on a big-screen TV with a Surround sound system in place — it's amazing. You can even get a full HDTV (high-definition TV) picture on the Xbox, with certain games. And, because these gaming consoles are really nothing more than specialized computers, they can offer the same kind of networking capabilities that a PC does; in other words, they can fit right into your wireless home network.

You can't just take your console out of the box and connect it to your wireless network, however. Here are three steps you need to take; we talk about each one in more detail in this section:

1. Get the networking kit appropriate to your console.

2. Get signed up with an online gaming service.

3. Get a wireless Ethernet bridge (see Figure 12-1) to make the connection.

Console online gaming services and equipment

In this section, we conjoin our discussion of the first two requirements listed previously: the networking kit and the online gaming service. For the Xbox, these two items are one and the same. Conversely, for PlayStation and GameCube, they're separate steps, as we discuss shortly.

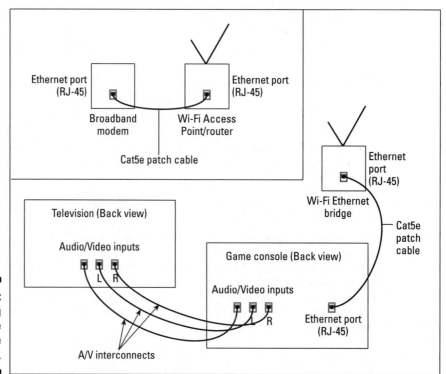

Figure 12-1:
Connecting a game console wirelessly.

Game consoles: the next generation

They're coming. And, they will be spectacular. We're talking about the forthcoming PS3 (PlayStation 3), Xbox 360, and Nintendo Revolution — the three next-generation gaming consoles from the three big gaming manufacturers. We've not gotten our hands on any of these next-generation consoles yet (they're not available as we write in late 2005), but we've read the press releases and the almost breathless coverage in the press.

We know only two things: that all the consoles will be really cool and that they all will support online gaming; and not just support it, but also encourage it, by including built-in Wi-Fi networking (it's standard on the Nintendo and Playstation 3 and an extra-cost option on the Xbox 360). We can't wait until all three are on the streets (we expect the Xbox 360 by the end of 2005 and the others sometime in 2006).

Can your games get online?

As you get into online gaming with your game console, keep one common requirement in mind: You need to have games that are online capable. Only a small percentage of games are online capable, so be sure the check the box. The Sony PS2, for example, has almost 200 games online, but it has more than 1200 games in its library. The Microsoft Xbox has about 150 games applicable to Xbox Live. The GameCube, unfortunately, brings up the rear of the pack with only one online game available.

Online-capable games cost about the same as regular games for these consoles — about $20–$50, and the price of the online service depends on the game and console you're using. Microsoft, for example, charges $50 per year for its gaming service, which covers all available games. Sony doesn't charge for its service, but individual games may have a fee to play online (none that we know of currently does, but it's possible that they will).

The cost of getting into online gaming is higher than just the price of the kit or service. You also need to account for the cost of new, online-ready games. Plus, none of the gaming services we discuss here includes the broadband Internet access that you need in order to make them work. You have to have a broadband Internet service, and *then* you need to buy the equipment and get the online gaming service set up.

Living large with Xbox

The Microsoft online gaming service, Xbox Live (www.xboxlive.com), is in our opinion the furthest along so far in terms of the overall experience: Although PS2 online games vary in their interface and experience game-by-game, Xbox Live offers a consistent online environment with *all* those more than 150 games readily available with one single sign-in and configuration procedure.

Xbox Live isn't just about playing against someone else, it's really almost a new lifestyle. With *Live*, you can

- ✔ Communicate in real time during games.
- ✔ Set up chats with your friends.
- ✔ Meet gamers from all over the world and put together a posse of your favorite teammates to go after others.
- ✔ Set up your own clans and start competitions with Xbox *Live* features.
- ✔ Join Xbox Live tournaments and show the world what you've got to show for all those hours of practicing.
- ✔ Download cool new stuff for your favorite games that's only available online — things like new maps, missions, songs, skins, vehicles, characters, and quests.
- ✔ Play games against hot celebs that Microsoft courts online.

To get online with Xbox Live, you need to buy a $69.99 kit (available at www. xbox.com/live), which is a combination of hardware and service. In other words, you get the components you need to get online as well as a year of gaming service. As of this writing, more than 150 Xbox Live-enabled games are on the market.

Microsoft doesn't provide the broadband service for Xbox Live (none of the gaming companies does) — just the gaming service itself. Thus, you need to already have a cable or DSL modem set up in your home. What Microsoft *does* do — and this is a bit different from what Sony and Nintendo do with their online gaming — is host its own online service that you connect to when you sign on to Xbox Live. You need to sign up for only one service to play online games with your Xbox. Sony and Nintendo rely on game software vendors to set up their own online gaming services, so you may need to subscribe to one service for Game A and another for Game B.

Xbox Live includes a software disc to get things set up on your console as well as a headset that plugs into one of the Xbox controller ports. This headset enables a really cool feature of Xbox Live: voice chat during game play. With this headset, you can add your own running commentary to the game while you blow past your opponent on the race course or blow up her tank.

Because the Xbox comes out of the box with a built-in Ethernet port, the Xbox Live kit doesn't contain any other networking hardware. You just need to connect your Xbox to the wireless network (using a wireless Ethernet bridge, as we discuss in the upcoming section "Console wireless networking equipment"), insert the Xbox Live disc into your Xbox, and follow the onscreen instructions. You're prompted to enter a *Gamertag* — your online "handle" or screen name — as well as your real name, address info, credit card number, and subscription code (you usually find it inside the disc case that your Xbox Live disc came in). After you do all this, your account is registered and you're ready to game.

Microsoft doesn't let you change your Gamertag after the fact, so pick one you like — you're stuck with it.

If you're going to play Xbox Live, you need to make sure that your router is Xbox Live Compatible: www.xbox.com/en-US/live/connect/routerlanding.htm. On this page, Microsoft lists routers that don't work with its Live service, so be sure to check the list before you buy. If your router isn't on the Works or Does Not Work lists, it's in a huge gray area of "we have no clue, but don't blame us if it doesn't work." Microsoft always loves a scapegoat!

If your current router isn't on this list, don't despair. Check the router manufacturer's Web site — often, it has specific steps (such as installing a *firmware* update — updating the router's software) which makes it work just fine. Some routers work just as they are, but they simply haven't been certified for some reason.

PSP: Your passport to Wi-Fi gaming

If you're into handheld gaming devices, the Sony PSP (Playstation Portable) may be just the ticket. For about $250 (for a Value Pack including a couple of games and accessories), this slick little handheld lets you take your gaming with you. But, there's more to the PSP than just gaming. The PSP is designed to be an all-purpose media player, with a Memory Stick DUO slot designed to let you carry photos, music, and even video along with you.

That's all cool, but what's cooler is that the PSP has a built-in Wi-Fi (802.11b) adapter that lets you connect to any 802.11b or 802.11g Wi-Fi network. The initial PSPs shipped with only support for WEP encryption, but the latest (as we write in late 2005) 2.0 firmware upgrade lets you connect to a properly secured WPA network. When connected via Wi-Fi, you can play online games against others on your network or over the Internet. There's even a built-in Web browser, so that when your thumbs need a break from all that hot game action, you can surf your favorite Web sites.

Playing online with PlayStation 2 (PS2)

Although the Xbox, with its Xbox Live service, is probably the most advanced online gaming console, it has one big disadvantage when compared with the Sony PS2 console — many fewer users. The PlayStation is the numero uno, most popular gaming console these days, with tens and tens of millions of users. This popularity led to a greater number of game software companies creating a greater number and variety of games for the PS2 console.

As we discuss in the earlier section "Can your games get online?," most existing games don't work online. As we write this chapter, almost 200 PS2 games allow online gaming.

If you've recently bought your PS2 (the slimline model), you have all the hardware you need to connect to your Wi-Fi Ethernet bridge. But, for older PS2s, you need to buy a kit. Because the original PS2 didn't come from the factory with an Ethernet port, you need to spend 40 bucks for the Sony PlayStation 2 Network Adaptor to get into online gaming. The adaptor plugs into a port on the back of the PS2 and has an Ethernet port (like the port that's already on the back of an Xbox) for connecting to your wireless home network using a wireless Ethernet bridge. The network adaptor also has a dial-up modem built in, so even if you don't have broadband, you can still get into online gaming (unlike with Xbox Live, which is broadband only).

We think that you really need broadband to do online gaming right; otherwise, the play is just too choppy and lagging. If you don't have broadband, we also recommend that you don't bother connecting your PS2 to your wireless LAN. Just plug the network adapter into the nearest phone jack. If you don't have a phone jack near your PS2, consider getting one of the RCA wireless phone jacks. (Search for this term on Amazon.com or Google.com to find more information.) Although these items aren't wireless LAN equipment, they're a cheap way (about $50) to put a phone jack where one isn't.

You can find more information about PS2 online gaming at the Sony site (www.us.playstation.com/onlinegaming). As we mention in the preceding section, the big difference between PS2 and Xbox Live online gaming relates to who provides the online gaming service itself. With the Xbox, you sign up for your account with Microsoft, and you can then play any Xbox Live game using that account. With the PS2, you need to sign up for accounts with the individual game developers. So, if you want to be the Duke Blue Devils in the Electronic Arts NCAA March Madness 06 Hoops game, you need to sign up for the Electronic Arts online game-hosting service. Luckily, the game manufacturers aren't currently charging for this service, but you may end up having to remember account names and passwords for multiple services when your game collection grows.

GameCube

Without a doubt, the Nintendo GameCube is the cutest of the three major game console systems. Although it's positively tiny compared with the PS2 (excluding the newest slim version) — and especially when compared with the huge Xbox — it's still loaded with powerful computer chips that give you some big gaming fun. Like the other two consoles, the GameCube can be a part of your wireless LAN, with just a few additions.

Like the PS2, the GameCube doesn't have a built-in Ethernet port with which you can connect the console directly to a wireless Ethernet bridge. So (as with the PS2), you need to buy an adapter — a broadband adapter, to be precise, which costs about $34.95 — that plugs into the back of the GameCube and contains an Ethernet port you can use for hooking the console into your wireless home network. You can find more details about this network adapter — as well as lots of info about the GameCube itself — at the Nintendo Web site (www.gamecube.com).

Going Wi-Fi and portable with Nintendo DS

Nintendo has a nifty handheld gaming console called the Nintendo DS (it's Nintendo's competitor to the Sony PSP) that features, among many things, *two screens*. (Imagine driving in a race while simultaneously looking out of your windshield and also at a bird's eye view of your car on the track.)

Like the PSP, the DS has built-in support for Wi-Fi network connectivity. This connectivity is now used for hooking up with other nearby DS users — using a feature of the DS called *PictoChat*, which allows you to share drawings and have text chats.

A new feature, available by the time you read this book, will be added when Nintendo launches its *free* Nintendo Wi-Fi Connection service. This service will allow you to connect the DS to your home Wi-Fi network to play a number of online games being launched in conjunction with the service. If you don't have Wi-Fi in your home (we suspect that you do, because you're reading this book, but just in case), you can buy a Nintendo USB Wi-Fi adapter to plug into your broadband-connected PC — this adapter doesn't create a normal Wi-Fi network throughout your home, but does let you connect your DS to the Internet.

The coolest part of this service is that Nintendo is planning on launching "thousands" of free Nintendo DS-accessible *hot spots* around the United States to connect to online gaming when you're on the road.

All the details are still pending as we write, but keep an eye on the Nintendo Web site for the details. This Wi-Fi Connection service will also serve as the basis for Wi-Fi gaming when the new Nintendo Revolution console launches in 2006, so expect this service to get huge!

At the time this book is being written, you can play only one GameCube game online — the Sega *Phantasy Star Online Episodes I&II* or *Phantasy Star Online Episode III: C.A.R.D. Revolution* — that requires an $8.95 per month subscription and works with most online services. (Unfortunately, with the biggest one — AOL — you can play only via AOL Broadband, not AOL Dialup). We expect more GameCube online games to become available, but so far, that's it.

Console wireless networking equipment

In case we don't make it abundantly clear in our discussion, we reiterate: *None* of the consoles that are now available comes with any kind of built-in wireless LAN capabilities, and *none* of the networking kits or adapters you need to buy from the console maker includes wireless LAN equipment. What all these consoles do have, when outfitted for online gaming, is an Ethernet port. This situation will undoubtedly change, but for now, that's it.

Really, that's all you need, thanks to the availability of relatively inexpensive wireless Ethernet bridges. The deeper you get into the networking world, the more likely you are to run into the concept of a *bridge,* which is simply a device that connects two segments of a network. Unlike hubs or switches or routers or most other network equipment (we talk about much of this stuff over in Chapters 2 and 5), a bridge doesn't do anything with the data flowing through it. It basically just passes the data straight through without manipulating it, rerouting it, or even caring what it is. A wireless Ethernet bridge's sole purpose in life, then, is to send data back and forth between two points. (It's not too tough to see where the name came from, huh?)

 While we're discussing these wireless Ethernet bridges in terms of game console networks in this chapter, they're quite handy devices that can be used for lots of different applications in your wireless LAN. Basically, any device that has an Ethernet port — such as a personal video recorder (PVR), an MP3 server (such as the AudioReQuest), and even an Internet refrigerator (such as the Samsung Internet Refrigerator) — can hook into your wireless home network by using a wireless Ethernet bridge.

The great thing about wireless Ethernet bridges, besides the fact that they solve the very real problem of getting noncomputer devices onto the wireless network, is that they're the essence of Plug and Play. You may have to spend three or four minutes setting up the bridge itself (to get it connected to your wireless network), but you don't need to do anything special to your game console other than plug the bridge in. All the game consoles we discuss in this chapter (at least when equipped with the appropriate network adapters and software) "see" your wireless Ethernet bridge as just a regular Ethernet cable. You don't need any drivers or other special software on the console. The console doesn't know (nor does it care in its not-so-little console brain) that there's a wireless link in the middle of the connection. It just works!

If you have encryption (like WPA) set up on the network, you need to complete one step before just plugging your wireless bridge into your gaming console's Ethernet port. First, you need to plug the bridge into one of the wired Ethernet ports on your router and access the bridge's built-in Web configuration screens. There, you find the location to enter your WPA passphrase (or WEP key if you're using WEP), and network name (or ESSID). After you've made these settings, you're ready to plug the bridge into your console and get online. It's that simple!

Not all the wireless Ethernet bridges on the market support the (much more secure) WPA encryption technology that we discuss in Chapter 10 (and which we highly recommend you use on your wireless network. If you're using WPA, make sure that you choose a wireless Ethernet bridge that supports this encryption method: You can't mix and match WPA and lesser encryptions systems like WEP, so you would have to make your whole network less secure if you mixed in a lesser wireless Ethernet bridge.

D-Link DGL-3420 Wireless 108AG Gaming Adapter

D-Link (www.dlink.com) has developed this product with gaming consoles in mind. In fact, D-Link even has its own online GamerLounge site with lots of great gaming information on it (games.dlink.com). The $99 list price DGL-3420 (see Figure 12-2) doesn't need any special drivers or configuration, but does include a Web-browser-based configuration program that enables you to do things like enter your Wi-Fi Protected Access (WPA) passphrase. (Check out Chapter 10 for more information on this topic.)

Figure 12-2:
The D-Link
DGL-3420
Gaming
Adapter.

The DGL-3420 is a loaded Ethernet bridge that supports both 802.11a and 802.11g (most folks use 802.11g) and even supports the higher-speed Super G 108 Mbps variant of 802.11g — if your router also supports it.

There's even some special "secret sauce" for making gaming faster — the D-Link GameFuel prioritization technology, as discussed in the nearby sidebar, "Getting your router optimized for gaming."

SMC SMCWEBT-G EZ Connect g Wireless Ethernet Bridge

The SMC Network SMCWEBT-G Wireless Ethernet bridge is an inexpensive Swiss army knife of an Ethernet bridge. First of all, it's an 802.11g wireless Ethernet bridge with a theoretical 108 Mbps maximum speed (you need a router that also supports the "Super G" protocol). Like the D-Link bridge we discuss in the preceding section, the SMCWEBT-G supports WPA encryption, which means that it plays nicely on your well-secured wireless network.

There's more to it, though: The SMCWEBT-G can be configured to work as an access point all on its own (so that you can plug it into a stand-alone router to provide wireless access) and even as a *WDS repeater* that can extend the range of your network if your primary router is one of the SMC wireless routers. For only $79.99, it's a relative bargain and well worth checking out.

Getting your router optimized for gaming

A few vendors have begun to sell wireless routers (or gateways, depending on their terminology) especially tweaked to support gaming. A wireless router manufacturer can do two things to ensure that gaming works well:

✔ Make it easier to support online game play: Routers can be designed to work specifically with online gaming applications. For example, a router may include more built-in game application support in its Web configuration, so you can easily "turn on" game support in the firewall and NAT routing functionality, without having to go through lots of trouble setting up port forwarding and DMZs (discussed in the final two sections of this chapter). Many gaming-specific routers support Universal Plug and Play (UPNP), also discussed in those sections, which makes the configuration of game applications automatic.

✔ Provide *prioritization* to game applications: For the ultimate in gaming experience,

some routers prioritize gaming applications over other traffic flowing through the router. Therefore, if two (or more) different applications are trying to send traffic through your router at the same time (like your game and your spouse's e-mail application sending a work document to the server), the router makes sure that the gaming data gets through to the Internet first. This concept can reduce the *latency* (or delay) you experience in playing online games and make the experience better (you can blow up the other guy faster!).

An example of this kind of wireless router is the D-Link DGL-4300 Wireless Gaming Router (`http://games.dlink.com/products/?pid=370`, $149.99). This router includes the D-Link *GameFuel* prioritization technology, a 108 Mbps 802.11g AP (using the Super G technology discussed in Chapter 3), and a wired switch supporting Gigabit (1000BaseT) connections for your wired PCs and consoles.

Dealing with Router Configurations

So far in this chapter, we talk a bit about the services and hardware you need to get into online gaming using your wireless network. What we haven't covered yet — getting online and playing a game — is either the easiest or the hardest part of the equation. The difficulty of this task depends on two things:

✔ **The platform you're using:** If you're trying to get online with a PC (whether it's Windows-based or a Mac) — well, basically there's nothing special to worry about. You just need to get it connected to the Internet as we describe in Chapter 9. For certain games, you may have to do a few fancy things with your router, which we discuss later in this chapter. If you're using a gaming console, you may have to adjust a few things in your router to get your online connection working, but when you're using a game console with many routers, you can just plug in your wireless equipment and go, too.

✔ **What you're trying to do:** For many games, after you establish an Internet connection, you're ready to start playing. Some games, however, require you to make some adjustments to your router's configuration. If you're planning to host the games on your PC (which means that your online friends will be remotely connecting to your PC), you definitely have to do a bit of configuration.

Don't sweat it, though. It's usually not all that hard to get gaming set up, and it's getting easier every day. We say that it's getting easier because the companies that make wireless LAN equipment and home routers realize that gaming is a growth industry for them. They know that they can sell more equipment if they can help people get devices like game consoles online.

You need to accomplish two things to get your online gaming — well, we can't think of a better term — online:

1. **Get an Internet Protocol (IP) address.**

   Your access point needs to recognize your gaming PC's or console's network adapter and your console's wireless Ethernet bridge, if you have one in your network configuration. If you have WEP configured (refer to Chapter 10), your game machine needs to provide the proper password. Your router (whether it's in the access point or it's separate) needs to provide an IP address to your gaming machine.

2. **Get through your router's firewall.**

   The preceding step is really pretty easy. The step that takes some time is configuring the firewall feature of your router to allow gaming programs to function properly.

Getting an IP address

For the most part, if you've set up your router to provide IP addresses within your network using DHCP (as we discuss in Chapters 5 and 7), your gaming PC or gaming console automatically connects to the router when the device is turned on and sends a Dynamic Host Configuration Protocol (DHCP) request to the router asking for an IP address. If you've configured your gaming PC like we discuss in Chapters 7 and 8, your computer should get its IP address and be online automatically. Or, as we like to say about this kind of neat stuff, auto*magically*. You may need to go into a program to select an access point and enter your WEP password, but, otherwise, it should just work without any intervention.

If you have a game console with a wireless Ethernet bridge, the process should be almost as smooth. The first time you use the bridge, you may need to use a Web-browser interface on one of your PCs to set up WEP passwords; otherwise, your router should automatically assign an IP address to your console. Sometimes, however, a router may not be completely compatible with a gaming console. Keep in mind that online console gaming was introduced in November 2002, and many home router models have been around much longer than that.

Before you get all wrapped around the axle trying to get your game console connected to your router, check out the Web site of your particular console maker *and* your router manufacturer. We have no doubt that you can find lots of information about how to make this connection using those resources. In many cases, if you're having troubles getting your router to assign an IP address to your console, you need to download a firmware upgrade for your router. *Firmware* is the software that lives inside your router and tells your router how to behave. Most router vendors have released updated firmware to help their older router models work with gaming consoles.

Some older router models simply don't work with gaming consoles. If online gaming is an important part of your plans, check the Web sites we mention earlier in this chapter *before* you choose a router.

In most cases, if your console doesn't get assigned an IP address automatically, you need to go into your router's setup program — most use a Web browser on a networked PC to adjust the configuration — and manually assign a fixed IP address to the console. Unlike DHCP-assigned IP addresses (which can change every time a computer logs on to the network), this fixed IP address is always assigned to your console.

Every router has a slightly different system for doing this, but typically you simply select an IP address that isn't in the range of DHCP addresses that your router automatically assigns to devices connected to your network.

You need to assign an IP address that isn't in the range of your router's IP address pool but is within the *same subnet.* In other words, if your router assigns IP addresses in the 192.168.0.*xxx* range, you need to use an IP address beginning with 192.168.0 for your game console. For example, if your router uses the range of 192.168.0.0 to 192.168.0.32 for computers connected to the network, you want to choose an IP address like 192.168.0.34 for your console. Every router's configuration program is different, but you typically see a box that reads something like `DHCP Server Start IP Address` (with an IP address next to it) and another box that reads something like `DHCP Server Finish IP Address` with another box containing an IP address. (Some routers may just list the start address, followed by a *count,* which means that the finish address is the last number in the start address plus the count number.)

The key thing to remember is that you only have to come up with the last number in the IP address, the number after the third period in the IP address. The first three (which are usually 192.168.0) don't change. All you need to do to assign this IP address is to pick a number between 1 and 254 that *is not* in the range your router uses for DHCP. (Most routers use the .1 address, so you should use a number between 2 and 254.)

Dealing with port forwarding

After you have your gaming PC or game console assigned an IP address and are connected to the Internet, you may well be ready to start playing games. Our advice: Give it a try and see what happens. Depending on the games you play, any additional steps may not be needed.

The steps we're about to discuss shouldn't be required for a game console. And, although we haven't checked out every single game out there, we haven't run into any incidences where you need to get involved with the port forwarding that we're about to discuss with a game console. After you get your console assigned an IP address and connected to the Internet, you should be ready to start playing. If you have an older router that doesn't work well with console games, you may consider putting your console on the router's DMZ, as we discuss in the upcoming section "Setting Up a Demilitarized Zone (DMZ)."

If, however, your games don't work, you may need to get involved in configuring the firewall and Network Address Translation (NAT). As we discuss in Chapters 5 and 9, home network routers use a system called NAT to connect multiple devices to a single Internet connection. What NAT does, basically, is translate between public Internet IP addresses and internal IP addresses on your home's network. When a computer or other device is connected to your home network (wirelessly or even a wired network), the router assigns it an internal IP address. Similarly, when your router connects to the Internet, it's assigned its own public IP address: that is, its own identifying location on the Internet. Traffic flowing to and from your house uses this public IP address to find its way. After the traffic (which can be gaming data, an e-mail, a Web page — whatever) gets to the router, the NAT function of the router figures out to which PC (or other device) in the house to send that data.

One important feature of NAT is that it provides firewall functionality for your network. NAT knows which computer to send data to on your network because that computer has typically sent a request over the Internet for that bit of data. For example, when a computer requests a Web page, your NAT router knows which computer made the request so that when the Web page is downloaded, it gets sent to the right PC. If no device on the network has made a request — meaning that an unrequested bit of data shows up at your public IP address — NAT doesn't know where to send it. This process provides a security firewall function for your network because it keeps this unrequested data (which could be some sort of security risk) off your network.

NAT is a cool thing because it lets multiple computers share a single public IP address and Internet connection and helps keep the bad guys off your network. NAT can, however, cause problems with some applications that may require this unrequested data to work properly. For example, if you have a Web server on your network, you would rightly expect that people would try to download and view Web pages without your PC sending them any kind of initial request. After all, your Web server isn't clairvoyant. (At least ours isn't!)

Gaming can also be an application that relies on unrequested connections to work properly. For example, you may want to host a game with your friends on your PC, which means that their PCs will try to get through your router and connect directly with your PC. Even if you're not hosting the game, some games send chunks of unrequested data to your computer as part of the game play. Other applications that may do this include things such as audio- and videoconferencing programs (such as Windows Messenger) and remote control programs (such as pcAnywhere).

To get these games (or other programs) to work properly over your wireless home network and through your router, you need to get into your router's configuration program and punch some holes in your firewall by setting up NAT port forwarding.

Of the many routers out there, they don't all call this process *port forwarding*. Read your manual. (Really, we mean it. Read the darn thing. We know it's boring, but it can be your friend.) Look for terms like *special applications support* or *virtual servers*.

Port forwarding effectively opens a hole in your firewall that not only allows legitimate game or other application data through but may also let the bad guys in. Set up port forwarding only when you have to and keep an eye on the logs. (Your router should keep a log of whom it lets in — check the manual to see how to find and read this log.) We also recommend that you consider using personal firewall software on your networked PCs (we like ZoneAlarm, www.zonelabs.com) and that you keep your antivirus software up to date.

Some routers let you set up *application-triggered* port forwarding (sometimes just called *port triggering*), which basically allows your router to look for certain signals coming from an application on your computer (the triggers) and then enable port forwarding. This option is more secure, if it's available to you, because when the program that requires port forwarding (your game, in this case) isn't running, your ports are closed. They open only when the game (or other application) requires them to be opened.

When you set up port forwarding on your router, you're selecting specific ports (ports are subsegments of an IP address — a computer with a specific IP address uses different numbered ports to connect different applications to the network) and sending all incoming requests using those ports to a specific computer or device on your network. When you get involved in setting up port forwarding, you notice two kinds of ports: TCP (Transmission Control Protocol) and UDP (User Datagram Protocol). These names relate to the two primary ways by which data is carried on the Internet, and you may have to set up port forwarding for both TCP and UDP ports, depending on the application.

Every router or access point will have its own unique system for configuring port forwarding. Generally speaking, you find the port forwarding section of the configuration program and simply type into a text box on the screen the port numbers you want to open. For example, Figure 12-3 shows port forwarding being configured on a NETGEAR WPN824 router/access point.

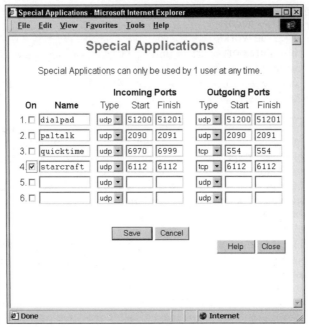

Figure 12-3:
Setting
up port
forwarding.

As we mention earlier in this chapter, ports are assigned specific numbers. To get some gaming applications to work properly, you need to open (assign) port forwarding for a pretty big range of port numbers. The best way to find out which ports need to be opened is to read the manual or search the Web page of the game software vendor. You can also find a relatively comprehensive list online at `practicallynetworked.com/sharing/app_port_list.htm`.

If your router is UPnP-enabled (Universal Plug and Play, a system developed by Microsoft and others, that — among other things — automatically configures port forwarding for you) and the PC game you're using uses Microsoft DirectX gaming, the router and the game should be able to talk to each other and automatically set up the appropriate port forwarding. Just make sure that you enable UPnP in your router's configuration system. It's usually a check box in the router's configuration program.

Setting Up a Demilitarized Zone (DMZ)

If you need to do some special port forwarding and router tweaking to get your games working, you may find that you're spending entirely too much time getting it all up and running. Or, you may find that you open what *should* be the right ports — according to the game developer — and that things still just don't seem to be working correctly. It happens; not all routers are equally good at implementing port forwarding.

Here's another approach you can take: set up a *demilitarized zone* (DMZ). This term has been appropriated from the military (think the North and South Korean borders) by way of the business networking world, where DMZs are used for devices such as Web servers within corporate networks. In a home network, a DMZ is a virtual portion of your network that's completely outside your firewall. In other words, a computer or device connected to your DMZ accepts all incoming connections — your NAT router forwards all incoming connections (on any port) to the computer connected to the DMZ. You don't need to configure special ports for specific games because everything is forwarded to the computer or device you have placed "on the DMZ."

Most home routers we know of set up a DMZ for only one of your networked devices, so this approach may not work for you if you have two gaming PCs connected to the Internet. However, for most people, a DMZ does the trick.

Although setting up a DMZ is perhaps easier to do than configuring port forwarding, it comes with bigger security risks. If you set up port forwarding, you lessen the security of the computer that the ports are being forwarded to — but if you put that computer on the DMZ, you've basically removed all the firewall features of your router from that computer. Be judicious when using a DMZ. If you have a computer dedicated only to gaming, a game console, or a kid's computer that doesn't have any important personal files configured to be on your DMZ, you're probably okay — but you run a risk that even that computer can be used to attack the others on your network. DMZs are perfectly safe for a console, but should be used for PCs and Macs only if you can't make port forwarding work.

Depending on the individual router configuration program that comes with your preferred brand of router, setting up a DMZ is typically quite simple. Figure 12-4 shows a DMZ being set up on a Siemens SpeedStream router/ access point. It's a dead-simple process. In most cases, you need only to mark a check box in the router configuration program to turn on the DMZ and then use a pull-down menu to select the computer you want on the DMZ.

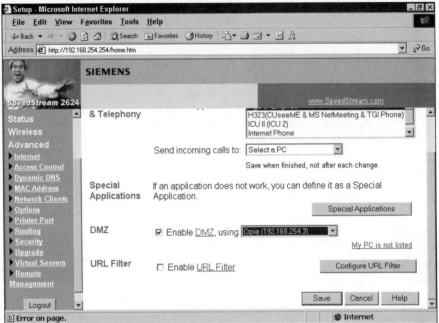

Figure 12-4:
Setting up
a DMZ.

Chapter 13

Networking Your Entertainment Center

*W*ithout doubt, the most significant news in wireless home networking — outside of the general price drops that are driving growth in the industry — is the movement of the 802.11-based networking outside of the realm of computers and into the realm of entertainment.

The linkage of the two environments yields the best of both possible worlds. You can use your hard drive on your PC to store audio and video tracks for playback on your TV and through your stereo. You can stream movies from the Internet and play them on your TV. You can take pictures with your digital camera, load them on your PC, and view them on your TV. You get the picture (oops, pun).

You will simply not believe how much the ability to link the home entertainment center with the PC will affect your computing and entertainment experience. It could affect which PC you buy. For example, Microsoft has teamed up with leading hardware manufacturers, such as Hewlett-Packard (HP) and Gateway to offer Windows XP *Media Center Edition* PCs, designed to power your home entertainment system (it's too irresistible). It could affect how you rent movies: Why go all the way to Blockbuster when you can just download a movie over the Internet from Movielink (www.movielink.com) with a single click? It could even affect how you watch your favorite shows because with PC-based personal video recorders (PVRs), you can record the shows you want to watch — but always miss because you could never figure out how to record on the VCR. Whew. That's *some* change.

In this chapter, we expose you to some of the ways wireless home networking is enabling this revolution toward a linked TV/PC world. You will find that much of what we talk about throughout this book serves as the perfect foundation for linking PCs and audio/video systems.

You may be thinking, "Whoa, wait a minute, I thought wireless was just for data. Are you telling me that I need to move my PC to my living room and put it next to my TV?" Rest assured: We're not suggesting that, although you may find yourself putting a PC near your TV sometime soon. You could indeed put your PC next to your TV, link it with a video cable, and run your Internet interconnection to the living room. But, if that's your only PC and your spouse wants to watch the latest basketball game, you may find it hard to do your work!

The revolution we're talking about — and are just getting started with in this chapter and the ones that follow — is the whole-home wireless revolution, where that powerful data network you install for your PCs to talk to one another and the Internet can also talk to lots of other things in your home. You hear us talk a great deal about your *whole-home audio network* or a *whole-home video network*. That's our code for "you can hear (view) it throughout the house." You built that wireless network (in Part III), and now other devices will come and use it. And coming they are, indeed — by the boxful. Be prepared to hear about all these great devices — things you use every day, such as your stereo, refrigerator, and car — that want to hop onboard your wireless home highway.

Wirelessly Enabling Your Home Entertainment System

If you're like most of us, your home entertainment system probably consists of a TV, a stereo receiver, some components (like a record player, tape deck, or CD/DVD player), and a few speakers. For most parties, this setup is enough to make for a memorable evening!

And, if you're like most of us, you have a jumble of wires linking all this audio/visual (A/V) gear together. The mere thought of adding more wiring to the system — especially to link, for example, your receiver to your computer to play some MP3s — is a bit much.

We have some good news for you. Regardless of whether you have a $250 television set or a $25,000 home theater, you can wirelessly enable almost any type of A/V gear you have. Before we get into the specific options now on the market, we need to discuss at a high level the wireless bandwidth requirements for the two major applications for your entertainment system: audio and video. Talking in general terms about this topic is okay because the differences among the bandwidth options are fairly great (so applications fall into clear camps), and we believe that 802.11a and g access points (APs) have more than enough bandwidth to handle most of your audio and (to a lesser degree) video needs.

Here are the two predominant ways that audio and video files are handled with your entertainment/PC combo:

- ✔ **Streaming:** The file is played on your PC and sent via a continuous signal to your stereo for live playback.

- ✔ **File transfer:** The file is sent from your PC to your stereo system componentry, where it's stored for later playback.

These two applications are very different. The big issue here is where the file is played from. If it's played on the PC, for example, it's streamed to the stereo for speaker amplification. If it's played on a source stereo system component, you just need to transfer the file. The wireless requirements are quite different.

With file transfer, lots of transmissions take place in the background. For example, many audio programs allow for automatic synchronization between file repositories, which can be scheduled during off hours to minimize the impact on your network traffic when you're using your home network. And, in these cases, you're not as concerned with how long it takes as you would be if you were watching or listening to it live while it plays.

However, a streaming application is very sensitive to network delays and lost data packets. You tend to notice a bad picture pretty quickly. Also, with a file

Getting to the (access) point

Your wireless signal degrades the farther you get from your access point, regardless of which protocol you're using. Thus, you may have a great signal near your AP, a pretty good signal 30–50 feet away, and an increasingly poor signal as you get farther and farther away. The quality of signal isn't measured just in speed but also in the strength of the signal so that the data packets — whether they're carrying voice, data, video, audio, or whatever — are received and understood the first time by the recipient. (Check out Chapters 4 and 5 for more info about choosing an AP and where to place it in your home for best performance.)

There's no good absolute definition of what constitutes a good-quality signal; but for our purposes here, it means that the signal is consistent (not varying up and down) and has at least enough throughput to be able to match the bandwidth of the source signal. So, if you're streaming a 192 Kbps MP3 file, you want to make sure that you have at least that much throughput available on a consistent basis for that streaming file. In most instances, when streaming content from the Internet, your wireless network speeds exceed that of your Internet connection, so your wireless connection probably isn't the cause of the bottleneck.

transfer, any lost data can be retransmitted when its loss was detected. But, with streaming video and audio, you need to get the packets right the first time because most of the transmission protocols don't even allow for retransmission, even if you want to. You just get clipped and delayed sound, which sounds bad.

A good-quality 802.11b signal is fine in most instances for audio or video file transfers and is acceptable for audio streaming. Whether it's okay for *video* streaming depends a great deal on how the video was encoded and how big the file is. The larger the file size for the same amount of running time, the larger the bandwidth that's required to transmit it for steady video performance. As a result, people tend to talk about 802.11g and 802.11a protocols for video simply because a great deal of available bandwidth exists for any problems that may occur when sending the data over the airwaves. Most wireless audio and video gear now available on the market is shipping with 802.11g on board.

In general, here are four generic ways you can wirelessly enable your A/V system, each somewhat dependent on where the source content resides.

If the source content resides in the entertainment center:

✔ **Buy wirelessly functional equipment.** Some gear comes with wireless inboard. For example, the SoundBridge Radio, from Roku Labs (www.rokulabs.com, $400), lets you stream your music library or Internet Radio (it comes with 20 preset Internet radio stations already set up for you), and can act as an AM/FM radio with an alarm clock built in. (That retro Internet thing is happening here.) You just need to provide such wireless A/V equipment with the right service set identifier (SSID) and Wi-Fi Protected Access (WPA) settings (or WEP if it doesn't support WPA), and it's on your wireless home network. (Chapters 6, 7, and 8 cover SSID; Chapter 10 has the scoop on WPA/WEP.)

This arrangement typically gives the equipment access to the Internet and users remote access to the device itself over these Internet connections. (In the next section, we introduce you to some of the ways that current entertainment gear is getting wirelessly enabled.)

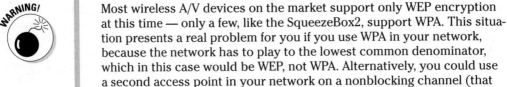

Most wireless A/V devices on the market support only WEP encryption at this time — only a few, like the SqueezeBox2, support WPA. This situation presents a real problem for you if you use WPA in your network, because the network has to play to the lowest common denominator, which in this case would be WEP, not WPA. Alternatively, you could use a second access point in your network on a nonblocking channel (that is, you can use Channel 6 for your main AP and Channel 1 or 11 for the new AP) that is applicable just to your music and other WEP devices.

✔ **Buy a wireless adapter or bridge.** Some A/V equipment is _network enabled_ (it has some basic network interface capability, such as an Ethernet or a Universal Serial Bus [USB] port) but lacks wireless functionality. In these instances, you can buy a wireless adapter to interface with that port to get the device on the home network. It typically has an RCA jack on one end of the wireless connection and an Ethernet connection on the other. A wireless bridge is a perfect way to get it online. Gaming equipment, which we cover in detail in Chapter 12, commonly has an Ethernet port but no wireless capability; wireless bridges are perfect to allow multiplayer gaming over the Internet. Later in this chapter, we talk about the range of wireless adapters and bridges available for the home user.

If the source content resides in the personal computing center:

✔ **Buy a wireless media player.** Some A/V gear is complemented by a media player whose main goal is to coordinate the flow of audio, video, and other data between the PC/Internet environment and the entertainment system. A good example is the $199 SqueezeBox2 (www.slimdevices.com) — a wireless, digital audio receiver that enables you to stream audio from your PC or the Internet (through your broadband connection) directly to your home stereo (see Figure 13-1). We introduce you to some of the leading media players on the market in a few moments.

Figure 13-1: The Squeeze-Box2 digital audio music adapter is one of our favorites.

✔ **Buy a wireless media server.** You may want to move your digital content off the PC and onto a specialized device that can serve up your photos, music, and videos — without affecting your PC's performance every time you want to play something. These are called *media servers*, and we will tell you later in this chapter about some of the best ones available.

✔ **Buy a home theater PC.** A high-powered PC designed to interact with the entertainment center is a perfect complement to your home. Rather than spend money on a new DVD player, why not use that CD/DVD player in your PC? In place of a bunch of home-created CDs, why not just leave them on a high-capacity hard drive on your PC and let the songs play through your stereo whenever you want? We talk about the home theater PC later in this chapter.

Getting at Your Entertainment System-Based Content

Ideally, all your stereo equipment would come with 802.11 chips onboard so that they could just hop onto your wireless *backbone* (a technogeek way of talking about your wireless signal footprint in your home) and get to work. Although we think that's not all that unlikely as technology moves forward, it's not the case now.

Instead, what you find now is that lots of home entertainment accessories are going wireless, like your MP3 players and portable speakers. One of the most major pieces of your home entertainment system going wireless is your TV's set-top box. Typically, to distribute video around the house, you had to wire a home with coaxial cable. The cable companies know that they don't make much (if any) money on that part of the equation, so they would just as soon run a cable into the home gateway set-top box and then use wireless signals from there. Want to watch TV by the pool? No problem — your wireless TV signal can help you out. We expect that satellite, cable, and telephone company video set-top boxes will all sport wireless options fairly soon. Instead of them being hard-wired to your cable box, you can just pick up your TV (outfitted with a compatible wireless adapter) and carry it to the pool. And, with your wireless remote control controlling the set-top box back inside the house, you may think that you're in heaven. (Just keep the TV out of the hot tub, or you may really be in heaven.)

Many competing technologies carry video signals around the house, and Wi-Fi is just one of them. You may possibly also be sending these signals around via your electrical, phone, and coaxial lines; wireless will be in the mix somewhere, we bet, but the jury is still out.

In Chapter 14, we introduce you to the next wave of remote controls — 802.11b-based remotes that control signals in other rooms. Right now, these signals go to infrared (IR) devices that mimic an IR remote control in that room. In the near term, you may see onboard wireless interfaces in the set-top boxes themselves, which will again allow remote control and access to files.

Alas, for now, only a few pieces of audio and video gear have standards-based wireless interfaces. You're starting to see video projectors sport 802.11g interfaces; for example, the Panasonic PT-LB20NTU (www.panasonic.com, $1,400) can communicate continuously and in real time from a PC to the projector through a wireless system via 802.11g or b. The wireless option makes it easy to connect to the video projector from anywhere nearby, without the hassles of cables to trip over. Although this particular projector can double for home or office use, many home theater projectors are moving toward wireless connectivity, too.

Online sites like www.projectorpeople.com let you search for projectors specifically with wireless interfaces. We think that projectors are great for all sorts of entertainment. If you want to know more, check out our *HDTV For Dummies* and *Home Theater For Dummies* books, both published by Wiley Publishing, Inc.

Yamaha (www.yamaha.com) has an 802.11b-enabled audio server called the MusicCAST (see Figure 13-2). This system consists of a couple of pieces. The server, the centerpiece of the system, uses a large computer hard drive and a built-in CD drive to *rip* (convert to MP3) all your CDs and store the music. The server then uses 802.11b to send streaming music files to separate receivers throughout your home. The receivers contain built-in audio amplifiers, so you can plug a set of standard stereo speakers into them. Or, if you have an existing stereo system in the room where the receiver is located, you can plug the receiver directly into that unit and use the speakers you already have. The MusicCAST system isn't cheap: The price of a server and a single receiver is about $2,200, and additional receivers (for other rooms in the house) go for about $600.

Figure 13-2:
The Yamaha
MusicCAST
enables
whole-home
audio
through
wireless.

The Yamaha MusicCAST system isn't as open as other systems we discuss. It only supports MP3 on its system and isn't designed to work with any Internet music services, like Rhapsody.

Expanding Your Home Entertainment Center with Wireless Adapters

Wi-Fi has been slow to enter the innards of the A/V gear unless driven by business applications or companies with a vision to have very open applications. With the pace of change happening, most A/V gear makers don't want to get caught with an obsolete receiver because it has yesterday's wireless standard on board. So, most Wi-Fi-enablement of A/V gear has been through add-on wireless adapters.

Indeed, nothing is worse than having a great piece of entertainment gear that you want to get onto your home network, but the nearest outlet is yards away, and you don't have a cable long enough to plug it in. So, you can imagine Danny's face when he had his brand-new, networking-capable ReQuest,

Inc., AudioReQuest system (www.request.com) with no Ethernet connection near it to plug it into. Argh!

To get this gear on your net, you need a wireless *bridge*. A popular model is the D-Link (www.d-link.com, $80) DWL-G810 Wireless Ethernet Bridge (802.11g) that comes with Wi-Fi Protected Access (WPA) and 128-bit WEP security. On the back is a simple Ethernet port that enables you to bring any networkable device onto your wireless backbone. Another popular product is the Apple Airport Express (www.apple.com, $129), which is a great little multipurpose device that is a media adapter, a travel router, an access point, and a printer server all in one slick white package. Oh, and it can play music purchased at the iTunes store (and it supports WPA).

Other Ethernet bridge products include the Linksys WET-54G Wireless-G Ethernet Bridge (www.linksys.com, $120), the Belkin F5D7330 802.11g Wireless Ethernet Bridge & Game Adapter (www.belkin.com, $110) and the NETGEAR ME101 802.11b Wireless Ethernet Bridge (www.netgear.com, $50).

Here are some tips for buying these devices:

- ✔ **Buy 802.11g, not b, for this application.** You need the bandwidth. Video doesn't work well at 802.11b speeds.

- ✔ **Check out the specs.** Note that some products refer to gaming in their product names. Indeed, you also see lower-cost so-called gaming adapters, like the Linksys WGA54G, which is only $80 from Linksys. These devices also allow for Ethernet-to-wireless connections. Why the $40 discount? The major differences between these bridges and gaming adapters can often be subtle and not worth the extra money. In this case, the WGA54G game adapter is merely a lower-security device — it only supports WEP and is designed to be as hands-free as possible. The WET54G supports both WEP and WPA and can be powered via a *PoE* (powered via the Ethernet cable) connection from the computer or an adapter you place next to the computer. This gives you the option of putting this device a good 100 meters away from its end point. You may or may not care, and the lower-cost item may be fine for your use.

- ✔ **Check out your options.** You may also ask "What's the difference between these and a full access point — the access points are much cheaper." How wise you are, young grasshopper — access points can be had for less than $50. If you can stomach configuring a full access point into bridge mode (not all can be configured this way, so read the specifications clearly) and don't mind the larger device, you get way more for your money in getting an access point.

There are also wireless adapters for non-Ethernet devices. Instead of connecting to an Ethernet port like a normal AP, the device is equipped with audio-video connectors. Creative Labs Sound Blaster Wireless Music (www. creative.com, $200) works with home stereo and stand-alone speakers featuring digital optical (SPDIF) and standard RCA connectors. The remote control features a large LCD screen that lets you view and choose songs and playlists without needing a TV (nice!). Setup is fairly easy. You just install the included software on your computer, hook it up to the Sound Blaster with the included USB cable, follow the setup wizard's instructions, and then disconnect and attach the receiver to a stereo or powered speakers. (See Figure 13-3).

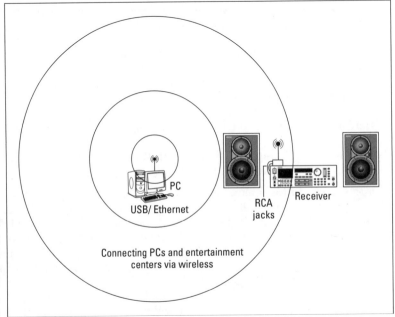

PC

USB/ Ethernet

RCA jacks

Receiver

Connecting PCs and entertainment centers via wireless

Figure 13-3:
Linking a PC
with any
piece of
stereo gear.

If you want to stream video over WiFi, check out the Onkyo WL-TR100 (www.onkyo.com, $765). This system can transmit composite, S-video, and analog audio signals. The base unit plugs into your video source, such as a DVD player or PVR, and the remote unit plugs into your TV. The video is compressed to MPEG-2 for transmission over its 802.11a wireless link.

The *AudioReQuest* — a digital music server; see Figure 13-4 to see how the server sends music throughout the house — is a great example of the type of network-enabled (but not wireless) audio gear you want to get on your home net. Capable of storing as many CDs as you have (you can add additional storage by using their swappable hard drives or getting higher-capacity units), it's the ultimate in CD listening pleasure.

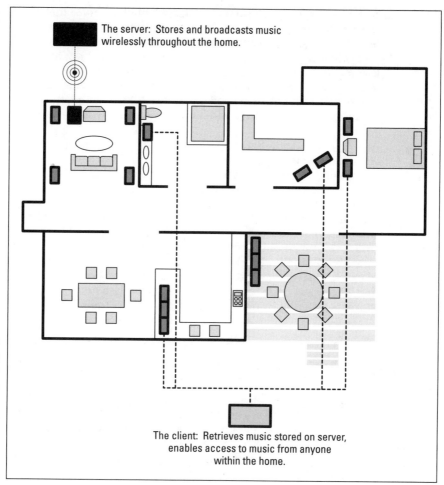

The server: Stores and broadcasts music wirelessly throughout the home.

The client: Retrieves music stored on server, enables access to music from anyone within the home.

Figure 13-4:
Wirelessly
serving up
digital music
around the
house with
Audio-
ReQuest.

With a device like the AudioReQuest TV Navigator Interface, you can use your TV screen as the interface to your music collection. A bright, TV-screen-based user interface enables you to select and play your music, create playlists from albums and artists stored in the system, and enjoy pulsating, music-driven graphics on the TV set's display. That's much better than a two-line liquid crystal display (LCD) screen. And, it's easy to use: Loading (ripping) a new CD into the system is as easy as opening the CD tray and closing it. The AudioReQuest determines whether the CD is already loaded in your system and then looks up the name of the album and artist in its internal database of 650,000 albums; if the system can't find the CD, it checks a master database on the Internet.

The AudioReQuest has an onboard internal Web server that allows access to this music from wherever you want, whether it's in the house or over the Internet. You can also add other units to the system and network them. Danny has one unit in his house in Maine and another in his house in Connecticut, and they stay synchronized. What's more, multiple units enable you to have a backup of your collection in case your hard drive crashes. Danny has even linked/synced his AudioReQuest with his Omnifi car digital media system, too — over wireless computer network connections.

An entry-level AudioReQuest Nitro system costs about $2,500 and scales up from there depending on storage capacity and extra features. This is the box you put in your home if you're serious about music! It's truly the future of music in the entertainment center.

The only problem? No wireless connectivity is built into the system. But because the AudioReQuest has an Ethernet outlet, it's easy to use a wireless bridge to bring it onboard to your wireless home network. Danny's using a D-Link DWL-G810 Wireless Ethernet Bridge (802.11g) to link it into his wireless network. Entertainment devices, such as the Microsoft Xbox (www.xbox.com) and TiVo (www.tivo.com), can also connect to a network with the D-Link Wireless Ethernet Bridge (or similar device) via their built-in Ethernet ports.

Other wireless ways (Where there's a will. . . .)

We are obviously biased toward the 802.11x technologies because we believe in a wireless home network backbone. We think that with all the focus on standards, costs will decrease, new features will evolve, and the overall capability will continue to get better. Collectively, it simply gives you more options for the home.

That doesn't mean that standards are the only way to go. Plenty of proprietary 900 MHz, 2.4 GHz, and 5 GHz approaches — as well as other frequency bands — are popular because they're just cheap to manufacture and cheap to implement. For example, check out the Terk (www.terk.com, $99) Leapfrog Series Wireless A/V System (Model LF-30S, for example), which uses the same 2.4 GHz frequency spectrum as does 802.11b and 802.11g to carry audio and video around the house. The gear we've tested in this space, like the X10 Entertainment Anywhere and various Radio Shack 900MHz models, has been somewhat of a disappointment.

So, 802.11 isn't the only way, but we prefer it based on experience. Just remember: The more signals you put in the 2.4 GHz and 5 GHz ranges to compete with your 802.11 signals, the more problems you have. The 802.11 products are building in new quality-of-service capabilities designed to deal with multiple simultaneous audio and video transmissions, and over time will be more robust, accessible and reliable, we think. Look for the Wi-Fi icon when you buy.

Getting at Your PC-Based Content

A great deal of content is found on your PC or on the Internet — getting that into your entertainment center requires a new intermediary device — *media player* — which has thrust itself onto the scene with a goal of simplifying the PC-to-entertainment system interface. Simply, these boxes give you an easy way to get at information on your PC, for playing or viewing on your TV and stereo system, by giving you an onscreen display, a remote control, and even a wireless keyboard.

Specifically, this device sits between your TV and your PC. And, rather than use your computer display to see what's going on, the media player displays its own user interface on the TV set — much like the AudioReQuest, which we mention earlier in this chapter. Thus, they can make it much simpler to merely play a song (much better than having to boot up a computer, open a program, and scroll around!). It interfaces with your PC via a wireless (or wired) connection.

Roku Labs (www.rokulabs.com) has a great line-up of devices under its SoundBridge product line ($149-$399) that seamlessly marry the content in your PC and the Internet with your stereo system (see Figure 13-5). SoundBridge plays your PC or Mac digital music files anywhere in the house, by connecting your stereo or powered speakers to your computer's digital music library. You can also listen to a variety of Internet Radio stations, without even turning on your computer. It's network-ready with wired Ethernet or Wi-Fi onboard. It supports a range of file formats, including WMA, MP3, AAC, AIFF, and WAV music formats plus Apple iTunes, Windows Media Connect, Windows Media Player 10, and Windows Media DRM 10. It's pretty complete, we think.

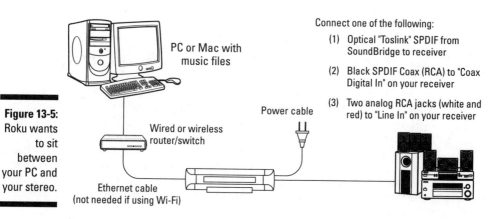

Figure 13-5: Roku wants to sit between your PC and your stereo.

Roku also offers the first digital media player — the PhotoBridge HD ($300) — built from the ground up to support high-definition television (HDTV) — and the results, if you have an HDTV display, yield stunning image quality.

PhotoBridge is probably not the best product name for this product because it can play stored audio and video as well. It supports MP3, AAC*, WAV, and AIFF audio files as well as MPEG2 video files.

What's neat about the Roku PhotoBridge HD is that Roku offers a library of images you can purchase to turn your high-definition TV into a true museum, photo album, or even something quite fishy. That's right, downright fishy. The Roku Aquarium Art Pack ($69) contains a stunning, high-definition, 30-second MPEG video loop on a 64MB Compact Flash card, plus a 3-minute bonus loop on CD-ROM, of a virtual aquarium that looks insanely real. It was created by Roku in 3D using a professional "Hollywood" special effects house.

Other players are getting into the act, too. The D-Link MediaLounge DSM-320 Wireless Media Player (www.dlink.com, $189) extends digital music and photos on your PC to your TV and stereo systems. By using a standard remote control, the receiver enables you to browse through your favorite music and photos and choose what you want to view or listen to without having to go to your PC and use your mouse and keyboard. The D-Link MediaLounge provides access to digital content from a PC on a user's wired Ethernet or wireless 802.11b/g home network. The device has wide support for MP3, WMA and WAV audio files; music playlists, such as M3U and PLS; video formats in MPEG1/2/4, AVI, or XviD format; and photos in JPEG, JPEG2000, TIFF, GIF, BMP, or PNG formats.

The photos section will appeal to those with a digital camera. Digital photography enthusiasts can access images and share their favorite moments with others in picture shows displayed on their TVs in the living spaces of their choice rather than on PC monitors.

My name is Media, and I'll be your server

HTPCs (Home Theater PCs) and Windows XP Media Center Edition PCs are what their names say they are: *PCs*. Look to the horizon for a new generation of computer-like devices that serve up media. A *media server* (creative name, no?) is really just a souped-up version of a stand-alone PVR (think TiVo) or a stand-alone MP3 server (like AudioReQuest). They don't run a PC operating system or do typical PC stuff. They just serve up media, and wireless is a key way, usually by using 802.11a/g technology. You can hook media servers into your PC network *and* into your home theater, by using them to store music, video, digital photographs, and more.

A number of the media servers on the market were designed to sit right next to your stereo system. Most are wired, not wireless. You can add them to your network, however, by using a wireless Ethernet bridge, as we discuss earlier in this chapter, in the section "Expanding Your Home Entertainment Center with Wireless Adapters."

We focus on a leading-edge wireless media server product, the Sonos Music System (www.sonos.com, about $1,100 for a two-room system), as shown in Figure 13-6. This technogeek's dream system consists of a controller (the brains of the system), a "zone" player (the endpoints of the system where all the speaker and system interfaces are housed, as well as a four-port switch so that you can network other items in the vicinity — nice!), and matching speakers you can use if you want everything to match.

Figure 13-6:
The Sonos Music System is advanced stuff!

Most buyers of the Sonos also buy a local *NAS* (Network Attached Storage) hard drive because the Sonos itself doesn't have one — a non-NAS system just plays music found elsewhere, like on your PC. You can also have more than one Sonos zone player; the players talk to each other and the controller in a mesh-like fashion, so if you have a really long house, you can still use the Sonos system. In such instances, the Sonos system synchronizes the music so that it all plays at the same time, avoiding any weird echo-type sounds around the house. Sonos uses 802.11g for its wireless protocol — but doesn't connect to your Wi-Fi access points (it creates its own "mesh" network) hopping from Sonos to Sonos throughout your home.

The ultimate: A home theater PC

When you talk about your home entertainment center, you often talk about *sources:* that is, devices such as tape decks, AM/FM receivers, phono players, CD units, DVD players, and other consumer electronics devices that provide the inputs of the content you listen to and watch through your entertainment system.

When you think about adding your networked PC, or PCs, to your entertainment mix, the PC becomes just another high-quality source device attached to your A/V system — albeit wirelessly. To connect your PC to your entertainment system, you must have some special audio/video cards and corresponding software to enable your PC to "speak stereo." When it's configured like this, you effectively have a *home theater PC* (or *HTPC*, as all the cool kids refer to them). In fact, if you do it right, you can create an HTPC that funnels audio and video into your system at a higher-quality level than many moderately priced, stand-alone source components. HTPC can be that good.

You can either buy an HTPC ready-to-go right off the shelf, or you can build one yourself. Building an HTPC, obviously, isn't something we recommend unless you have a fair amount of knowledge about PCs. If that's the case, have at it. Another obvious point: It's much easier to buy a ready-to-go version of the HTPC off the shelf. You can find out more about HTPCs in *Home Theater For Dummies* (Pat and Danny wrote that one, too) by Wiley. What we include here is the short and sweet version of HTPC.

What you expect from your home theater PC is quite different from what David Bowie might expect from his HTPC. Regardless of your needs, however, a home theater PC should be able to store music and video files, play CDs and DVDs, let you play video games on the big screen, and tune in to online music and video content. Thus, it needs ample hard drive space and the appropriate software (see the following section). Also, your HTPC acts as a PVR (see the nearby sidebar, "Checking out PC PVRs," for the lowdown on PC-based PVRs). In addition, an HTPC can

- ✔ **Store audio (music) files:** Now you can easily play your MP3s anywhere on your wireless network.

- ✔ **Store video clips:** Keeping your digital home video tapes handy is quite the crowd pleaser — you can have your own *America's Funniest Home Videos* show.

- ✔ **Play CDs and DVDs:** The ability to play DVDs is essential in a home theater environment.

- ✔ **Act as a PVR (personal video recorder):** This optional (but almost essential, we think) function uses the HTPC's hard drive to record television shows like a TiVo (www.tivo.com).

✔ **Let you play video games on the big screen:** With the right hardware, PCs are sometimes even better than gaming consoles (which we cover in Chapter 12).

✔ **Tune in to online music and video content:** Grab the good stuff off the Internet (yes, and pay for it) and then enjoy it on the big screen with good audio equipment.

✔ **Provide a high-quality, progressive video signal to your TV video display:** This is behind-the-curtain stuff. Simply, an HTPC uses special hardware to display your PC's video content on a TV. Sure, PCs have built-in video systems, but most are designed to be displayed only on PC monitors, not on TVs. To get the highest possible video quality on your big-screen HDTV, you need a special video card that can produce a high-definition, progressive-scan video signal. (This investment also gives you better performance on your PC's monitor, which is never bad.)

✔ **Decode and send HDTV content to your high-definition TV display:** HTPCs can provide a cheap way to decode over-the-air HDTV signals and send them to your home entertainment center's display. You just need the right hardware (an HDTV-capable video card and a TV tuner card). If you have HDTV, this is a cool optional feature of HTPC.

For example, the HP z555 Digital Entertainment Center (www.hp.com, $2,000) is a full-fledged digital media center PC with onboard 802.11g functionality. From regular and high-definition TV broadcasts to movies, music, games, and digital photos, this baby has it all, and you can wirelessly connect to it. What more could you want?

The term *Media Center PC* is often used generically, but it can mean two different things: a PC configured to be a repository and driver for media applications and a PC that is sold with the Microsoft Windows XP Media Center Edition software on board. This software can only be gotten by buying a new specially configured Media Center PC. Not all Media Center PCs have Windows XP Media Center Edition software on them, so read the fine print.

If you have a Windows XP Media Center PC, you want to link it to other TVs. The Linksys WMCE54AG Dual-Band Wireless A/G Media Center Extender (www.linksys.com; $120) is an 802.11a- or g-based transmitter for extending your Media Center PC around the house. It resides in home entertainment centers, next to the television and stereo. The device looks more like a piece of stereo gear than a wireless device, except for the antenna (see Figure 13-7). Using the included remote control and the user-friendly menus on your TV, you can quickly find digital movies, TV shows, pictures, or music stored on your Windows Media Center PC. You can even chat with friends through Microsoft Windows Messenger while watching movies on the same screen. It's pretty neat, we think.

Figure 13-7:
Linksys
wants the
WMCE54AG
to be your
next piece
of stereo
gear.

Internet Content for Your Media Players and HTPCs

If you're really into this HTPC thing, think about whether setting up an HTPC is really worth the trouble just to play back DVDs (although the quality would be way high). Probably not, huh? "So," you may ask yourself, "what else is in it for me?" What makes an HTPC useful is its ability to provide a portal to all sorts of great Internet-based content — that is, music and video content. A *portal* is simply a one-stop shop for movies, songs, animation clips, and video voice mail. Think of it as a kind of a Yahoo! for your audio and video needs. (In fact, Yahoo!, a portal itself, is trying to position itself to be just that! You can play great music videos from its Web site, at `launch.yahoo.com`.)

You're not getting much Internet content if your HTPC isn't connected to the Internet. And, don't forget that a connection to your high-speed Internet access (digital subscriber line [DSL] or cable modem) is part of the overall equation. (Yup, a regular ol' vanilla dial-up connection works, but — we can't stress this enough — not nearly as well. Pony up the cash and come on into this century.)

Checking out PC PVRs

Using the HTPC's hard drive to record television shows like the way a TiVo does is an optional (but almost essential, we think) function. And, using an HTPC as a PVR is a standard feature in a Windows XP Media Center PC — and something that we think you should consider adding to your home-built HTPC. Even if this were the only thing you wanted to do with your HTPC, it would be worth it. You can simply install a PC PVR kit and skip much of the other stuff (such as the DVD player, decoder, and software).

Tip: Because the biggest limitation to any PVR system is the amount of space on your hard drive for storing video, consider a hard drive upgrade regardless of your other HTPC intentions.

PC PVR kits on the market include the ATI All-In-Wonder 2006 Edition (www.ati.com), SnapStream Beyond TV (www.snapstream.com), and Pinnacle PCTV (www.pinnaclesys.com).

You've undoubtedly read about Hollywood's drive to rid the Internet of peer-to-peer file-sharing programs, to halt the *ripping* (copying) of DVDs from rented DVD discs, and so on. For the rest of us, who have better things to focus on, a slew of great online music stores and services are legal, economical, and easy to use — you just have to try them.

You find three types of online music offerings:

- ✔ Online music stores where you download music, like iTunes.com, to your PC or network-capable device. There are limits to what you can do with these songs after they're downloaded, but generally you can play them anywhere on your network.

- ✔ Online music jukeboxes, where you can play any songs available in their catalogs, like Rhapsody and Yahoo! Music. These are streaming audio songs that you play as often as you like, wherever you want, as long as you have Internet access. For many of these services, if you want to play them *off* your PC, you need a media adapter or player specifically designed for that particular service.

- ✔ A combination of the preceding two items where you can play any you want, and download for an extra fee.

Some of the most popular online music hangouts include

- ✔ Apple iTunes Music Store (www.itunes.com)
- ✔ Real Network's Rhapsody (www.rhapsody.com)

✔ Napster (newly relaunched at www.napster.com)

✔ eMusic (www.emusic.com)

✔ Yahoo! Music (music.yahoo.com)

Some sites require monthly fees to join, typically around $10 per month; others have their business model driven by download fees.

The cellular phone companies are getting into the act too, by turning your cell phone into an audio player of downloaded music. There's even an iTunes phone on the market, from Motorola (the E790 model).

You don't have to pay to get some music from the Internet — lots of Internet radio stations are out there. You can find Internet-only stations (Pat's favorite is Radio Paradise, at www.radioparadise.com) and simulcasts from traditional broadcasters, like National Public Radio, at www.npr.org. To find online radio stations, check out SHOUTcast (www.shoutcast.com), Live365 (www.live365.com), Radio-Locator (www.radio-locator.com), or just do a Web search on Yahoo! or Google.

We're usually complaining about Microsoft being closed and proprietary, but this time we're picking on Apple and its iTunes service. If you download songs from iTunes, they're encoded in protected *AAC* format files, and that means there are few places you can play them. If you use iTunes and want to play those songs elsewhere, you need to really dig to make sure. For example, the Roku Labs SoundBridge Radio, mentioned earlier in this chapter, can play AAC files created by importing your own CDs. However, iTunes Music Store files ("Protected AAC files") aren't supported unless you first save them to a CD and then re-rip them. What a pain. So look to see whether a device specifically supports AAC file formats so that you're not surprised. In fact, look to make sure that any service you have is supported by the device you intend to buy, because if you like Rhapsody (we simply love this "any music, any time, fixed price" approach), you want an adapter that specifically supports this as well, like the NETGEAR adapters.

This copy prevention system (the Apple system is called *FairPlay*) isn't part of *all* AAC files. Similarly, the Microsoft Windows Media DRM (*Digital Rights Management* — the term used to mean copy prevention) isn't part of all WMA Windows Media Files. But, if you get music from an online store, it *will* have some DRM attached to it that restricts how you use it on your network. The only exception here is eMusic, which provides users with unprotected MP3 files with which they can do anything they want (restricted only by laws, not by awkward and restrictive DRM systems).

Chapter 14

Other Cool Things You Can Network

In This Chapter

▶ Cruisin' with wireless onboard

▶ Looking good on *Candid Camera,* 802.11-style

▶ Controlling your home from the couch (or bed or backyard)

▶ Talking to your robo-dog (and having him talk back)

*T*he wireless age is upon us, with all sorts of new devices and capabilities that you can add to your network that save you time and enhance your lifestyle and are simply fun. After you have your wireless local-area network (LAN) in place, which we show you how to do in Parts II and III, you can do a nearly unlimited number of things. It sort of reminds us of the Dr. Seuss book *Oh, the Places You'll Go!*

In this chapter, we introduce you to some of the neater things that are available now for your wireless home network. In Chapter 19, we talk about those things that are coming soon to a network near you! Together, with the gaming and A/V discussion in Chapters 12 and 13, you see why we say that wireless home networking isn't just for computers any more.

In this chapter, we give you an overview of many new products, but we can't really give you much specific information about how to set up these products. In general, you have to provide your service set identifier (SSID) and WPA (or WEP, if your network doesn't support WPA) passphrase, and that should be 95 percent of what you need to do to set up your device for your wireless network. In this chapter and in Chapter 19, we feel that it's important to expose you to the developments happening now so that you can look around and explore different options while you wirelessly enable your home. To say that your whole house will have wireless devices in every room within the next three years is *not* an understatement — it's truly coming on fast (so hold on tight!).

The wireless-enablement of consumer goods is spreading faster than a wildfire. As we write, products are coming out daily. Many products that we mention in this chapter represent some of the early forms of addressing the wireless enablement of some area of your home. If you're interested in seeing what else has popped up since we wrote this book, try searching Google (www.google. com), as well as our book-update site, at www.digitaldummies.com, for the products we mention. The press likes to compare different items in articles, and you're likely to find other new products along with those referenced in this book.

Making a Connection to Your Car

For many people, their cars are something more than mechanisms to get them from Point A to Point B. Some folks spend a considerable amount of time each day commuting — we know people who spend 1.5 hours in the car *each way* in a commute. For others, like those with RVs, their vehicles represent entire vacation homes.

If you think about the things you do in your car — listen to music, talk on the phone, let your kids watch movies — they're not all that different from things you do around the house. Because your home's wireless connection can reach outside your walls and into your driveway or garage, your car can go online with your home network and access data ranging from your address book on your PC to your latest MP3s in your stereo. You can download them to your car, thus simplifying your life and making the car truly a second home. (No more calls home, saying "Honey, can you look on my computer for the number for. . . .?")

Your car's path to wireless enlightenment

Although you may think that wireless is a new topic for your car, in fact, your car has been wirelessly enabled for years. Your car stereo gets wireless AM/FM signals from afar, and with the advent of satellite radio, now even farther than ever. (See the nearby sidebar, "Satellite radio.") Wireless phone options — cellular and Bluetooth-based technologies — are quickly filtering into the car. (We discuss Bluetooth and cars more in Chapter 15.) And then there's the new wave of electronic toll systems that also predominantly use short-range wireless technology to extract from your bank account that quarter (or dollar) every time you cross a toll bridge. Wireless is all over your car — but just not centralized on any sort of wireless backbone, like we talk about for your home.

Your car is also becoming more outfitted for computing and entertainment devices and functionality as manufacturers add as standard and optional features such items as CD and DVD playback systems, global positioning systems (GPSs), and even computers to operate your car.

All this spells "opportunity" for wireless. Bluetooth and 802.11 technologies are infiltrating the car and creating the same wireless backbone as in your home — a universal wireless network that any device or function can access to talk to other parts of the car, like your stereo, and to points outside the car. In fact, your wireless *home* network plays an important part in helping consolidate and integrate your *car's* wireless network within the car and with your home as these two areas converge toward each other.

The response has been a flurry of activity by auto manufacturers and others to network-enable cars with wireless phone, data, video, audio, and control mechanisms that resemble (in many ways) the same efforts going on inside your house by the other consumer goods manufacturers. In fact, you're starting to see whole product lines that include home and car wireless network products.

Satellite radio

Your wireless home isn't always just about 802.11 technologies — other forms of wireless scan enhance your home, and satellite radio is one of them, particularly for your car. If you're like us, you live somewhere where there isn't a whole lot of programming you really want to listen to. Check out satellite radio, which offers a huge number of stations (more than 100 each) beamed to your house or car from a handful of geostationary satellites hovering above the equator. We find a ton more diverse and just plain interesting stuff coming across these space-based airwaves than we now find on our local radio. Satellite radio services, from start-ups such as XM Radio or SIRIUS, require you to (gasp) *pay* for your radio (about $12.95 per month).

Check out the Web sites of the two providers (XM Radio, www.xmradio.com; and SIRIUS, www.sirius.com) to find the programming you prefer. Then, get your hands on a satellite radio tuner. (You can find a bunch of different models listed on each company's Web page.) The majority of these satellite tuners are designed for in-car use (because people tend to listen to the radio most while they're driving), but XM Radio offers some really cool tuners (from Sony and Delco) that can do double duty: You can put these tuners in your car, and when you get home, pull them out and plug them into your A/V receiver or into a portable boombox.

We like the Delphi XM MyFi (www.xmradio.com/myfi/, $299.99) which is an iPod-like portable XM receiver that also can store as much as 5 hours worth of XM content, so you can catch up on those car hack shows you missed! XM Radio has also launched a version of its service that wirelessly transmits weather conditions to a specialized receiver as well, although it's pricey at $99 per month. (For that price, you can get a good PDA with wireless EVDO access from a carrier like Sprint (www.sprint.com) and get all the weather plus Internet access — that's probably a better deal).

Tip: Check out the annual pricing plans where you can save a good deal of money by paying in advance for a whole year. Also, each of these two satellite radio companies offers family plans for multiple receivers, where the price per extra receiver subscription can drop to as low as $6.99 per month — pretty good if you have lots of kids.

Synching your car stereo with home

The major area where 802.11 is just beginning to show up is in third-party add-ons to the car — a typical precursor to manufacturers directly bundling these add-ons into the car (in-car VCRs started the same way). One example is in the A/V arena. We show in Chapter 13 how simple it is to synchronize your audio and video server across the house and over the Internet — why not with your car, too? (See Figure 14-1.)

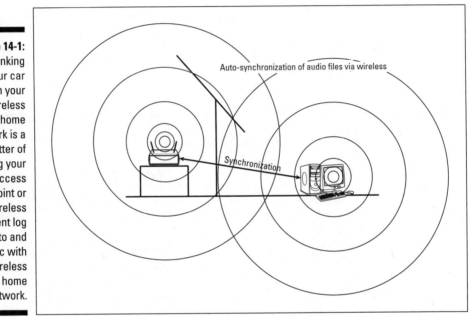

Figure 14-1: Linking your car with your wireless home network is a matter of having your car's access point or wireless client log on to and sync with the wireless home network.

Rockford Fosgate (www.omnifimedia.com) sold until late 2005 an 802.11b-based car product, Omnifi, that enabled you to wirelessly transfer tunes from your home PC to the car, where they can be played on your in-dash stereo. We were sorry to see this product taken off the market — because it's really the only auto-updating automobile-based Wi-Fi wireless system we've seen — but you can still find it on eBay and in various online stores. The Omnifi has an in-dash device that can store as many as 20GB of files; the home component is a stand-alone receiver capable of streaming media dispatched from the PC (see Figure 14-2).

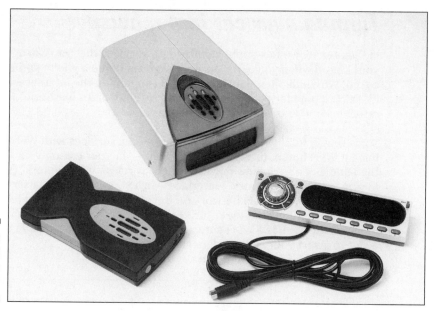

Omnifi eliminates the legwork (the need to burn CDs) to listen to digital music in the car. It gives consumers the ability to download and transfer music and programs from the Internet to the PC hard drive to the consumer's car and home stereo and theater systems — using wireless technologies. You can also subscribe to services like audiobooks, from www.audible.com, so that you can listen to your favorite mystery book while you drive down the road. iTunes work as well. Very cool.

Kenwood has its KHD-CX910 Excelon Music Key (www.kenwoodusa.com, $700), which is a portable hard-disk-based system that enables you to move music and other content from your home to your car — but it's not wireless, and because we're wireless bigots, we mention this solely for completeness when talking about getting your home's music to your car.

Other vendors say that they're entering the marketplace, so expect your car to become a hot zone for wireless technologies soon. Delphi Corp., a well-known brand in car electronics, has been working with Comcast to try to bring some sort of home-car integration to the market. It has demonstrated Wi-Fi enabled devices that sync with cable set-top boxes in your living room, and are working to bring audio and video downloads to the car — but products are not expected before 2007. Other car manufacturers have likewise shown prototypes of various systems, but the Omnifi remains the only product we've seen that's explicitly designed for the home-car linkage — that remains your best bet, if you can find one.

Turning your car into a hotspot

In Chapter 16, we talk about cellular data services that you can access with
your laptop when you're on the go — or from home if you're sitting on the
couch. With unlimited data access, you can hop on the Internet anywhere.
EV-DO is a popular data service offered by companies like Sprint (www.
sprint.com) and Verizon (www.verizon.com).

Some brainy folks thought to marry these data services with Wi-Fi to create
instant Wi-Fi hotspots anywhere you want — in your car, on your boat, or in
the middle of a park. New devices called "wireless WAN routers" (where WAN
means "wide-area network") interfaces with your cellular data service on the
one hand and your Wi-Fi network on the other. One popular model on the
market is from Junxion (www.junxion.com, $599; see Figure 14-3). Its lime-
green metal box has a Wi-Fi antenna for broadcasting your 802.11 signals, and
a slot to insert your cellular data carrier's PC card.

Figure 14-3:
The Junxion
Wireless
WAN Router
is trans-
portable
wherever
you want
to go.

What can you do with a portable wireless router? Just about anything you
want. Stick it in your car and you can have Wi-Fi access for anyone in your
car — and those around you. You can even have a virtual party with the cars
in front of and behind you, linked via Wi-Fi.

An enterprising guy named Mike Outmesguine decided to put one in his backpack so that he could always have a hotspot wherever he went. He and his friends can play multiplayer games while sitting in the middle of a nice park, courtesy of this solar-powered portable contraption. (How's that for trying to be the center of attention wherever you go!)

To build one yourself, you need three major components: a wireless WAN router, such as the Junxion Box; a cellular data PC card, such as the Sprint EVDO PCMCIA card; and a Voltaic Systems solar-charging backpack or case (www.voltaicsystems.com, $200). That and about $35 of additional items from Radio Shack, and you're ready to hit the trail wirelessly. Check out Mike's step-by-step *Popular Science Magazine* article:

```
www.popsci.com/popsci/how20/6a278ca927d05010vgnvcm1000004e
                      ecbccdrcrd.html
```

Wireless WAN routers are brand-new devices and follow a sharply descending price curve, so search Google for **EVDO Router** to see what's available. We expect all the major vendors of wireless gear to have one, but as of the time of this update, most have only announced their intentions to launch products sometime in 2006. We know that D-Link (www.dlink.com) and Kyocera (www.kyocera.com) will be among the first to come out with much lower-cost products, expected to be in the sub-$200 range. Figure 14-4 shows a cool design that someone came up with for a portable wireless WAN router — take your hot spot on the road with you!

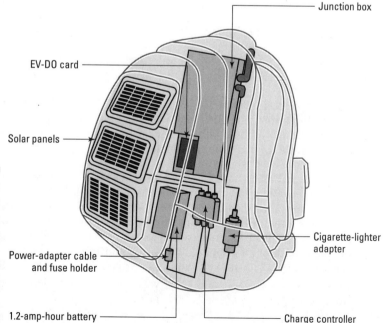

Figure 14-4: A wireless WAN router, a backpack, and solar power — the mobile access point.

Junction box

EV-DO card

Solar panels

Cigarette-lighter adapter

Power-adapter cable and fuse holder

1.2-amp-hour battery

Charge controller

Getting online with your own car PC

Pretty soon, downloading audio or video to the car won't be enough — you will want a full-fledged PC onboard. Luckily for you, some cool, wireless-capable auto PCs are now on the market.

With a PC in your car (I don't recall seeing any of those plastic traffic signs in any car windows saying "PC on Board" — do you?), you can mimic your wireless home network in your car, almost in its entirety. You can sync up with your PC for audio and video to play over your car's radio and video display system. You can play computer games over those same systems. You can access your address books and calendars, just like at your desk. You can even use wireless keyboards.

Colloquially known as a *carputer* — a computer specifically designed to be installed in a car — these small-footprint devices use less power and are better prepared for the rugged car experience. When we say *small,* we mean it: We have seen them no bigger than a paperback book. After you install one, you use a wireless keyboard, touch-screen interface, remote control, and other similar devices to run specific applications on your PC.

Carputers are definitely in the hobbyist stage, in the sense that you install one and then keep adding devices. We've seen setups with Wi-Fi cameras, multiplayer gaming, and other such fun stuff scattered throughout the car.

It starts with the basic unit, however, and you can find a couple of good online sources for basic parts and systems: CarCPU.com (www.carcpu.com) and MP3Car.com (www.mp3car.com). You can get additional accessories to boost your enjoyment of your car PC. A wireless keyboard makes it simple to interface with the PC for text-oriented tasks (as is common with kids' games) and for surfing the Internet. You can wirelessly connect to the Internet while driving by using a cellular data PC Card, like the Sierra Wireless AirCard 750.

So, you can now pull up to a hot spot and log on. (Check out Chapter 16 for more about hot spots.) Or, auto-sync when you enter your garage. It's just a matter of time until you can play games car-to-car with another wirelessly enabled car while driving down the road.

Installing your car PC is both easy and hard. It's easy in the sense that you screw the unit to your car and run power to the unit. It's hard in the sense that other than the wireless connections, any connections to your car stereo or video system may entail running wires, just like with the audio wireless car servers we describe earlier in this chapter. After you have all this in place, though, using a different application is just a matter of installing new software on your car PC. It's just like with your home PC: After you install your printer, your monitors, and all the other parts of your system, the hard work is done. Just install new software to do new things.

We think that every car should have one of these wireless PCs! At least any car that has passengers in it — you don't want to be surfing the Web while you're driving.

If you need to remove your car's stereo system in order to do the install, we highly recommend `www.carstereohelp.com` to find out how to safely and correctly take your dashboard apart — with instructions for each car's make and model.

Picking wireless gear for your car

The integration of external wireless connectivity options to cars is definitely in its infancy. However, some things to look for when shopping for auto-based audio and video gear include the following:

- ✔ **PC Card (PCMCIA) slots:** You get the ultimate in flexibility with PC Card slots because you can put any card you want into the system. You need these for connecting to the home when parked in the yard and accessing the Internet when traveling. Ideally, you would have two PC Card slots because it probably will be a while before many dual-mode Wi-Fi/cellular cards are on the market.

- ✔ **FM modulator:** Some systems have an optional FM modulator that enables you to merely tune into an unused FM band in your area and broadcast your music from the server to your stereo system. Because some audio and video systems require you to have specific receivers (that is, your actual audio component where you listen to the music) for your car to make full use of the new functionality, it can get expensive to install a system. FM modulators make it easy to put in a system without changing out your stereo; you lose some of the onscreen reporting that comes with a hard-wired installation, but you still get access to the music (which is the important part). Many new iPod car players use FM modulation to link to your car.

- ✔ **Upgradeable storage hard-disk space:** Look for systems that allow you to add storage space when you need to. Storage is getting cheaper and coming in smaller form factors all the time. You probably want to keep adding storage space as your audio and video collection increases.

- ✔ **Lots of interfaces:** After your system is installed, you want to plug a number of things into it. Make sure that you have a good supply of Universal Serial Bus (USB), FireWire, Ethernet, PC Card, serial, and RCA

Not to leave motorcyclists out!

The wireless bug is hitting motorcyclists too. Leading motorcycle helmet designers are adding Bluetooth to their products so that motorcyclists can talk on the phone while they ride. MOMO Design (www.momodesign.com, $300) has added the Motorola HS810 Bluetooth package to its helmets, to enable communication with any Bluetooth-enabled phone (not just Motorola phones). If you're a cyclist and love your helmet now, you can get a Bluetooth kit and just add it on — it's not that hard of a project. The Cardo Scala Rider Motorcycle Helmet Bluetooth kit (from many online shops like www.cellular accessory.com, $120) can put Bluetooth in your helmet (in fewer than five minutes, says the manufacturer!).

---

ports. You may have already installed a VHS tape deck or DVD player in your car; if you did, you may be able to easily install an audio or video server right beside it and use available In jacks on the video player to feed your existing screen and audio system.

All in all, expect a wireless LAN in your car soon — it just makes sense.

"Look, Ma, I'm on TV" — Video Monitoring over Wireless LANs

The heightened awareness for security has given rise to a more consumer-friendly grade of video monitoring gear for your wireless network, too — this stuff used to be the exclusive domain of security installers. You can get network-aware 802.11g-supporting videocameras that contain their own integrated Web servers, which eliminate the need to connect a camera directly to your computer. After installation, you can use its assigned Internet Protocol (IP) address on your network to gain access to the camera, view live streaming video, and make necessary changes to camera settings.

Network cameras are much more expensive than cameras you attach to your PC — because they have to have many of the elements of a PC in them to maintain that network connection. Expect to pay from $100 to more than $1,000 for network cameras, with the more expensive versions offering pan-tilt-zoom capabilities as well as extra features like two-way audio and motion detection.

D-Link is the leading vendor that has embraced the video aspects of wireless-based video surveillance. It has a special line of SecuriCam products designed just for surveillance as well as a large number of other wireless and wired network camera products. Its DCS-6620G Wireless G 10x Optical Zoom Internet Camera (www.dlink.com, $999) is on the higher end of the spectrum, but goes to show you how comprehensive these cameras have gotten. This 802.11g camera has motorized pan-tilt-zoom (so that you can look around an area and zoom in), two-way audio support (so that you can hear people and talk to them as well), dual-motion JPEG and MPEG-4 support (so that you can stream video using different bandwidth levels and quality), extreme low light sensitivity (so that you can take pictures in darker instances), and a frame capture rate of up to 30 FPS (see Figure 14-5). You can remotely monitor your camera using a Web-based interface or through the D-Link IP surveillance software. Your cameras can be accessed via the Web, with as many as 10 simultaneous users viewing the live feed. Using the IP surveillance program, you can monitor and manage as many as 16 cameras, set recording schedules, configure motion-detection settings, and change settings to multiple cameras — all from one place.

Figure 14-5:
The D-Link-SecuriCam DCS-6620G and DCS-900W wireless network cameras.

The other end of the pricing spectrum for D-Link is the DCS-900W ($120), which is an 802.11b-based camera offering simple, basic streaming video to the Web. The image is static, depending on where you point and focus it when you install the camera.

D-link has the best selection of wireless cameras — you can probably find the perfect camera for your needs there. D-Link even has a Wireless Internet Camera with 3G compatibility — the live camera feed can be pulled from the 3G cellular network by compatible cell phones with a 3GPP player! Cool.

Go to `www.dlink.com/products/liveDemo/?model=DCS-5300W` for a live demo of the D-Link DCS-5300 camera. See what it's like to pan, tilt, and zoom!

Panasonic is another vendor that has a large lineup of cameras. Its BL-C30A wireless network camera (`www.panasonic.com`; $299) is typical and offers SSID filtering and 64/128-bit WEP encryption to help protect your wireless network from illegal intrusion. (We talk more about SSIDs and WEP in Chapters 6 and 10, if you need to know more.) The BL-C30A allows as many as 20 simultaneous viewers to see as many as 15 frames per second (fps) of live-motion video. Resolution goes up to 640 x 480. Through a Web-based interface, you can perform remote pan and tilt functions and click to eight preset angles.

You can also get cameras from other players, like Linksys (`www.linksys.com`) and Actiontec (`www.actiontec.com`).

Installing a wireless network camera is incredibly simple. These network devices usually sport both an RJ-45 10Base-T wired network interface along with an 802.11b/g air interface. Installing the camera usually involves first connecting the camera to your network via the wired connection and then using the provided software to access your camera's settings. Depending on how complicated the camera is (whether it supports the ability to pan, to e-mail pictures on a regular basis, or to allow external access, for example), you may be asked to set any number of other settings.

To allow anyone from outside your home's LAN to view your camera feed directly (that is, they're not viewing it from a window pane published on your Web page), you need a static WAN IP address. Although you can probably get such an address from your broadband connection provider, it's likely to be pricey. More likely, you will use a Dynamic DNS service (DDNS). A dynamic DNS service allows you to assign a permanent Web address to the camera that is easier to remember than an IP address and is static. Your camera vendor should help you do this as part of the setup process. D-Link, for example, has a list of pre-approved partner DDNS providers that you can select from within the administration interface. So the DCS-5300G automatically updates your DDNS server every time it receives a different IP address. Linksys offers its own optional dynamic DNS provider service, called SoloLink, which is free for the first 90 days and costs $19.95 per year thereafter.

The wireless communication doesn't have to be 802.11b, although we would argue that it makes sense to use standards-based gear whenever you can. Danny likes his X10 FloodCam (www.x10.com; $80), which videotapes all activity around the house, night or day, and sends the images to a VCR or PC. That system uses 2.4 GHz to send the signals, but it's not standardized wireless LAN traffic. We believe that many of these systems will move, over time, to 802.11 or Bluetooth when those chip and licensing costs continue to come down.

Controlling Your Home over Your Wireless LAN

Another area of wireless activity is home control. If you got excited about going from the six remote controls on your TV set to one universal remote control, you ain't seen nothin' yet. (And, if you still have those six remote controls up there, we have some options for you, too.)

The problem with controlling anything remotely is having an agreed-on protocol between the transmitting functionality and the receiving functionality. In the infrared (IR) space, strong agreement and standardization exists for remote controls among all the different manufacturers, so the concept of a universal remote control is possible for IR. (IR remotes are the standard for the majority of home audio and video equipment.) But, in the *radio frequency* (RF) space, there has not been the same rallying around a particular format, thus making it difficult to consolidate control devices except for within the same manufacturer's line. And then you have the issues of controlling non-entertainment devices, such as heating and air conditioning, and security systems. Those have different requirements just from a user interface perspective.

The advent of 802.11b and Bluetooth — as well as touch-screen LCDs and programmable handheld devices — offers the opportunity to change this situation because, at the least, manufacturers can agree on the physical Transport layer of the signal and a common operating system and platform. Now we're starting to see the first moves toward collapsing control over various home functions toward a few form factors and standards. We talk about these topics throughout this section.

Using your cell phone as a remote control

One area that has seen some action is the personal digital assistant (PDA) marketplace. PDAs have a sophisticated operating system (OS), usually the Pocket PC or Palm OS. They have IR, 802.11, and sometimes Bluetooth wireless capabilities. And, they have a programmable onscreen interface, which makes it easy to show different buttons for different devices. These features make PDAs ideal for wireless remote control of any entertainment, computing, or other networked device. You can cue up an MP3 on your computer and play it on your stereo system in your living room. You can find out what's playing on DirecTV tonight by wirelessly accessing TV schedules on the Internet and then turn your DirecTV receiver to the right channel to watch. With the ability to play in both the PC and entertainment (as well as home control) worlds, the PDA can do lots of things, as demonstrated by these products:

 ✔ Universal Electronic's Nevo (www.mynevo.com) has a more onboard remote control operating system solution, initially built into the HP iPAQ Pocket PCs.

 ✔ NetRemote, from Promixis (www.promixis.com, $40), lets you control your music server as well as any other IR or Wi-Fi controllable device from any Pocket PC-driven PDA.

 ✔ The Griffin Technologies Total Remote software loads onto any Pocket PC PDA (www.griffintechnology.com/griffinmobile/totalremote/index.html, $25) and allows you to create virtual remotes for different devices or instances, (like one for your kids to use).

For people who want the flexibility of a big color screen, PDA-based programs allow you to take advantage of the dropping costs of PDAs to get a world-class universal remote. Many PDA manufacturers are looking at making it a standard feature on their systems. Check out your PDA's home page on the manufacturer's site for any information on remote-control software.

The stand-alone PDA is being phased out and replaced by Smartphone — where your cell phone has PDA-like software in addition to the ability to call Grandma. So, most of the PDA ability just mentioned is likewise available for cell phones, like the Treo line of products from Palm. For example, you can try out the NoviiRemote Deluxe (www.novii.com, $35) which lets you create your own customized universal remote control — using your Treo 650 and other cell phones. Now, if your spouse lets you have your cell phone in your bedroom, you can converge your remote and cell phone to one device.

TIP

Total *Harmony* with your wireless entertainment

A great idea demonstrating the power of consolidated remote controls is found in the Harmony Remote controls from Logitech (www.logitech.com/harmony). With their Smart State Technology capabilities, they can interface with your A/V gear through *macros*. Select Watch TV and the remote sequentially goes through all the motions to turn on the TV, turn on the receiver, select the TV mode, turn on the satellite receiver, and anything else that has to be activated to watch the television. What's more, these remotes have onscreen program guides to help you select what you want before you even turn on the TV. That's cool. You should check it out.

Whole-home 802.11-based IR coverage

Other devices — namely, Web tablets and stand-alone touch-screens, are sporting IR interfaces and can become remotes for your whole home, too. (*Whole-home* means that you can use it anywhere that your wireless net reaches for a broad range of devices anywhere in your home; check out Chapter 1 for more details about whole-home.)

One of the really cool wireless-enabled options is *iPronto* (www.pronto. philips.com, street prices as low as $800), which is a Web tablet-like device that enables you to do all sorts of chores. Phillips describes this wireless mobile device as a "dashboard for the digital home" that combines home entertainment, security, and other systems control as well as 802.11b wireless LAN and broadband Internet access. That's a lot to pack in one device.

With iPronto (model TSi6400), you can control your A/V system components, check out program guides, and surf the Web — all while connected wirelessly to your home 802.11b network. Users can easily control devices via the high-resolution, touch-screen LCD, combined with a customizable user interface and exterior hard buttons. The system features a built-in microphone and stereo speakers, which allow users to listen to MP3s from the Internet and to future-proof themselves for applications such as voice recognition and telephony. Way cool.

One really neat capability of iPronto is its ability to link with your home's 802.11b network to communicate with IR-enabled, network-extender devices in other rooms. Suppose that you're in your master bedroom and you're listening to a AudioReQuest Nitro audio music server (www.request.com; $3,000) through your remote wireless speakers, and you want to change the music that's playing. Just grab your iPronto and tap-tap-tap, you can change the song that's playing. Because the Nitro isn't wireless, you would have to go all the way downstairs to point the remote at the Nitro to change stations. That's the whole-home advantage!

In an iPronto model, you could have a network extender in the room that has IR-emitter capability. The iPronto can communicate via 802.11b to the network extender, to give it the proper codes to send to the AudioReQuest via IR, and — voilà! (or wall*a*! as a former employee once wrote in a presentation), you can change stations without leaving your bed. You could have whole-home infrared-capability linked via 802.11. That's really neat.

Whole-home RF-based IR blasters are coming more into vogue at the low end as well. Many low-end devices are point-to-point devices, designed to allow access to the devices in one room — the living room, for example — from another room, such as the kitchen. SmartHome (www.smarthome.com) has a number of these for sale.

See me, feel me, hear me, touch me

Other neat touch panels are ideal for whole-home wireless control. You're probably familiar with touch screens, if you've ever used a kiosk in a mall to find a store or at a hotel to find a restaurant. Touch panels are smaller (typically 6- to 10-inch screens) and are wall mounted or simply lie on a table; you touch the screen to accomplish certain tasks.

Touch panels have become a real centerpiece for expensive home control installations, where touch panels allow you to turn the air conditioning on and off, set the alarm, turn off the lights, select music, change channels on the TV — and the list goes on. These are merely user interfaces into often PC-driven functionality that can control almost anything in your house — even the coffee maker.

Crestron (www.crestron.com) rules the upper end of touch panel options with a whole product line for home control that includes wireless-enabled touch panels. The Crestron color touchpad systems are to die for (or at least to second-mortgage for). We would say, "The only thing these touch panels cannot do is let the dog out on cold nights," but as soon as we said it, someone would retort, "Well, actually, they can."

For example, Crestron has the Isys i/O WiFi, TPMC-10. It's a modified tablet-style PC with a 10-inch screen; This product runs a specially modified version of Windows and communicates using 802.11g. With this device, you can control your home theater and home automation system, turn on lights, and basically control anything in an "automated house." You can also listen to music files and view streaming video directly on the tablet itself!

Crestron is definitely high end: The average Crestron installation tops $50,000. But, if you're installing a home theater, a wireless computing network, a slew of A/V, and home automation on top of that, you probably will talk to Crestron at some point.

An up-and-coming, lower-cost alternative to Crestron is CorAccess (www.coraccess.com), which offers a line of products that are 802.11b/g enabled. Dubbed the CorAccess Companion line of products, these products are a pretty sleek and convenient way to interface with various home automation products, such as the HAI Omni and OnQ HMS home-control software systems that allow you to manage the systems in your home (see Figure 14-6).

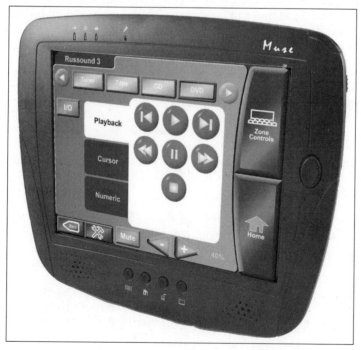

Figure 14-6:
The CorAccess Companion Muse.

CorAccess also has added some nifty applications to boost this from just being a touch panel for controls. Its PhotoMate software turns the Companion into a digital picture frame. When it's not in control mode, it displays a single picture or slideshow; images of the kids, your last vacation, or even updates of news and weather downloaded from the Internet. You can manage your Companion and its photo presentations from CorPhoto (`www.corphoto.com`), which is the CorAccess digital photo exchange site.

The Companion also comes equipped with a full camera monitoring application, where you can view as many cameras as you want, one or four at a time. With just a touch, you can go to full screen, stop on particular cameras, or change the delay time between camera views. Or, you can add camera views available through the Internet to see local traffic, weather, or any other IP-based camera (such as the Panasonic or D-Link cameras that we discuss earlier in this chapter).

The optional AudioMate application, from CorAccess, can be used to play music from your home network or streaming content from the Internet and can even become your home intercom system. An AudioMate intercom isn't limited to just inside the home, however. The CorAccess Voice over IP (VoIP)–based communication system allows Companion to talk to a multitude of other devices — from the Companion in the entryway to a laptop downtown or a PC halfway around the world.

When the Companion is used with the HAI Omni system (`www.homeauto.com`), you add in an automation and security controller. Omni coordinates lighting, heating and air, security, scenes, and messaging based on activity and schedules. Omni comes with several standard modes, such as Day, Night, Away, and Vacation, and can accept customized scenes such as Good Night, Good Morning, or Entertainment that set temperatures, lights, and security to the desired levels — all with just one touch. Security and temperature sensors can be used to adjust lights, appliances, and thermostats; monitor activity; and track events.

So much control, so little time. The CorAccess products come in a wall mount (Companion 8) or Wi-Fi-driven tablet version (Companion Muse). Pricing ranges from about $2,000 to $2,500. An HAI system adds about $1,500 to $3,500 to the mix.

If you're really interested in home automation and linking the various aspects of your home together, try *Smart Homes For Dummies,* from Wiley Publishing, Inc. It's the best book on the topic. (Can you tell that Pat and Danny wrote it?)

Sit, Ubu, Sit . . . Speak!

Your wireless network can help with your pet tricks, too! Although we're not sure that this is what the pet trainer meant when she said that she would teach your dog to speak, speak he can if he's Sony's AIBO robotic dog (www.aibo.com; $1,500 and up). Don't be misled and think of this as a cute expensive toy — this is one incredible robot. If you don't know much about the AIBO, check out its Web site to find out about this robotic puppy. It's neat how Sony has wirelessly enabled its robo-dog with 802.11b.

All you need to do is buy an AIBO wireless LAN 802.11b card and a programming memory stick (assuming that you already have an AIBO), and your pooch roves about, constantly linked to your wireless home network. With AIBO Messenger software, AIBO can read your e-mail and home pages. AIBO tells you when you receive e-mail in your inbox. AIBO reads your e-mail messages to you. ("Hey, Master, you got an e-mail from your girlfriend. She dumped you.") You can send an e-mail to AIBO asking it to take a picture on demand and send it back to you via e-mail. AIBO can read as many as five pre-registered Web sites for you. And, AIBO reminds you of important events.

With AIBO Navigator software, your computer becomes AIBO's remote-control unit. From the cockpit view on your PC, you can experience the world from AIBO's eyes in real-time. (You know, there are just some things that a dog sees that we really would rather not see!)

Through the control graphical user interface (GUI) on your PC, you can move your AIBO anywhere you want. Use a joystick or your keyboard and mouse to move AIBO about. By using the sound transmission feature, you can make AIBO speak instead of you from a remote location. ("Hey, baby, how's about you and me going out for a cup of coffee?")

We're not sure that you're ready to start telling people that your dog has an SSID ("AIBONET"), but this is one good example of robots now using your wireless home highway. Above all, make sure that you turn on WEP and follow the security suggestions we give you in Chapter 10. (Can you imagine taking control of your neighbor's unsecured AIBO — now, *that* could be fun!) You can find out more about setting up an AIBO on your wireless LAN, at http://esupport. sony.com/perl/model-documents.pl?mdl=ERS7M2.

Chapter 15

Using a Bluetooth Network

Most of the time, when people talk about wireless networks, they're talking about wireless local-area networks (LANs). LANs, as the name implies, are *local*, which means that they don't cover a wide area (like a town or a city block). Wide-area networks (WANs), like the Internet, do that bigger job. For the most part, you can think of a LAN as something that's designed to cover your entire house (and maybe surrounding areas, like the back patio).

Another kind of wireless network is being developed and promoted by wireless equipment manufacturers. The *personal-area network* (PAN) is designed to cover just a few yards of space and not a whole house (or office or factory floor or whatever). PANs are typically designed to connect personal devices (cell phones, laptop computers, handheld computers, and personal digital assistants [PDAs]) and also as a technology for connecting peripheral devices to these personal electronics. For example, you could use a wireless PAN technology to connect a mouse and a keyboard to your computer without any cables under the desk for your beagle to trip over.

The difference between LANs and PANs isn't all that clear cut. Some devices may be able to establish network connections by using either LAN or PAN technologies. The bottom-line distinction between LANs and PANs is this: If something connects to a computer by a network cable, its wireless connection is usually a LAN; if it connects by a local cable (like Universal Serial Bus [USB]), its wireless connection is usually a PAN.

In this chapter, we discuss the most prominent wireless PAN technology: Bluetooth, which we introduce in Chapter 3. The *Bluetooth* technology has been in development for years and years. We first wrote about it in our first edition of *Smart Homes For Dummies* (Wiley Publishing, Inc.) in 1999. For a while, it seemed that Bluetooth may end up in the historical dustbin of wireless networking — a great idea that never panned out — but these days Bluetooth seems to be *everywhere*. Watch a few TV cell phone ads and you hear the term — or check out the ads for new Lexus, Toyota, BMW, or Acura cars (these cars have Bluetooth built right in for hands-free cell phone operation).

The most common use of Bluetooth these days is connecting mobile phones to hands-free systems. If you have that Toyota Prius, the hands-free system is built right into the car (using a microphone and the car's audio speakers). You've probably also seen an even more popular example of Bluetooth in action: the cool (well, cool if you're a nerd like us) cordless Bluetooth headsets that let you leave your phone in your pocket while making a call. Now you can finally talk on the cell phone and use both hands to gesticulate!

Discovering Bluetooth Basics

Let's get the biggest question out of the way first: What the heck is up with that name? Well, it has nothing to do with what happens when you chew on your pen a bit too hard during a stressful meeting. Nor does it have anything to do with blueberry pie, blueberry toaster pastries, or any other blue food. Bluetooth — www.bluetooth.com is the Web site for the industry group — is named after Harald Blåtand (Bluetooth), King of Denmark from A.D. 940 to 981, who was responsible for uniting Denmark and Norway. The idea here is that Bluetooth can unite things that were previously un-unitable. (We're a little rusty on our medieval Scandinavian history, so if we're wrong about that, blame our high school history teachers. If you're a Dane or a Norwegian, feel free to e-mail us with the story!)

The big cell phone (and other telecommunications equipment) manufacturer Ericsson was the first company to promote the technology (back in the 1990s, as we mention earlier), and other cell phone companies joined in with Ericsson to come up with an industry de facto standard for the technology. The *Institute of Electrical and Electronics Engineers* (IEEE) — the folks who created the 802.11 standards that we talk about throughout *Wireless Home Networking For Dummies,* 2nd Edition — have since become involved with the technology under the auspices of a committee named *802.15.*

The initial IEEE standard for PANs, 802.15.1, was adapted from the Bluetooth specification and is fully compatible with Bluetooth 1.1, the most common variant of Bluetooth (there are 1.2 and 2.0 versions of the technology, discussed over in Chapter 3 — they're both compatible with Bluetooth 1.1, and add some additional features and performance).

If you're looking for a few facts and figures about Bluetooth, you've come to the right chapter. Here are some of the most important things to remember about Bluetooth:

✔ **Bluetooth operates in the 2.4 GHz frequency spectrum.** It uses the same general chunk of the airwaves as do 802.11b and 802.11g. (This means that interference between the two technologies is indeed a possibility.)

✔ **The Bluetooth specification allows a maximum data connection speed of 723 Kbps.** A few of the most recent Bluetooth 2.0 devices can go three times faster (2.1 Mbps), but these devices are still pretty rare. Compare this with the 54 Mbps of 802.11g. Bluetooth is much slower than wireless LAN technologies.

✔ **Bluetooth uses much lower power levels than do wireless LAN technologies (802.11x).** Thus, Bluetooth devices should have a much smaller impact, power-wise, than 802.11 devices. This is a huge deal for some of the small electronic devices that are being Bluetooth-enabled because it means that Bluetooth will eat up a whole lot less battery life than will 802.11 systems.

Because Bluetooth uses a lower power level than does 802.11, it can't beam its radio waves as far as 802.11 does. Thus, the range of Bluetooth is considerably less than that of a wireless LAN. Theoretically, you can get up to 100 meters (these are called *Class 1* devices), but most Bluetooth systems use less than the maximum allowable power ratings, and you typically see ranges of 30 feet or less with most Bluetooth gear — which means that you can reach across the room (or into the next room), but not all the way across the house.

✔ **Bluetooth uses a peer-to-peer networking model.** This means that you don't have to connect devices back through a central network hub like an access point (AP). Devices can connect directly to each other by using Bluetooth's wireless link. The Bluetooth networking process is highly automated; Bluetooth devices actively seek out other Bluetooth devices to see whether they can connect and share information.

✔ **Bluetooth doesn't require line of sight between any of the connected devices.**

✔ **Bluetooth can also connect multiple devices in a point-to-multipoint fashion.** One *master* device (often a laptop computer or a PDA) can connect with as many as seven slave devices simultaneously in this manner. (*Slave* devices are usually things such as keyboards and printers.)

The really big deal you should take away from this list is that Bluetooth is designed to be a low-power (and low-priced!) technology for portable and mobile devices. Bluetooth (do they call it *Bleutooth* in France?) isn't designed to replace a wireless LAN. It's designed to be cheaply built into devices to allow quick and easy connections.

Some of the PAN applications that Bluetooth has been designed to perform include

- **Cable replacement:** Peripheral devices that use cables today — keyboards, mice, cell phone headsets, and the like — can now (or will soon, in the near future) cut that cord and use Bluetooth links instead.

- **Synchronization:** Many people have important information (such as address books, phone number lists, and calendars) on multiple devices (such as PCs, PDAs, and cell phones), and keeping this information *synchronized* (up-to-date and identical on each device) can be a real pain in the butt. Bluetooth (when combined with synchronization software) allows these devices to wirelessly and automatically talk with each other and keep up to date.

- **Simple file sharing:** If you've ever been at a meeting with a group of technology geeks (we go to these meetings all the time, but then, we're geeks ourselves), you may have noticed these folks pulling out their Windows Mobile and Palm PDAs and doing all sorts of contortions with them. What they're doing is exchanging files (usually electronic business cards) via the built-in infrared (IR) system found on Palms. This system is awkward because you need to have the Palms literally inches apart with the IR sensors lined up. Bluetooth, because it uses radio waves, has a much greater range, which doesn't require that direct IR alignment — and is much faster to boot.

Look for even more cool applications in the future. For example, Bluetooth could be used to connect an electronic wallet (located on your PDA or cell phone — the line between these devices is becoming blurred, so perhaps your PDA/cell phone-combo device — the *Smartphone*) to an electronic kiosk. For example, a soda machine could be Bluetooth enabled, and if you wanted a soda, you wouldn't need to spend ten minutes trying to feed that last, raggedy dollar bill in your wallet into the machine. You would just press a button on your PDA or cell phone, and it would send a buck from your electronic wallet to the machine and dispense your soda. (Pat will have a root beer, thank you very much.)

Another common future application may be customized information for a particular area. Ever go to one of those huge conferences held in places like Las Vegas? The booth numbers tend to go from 0 to 20,000, and the convention floor is about the size of 50 football fields — in other words, it's a real pain in the rear to find your way around. With Bluetooth, you can simply walk by an info kiosk and have a floor map and exhibitor display downloaded to your PDA. We're hoping that this feature is in place next time we go to the Consumer Electronics Show; we hate being late for appointments because we're spending an hour searching for a booth.

Bluetooth Mobile Phones

The first place where Bluetooth technology is really taking off is in the cell phone world. This statement probably shouldn't be a surprise because Ericsson (a huge cell phone maker) was the initial proponent of the technology, and other big (huge, actually) cell phone companies, such as Nokia, are also huge proponents of the technology.

In 2005, just about every new phone being announced (except for the cheap-o ones) includes Bluetooth technology. Sony Ericsson, Nokia, Motorola, Samsung, and Siemens, among others, have all begun selling Bluetooth-enabled phones. The adoption of the technology has been spectacular. A couple of years ago, Bluetooth was a rarity; now, it's just about standard.

You can do many things with Bluetooth in a cell phone, but the five most common applications are

- ✔ **Replace cables:** Many people use headsets with their cell phones. It's much easier to hear with an earpiece in your ear than it is to hold one of today's miniscule cell phones up to your ear — and much more convenient. The wire running up your torso, around your arm, and along the side of your head into your ear is a real pain, though. (Some people go to great lengths to keep from being tangled up in this wire — check out the jackets at www.scottevest.com.) A better solution is to connect your headset wirelessly — using Bluetooth, of course. Literally dozens of Bluetooth headsets are on the market, from specialized headset manufacturers like Plantronics (www.plantronics.com) and Jabra (www.jabra.com) as well as from the cell phone manufacturers themselves.

If you have a Motorola V3 RAZR phone and you like wearing cool sunglasses, check out the RAZRWIRE from Motorola and Oakley. It combines a Bluetooth headset (you don't need a RAZR; it should work with any Bluetooth phone that supports the headset or hands-free profiles — we talk about profiles in the later section "Understanding Pairing and Discovery") built right into (okay, *onto*) the frames of a killer set of Oakley shades. Very cool!

- ✔ **Synchronize phone books:** Lots of us keep a phone book on our PC or PDA — and most of us who do have been utterly frustrated by the difficulty we face when we try to get these phone books onto our cell phones. If you can do it at all (and you often can't), you end up buying some special cable and software and then you still have to manually correct some of the entries. But, with Bluetooth on your cell phone and PC or PDA, the process can be automatic. (In the meanwhile, we've been using SnapSync, from FutureDial, Inc. [www.futuredial.com; $24.95]. This phone synchronization software loads numbers into our phones. It's the first software we've found that does the trick easily and without error. Buy it until you get a Bluetooth phone!)

✔ **Get the pictures off of your camera phone:** Many new cell phones are camera phones with a built-in digital camera. The cell phone companies promote this concept because they can charge customers for multimedia messaging services (MMS) and allow people to send pictures to other cell phone customers. But, if your PC has Bluetooth capabilities, you can use Bluetooth to send the picture you just snapped to your PC's hard drive (or even use Bluetooth to transfer the file directly to a buddy's cell phone when he's within range (for free!).

✔ **Go hands-free in the car:** Face it — driving with a cell phone in your hands isn't a safe thing to do. Using a headset is better, but the best choice (except not using your phone while driving) is to use a completely hands-free system in your car, which uses a microphone and speakers (the speakers from your car audio system). This used to take a costly installation process and meant having someone rip into the wiring and interior of your car. If you bought a new phone, you probably needed to have the old hands-free gear ripped out and a new one installed. No more — Bluetooth cars are here, and they let you use any Bluetooth-enabled cell phone to go hands-free. Just set the phone in the glove box or dashboard cubbyhole and don't touch it again. Keep your hands and eyes on the road!

If your current car isn't outfitted with Bluetooth, don't despair. Dozens of Bluetooth retrofit kits are available on the market — ranging from simple speaker/microphone devices that plug into your 12-volt power source (the lighter, in other words) to custom-installed, fully integrated systems that can even use your car's steering wheel controls.

✔ **Get your laptop on the Internet while on the road:** We think that the best way to connect your laptop to the Internet, when you're out of the house, is to find an 802.11 hot spot (we talk about them in Chapter 16), but sometimes you're just not near a hot spot. Well, worry no more because if you have a cell phone and laptop with Bluetooth, you can use your cell phone as a wireless modem to connect to the Internet. With most cell phone services, you can establish a low-speed, dial-up Internet connection for some basic stuff (like getting e-mail or reading text-heavy Web pages). If your cell phone system (and plan) includes a high-speed option (one of the 2.5 or 3G systems we talk about in Chapter 16), you can get online at speeds rivaling (although not yet equaling) broadband connections like digital subscriber line (DSL) — all without wires!

Some cell phones have Bluetooth capabilities but have been artificially limited by the cell phone companies. For example, some Bluetooth phones have had their software configured by your cell phone company in such a way that you can't use the phone as a modem for your laptop, as described in the preceding bullet. There's not any easy way to know this up front — but it's a good reason to read the reviews in sources like CNET (www.cnet.com) before taking a leap.

The list of Bluetooth-enabled cell phones and accessories is already too long for us to list here. The Bluetooth Web site (listed earlier) maintains an up-to-date listing of all available Bluetooth cell phones and cell phone accessories. We expect that list to go from merely large (today) to huge very soon.

Bluetooth PDAs

In addition to cell phones, the other category of device that's seeing a great deal of action in the Bluetooth arena is the PDA category. In case you're not familiar with the concept, the term *PDA* (personal digital assistant) encompasses a wide range of handheld computing devices — and therefore, PDAs are also often referred to as *handhelds*.

The most common types of PDAs are

- **PDAs that use the Palm operating system (OS):** These are the granddaddies of the PDA space. Palm's original model, the Palm Pilot, basically created the entire multibillion-dollar PDA market back in the 1990s. Palm has since been split into two separate groups: Palm, Inc. (www.palm.com), which makes a line of PDAs; and PalmSource, Inc. (www.palmsource.com), which develops the Palm OS. One reason that the company has been split in two is the fact that a number of other companies also manufacture and sell Palm OS-based PDAs. Speaking very generally (there are a few notable exceptions), Palm OS PDAs are the cheapest and easiest but also the least powerful (in terms of raw computing power) of the PDAs now available.

- **Handhelds that use the Microsoft Windows Mobile operating system:** Windows Mobile handhelds are typically (though not always) a bit more expensive and faster than Palm OS PDAs. The major manufacturers of Windows Mobile systems include Hewlett-Packard (HP; www.hp.com), Toshiba (www.toshiba.com), and Dell (www.dell.com). In many ways, down to the user interface, Windows Mobile models tend to mirror Windows-based desktop and laptop computers in a smaller, shrunken-down form. Windows Mobile handhelds used to be considerably more expensive than Palm handhelds, but because of a price war among the vendors, the price differential has greatly decreased.

- **Smartphones:** As we mention earlier in this chapter, in the section "Discovering Bluetooth Basics," the line between PDAs and cell phones becomes a bit more blurry with each passing day, and in fact *Smartphones,* which combine PDA and cell phone in one device, are taking over the PDA world. Companies such as Palm are building Palm OS devices that are cell phones and PDAs in one (the famous Treo phones), and other companies such as Samsung (www.samsung.com) sell Windows Mobile-based combos. Some cell smartphone devices use entirely different operating systems (such as Symbian, Blackberry, or even the open-source Linux operating system used on many business server computers).

Despite the variation in and among the PDA world, there's also a commonality — PDAs work much better as "connected" devices that can talk to computers and other PDAs. And, because PDAs and cell phones are increasingly *converging*, or taking on the same functionality, any of the applications we discuss in the preceding section may come into play with a PDA.

In particular, the synchronization application we discuss in that section is especially important for PDAs because they tend to be mobile, on-the-road-again (thanks to Willie Nelson) extensions of a user's main PC. Most PDAs now require either a *docking cradle* (a device you physically set the PDA in, which is connected via a cable to the PC), or at least a USB or another cable to synchronize contacts, calendars, and the like with the PC. With Bluetooth, you just need to have your PDA in the same room as the PC, with no physical connection. You can even set up your PDA to automatically synchronize when it's within range of the PC.

Accordingly, we've begun to see Bluetooth functionality built into an increasing number of PDAs. For example, the newest Palm model, the Tungsten E2, includes a built-in Bluetooth system, as does the Dell Windows Mobile OS Axim series of Windows Mobile handhelds.

You can also buy some cool Bluetooth accessories for handhelds. One big issue with handhelds is the process of entering data into them. Most either have a tiny keyboard (a thumb keyboard, really, which is too small for using all your fingers and touch typing) or use a handwriting system, where you use a stylus and write in not-quite-plain English on the screen. Both these systems can work really well if you spend the time required to master them, but neither is optimal, especially if you want to do some serious data entry — like writing a book! In that case, you really need a keyboard. Check out the Freedom Input Bluetooth keyboards (www.freedominput.com). These devices, available for PDAs, Windows Mobile devices, and smart phones, are compact (some even fold up) but give you a nearly full-size typing area for going to town.

If you already own a PDA and it doesn't have Bluetooth built in, what to do? Do you really have to go and replace that six-month-old PDA with a new model? Maybe not. Several manufacturers have begun selling add-on cards for existing PDAs that enable Bluetooth communications. For example, Socket Communications (www.socketcom.com/product/bluetooth.asp) sells SDIO and Compact Flash (CF) Bluetooth cards for Windows Mobile PDAs. Speaking more generally, most PDAs and Smartphones have a slot like this — SD, Compact Flash, or Memory Stick — that is most often used to expand the amount of memory in the PDA but can be used for other purposes. Just like the 802.11 cards in these formats we discuss in Chapter 5, you can now (or will soon be able to) find Bluetooth cards in these formats.

Getting a Bluetooth card installed and set up on your PDA is supereasy. The first thing you may (or may not) have to do is to install some Bluetooth software on your handheld. If this step is required, you simply put the software CD in your PC and follow the onscreen instructions, which guide you through the process of setting up the software. After the software is on your PC, it should be automatically uploaded to your PDA the next time you sync it (using your cable or cradle). After the software is on your PDA, just slide the Bluetooth card into the PDA. The PDA recognizes it and may (or may not — this process is so automated that you may not notice anything happening) guide you through a quick setup wizard-type program. That's it — you're Bluetooth-ed!

After you get Bluetooth hardware and software on your PDA, you're ready to go. By its nature, Bluetooth is constantly on the lookout for other Bluetooth devices. When it finds something else (like your Bluetooth-equipped PC or a Bluetooth printer) that can "talk" Bluetooth, the two devices communicate with each other and let each other know what their capabilities are. If there's a match (like you have a document to print, and there's a printer nearby with Bluetooth), a dialog box pops up on your screen through which you can do your thing. It's usually really easy. In some cases (like syncing mobile phone address books with your PC), you need to finesse some software on one side or the other. We find that this is a good time to consult the owner's manual and the Web sites of the software and hardware companies involved.

Check out the section "Understanding Pairing and Discovery," at the end of this chapter, for more details on making Bluetooth connections.

Other Bluetooth Devices

Cell phone and PDAs aren't the only devices that can use Bluetooth, of course. In fact, the value of Bluetooth would be considerably lessened if they were. It's the *network effect* — the value (to the user) of a networked device that increases exponentially as the number of networked devices increases. To use a common analogy, think about fax machines (if you can remember them — we hardly ever use ours any more). The first guy with a fax machine found it pretty useless, at least until the second person got hers. As more and more folks got faxes, the fax machine became more useful to each one of them because they simply had many more people to send faxes to (or receive them from).

Bluetooth is the same way. Just connecting your PDA to your cell phone is kind of cool, in a geek-chic kinda way, but it doesn't set the world on its ear. But, when you start considering wireless headsets, printers, PCs, keyboards, and even global positioning system (GPS) receivers — if you're a surveyor, check out Trimble's (www.trimble.com) GPS receivers with BlueCap technology — and the value of Bluetooth becomes much clearer.

In this section of the chapter, we discuss some of these other Bluetooth devices.

Printers

We talk about connecting printers to your wireless LAN in Chapter 11, but what if you want to access your printer from all those portable devices that don't have wireless LAN connections built into them? Or, if you haven't got your printer connected to the wireless LAN, what do you do when you want to quickly print a document that's on your laptop? Well, why not use Bluetooth?

You can get Bluetooth onto your printer in two ways:

✔ **Buy a printer with built-in Bluetooth.** This item is relatively rare as we write, but is becoming more widely available. An example comes from HP (www.hp.com), with its DeskJet 450wbt printer ($349 list price). In addition to connecting to laptops, PDAs, and other mobile devices using Bluetooth, this Mac- and Windows-compatible printer can connect to your PCs with a standard USB cable. So, you can connect just about any PC or portable device directly to this printer, with wires or wirelessly.

✔ **Buy a Bluetooth adapter for your existing printer.** Many printer manu-facturers haven't gotten around to building printers with built-in Bluetooth yet, but that doesn't have to stop you. D-Link, for example, offers a Bluetooth printer adapter (the DBT-320) for about $65 that plugs into the USB port and works with most inkjet printers.

What we really expect to see happen in the printer world while the prices for the chips that allow Bluetooth and 802.11 wireless LAN technologies continue to plummet — you read our minds! — is printers that have both 802.11 *and* Bluetooth built into them.

Audio systems

An area where Bluetooth is starting to make some inroads is in the realm of audio systems. This really should come as no surprise, considering that cell phone audio (for example, hands-free and headset systems) is where the vast majority of Bluetooth action occurs.

What we're talking about here is Bluetooth devices that carry higher-quality audio signals — hi-fi (as opposed to Wi-Fi), as it were. Well, this is an exciting new area for the Bluetooth world because Bluetooth is designed for audio and supports relatively high-quality digital audio transmissions.

You may find Bluetooth audio devices in two distinct places:

✔ **Headphones:** Many of us now carry iPods or other portable digital audio players (MP3 players, as they're commonly known) wherever we go. You can identify us by our ubiquitous (at least among the 80 percent or so of MP3 player owners who use iPods) white headphone cords snaking up out of our pockets and into our ears. Well it's time to cut *that* cord too. With systems like the Logitech Wireless Headphones for iPod ($149.99, `www.logitech.com`), you can be up to 30 feet from your iPod while grooving to the White Stripes' latest single. The Logitech system even includes integrated iPod controls so that you can not only listen, but also adjust volume, pause, or even skip back to the beginning of "Blue Orchid."

✔ **Speaker systems:** If you have a stereo or multichannel audio system in your house, you know the Achilles heel of all such systems: those ugly speaker wires running from the back of your receiver or amplifier to the speakers. For home theater systems, this problem is particularly acute because you have speakers in the *back* of the room (we wrote *Home Theater For Dummies* and even we have trouble dealing with that speaker wire run). Well, Bluetooth can come to the rescue. Bluetake (`www.bluetake.com`) sells a system called the Bluetake Hi-PHONO BT460EX, which includes a Bluetooth transceiver (which connects to your audio source like a receiver) and receiver (which receives the Bluetooth audio) and an amplifier that connects to the receiver and hooks up to your speakers with a *short* speaker wire. You can, for less than $175 street price, cut the cord and still enjoy your music. In the future, we think that more manufacturers will include Bluetooth right in their powered speakers, so you don't need a setup quite as elaborate as the Hi-PHONO.

Where are the Bluetooth cameras?

When we first wrote *Wireless Home Networking For Dummies* a few years ago, there was what seemed at the time to be the beginning of a wave of Bluetooth digital cameras and video camcorders hitting the market. (Sony, in particular, had several models, though not too many in the North American market.) It seemed like a good idea: why not cut the cord and transfer your pictures and videos wirelessly?

Unfortunately, it never really panned out, and only a small handful of (not so highly reviewed) Bluetooth cameras are on the market. We think that the reason is that camera image sizes have simply ballooned way past the point where they can be transferred across a Bluetooth link (remember that most Bluetooth connections are less than 800 Kbps at best). We think that most camera and camcorder manufacturers are now considering Wi-Fi or waiting for Ultra Wideband, or UWB (refer to Chapter 3).

Remember, however, that most cell phones these days have decent (not great, but decent) digital cameras built in, and many of these phones also sport Bluetooth connections!

Keyboards and meeses (that's plural for mouse!)

Wireless keyboards and mice have been around for a while (Danny has been swearing by his Logitech wireless mouse for years and years), but they've been a bit clunky. To get them working, you had to buy a pair of radio transceivers to plug into your computer, and then you had to worry about interference between your mouse and other devices in your home. With Bluetooth, things get much easier. If your PC (or PDA, for that matter) has Bluetooth built in, you don't need to buy any special adapters or transceivers. Just put the batteries in your keyboard and mouse and start working. You probably don't even need to install any special software or drivers on your PC to make this work. For example, if you have a Mac, check out the Apple Wireless Keyboard and Mouse (`www.apple.com/keyboard`) — they're very slickly designed (of course they are — they're from Apple!) and go for months on their batteries without any cords.

If your PC isn't already Bluetooth equipped, you may consider buying the Microsoft Wireless Optical Desktop Elite for Bluetooth (`www.microsoft.com/hardware/mouseandkeyboard/productdetails.aspx?pid=033`; about $140). This system includes both a full-function wireless keyboard (one of those cool Microsoft models with a ton of extra buttons for special functions such as audio volume, MP3 fast forward/rewind, and special keys for Microsoft Office programs), a wireless optical mouse (no mouse ball to clean — as an aside, if you haven't used an optical mouse yet, you really need to try one!) with the cool 4-way scrolling feature (you can scroll from side to side as well as up and down!), and a Bluetooth adapter that plugs into one of your PC's USB ports. This adapter turns your PC into a Bluetooth PC. In other words, it can be used with any Bluetooth device, not just with the keyboard and mouse that come in the box with it. This kit is a great way to unwire your mouse and keyboard *and* get a Bluetooth PC, all in one fell swoop.

The Wireless Optical Desktop Elite for Bluetooth is really easy to set up. You just need to plug the receiver into a USB port on the back of your computer and install the keyboard and mouse driver software. (This isn't really even a Bluetooth requirement, but rather, it allows you to use all the special buttons on the keyboard and extra mouse buttons on the mouse.) You do, however, have to have an up-to-date version of Windows XP (which you can update by using the Windows XP built-in software update program) or a Macintosh with OS X version 10.2 or later.

Bluetooth adapters

If your PC doesn't have built-in Bluetooth (and many don't, but a large number of laptops and an increasing number of desktop computers — like most of the Apple product line — do), you need some sort of adapter, just like you need an 802.11 adapter to connect your PC to your wireless LAN. The most common way to get Bluetooth onto your PC is by using a USB adapter (or *dongle*). These compact devices (about the size of your pinkie — unless you're in the NBA, in which case, we say *half* a pinkie) plug directly into a USB port and are self-contained Bluetooth adapters. In other words, they need no external power supply or antenna. Figure 15-1 shows the D-Link DBT-120 USB Bluetooth adapter.

Figure 15-1:
The D-Link
USB
Bluetooth
adapter is
tiny —
about the
size of a
small pack
of gum.

Because Bluetooth is a relatively low-speed connection (remember that the maximum speed is only 732 Kbps in most cases, and a maximum of 2.1 Mbps for the fastest USB devices), USB connections will always be fast enough for Bluetooth. You don't need to worry about having an available Ethernet, PC Card, or other high-speed connection available on your PC.

Because many people have more USB devices than USB ports on their computers, they often use USB *hubs,* which connect to one of the USB ports on the back of the computer and connect multiple USB devices through the hub to that port. When you're using USB devices (such as Bluetooth adapters) that require power from the USB port, you should plug them directly into the PC itself and not into a hub. If you need to use a hub, make sure that it's a *powered* hub (with its own cord running to a wall outlet or power strip). Insufficient power from an unpowered hub is perhaps the most common cause of USB problems.

If you have lots of USB devices, using a USB hub is simple. We've never seen one that even required any special software to be loaded. Just plug the hub (use a standard USB cable — there should be one in the box with the hub) into one of the USB ports on the back of your PC. If it's a powered hub (which we recommend), plug the power cord into your power strip and into the back of the hub (a designated power outlet is there), and you're ready to go! It's easy as can be. Now you can plug any USB device you have (keyboard, mouse, digital camera, printer — you name it) into the hub and away you go.

(Un)plugging into Bluetooth access points

Although most people use Bluetooth to connect to devices in a *peer-to-peer* fashion — connecting two devices directly by using a Bluetooth airlink connection — in some situations you may want to be able to connect Bluetooth devices to your wireless home network itself (or to the Internet through your wireless home network). Enter the Bluetooth access point. Like the wireless access points we discuss throughout this book, Bluetooth access points provide a means of connecting multiple Bluetooth devices to a wired network connection.

Bluetooth APs, like the Belkin Bluetooth Access Point with USB Print Server ($199), have a high-powered Bluetooth radio system (which means that they can reach as far as 100 meters,

although your range is limited by the range of the devices you're connecting to the AP, which is typically much shorter) and connect to your wireless home network with a wired Ethernet connection. The Belkin AP also includes a USB print server, so you can connect any standard USB printer to the AP and share it with both Bluetooth devices and any device connected to your wireless home network (including 802.11 devices — as long as your wireless home network is connected to the same Ethernet network).

Moving forward, we expect to see access points with both 802.11 *and* Bluetooth functionality built in — multipurpose access points that can connect to any wireless device in your home.

Street prices for these USB Bluetooth adapters generally run under $40, and you can find them at most computer stores (both online and the real brick-and-mortar stores down the street). Vendors include companies such as D-Link (www.dlink.com), Belkin (www.belkin.com), and Sony (www.sony.com).

Understanding Pairing and Discovery

A key concept to understand when you're dealing with a Bluetooth device (like a cell phone or cordless headset) is pairing. *Pairing* is simply the process of two Bluetooth-enabled devices exchanging an electronic *handshake* (an electronic "greeting" where they introduce each themselves and their capabilities) and then "deciding," based on their capabilities and your preferences (which you set up within the Bluetooth preferences menu on your device) how to communicate.

A typical Bluetooth cell phone has three key settings you need to configure in order to pair with another Bluetooth device:

 ✔ **Power:** First, you need to make sure that Bluetooth is turned on. Many phones (and other battery-powered devices) have Bluetooth turned off by default, just to lower power consumption and maximize battery life. On your phone's Bluetooth menu, make sure that you have turned the power on.

✔ **Discoverable:** With most Bluetooth devices (such as cell phones or PCs and Macs), you can configure your Bluetooth system to be *discoverable,* which means that the device openly identifies itself to other nearby Bluetooth devices for possible pairings. If you set your device to be discoverable, it can be found — if you turn off this feature, your phone can still make Bluetooth connections, but only to devices with which it has previously paired.

This setting has different names on different phones. On Pat's Motorola phone, it's Find Me — yours may be different.

Some phones and other devices aren't discoverable *all the time*. For example, Pat's RAZR phone becomes discoverable for 60 seconds when you select Find Me.

✔ **Device name:** Most devices have a generic (and somewhat descriptive) name identifying them (like Motorola V3 RAZR). You can modify this name to whatever you want ("Pat's phone," for example) so that you recognize it when you establish a pairing.

One other important Bluetooth concept affects the ability of two Bluetooth devices to "talk" to each other: Bluetooth profiles. A *profile* is simply a standardized *service,* or function, of Bluetooth. There are more than 2 different profiles for Bluetooth devices, such as *HFP* (Hands Free Profile) for hands-free cell phone use, or *FTP* (File Transfer Profile) for sending files (like pictures or electronic business cards) from one device to another.

For two devices to communicate using Bluetooth, they *both* must support a common profile (or profiles). And, for two Bluetooth devices to not only communicate but also do whatever it is that you want to do (like send a picture from your camera to your Mac), they both need to support the profile that supports that function (in this case, the FTP profile).

Making all this happen is, we're sorry to tell you, highly dependent on the particular Bluetooth devices you're using — and more than a thousand Bluetooth devices are available, which means that we can't account for every possibility here. This is one of those times where you should spend a few minutes reading the manual (sorry)! and figuring out exactly which steps your devices require. (We hate having to tell you that, but it's true!)

We don't totally leave you hanging here though. Here are some generic steps you need to take:

1. **Go to the Bluetooth setup or configuration menus of both devices and do the following:**

   a. Turn on the Bluetooth power.

   b. (Optional) Customize your device name to something you recognize.

   c. Make the devices discoverable. Typically, you set up one device to be discoverable and the other to "look" for discoverable devices. For example, you may press a button on a Bluetooth cordless headset to make it discoverable and invoke a menu setting on your phone to allow it to discover compatible Bluetooth devices.

   One device notifies you with an alert or onscreen menu item that it has discovered the other, and asks whether you want to pair. For example, if you press the button on your headset, your cell phone displays a message asking whether you want to pair.

2. **Confirm that you do by pressing Yes or OK (or whatever positive option *your* device offers).**

3. **Enter the passkey and press Yes or OK.**

   Most Bluetooth devices use a *passkey* (a numeric or alphanumeric code), which allows you to confirm that it is your device that's pairing and not the device belonging to the guy in the trench coat who's hiding behind a newspaper across the coffee shop. You find the passkey for most devices in their manuals (drat! — the dreaded manual pops up again). In some cases (like pairing with a PC or Mac), one device generates and display a passkey, which you then enter into the other device.

   Your devices verify the passkey and pair. That's all you have to do in most cases — you now have a nice wireless Bluetooth connection set up, and you're ready to do whatever it is you want to do with Bluetooth (like talk on your phone hands free!).

After you've paired two devices, they *should* be paired for good. The next time you want to connect them, you should only have to go through Steps 1 and 2 (maybe even just Step 1) and skip the whole passkey thing. Bluetooth devices are supposed to mate for life (like penguins). Sometimes, however, Bluetooth is just a bit funky and things don't work as you had planned. Don't be surprised if you have to repeat all these steps the next time you want to connect. A great deal of work is going on to make Bluetooth more user friendly, and making pairing easier and more consistent is the primary focus.

Chapter 16

Going Wireless Away from Home

*T*hroughout this second edition of *Wireless Home Networking For Dummies,* we focus (no big surprise here) on wireless networks located within your home. But, wireless networks aren't just for the house. For example, many businesses have adopted wireless networking technologies in order to provide network connections for workers roaming throughout offices, conference rooms, and factory floors. Just about every big university has built a campuswide wireless network that enables students, faculty, and staff members to connect to the campus network (and the Internet) from just about every nook and cranny on campus. Entire cities are beginning to go "unwired," by setting up metropolitan Wi-Fi networks that provide free or cheap wireless access to residents, workers, and visitors.

These networks are great and very useful if you happen to work or teach or study at a business or school that has a wireless network. But, you don't need to be in one of these locations to take advantage and get online wirelessly. You can find literally tens of thousands of *hot spots* (places where you can log on to publicly available Wi-Fi networks) across the United States (and the world, for that matter) where you can connect your laptop or handheld computer to the Internet via wireless local-area network (LAN) technologies.

In this chapter, we give you some general background on public hot spots, and we discuss the various types of free and for-pay networks out there. We also talk about tools you can use to find a hot spot when you're out of the house. Finally, we talk in some detail about some of the bigger for-pay hot spot providers out there and how you can get on their networks. The key thing to remember about hot spots — the really cool part — is that they use 802.11 wireless networking equipment. In other words, they use the same kind of equipment you use in your wireless home network, so you can take basically any wireless device in your home (as long as it's portable enough to lug around) and use it to connect to a wireless hot spot.

Discovering Public Hot Spots

A wide variety of people and organizations have begun to provide hot spot services, ranging from individuals who have opened up their wireless home networks to neighbors and strangers to multinational telecommunications service providers who have built nation- or worldwide hot spot networks containing many hundreds of access points. There's an in-between here, too. Perhaps the prototypical hot spot operator is the hip (or wannabe hip) urban cafe with a digital subscriber line (DSL) and an access point (AP) in the corner. In Figure 16-1, you can see a sample configuration of APs in an airport concourse, which is a popular location for hot spots because of travelers' downtime when waiting for flights or delays.

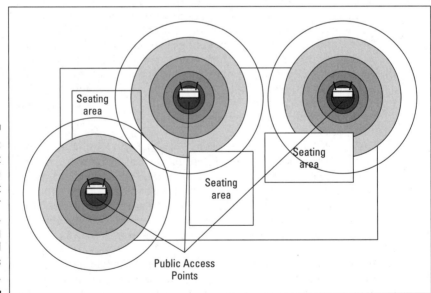

Figure 16-1:
An airport concourse is a perfect location for a hot spot, using several access points.

Seating area

Seating area

Seating area

Public Access Points

Most hot spot operators use the 802.11b standard for their hot spot access points — though some newly installed hot spots are beginning to use 802.11g. Even though 802.11b isn't the latest and greatest, it's the most compatible standard — so that you can, in most cases, connect to the hot spot with your computer. If you use 802.11g equipment in your PC, for example, you can still connect because the equipment is backward compatible with 802.11b. *Note:* If your laptop or handheld computer has an 802.11a-only network adapter in it, you can't connect these hot spot operator's networks. Head to Chapter 2 for a refresher on the 802.11 Wi-Fi standards.

Of the myriad reasons that someone (or some company or organization) may open up a hot spot location, the most common we've seen include

- ✔ **In a spirit of community-mindedness:** Many hot spot operators strongly believe in the concept of a connected Internet community, and they want to do their part by providing a hop-on point for friends, neighbors, and even passers-by to get online.

- ✔ **As a municipal amenity:** Not only individuals want to create a connected community. Many towns, cities, and villages have begun exploring the possibility of building municipality-wide Wi-Fi networks. A cost is associated with this concept, of course, but they see this cost as being less than the benefit the community will receive. For example, many towns are looking at an openly accessible "downtown Wi-Fi network" as a way to attract business (and businesspeople) to downtown areas that have suffered because of businesses moving to the suburbs.

- ✔ **A way to attract customers:** Many cafes and other public gathering spots have installed free-to-use hot spots as a means of getting customers to come in the door and to stay longer. These businesses don't charge for the hot spot usage, but they figure that you will buy more double espressos if you can sit in a comfy chair and surf the Web while you're drinking your coffee — in many cases, the business provides you with free access after you buy something (like that double espresso).

- ✔ **As a business in and of itself:** Most of the larger hot spot providers have made public wireless LAN access their core business. They see (and we agree with them) that hot spot access is a great tool for traveling businesspeople, mobile workers (such as sales folks and field techs), and the like. They've built their businesses based around the assumption that these people (or their companies) will pay for Wi-Fi access mainly because of the benefits that a broadband connection offers them compared with the dial-up modem connections that they've been traditionally forced to use while on the road.

Another group of hot spot operators exists that we like to call the *unwilling* (or *unwitting!*) hot spot operators. These are often regular Joes who have built wireless home networks but haven't activated any of the security measures we discuss in Chapter 10. Their access points have been left wide open, and their neighbors (or people sitting on the park bench across the street) are taking advantage of this open access point to do some free Web surfing. Businesses, too, fall into this category: You would really be shocked at how many businesses have access points that are unsecured — and in many cases that their IT staff doesn't even know about. It's all too common for a department to install its own access point (a *rogue access point*) without telling the IT staff that they've done so.

Going onto one of these not-really-a-hot-spot hot spots with your PC is an iffy legal proposition. On the one hand, if you're sitting somewhere (like your home) and your computer automatically associates itself with someone's unsecured AP, there's no real harm. But, if you actively seek out and get onto someone's unsecured access point that they *haven't* explicitly set up as a hot spot, the jury's still out on that one. Florida has a pending court case where someone has been charged with a felony for doing just that — and it's too soon to tell how it will end.

We tend to divide hot spot operators into two categories: free networks (*freenets*) that let anyone associate with the hot spot and get access without paying; and *for-pay* hot spots that require users to set up an account and pay per use or a monthly (or yearly) fee for access. In this section, we talk a bit about these two types of operators.

Freenets and open access points

Most open access points are just that: individual access points that have been purposely (or mistakenly) left open for others to use. Because this is essentially an ad hoc network created by individuals, without any particular organization behind them, these open hot spots can be hard to find. (***Note:*** This is different from an ad hoc network that doesn't use an access point; refer to Chapter 7.) In some areas, the owners of these hot spots are part of an organized group, which makes these hot spots easier to find. But, in other locations, you need to do some Web research and use some special programs on your laptop or handheld computer to find an open access point.

The more organized groups of open access points — often called *freenets* — can be found in many larger cities. See a listing in Chapter 20 of the Web sites of some of the most prominent of these freenets. A few of the bigger and better-organized ones include

- ✔ **NYCwireless (www.nycwireless.net):** A freenet serving Manhattan, Brooklyn, and other areas of the metro New York City region

- ✔ **Bay Area Wireless Users Group (www.bawug.org):** A freenet in the San Francisco Bay area

- ✔ **AustinWireless (www.austinwireless.net):** Serving the Austin, Texas, region

Many freenets are affiliated with larger, nation- or even worldwide efforts. Two of the most prominent are FreeNetworks.org (www.freenetworks.org) and the Wireless Node Database Project (www.nodedb.com). These organizations run Web sites and provide a means of communications for owners of hot spots and potential users to get together.

These aren't the only sources of information on open hot spots. The folks at Wi-Fi Planet (one of our favorite sources of industry news) run the Web site Wi-FiHotSpotList.com (www.wi-fihotspotlist.com), which lets you search through its huge worldwide database of hot spots. You can search by city, state, or country. Wi-FiHotSpotList.com includes both free and for-pay hot spots, so it's a comprehensive list.

Another great site is JiWire (www.jiwire.com). This site includes a comprehensive listing of free and for-pay hot spots, a Wi-Fi news site that's really great (Wi-Fi Net News), and even special software you can download to help you locate hot spots (that part is free), or to secure your hot spot connections (you have to pay to activate that feature). We talk about this software more in the upcoming section "Tools for Finding Hot Spots."

You have much more luck finding freenets and free public access points in urban areas. The nature of 802.11 technologies is such that most off-the-shelf access points reach a few hundred feet with any kind of throughput. So, when you get out of the city and into the suburbs and rural areas, the chances are that an access point in someone's house won't reach any place you're going to be — unless that house is right next door to a park or other public space. There's just a density issue to overcome. In a city, where numerous access points may be on a single block, you will just have much better luck getting online.

Although these lists are pretty good, none of them is truly comprehensive because many individuals out there who have open hot spots haven't submitted them. If you're looking for a hot spot and haven't found it through one of these (or one of the many, many others online) Web sites, you may try using one of the hot spot-finding programs we discuss in the upcoming section "Tools for Finding Hot Spots."

Opening up to your neighbors

We're not talking about group therapy or wild hot tub parties. Wireless networks can carry through walls, across yards, and potentially around the neighborhood. Although wireless LANs were designed from the start for in-building use, the technology can be used in outdoors settings. For example, most college campuses are now wired with dozens or hundreds of wireless access points so that students, staff members, and professors can access the Internet from just about anywhere on campus. At UC San Diego, for example, freshmen are outfitted with wireless personal digital assistants (PDAs) to schedule classes, send e-mails, and instant messages, and even find their friends at the student center (by using a locator program written by a student). Many folks are adapting this concept when it comes to access in their neighborhood, by setting up community wireless LANs.

Some creators of these community LANs have taken the openness of the Internet to heart and have opened up their access points to any and all takers. There's even an Internet subculture with Web sites and chalk markings on sidewalks identifying these open access points. In other areas, where broadband access is scarce,

neighbors pool money to buy a T1 or other business-class, high-speed Internet line to share it wirelessly.

We think that both these concepts make a great deal of sense, but we have one warning: Many Internet service providers (ISPs) don't like the idea of you sharing your Internet connection without them getting a piece of the action. Beware that you may have to pay for a more expensive commercial ISP line. Before you share your Internet connection, check your ISP's Terms of Service (TOS) or look at the listing of wireless-friendly ISPs on the Electronic Frontier Foundation Web page (www.eff.org). The same is true of DSL and cable modem providers. Your usage agreement with the provider basically says that you won't do this, and ISPs are starting to charge high-use fees to lines that have *extranormal* traffic (that is, those lines that seem like a bunch of people on the broadband line are sharing the connection).

One ISP that not only *allows* you to share your Internet connection by hot spot but also *encourages it* is Speakeasy (www.speakeasy.net).

Some of the hot spots you find by using these tools, or some of the online Web pages that collect the reports of people using these tools, are indeed open, albeit unintentionally. As we discuss in Chapter 10, a whole wireless LAN subculture is out there — the *wardrivers* — who recreationally find open access points that should be closed. (Check out www.wifimaps.com for some results of their handiwork.) We don't get involved in a discussion of the morality or ethics of using these access points to get yourself online. We would say, however, that some people think that locating and using an open access point is a bad thing, akin to stealing. So, if you're going to hop on someone's access point and you don't know for sure that you're meant to do that, you're on your own.

For-pay services

Freenets are cool. And, although we think that freenets are an awesome concept, if you have an essential business document to e-mail or a PowerPoint presentation that you absolutely have to download from the company server before you get to your meeting, you may not want to rely solely on the generosity of strangers. You may even be willing to pay to get a good, reliable, secure connection to the Internet for these business (or important personal) purposes.

Trust us: Someone out there is thinking about how he can help you with that need. In fact, a bunch of companies are focusing on exactly that business. It's the nature of capitalism, right? You have a need that you're willing to part with some hard-earned cash to have requited. And some company will come along, fulfill that need and separate you from your money.

The concluding sections of this chapter talk about a few of these companies, but for now, we just talk in generalities. Commercial hot spot providers are mainly focused on the business market, providing access to mobile workers and road-warrior types. Many of these providers also offer relatively inexpensive plans (by using either prepaid calling cards or pay-by-the-use models) that you may use for nonbusiness (your personal) connectivity (at least if you're like us, and you can't go a day without checking your mail or reading DBR — www.dukebasketballreport.com — even when you're on vacation.)

Unless you're living in a city or town right near a hot spot provider, you probably don't pick up a hot spot as your primary ISP, although in some places (often, smaller towns), ISPs are using Wi-Fi as the primary pipe to their customers' homes. You can expect to find for-pay hot spot access in lots of areas outside the home. The most common include

✔ Hotel lobbies and rooms

✔ Coffee shops and Internet cafes

✔ Airport gates and lounges

✔ Office building lobbies

✔ Train stations

✔ Meeting facilities

Basically, anywhere that folks armed with a laptop or a handheld computer may find themselves is a potential for a hot spot operator to build a business.

Pretty soon, you will even be able to plug into a Wi-Fi network on an airplane. Boeing (you know, the folks who make jets) has started a service called Connexion by Boeing. This service started on a single plane (a Lufthansa 747 that makes regular trips between Frankfurt, Germany, and Washington, D.C.) and has grown to incorporate dozens of flights (almost all the international flights). The system connects to a satellite ISP and gives passengers a high-speed connection (up to 1 Mbps) in any seat on the plane (even back in 52D, that awful middle seat by the lavatory!). Here's a cool aside about this system: On the inaugural flight, a reporter wrote and submitted his story entirely online while flying on the plane. To learn more about Connexion, go to `www.connexionbyboeing.com`.

The single biggest issue that has been holding back the hot spot industry so far — keeping it as a huge future trend rather than as a use-it-anywhere-today reality — has been the issue of roaming. As of this writing, no single hot spot operator has anything close to ubiquitous coverage. Instead, dozens of different hot spot operators, of different sizes, operate in competition with each other. As a user, perhaps a salesperson who's traveling across town to several different clients in one day, you may run into hot spots from three or four different hot spot providers — and need accounts from three or four separate providers to get online with each one.

This situation is much different, of course, from the cell phone industry, in which you can pretty much take your phone anywhere and make calls. The cell phone providers have some elaborate roaming arrangements in place that allow them to bill each other (and in the end, bill you, the user) for these calls. Hot spot service providers haven't quite reached this point. However, a couple of trends will help bring about some true hot spot roaming:

✓ **Hot spot aggregators, such as Boingo Wireless, are bringing together thousands of hot spots.** Boingo (founded by Sky Dayton, who also founded the huge ISP EarthLink), doesn't operate any of its own hot spots, but instead has partnered with a huge range of other hot spot operators from little mom-and-pop hot spot operators to big operations, such as Wayport. Boingo provides all the billing and account management for users. Thus, a Boingo customer can go to any Boingo partner's hot spot, log on, and get online. (We talk about both Boingo and Wayport in more detail later in this chapter.)

✓ **Cell phone companies are getting into the hot spot business.** Led by T-Mobile (which has hot spots in almost every Starbucks coffee shop), cell phone companies are beginning to buy into the hot spot concept, by setting up widespread networks of hot spots in their cellular phone territories. Although these networks aren't yet ubiquitous — the coverage isn't anywhere close to that of the cellular phone networks yet — it's getting better by the day.

Besides improving coverage and solving the roaming problem, commercial hot spot providers are beginning to look at solutions that provide a higher grade of access — offering business class hot spot services, in other words. For example, they're exploring special hot spot access points and related gear that can offer different tiers of speeds (you could pay more to get a faster connection) or that can offer secure connections to corporate networks (so that you can safely log on to the office network to get files).

In the following section, we talk about some of the most prominent commercial hot spot providers operating in the United States. We don't spend any time talking about the smaller local hot spot providers out there, although many of them are hooking up with companies like Boingo. We're not down on these smaller providers, but we're aiming for the maximum bang for our writing buck. If you have a local favorite that meets your needs, go for it!

Using T-Mobile Hot Spots

The biggest hot spot provider in the United States — at least in terms of companies that run their own hot spots — is T-Mobile (www.t-mobile.com). T-Mobile has hot spots up and running in more than 5,400 locations, primarily at Starbucks coffee shops throughout the United States. T-Mobile got into the hot spot business when it purchased the assets of a start-up company named Mobilestar, which made the initial deal with Starbucks to provide wireless access in these coffee shops.

T-Mobile has branched out beyond Starbucks and is also offering access in American Airlines Admirals Clubs in a few dozen airports as well as in a handful of other locations. T-Mobile charges $29.99 per month for unlimited national access, if you sign up for a year, and $39.99 monthly if you pay month to month. You can also pay by the day (about $10) or by the hour ($6 per hour).

T-Mobile also offers some corporate accounts (for those forward-thinking companies that encourage their employees to drink quadruple Americanos during working hours — Danny, are you listening?), prepaid account options, and pay-as-you-go plans.

To try out T-Mobile hot spots for free, register on the T-Mobile site, at www.t-mobile.com/hotspot.

T-Mobile, like most hot spot companies, uses your Web browser to log you in and activate your service. You need to set the service set identifier (SSID) in your wireless network adapter's client software to tmobile to get on the network. (Check out Part III of this book for information on how to do that on your laptop or handheld.)

One cool feature of T-Mobile hot spots is that they have begun to support WPA and 802.1X security (refer to Chapter 10) so that you can connect to them and feel safe and secure about your wireless connections.

Using Wayport Hot Spots

Another big commercial hot spot provider is Wayport (www.wayport.com). Wayport has made business travelers its number-one focus: The company has more than 7,000 hot spots around the world. Besides just offering Wi-Fi access, Wayport offers wired Internet access in many hotels and airports. (You see Wayport Laptop Lane kiosks in many airports when you scurry from your security strip search to the gate.)

Wayport, like T-Mobile, offers a range of service plans, ranging from one-time, pay-as-you-go plans using your credit card to prepaid calling card plans. You can sign up as an annual customer for $29.95 per month (if you sign up for a year's worth of service; otherwise, it's $49.95 for a month-to-month plan) to get unlimited access to any of the Wayport Wi-Fi locations nationwide. Wayport also offers corporate plans, so consider bribing your IT manager if you travel often.

Like T-Mobile, Wayport uses your Web browser to authenticate you and collect your billing information. You need to set your SSID to Wayport_Access to get logged on to the access port.

Using Boingo Hot Spots

Boingo (www.boingo.com) made a big splash in 2002 when the company was launched, because it was the first company to bring a solution to the hot spot roaming issue. Boingo doesn't own its own network of hot spots; instead, it has partnered with a number of other hot spot providers (including Wayport, which we discuss in the preceding section). Boingo provides you, the user, with some cool software, and gives you access to all the hot spots of its partners with a single account, a single bill, and not much hassle on your part.

As of this writing, Boingo has more than 20,000 hot spots up and running on its network. Like the other providers, Boingo offers monthly plans ($21.95 for unlimited access) as well as pay-as-you-go plans and corporate accounts. (Keep buttering up your IT manager at work!)

The big difference between Boingo and the other services is that Boingo uses its own software to control and manage the connection process. You download the Boingo software (available for most Windows and Mac computers and also for Pocket PC handhelds) and use the software to sign on to a Boingo hot spot. This arrangement allows Boingo to offer a more consistent user experience when you roam around using its service. Boingo is also taking advantage of this software to offer a Virtual Private Network, or VPN, service for business customers. *VPN* is a secured network connection that can't be intruded on by others. (Refer to Chapter 10 for more information on VPNs.)

If you use a Mac PowerBook or iBook, Boingo can be for you — a Boingo client software download is available on the Boingo Web site for any Mac OS X PC.

We talk a bit more about the Boingo software in the following section because you can use it to sniff out open access points around you, regardless of whether they're Boingo's.

Tools for Finding Hot Spots

When you're on the road looking for a freenet, a community hot spot, or a commercial provider, here are a couple of ways that you can get your laptop or handheld computer to find available networks:

- ✔ **Do your homework:** If you know exactly where you're going to be, you can do some online sleuthing, find available networks, and write down the SSIDs or WPA passphrase or WEP keys (if required) before you get there. We talk about these items in more detail in Chapter 10. Most hot spots don't use WPA or WEP (it's too hard for their customers to figure out), but you can find the SSID on the Web site of the hot spot provider you're planning to use. Just look in the support or how-to-connect section.

- ✔ **Look for a sign:** Providers that push open hot spots usually post some prominent signs and otherwise advertise this service. Most are providing you with Wi-Fi access as a means of getting you in the door as a paying customer, so they find a way to let you know what they're up to.

- ✔ **Rely on your network adapter's client software:** Many network adapter software systems give you a nice pull-down list of available access points. In most cases, this list doesn't really tell you any details about the access points, but you can do the trial-and-error thing to see whether you can get online.

> ✔ **Use a network sniffer program:** These programs work with your network adapter to ferret out the access points near you and provide a bit of information about them. In this section, we describe sniffers from two companies: Netstumbler.com and Boingo. (*Note:* In most cases, *network sniffer programs* are used to record and decode network packets — something the highly paid network analysts at your company may use. In this case, we're referring to programs designed solely for wireless LANs and that sniff out radio waves and identify available networks.)

We find sniffer programs to be quite handy because they're a great way to take a quick survey of our surroundings when we're on the road. For example, Pat (one of the authors of this book) was recently staying at a hotel that belonged to a chain partnered with Wayport, but Wayport hadn't officially started offering service yet — and the hotel staff was clueless. No problem! A quick session using the Network Stumbler software (see the following subsection), and, lo and behold! The Wayport access point in the lobby was up and running, and with a quick flip of the wallet (to pull out his prepaid card), Pat was up and running on high-speed wireless Internet. Take that, dial-up!

Network sniffer programs are also a good way to help you evaluate the security of your own network. In fact, it's the main reason that the developers of Network Stumbler created the program. After you implement some of the security steps we discuss in Chapter 10, you can fire up your favorite sniffer program and see whether you've been successful.

Netstumbler.com

The granddaddy of wireless network sniffer programs is Network Stumbler (www.netstumbler.com), which is a Windows program (it works with Windows 95/98/Me/2000/XP) that connects to the PC Card network adapter in your laptop and lets you survey the airwaves for available Wi-Fi access points. Network Stumbler lists all available access points and gives you relatively detailed information about things such as the SSID and Media Access Control (MAC) address of the AP, whether WEP is enabled, the relative power of the signal, and more. You can even combine Network Stumbler with a global positioning system (GPS) card in your laptop to figure out exactly where you and the access point are located.

Network Stumbler users can upload their surveys to the Netstumbler.com Web page and contribute to a database of available access points that the Netstumbler.com folks maintain. You can see a map at www.netstumbler.com/nation.php, to get an idea of places where people have already used the program. You can submit search queries on this Web page if you want to see other people's survey results.

Network Stumbler doesn't work with every Wi-Fi card. You can find a list of compatible cards on the Netstumbler.com Web site.

Figure 16-2 shows Network Stumbler in action in Pat's house, tracking down his two access points (and one of his neighbor's APs, too!).

Figure 16-2: Net-stumbling Pat's house — lots of access there!

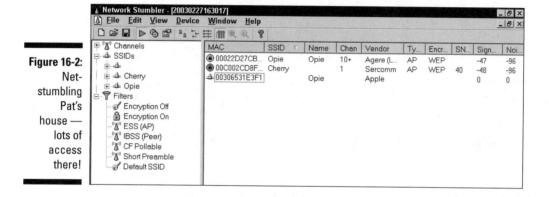

If you use a Pocket PC handheld computer, the folks at Netstumbler.com have a program for you: Mini Stumbler, available at the same Web site (www.netstumbler.com). A similar program is available for Mac OS X computers, called MacStumbler (www.macstumbler.com).

In fact, a growing number of these network sniffer programs are available, and most of them are free to download. You can find a list at the Personal Telco Project, at www.personaltelco.net/index.cgi/WirelessSniffer.

Boingo

The Boingo client software (available at www.boingo.com) can also be used as a network sniffer program (as long as you're using a compatible operating system and network adapter). The primary purpose of this software, of course, is to manage your connections to the Boingo network, but Boingo has also designed the software (and encourages the use of it) as a means of finding and connecting to freenets and other public open networks.

You can even use the Boingo software as a manager for all your Wi-Fi network connections. If you have a wireless network at home, one or more in the office, plus some public networks you want to connect to, try out the Boingo software. It's pretty cool.

Figure 16-3 shows the Boingo software in action.

On the Go with EV-DO!

If you're a wireless power user — and you tend to travel on the main thorough-fares and metro areas — you may be interested in another on-the-road (heck, you can even use it while you're at home!) option for wireless connectivity: *wireless WAN services*. These wireless *wide-area network* services are offered by cellular carriers in more and more places around the United States as they build out their networks for the next generation of audio and video (yes, TV on your phone) services.

Wireless WAN services come in different flavors depending on the technology each carrier is deploying and where each flavor is available. Some of the most common of these connections are

- **1xRTT:** Stands for *single carrier (1x) radio transmission technology*, a 3G (third-generation) wireless technology based on the *CDMA* (code division multiple access, if you must know) platform. (1xRTT is also referred to as *CDMA2000*.) 1xRTT has the capability to provide speeds of as much as 144 Kbps (but usually in the 60Kbps–90Kbps range). Carriers such as Sprint and Verizon offer this service.

- **EV-DO:** Stands for *Evolution Data Only*. This CDMA-based wireless data platform, the fastest wireless WAN technology available on the mass market, is capable of transmitting more than 2 Mbps, but typically more likely in the 400Kbps–700Kbps range. It's offered by Sprint and Verizon.

✔ **GPRS/EDGE:** The competitor to CDMA is a European standard named *Group System for Mobile Communications*, or *GSM,* for short. The high-speed WAN version of GSM is called *GPRS* (*General Packet Radio Service*), offered by Cingular and T-Mobile in the United States. GPRS is often described as "2.5G" — that is, a technology between the second (2G) and third (3G) generations of mobile telephony. Although speeds can theoretically top 170 Kbps, a more likely range is 30Kbps–70Kbps — not that fast. A slightly faster version, called *EDGE*, is rolling out across the United States as well.

✔ **WiMAX:** The up-and-coming wireless WAN technology is called *WiMAX* (*Worldwide Interoperability for Microwave Access*), which some people believe could act as your home's broadband connection too because it can hit speeds of up to 70Mbps! Wow, we can't wait. Look for actual services you can purchase based on WiMAX starting in 2007.

Using these data services is easy. You just plug your PC card into your laptop (just like an 802.11 PC card) and launch your carrier's cellular access program, and you're online, surfing away (refer to Figure 16-3).

Wireless WAN chips are starting to ship within laptops now, in the same way that Intel seeded the growth of the Wi-Fi space with 802.11 capabilities embedded on the motherboard (with its Centrino products). So you can, if you want, order a Dell laptop with Verizon EV-DO on board (Wi-Fi too!) — no hassling with PC cards any more!

The biggest issues for these services are now *cost* (an unlimited plan sets you back $60–$80 per month, and that's on top of whatever you pay for your mobile voice services) and *availability* (mostly in the major metro areas and on interstate highways). Still, if you can get it, it's great. We love our Sprint EV-DO service!

Part V
The Part of Tens

The 5th Wave   By Rich Tennant

"We take network security very seriously here."

In this part . . .

Part V is the one you have been waiting for, right? We have included four top-ten lists here that we hope you will find interesting as well as helpful: ten frequently asked questions about wireless home networking; ten ways to improve the performance of your wireless home network; ten way-cool devices that you will (eventually) connect to your wireless home network; and the top ten sources for more information about wireless networking.

Chapter 17

Ten FAQs about Wireless Home Networks

*W*ireless networks are increasingly easy to set up, configure, and connect to. But they are, unfortunately, far from foolproof and dead simple. Despite some great efforts by vendors and industry organizations to simplify the whole wireless buying, installing, and using experience, things simply can get a bit confusing, even to those in the know.

In this chapter, we look at ten issues we hear the most often when friends and family ask us for help with getting started in the wireless LAN world. We also talked to our helpful friends at several of the most popular vendors of wireless networking equipment and asked them what *they* hear (or what their customer service reps, sales partners, and others close to real-life users hear). Here's what we have put together (we spend the rest of the chapter answering these questions, by the way!):

✔ Which standard is right for me?

✔ Should I invest in Turbo/MIMO/Pre-N?

> ✔ I can connect to the Internet by using an Ethernet cable but not by using my wireless local-area network (LAN). What am I doing wrong?
>
> ✔ How do I get my video games to work on my wireless LAN?
>
> ✔ My videoconferencing application doesn't work. What do I do?
>
> ✔ How do I secure my network from hackers?
>
> ✔ What is firmware, and why might I need to upgrade it?
>
> ✔ Isn't Network Address Translation (NAT) the same as a firewall?
>
> ✔ How can I find out my Internet Protocol (IP) address?
>
> ✔ If everything stops working, what can I do?

If you don't see in this list the particular question you're asking, we recommend that you at least skim through this chapter anyway. You never know: You may find your answer lurking where you least expect it, or you may come across a tidbit of information that may come in handy later. Throughout this chapter, we also steer you to where in the book we further discuss various topics — which may in turn lead you to your answer (or to other tidbits of information that come in handy later). What we're saying is that reading this chapter can only help you. Also check out Chapter 18, where we give you some troubleshooting tips.

If you're new to *Wireless Home Networking For Dummies,* this chapter is a great place to start because you get a good overview to the things many people ask (when they haven't read the manual or this book!), and you can get to some meat (we hope that you're not vegetarian!) of the issues surrounding wireless. Don't feel bad if you feel like you're reading the book backward. (Just don't read it upside down.)

We firmly believe in the power of the Web and of using vendor Web sites for all they're worth. Support is a critical part of this process. When you're deciding on a particular piece of equipment for your home network, take a look at the support area on the vendor site for that device. Look at the frequently asked questions (FAQs) for the device; you may find some of those hidden "gotchas" that you wish you had known about *before* buying the gear.

Q: Which standard is right for me?

As we discuss in Chapters 2 and 4 (among other places), more than one standardized version of Wi-Fi wireless network exists. In fact, multiple variants exist: 802.11b, 802.11g, 802.11a, and, eventually, 802.11n. When you shop for wireless networking equipment, you find that the *vast* majority of wireless gear on the market now is based on the 802.11g standard. That's a good thing because it makes it easier to choose gear — we absolutely recommend that you pick equipment that's compatible with (and Wi-Fi certified for) 802.11g.

The bottom line is that 802.11g is not only a safe recommendation, but also a good one. Although it's far from perfect (the state of the art *always* moves forward), 802.11g provides a combination of range, compatibility, and speed that makes it good enough for most people. If you need *more* speed or range than standard 802.11g systems offer, check out some of the proprietary Turbo and MIMO systems discussed in the next section.

Q: Should I consider buying one of the new Turbo/MIMO/Pre-N systems rather than standard 802.11g?

In Chapter 2, we talk about some of the wide range of enhanced 802.11g products (often called Turbo) and the prestandard (built before the final standard has been ratified) 802.11n systems (usually called MIMO or Pre-N systems).

We have used a large number of these systems and have walked away from just about all of them impressed. The Turbo systems really do increase their speed over plain-Jane 802.11g, and the Pre-N systems do a great job with both speed and range.

If money is no object, we highly recommend that you at least *consider* using one of these systems in your network. We have found that the Pre-N or MIMO access points or routers that use 802.11g and then add the MIMO antenna systems on top of that baseline are a good deal for many folks.

For optimal results with these systems, you need to have Pre-N or MIMO (or Turbo) systems in use on all devices on your network. In other words, you need to have your chosen technology for both your AP and all client devices. But the good news is that many of the Pre-N and MIMO systems we have tested increase range and speed *regardless* of what type of client devices you have connected. This is good news when you're trying to connect devices that have built-in 802.11g client devices, like Centrino laptops or Apple PowerBooks.

What's the downside? In our minds, you have only two areas to worry about. The first is cost. You can expect to pay 50 percent more for the added capabilities of a Pre-N or MIMO system.

Q: I can connect to the Internet by using an Ethernet cable, but not by using my wireless LAN. What am I doing wrong?

You're almost there. The fact that everything works for one configuration and not for another rules out many potentialities. As long as your AP and router are the same device (which is most common), you know that the AP can talk to your Internet gateway (whether it's your cable modem, digital subscriber line [DSL] model, or dial-up routers, for example). You know that because, when you're connected via Ethernet, there's no problem. The problem is then relegated to being between your AP and your client on your PC.

Most of the time, this is a configuration issue dealing with your service set identifier (SSID) and your security configurations with Wi-Fi Protected Access (WPA) or Wired Equivalent Privacy (WEP). Your SSID denotes your service area ID for your LAN, and your WEP controls your encryption keys for your data packets. Without both, you can't decode the signals traveling through the air.

Bring up your wireless configuration program, as we discuss in Chapter 6, and verify again that your SSID is set correctly and your WPA passphrase or WEP key is likewise correct. Try typing the word **any** into the SSID to see whether it finds the AP at that point.

If neither of those issues is the problem, borrow a friend's laptop with a compatible wireless connection to see whether his card can find and sign on to your LAN when empowered with the right SSID and WPA/WEP codes. If it can, you know that it may be your client card. It could have gone bad.

Most cards (or any electronics, generally speaking), if they're going to go bad, have technical problems within the first 30 days.

If your friend's PC cannot log on, the problem may be with your AP. At this point, we have to say "Check out the vendor's Web site for more specific problem-solving ideas and call its tech-support number for further help."

Q: How do I get my video games to work on my wireless LAN?

This question has an easy answer and a not-so-easy answer. The easy answer is that you can get your Xbox, PlayStation 2, or GameCube onto your wireless LAN by linking the Ethernet port on your gaming device (if necessary, by purchasing a network adapter kit to add an Ethernet port on your system) with a wireless bridge — which gets your gaming gear onto your wireless network in an easy fashion. You just need to be sure to set your bridge to the same SSID and WEP key or WPA passphrase as your LAN.

That's the easy part, and you should now be able to access the Internet from your box.

The tough part is allowing the Internet to access you and your gaming system. This requirement applies to certain games, two-way voice systems, and some aspects of multiplayer gaming. You may need to open certain ports in your router to enable those packets bound for your gaming system to get there. This process is called *port forwarding* (or something like that — vendors love to name things differently among themselves). Port forwarding basically says to the router that it should block all packets from accessing your system except those with certain characteristics that you identify. (These types of data packets can be let through to your gaming server.) We talk a great deal about this topic in Chapter 12, in the section about dealing with port forwarding, so be sure to read up on that before tinkering with your router configuration.

If this process is too complex to pull off with your present router, you may consider just setting up a demilitarized zone (DMZ) for your gaming application, where your gaming console or PC sits fairly open to the Internet. This setup isn't a preferred one, however, for security reasons, and we recommend that you try to get port forwarding to work. We discuss setting up a DMZ in Chapter 12.

Q: My videoconferencing application doesn't work. What do I do?

In some ways, videoconferencing is its own animal in its own world. Videoconferencing has its own set of standards that it follows; typically has specialized hardware and software; and, until recently, has required special telephone lines to work.

The success of the Internet and its related protocols has opened up video-conferencing to a more mass market with IP standards-based Web cameras and other software-based systems becoming popular.

Still, if you have installed a router with the appropriate protection from the Internet bad guys, videoconferencing can be problematic for all the same reasons as in gaming, which we mention in the preceding section. You need to have packets coming into your application just as much as you're sending packets out to someone else.

Wait a minute. You may be thinking "Data packets come into my machine all the time (like when I download Web pages), so what are you saying?" Well, those packets are requested, and the router in your AP (or your separate router, if that's how your network is set up) knows that they're coming and lets them through. Videoconferencing packets are often unrequested, which makes the whole getting-through-the-router thing a bit tougher.

As such, the answer is the same as with gaming. You need to open ports in your router (called port forwarding) or set up your video application in a DMZ. Again, Chapter 12 can be a world of help here.

Q: How do I secure my network from hackers?

Nothing is totally secure from anything. The adage "Where there's a will, there's a way" tends to govern most discussions about someone hacking into your LAN. We tend to fall back on this one instead: "Unless you have some major, supersecret hidden trove of something on your LAN that many people would simply kill to have access to, the chances of a hacker spending a great deal of time to get on your LAN is minimal." This statement means that as long as you do the basic security enhancements we recommend in Chapter 10, you should be covered.

These basic enhancements cover the security of these items:

- ✔ **Your Internet connection:** You should turn on, at minimum, whatever firewall protection your router offers. If you can, choose a router that has *s*tateful *p*acket *i*nspection (SPI). You should also use antivirus software and seriously consider using personal firewall software on your PCs. It's defense in depth: After the bad guys get by your router firewall's Maginot line, you have extra guns to protect your PCs. (For a little historical perspective on defense strategies, read up on Maginot and his fortification.)

- ✔ **Your airwaves:** Because wireless LAN signals can travel right through your walls and out the door, you should strongly consider turning on WPA (and taking other measures, which we discuss in Chapter 10) to keep the next-door neighbors from snooping on your network.

Q: What is firmware, and why might I need to upgrade it?

Any consumer electronics device is governed by software that's seated in onboard chip memory storage. When you turn on the device, it checks this memory to find out what to do and loads the software in that area. This software turns the device on and basically "tells" it how to operate.

This *firmware* can be updated through a process that's specific to each manufacturer. Often, you see options in your software configuration program for checking for firmware upgrades.

Some folks advocate never, ever touching your firmware if you don't need to. Indeed, reprogramming your firmware can upset much of the logical innards of the device you struggled so hard to configure properly in the first place. In fact, you may see this advice on a vendor site, such as this statement from the D-Link site: "Do not upgrade firmware unless you are having specific problems" In other words: If it ain't broke, don't fix it. Many times, a firmware upgrade can cause you to lose all of the customized settings you've configured on your router. Although not all vendor firmware upgrades reset your settings to their defaults, many do. Also, it's always best to do a firmware upgrade with a *wired* connection to the router — if you lose the wireless signal during the upgrade, you could be forced to totally reset your router — you could even cause the router to become inoperable. Be careful!

Despite those warnings, we say "Never say never." Most AP and router vendors operate under a process of continuous improvement, by adding new features and fixing bugs regularly. One key way that you can keep current with these standards is by upgrading your firmware. Over time, your wireless network will fall out of sync with the latest bug fixes and improvements, and you will have to upgrade at some point. When you do so, follow all the manufacturer's warnings.

In Chapter 10, we discuss a forthcoming security enhancement for 802.11 LANs called Wi-Fi Protected Access 2 (WPA-2). Many existing APs and network adapters will be able to use WPA-2, but only after their firmware has been upgraded.

Q: Is NAT the same as a firewall?

If you find networking confusing, you're not alone. (If it were easy, we would have no market for our books!) One area of confusion is Network Address Translation (NAT). No, NAT isn't the same as a firewall. It's important to understand the difference, to make sure that you set up your network correctly. Firewalls provide a greater level of security than NAT routers and, as a result, are generally a bit more expensive than simple routers.

Often, you hear the term *firewall* used to describe a router's ability to protect LAN IP addresses from Internet snoopers. But, a true firewall goes deeper than that, by using SPI. It allows the firewall to look at each IP address and domain requesting access to the network; the administrator can specify certain IP addresses or domain names that are allowed to be let in while blocking any other attempt to access the LAN. (Sometimes you hear this term called *filtering*.)

Firewalls can also add another layer of protection, through a Virtual Private Network (VPN). It enables remote access to the private network through the use of secure logins and authentication. Finally, firewalls can help protect your family from unsavory content by enabling you to block content from certain sites.

Firewalls go well beyond NAT, and we highly recommend that you have a firewall in your home network. Check out Chapter 10 for more information on firewalls.

Q: How can I find out my IP address?

First off, you have two IP addresses: a public IP address and a private IP address. In some instances, you need to know one or the other (or both) of these addresses.

Your *private* IP address is your IP address on your LAN so that your router knows where to send traffic in and among LAN devices. If you have a LAN printer, that device has its own IP address, as does any network device on your LAN.

The address these devices have, however, is rarely the public IP address (the address is the "Internet phone number" of your network), mostly because public IP addresses are becoming scarce. Your Internet gateway has a public IP address for your home. If you want to access a specific device that's on your home network, but from a public location, you typically have to enable port forwarding in your router and then add that port number on the end of your public IP address when you try to make a connection. For example, if you had a Web server on your network, you would type an address 68.129.5.29:80 into your browser when you tried to access it remotely — 80 is the port used for HTTP servers.

You can usually find out your wide-area network (WAN; public IP address) and LAN (private IP address) from within your router configuration software or Web page, such as http://192.168.1.100. You may see a Status screen; this common place shows your present IP addresses and other key information about your present Internet connection.

If you have Windows 2000 or XP, you can find your computer's private IP address by choosing Start⇨Run. When the Run dialog box pops up, type **cmd** and then click OK. In the window that opens, type **ipconfig** at the command prompt and then press Enter. You see your IP address and a few other network parameters.

This IP address is your *internal,* or *private,* IP address, not the public address that people on the Internet use to connect to your network. If you try to give this address to someone (perhaps so that they can connect to your computer to do some videoconferencing or to connect to a game server you're hosting), it doesn't work. You need the public IP address that you find in the configuration program for your access point or router.

Q: If everything stops working, what can I do?

The long length of time it can take to get help from tech support these days leads lots of people to read the manual, check out the Web site, and work hard to debug their situation. But, what happens if you have tried everything and it's still a dead connection — and tech support agrees with you?

In these instances, your last resort is to reset the system back to its factory defaults and literally start over. If you do this, be sure to upgrade your firmware while you're at it because it resets your variables anyway. Who knows? The more recent firmware update may resolve some issues that could be causing the problems.

Resetting your device is considered a drastic action and should be taken only after you have tried everything else. Make sure that you at least get a tech-support person on the phone to confirm that you *have* tried everything else and that a reset makes sense.

Chapter 18

Ten Ways to Troubleshoot Wireless LAN Performance

Although troubleshooting any piece of network equipment can be frustrating, troubleshooting wireless equipment is a little more so because there's so much that you just can't check. After all, radio waves are invisible. That's the rub with improving the throughput (performance) of your wireless home network, but we're here to help. And, don't get hung up on the term *throughput* — it's just the effective speed of your network — when you take into account retransmissions attributable to errors, you find that the amount of data moving across your network is *lower* than the *nominal* speed of your network. For example, your PC may tell you that you're connected at 54 Mbps, but because of retransmissions and other factors, you may be sending and receiving data at about half that speed.

The trick to successfully troubleshooting anything is to be logical and systematic. First, be logical. Think about the most likely issues (no matter how improbable) and work from there. Second, be systematic. Networks are complicated things, which mandates a focus on sequential troubleshooting on your part. Patience is a virtue when it comes to network debugging.

Perhaps hardest of all is making sense of performance issues, which is the subject of this chapter. First of all, you can't get much great performance reporting from consumer-level access points, or APs. (The much more expensive ones sold to businesses are better at that.) Even so, debugging performance based on performance data in arrears is tough. Fixing performance issues is a trial-and-error, real-time process. At least most wireless client devices have some sort of signal-strength meter, which is one of the best sources of information you can get to help you understand what's happening.

Your signal strength meters (which are usually part of the software included with your wireless gear) are the best way to get a quick read on your network. These signal-strength meters are used by the pros, says Tim Shaughnessy, at NETGEAR: "I would highlight it as a tool." We agree.

It's a good idea to work with a friend or family member. Your friend can be in a poor reception "hole" with a notebook computer and the wireless utility showing the signal strength. You can try moving or configuring the access point to see what works. Just be patient — the signal meter may take a few seconds to react to changes.

Because not all performance issues can be tracked down (at least not easily), in this chapter we introduce you to the most common ways to improve the performance of your wireless home network. We know that these are tried-and-true tips because we have been there ourselves. We're pretty good at debugging this stuff by now. We just can't seem to figure out when it's not plugged in! (Well, Pat can't. Read the next section to see what we mean.)

Check the Obvious

Sometimes, what's causing you trouble is something simple — which you can fix simply.

For example, one of us (and we won't say who — *Pat*) was surprised that his access point just stopped working one day. The culprit was his beagle, Opie, who had pulled the plug out of the wall. As obvious as this sounds, it took the unnamed person *(Pat)* an hour to figure it out. Now, if someone told you, "Hey, the AP just stopped working," you would probably say "Is it plugged in?" *The moral:* Think of the obvious and check it first.

This section lists a couple more simple problems to think of first.

Problem: The power goes out and then comes back on. Different equipment takes different lengths of time to reset and restart, which causes the loss of connectivity and logical configurations in your network.

Solution: Sometimes, you need to turn all your devices off. Leave them all off for a minute or two, and then turn them all back on, working your way from the Internet connection to your computer — from the wide-area network (WAN) connection (your broadband modem, for example) back to your machine. This process allows each device to start up with everything upstream properly in place and turned on.

Problem: Your access point is working fine, with great throughput and a strong signal footprint, until one day it all just drops off substantially. No hardware problem. No new interferers installed at home. No new obstructions. No changes of software. Nothing. *The cause:* Your next-door neighbor got an access point and was using his on the same channel as yours.

Solution: This problem is hard to debug in the first place. How the heck do you find out who is charging invisible interference — by going door to door? "Uh, pardon me, I'm going door to door to try to debug interferers on my access point. Are you suddenly emitting any extraneous radio waves? No, I'm not wearing an aluminum foil hat, why?" Often, with debugging performance issues, you need to try many of the one-step solutions, such as changing channels, to see whether that has an effect. If you can find the solution, you have a great deal of insight into what the problem was. (If changing channels solved the problem, someone nearby was probably using the same channel, and you can then start tracking down whom!)

Speed: What to expect

Many of the newest technologies use multiple methods to greatly increase the effective speed and range of wireless connections. Unfortunately, much of that speed boost can be lost if you're in an area with lots of radio interference. If you have lots of noise in the area or many networks fighting for open channels, the base speed of what you're using — 54 Mbps for g/a and 11 Mbps for b — is the best you can hope for.

The wireless utility for the adapter may have a tab, called a *site survey* or *station list,* that lists the APs in range. The tab may show your neighbor's access point and the channel it's on.

Before you chase a performance issue, make sure that you *have* one. The advertised rates for throughput for the various wireless standards are pretty misleading. What starts out at 54 Mbps for 802.11a is really more like a maximum of 36 Mbps in practice (and less as distance grows). For 802.11b, it's more like 6 Mbps at best, rather than the 11 Mbps you hear bandied about. 802.11g is 54 Mbps — although some of the newer g models using MIMO can get you 30 to 40 percent greater speed. You *occasionally* see the high levels (like when you're within a few yards of the access point), but that's rare. *The moral:* If you think that you should be getting 54 Mbps, but you're getting only 38 Mbps, consider yourself lucky.

Move the Access Point

A wireless signal degrades with distance. You may find that the place you originally placed your access point, or AP, doesn't really fit with your subsequent real-world use of your wireless local-area network (LAN). A move may be in order.

After your AP is up and working, you will probably forget about it — people often do. APs can often be moved around and even shuffled aside by subsequent gear. Because the access connection is still up (that is to say, working), sometimes people don't notice that the AP's performance degrades when you hide it more or move it around.

Make sure that your AP is where you want it to be. Ensure that other gear isn't blocking it, that it isn't flush against a wall (which can cause interference), that its vertical orientation isn't too close to the ground (more interference), and that it isn't in the line of sight of radio wave interference (such as from microwaves and cordless phones).

Even a few inches can make a difference. The best location is in the center of your desired coverage area (remember to think in three dimensions!) and on top of a desk or bookcase.

For more information about setting up APs, check out Chapter 6.

Move the Antenna

Remember the days before everyone had cable or satellite TV? There was a reason that people would fiddle with the rabbit ears on a TV set — they were trying to get the antennas into the ideal position to receive signals. Whether the antenna is on the client or on the access point, the same concept applies: Moving the antenna can yield results. Because different antennas have different signal coverage areas, reorienting them in different declinations (or angles relative to the horizon) changes their coverage patterns. A strong signal translates to better throughput and performance.

Look at it this way: The antenna creates a certain footprint of its signal. If you're networking a multistory home and you're not getting a great signal upstairs, try shifting your antenna to a 45° angle, to increase a more vertical signal — that is, send more signal to the upstairs and downstairs, and less horizontally.

Change Channels

Each access point broadcasts its signals over portions of the wireless frequencies called *channels*. The 802.11b standard (the most common system at the time we wrote this chapter) defines 11 channels in the United States that overlap considerably, leaving only 3 channels that don't overlap with each other. The IEEE 802.11a standard specifies 12 (although most current products support only 8) non-overlapping channels. The 802.11g standard calls for the same 11 channels in the United States as 802.11b, again with overlapping channels.

This situation affects your ability to have multiple access points in the same area, whether they're your own or your neighbors'. Because channels can overlap, you can have the resulting interference. For 802.11b access points that are within range of each other, set them to different channels, five apart from each other (such as 1, 6, and 11), to avoid inter-access-point interference.

We discuss the channel assignments for wireless LANs, like 802.11b, further in Chapter 6.

Check for Dual-Band Interference

Despite the industry's mad rush to wirelessly enable every networkable device it makes, a whole lot hasn't been worked through yet, particularly interoperability. We're not talking about whether one vendor's 802.11b/g PC Card works with another vendor's 802.11b/g access point — the Wi-Fi interoperability tests usually make sure that's not a problem (unless one of your products isn't Wi-Fi certified). Instead, we're talking about having Bluetooth (see Chapter 15 for more on this technology) working in the same area as 802.11b/g, or having 802.11a modems and 802.11b/g modems operating in the same area. In some instances, like the former example, Bluetooth and 802.11b/g operate in the same frequency range, and therefore have some potential for interference. Because 802.11a and 802.11b/g operate in separate frequency bands, they're less likely to be exposed to interference.

Some issues also exist with how the different standards are implemented in different products. Some APs that support 802.11b and g, for example, really support one or the other — not both simultaneously. If you have all g in your house, that's great. If you have all b, that's great. If you have some g and the access point detects that b is in the house, it could downshift to b rates. You may be all set, but then your neighbor upstairs may buy a b network adapter (because you have said "Sure, no problem, you can share my Internet connection."). He's not only freeloading, but he also could be forcing your whole access point to shift down to the lower speeds.

To be fair, many of these very early implementation issues have gone away while vendors refine their solutions to the next level of 802.11n. Check out how any multimode access point that you buy handles dealing with more than one variant of 802.11 at the same time. Most newer APs compartmentalize their signals so that they can allow the faster 802.11g signals to connect at full (or nearly full) speed, while still allowing older 802.11b on the network, which is very nice and almost necessary.

Check for New Obstacles

Wireless technologies are susceptible to physical obstacles — and some more than others. In Chapter 4, Table 4-1 tells you the relative attenuation of your wireless signals (radio frequency; RF) as they move through your house. One person in our neighborhood noticed a gradual degradation of his wireless signal outside his house, where he regularly sits and surfs the Net (by his pool). The culprit turned out to be a growing pile of newspapers for recycling. Wireless signals don't like such masses of paper.

Move around your house and think about it from the eyes of Superman, using his X-ray vision to see your access point. If you have a bad signal, think about what's in the way. If the obstacles are permanent, think about using a SercoNet Wi-Fi extender or a HomePlug wireless access point (which we discuss in Chapter 3) to go around the obstacle by putting an access point on either side of the obstacle.

Another way to get around problems with obstacles is to switch technologies. In some instances, 802.11 Pre-N products could provide better throughput and reach than 802.11a/b/g when it comes to obstacles. Many Pre-N products use special radio transmission techniques that help "focus" the signal into the areas where your wireless client devices are. These "aimed" signals can help you overcome environments that just don't work with "regular" Wi-Fi gear. If you're in a dense environment with lots of clutter and you're using 802.11a/b or g, switching to Pre-N may provide some relief.

Install Another Antenna

In Chapter 5, we point out that a detachable antenna is a great idea because you may want to add an antenna to achieve a different level of coverage in your home. Different antennas yield different signal footprints. If your access point is located at one end of the house, putting an omnidirectional antenna on that access point is a waste because more than half the signal may prove to be unusable. A directional antenna better serves your home.

Antennas are inexpensive relative to their benefits and can more easily help you accommodate signal optimization because you can leave the access point in the same place and just move the antenna around until you get the best signal. Within a home, there's not a huge distance limitation on how far away the antenna can be from the access point.

Use a Signal Booster

Signal boosters used to be offered when 802.11g first came out a few years ago. The concept was that if you have a big house (or lots of interference), you can add a *signal booster,* which essentially turns up the volume on your wireless home network transmitter. Unfortunately, it does nothing for the wireless card in your computer, and that was the great failing in this product. Your base station would be stronger, but your workstation's signal would be the same. So, you could see your base station better, but couldn't communicate with it any better because your wireless card was at the same signal strength.

A signal booster was supposed to improve the range of your access point. The 802.11b and g products now typically have a range of 100 to 150 feet indoors mainly because 802.11b/g products operate at a relatively low frequency. 802.11a products have an even shorter reach — up to 75 feet indoors — because the higher frequencies that 802.11a uses lose strength faster with distance than do the lower frequencies used by 802.11g and b. The new Pre-N products from companies like Belkin reach at least another 25 to 50 feet, and many products using MIMO also achieve better range.

The signal range of the APs now on the market is steadily increasing because manufacturers are creating more efficient transceiver chipsets. We recommend reading the most recent reviews of products because products truly are improving monthly.

You can still find signal boosters for sale on eBay from companies such as Linksys, which sold the WSB24 Wireless Signal Booster that piggybacked onto a Linksys wireless access point (or wireless access point router).

Signal boosters have pretty much been discontinued and even though you can still get them, we strongly recommend staying away from them because you have many other options that are more versatile and compatible with what you already have and that keep you up-to-date with the newest technologies.

If you happen to come across one of these — or someone gives you one — you should know that signal boosters are *mated* devices, which means that they're engineered for specific products. Vendors have to walk a fine line when boosting signals in light of federal limits on the aggregate signal that can be used in the unlicensed frequencies. For example, the Linksys Wireless Signal Booster was certified by the Federal Communications Commission (FCC) for use with the WAP11 Wireless Access Point and BEFW11S4 Wireless Access Point Router only. Linksys says that using the WSB24 with any other product from either Linksys or another vendor voids the user's authority to operate the device.

The main reason that companies like Linksys sold their signal boosters for use with only their own products is certification issues. The FCC has to approve any radio transmission equipment sold on the market. A great deal of testing must be done for a piece of gear to get certified, and the certification testing must be done for the complete system — and vendors usually do this expensive testing only with their own gear.

As some reviews have pointed out, however, you *could* use the WSB24 with any wireless LAN product that operates in the 2.4 GHz band — notably, 802.11b and 802.11g products. You couldn't use it with 802.11a or any dual-band 2.4/5 GHz products; its design couldn't deal with the higher frequency.

Add an Access Point

Adding another access point (or two) can greatly increase your signal coverage, as shown in Figure 18-1. The great thing about wireless is that it's fairly portable — you can literally plug it in anywhere. The main issues are getting power to it and getting an Ethernet connection (which carries the data) to it.

The first item is usually not a problem because many electrical codes require, in a residence, that power outlets be placed every eight feet. However, if you're mounting an AP high up on a wall, you may not want an electrical power jack running to the spot. In that case, you may consider getting an AP that supports a Power over Ethernet (Power over Ethernet; PoE) option, which delivers power to run the unit over the same wiring that carries the data signal. Only one Cat 5e (standard Ethernet cabling) wire, therefore, has to be run to wherever you want your AP.

Leviton also has a neat product, the PowerJack (www.leviton.com/sections/prodinfo/newprod/powerjack/powerjack.htm; $25), that allows you to hide the power cable behind a four-conductor RJ-11 jack and avoid that AC adapter cable strung across the wall. Leviton doesn't yet have a version for an eight-conductor RJ-45 jack, although we expect one soon. Check the Leviton site to see whether one is available — and get one of them if you have problems with an AC adapter cable on your cordless phone.

The second issue (getting the Ethernet connection to your access point, or AP) used to be a matter of running all sorts of wiring around the house. Depending on the actual throughput you're looking to provide, however, you may be able to set up another AP by using the HomePlug, Home Phone Networking Alliance (HPNA), or even wireless repeater functionality that we mention in Chapter 3 and elsewhere in this chapter. We don't repeat those options here, but know that you have those options when you're moving away from your office or other place where many of your network connections are concentrated.

After you get the connectivity and power to the place you want, what do you need to consider when you're installing a *second* AP? Choose the right channel: If you have auto channel selection in your AP, you don't need to worry because your AP's smarts handle it for you. If you're setting the channel manually, don't choose the same one as your other AP is set to.

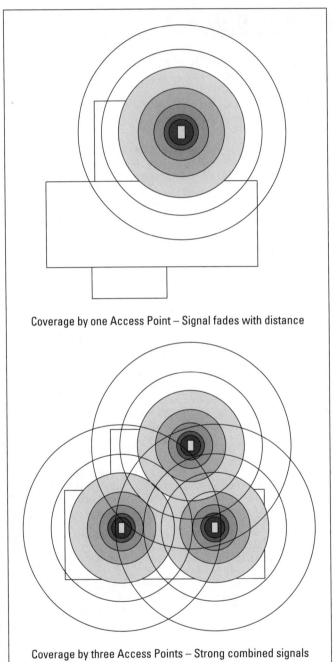

Coverage by one Access Point – Signal fades with distance

Figure 18-1:
Three APs provide a much stronger signal than a single AP.

Coverage by three Access Points – Strong combined signals

Carefully choose which channels you use for each of your access points. Make sure that you have proper spacing of your channels if you have 802.11b or 802.11g access points (which have overlapping bands). Read the section "Change Channels," earlier in this chapter, for more information on channels.

Add a Repeater or Bridge

Wireless repeaters are an alternative way to extend the range of an existing wireless network instead of adding more access points, or APs. We talk earlier in this book (refer to Chapter 2) about the role of bridges and repeaters in a wireless network. The topic of bridges can be pretty complex, and we don't want to rehash — be sure to read Chapter 2 for all that juicy detail.

Not many stand-alone repeaters are on the consumer market. However, what's important for our discussion is that repeater capability is finding its way into the AP firmware from many AP vendors. A wireless AP *repeater* basically does double duty — it's an AP as well as a wireless connection back to the main AP that's connected to the Internet connection.

At its most basic level, a repeater simply regenerates a wireless network signal in order to extend the range of the existing wireless LAN. You set the two devices to the same channel with the same service set identifier (SSID), thus effectively broadening the collective footprint of the signal.

If you have throughput performance issues because of interference or reach, putting an AP into repeating mode may help extend the reach of your network.

However, it's not clear that adding a repeater helps actual throughput in all situations, unfortunately. Some testing labs have cited issues with throughput at the main AP because of interference from the new repeating AP (which is broadcasting on the same channel). Others note that the repeater must receive and retransmit each frame (or burst of data) on the same RF channel, which effectively doubles the number of frames that are sent. This effectively cuts throughput in half. Some vendors have dealt with this issue through software and claim that it's not an issue.

It's hard at this juncture to make a blanket statement about the basic effectiveness of installing an AP in repeater mode, particularly versus the option of running a high-quality Ethernet cable to a second AP set on a different channel. If you can do the latter, that's preferable.

When you're using the bridging and repeating functions of APs and bridges, we recommend that you use products from the same manufacturer at both ends of the bridge, to minimize any issues between vendors. Most companies support this functionality only between their own products and not across multiple vendors' products.

Check Your Cordless Phone Frequencies

The wireless frequencies at 2.4 GHz and 5.2 GHz are unlicensed (as we define in Part I of this book), which means that you, as the buyer of an AP and operator of a wireless broadcasting capability, don't need to get permission from the FCC to use these frequencies as long as you stay within certain power and usage limitations as set by federal guidelines. It also means that you don't have to pay any money to use the airwaves — because no license is required, it doesn't cost anything.

Many consumer manufacturers have taken advantage of these free radio spectra and created various products for these unlicensed frequencies, such as cordless phones, wireless A/V connection systems, RF remote controls, and wireless cameras.

A home outfitted with a variety of Radio Shack and X10.com gadgets may have a fair amount of radio clutter on these frequencies. This clutter can cut into your network's performance. These sources of RF energy occasionally block users and access points from accessing their shared air medium.

As home wireless LAN use grows, people report more interference with home *X10 networks,* which use various wireless transmitters and signaling over electrical lines to communicate among their connected devices. If you have a home X10 network for your home automation and it starts acting weird (like the lights go on and off and you think that your house is haunted), consider your LAN as a potential problem source. A strong wireless LAN in your house can be fatal to an X10 network.

At some point, you have to get better control over these interferers, and you don't have many options. First, you can change channels, like we mention earlier in this chapter. Cordless phones, for example, use channels just like your local-area network does; you can change them so that they don't cross paths (wirelessly speaking) with your data heading toward the Internet.

Second, you can change phones. If you have an 802.11b or g network operating at home on the 2.4 GHz band, consider one of the newer 5 GHz cordless phones for your house. (Or, vice versa: If you have an 802.11a, 5 GHz network, get a 2.4 GHz phone.) *Note:* An old-fashioned 900 MHz phone doesn't interfere with either one, but finding one these days is a miracle.

You may find that your scratchy cordless phone improves substantially in quality and your LAN performance improves too. Look for other devices that can move to other frequencies or move to your 802.11 network. As we discuss in Chapter 19, all sorts of devices are coming down the road that will work *over* your 802.11 network and not compete with it. Ultimately, you need to keep the airwaves relatively clear to optimize all your performance issues.

At the end of the day, interference from sources outside your house is probably your own fault. If your neighbor asks you how your wireless connection works, lie and tell her that it works horribly. You don't want your neighbor getting one and sending any stray radio waves toward your network. Do the same with cable modems. You don't want your neighbor's traffic slowing you down because it's a shared connection at the neighborhood level. Interference is a sign of popularity — it means that lots of other people have caught on. Keep it your little secret.

Chapter 19

More Than Ten Devices to Connect to Your Wireless Network in the Future

*W*e tell you throughout this book to think bigger-picture than just net-working your home computers. In Chapter 11, we talk about adding various peripheral devices (such as a printer) to your home network. In Chapters 12 and 13, we talk extensively about all the gaming gear and audio-visual equipment that you would want to hook into your wireless home net-work. In Chapter 14, you hear about lots of things you can connect today, ranging from cameras to cars.

Clearly, the boom is on among the consumer goods manufacturers to net-work-enable everything with chips. You get the convenience (and cool-factor) of monitoring the health of your gadgets, and vendors want to sell you add-on services to take advantage of that chip. This transformation is happening to everything: clocks, sewing machines, automobiles, toaster ovens — even shoes. If a device can be added to your wireless home network, value-added services can be sold to those who want to track their kids, listen to home-stored music in the car, and know when Fido is in the neighbor's garbage cans again.

In this chapter, we expose you to some things that you could bring very soon to your wireless home network. These discussions aren't the pie-in-the-sky type because many of these products already exist. Expect in coming years that they will infiltrate your home. Like the Borg say on *Star Trek,* "Prepare to be assimilated."

Your Bath

Yup, wireless toys are everywhere now, having traversed their way into the innermost sanctuary of your home: the bathroom. We're not talking *Psycho*-type shots of people in the shower — we're interested in how to get audio, video, and data into the bathroom so that you can enjoy your privacy even more than you do today.

Not too many homes are wired for computer and video in the bathroom, and wireless may be the only way to get signals — like a phone — to some of these places. We have seen wireless-enabled toilets (don't ask) and all sorts of wireless controls for lighting in the bathroom to create just the right atmosphere for that bath.

It's the wireless enablement of the bathtub itself that gets us excited. Luxury bathing combined with a home entertainment bathing center into one outfitted bathroom set is probably the ultimate for a wireless enthusiast.

Jacuzzi (www.jacuzzi.com) is the leader in this foray. Jacuzzi sells the only wireless waterproof remote control we have seen (see Figure 19-1), but it's what comes with the remote control that gets us. The Jacuzzi Affinity hot tub comes standard with a built-in stereo/CD system, complete with four speakers, as well as an integrated 9-inch television. The multichannel unit is waterproof and includes a remote control. Cable ready, this feature allows you to enjoy the morning news or your favorite movie. A digital control panel offers easy access to the whirlpool operation, underwater lighting, and temperature readout. Talk about wired! All these features cost a mere $12,919, retail. Oh, and you get the hot tub part too — three fixed back jets per person and five fully directional jets around the perimeter.

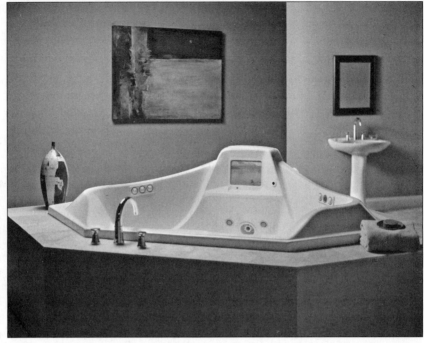

Figure 19-1:
The Jacuzzi Affinity hot tub can add to your home's wireless entertainment.

The problem is that most homes aren't wired for audio or video in their bathroom. That's where your wireless home network comes into play. You can use the same wireless A/V extension devices used to link your PC and your stereo system to reach into the bathroom and bring your Affinity online.

You can also get wireless speakers that are designed for the humidity and temperatures found in the bathroom — note that they're water-*resistant,* not waterproof, so don't expect to drop them in the water and have them work. (You can, though, check out underwater speakers, like those from Lubell Labs [www.lubell.com].)

Your Car

Your car will join the wireless revolution and in some neat ways. In Chapter 15, we discuss how cars are sporting Bluetooth interfaces to enable devices to interact with the car's entertainment and communications systems. In

Chapter 14, we discuss the range of aftermarket devices you can buy now that provide 802.11-based connectivity between your home's wireless LAN and your car, whenever it's in range. (We guess that makes your garage a really big docking station!)

Because most cars already have a massive computing and entertainment infrastructure, reaching out and linking it to both the Internet and your wireless home network is simply a no-brainer.

A wireless connection in the car enables you to talk to your car via your wireless network. Now, before you accuse us of having gone loony for talking to our car, think about whether your lights are still on. Wouldn't it be great to check on it from your 40th-floor apartment rather than head all the way down to the parking garage? Just grab your 802.11g-enabled handheld computer, surf to your car's own Web server, and check whether you left the lights on (again). Or, perhaps you're filling out a new insurance form and forgot to check the mileage on your car. Click over to the dashboard page and see what it says.

You can also, on request, check out your car's exact location based on global positioning system (GPS) readings. (*GPS* is a location-finding system that effectively can tell you where something is, based on its ability to triangulate signals from three or more satellites that orbit the Earth. GPS can usually spot its target within 10–100 meters of the actual location.) You can, again at your request, even allow your dealer to check your car's service status via the Internet. You can also switch on the lights or the auxiliary heating, for example, call up numbers in the car telephone or addresses in the navigation system, and unlock and lock the car — all from the wireless comfort of your couch (using some of those neat touch-panel remote controls that we talk about in Chapter 14). Just grab your wireless Web tablet, surf, and select. Pretty cool. The opportunities to wirelessly connect to your automobile are truly endless.

Look for the following near-term applications for wirelessly linking your car to your home:

- **Vehicle monitoring systems:** These devices — usually mounted under a seat, under the hood, or in the trunk — monitor the speed, acceleration, deceleration, and various other driving and engine performance variables so that you can determine whether your kids are racing down the street after they nicely drive out of your driveway. When you drive into your driveway, the information is automatically uploaded to your PC over your wireless home network.

   Devices like the Davis Instruments Corporation's DriveRight (`www.davisnet.com`, $375) and RoadSafety International's RS-1000 Teen Driver System (`www.roadsafety.com`, $280) can link to your home's network via any USB wireless client device.

✔ **E-commerce:** You hear a great new song on your radio. Maybe you didn't catch the artist or song title. You push the Buy button on your audio system, which initiates a secure online transaction, and a legal copy of the song is purchased and downloaded to the car at the next wireless hot spot your car senses. From now on, you can listen to the song over and over again, just like you would with a CD. When you get home, you can upload it to your home's audio system.

✔ **Remote control:** Use remote controls for your car to automatically open minivan doors or turn on the lights before you get in. A remote car starter is a treat for anyone who lives in very hot or cold weather (get that heater going before you leave your home). Fancier remote controls, like the AutoCommand Remote Starters and Security products from DesignTech International (`www.designtech-intl.com`, around $200), have a built-in car finder capability as well as a remote headlight control. AutoCommand can be programmed to automatically start your vehicle at the same time the next day, at low temperature, or at low battery voltage.

Okay, so these aren't necessarily new and don't require a wireless home network. But, when you can use wireless networks to connect these devices to the rest of your home's other systems, you can really start experiencing a whole home network. Imagine using that wireless connection to link to your home automation system, such as the one we discuss in Chapter 14. When you utter "Start the car," the system communicates with the car and gets it into the right temperature setting — based on the present temperature outside (it gets its readings from its Weatherbug backyard wireless weather station (`www.weatherbug.com`).

OnStar calling

Car manufacturers are sensing a business opportunity in providing connectivity to your car. Perhaps the most well-known service is OnStar (`www.onstar.com`), offered on a number of GM and other vehicles. OnStar offers emergency car services, such as the ones offered by the American Automobile Association (AAA), with GPS and two-way cellular communications thrown in. You can not only make cell phone calls with the system, but also get GM to unlock your car doors. It's a factory-installed-only option, so if it's not in your car when you bought it, you can't get it. You have to pay monthly service fees that start at $16.95 per month or $199 per year.

Other car manufacturers are following suit. BMW offers the similar BMW Assist, for example. We expect all car manufacturers to offer something similar within a few years — it makes too much sense. Check out some of the short movies on how OnStar has gotten people out of sticky situations, at `www.onstar.com/us_english/jsp/idemo/index.jsp`.

Your Exercise Gear

Parts of exercise regimens are becoming network aware, and wireless plays a part. One of the more interesting applications of the Internet to the world of exercise comes from Icon Fitness (iFIT; `www.ifit.com`), which links your exercise equipment, the Internet, live personal coaches, and a library of audio and video slide tours to make each day of exercising a brand-new adventure. (Try the 30-day trial, or pony up $9.99 per month for a yearlong contract.) Your iFIT-enabled exercise equipment can be controlled (either automatically by a preset program or live by a trainer) remotely via an Internet connection. The idea is to provide an environment where you can enjoy working out, be challenged, track your results, and learn about nutritional planning.

iFit.com can also remotely control more than 100 models of treadmills, elliptical trainers, stationary bikes, and incline trainers — from the Icon NordicTrack, Pro-Form, Reebok, HealthRider, and Image divisions (`www.iconfitness.com`). Each of these has an Ethernet connection into which you can put a wireless adapter to link your gear to the Internet.

If you don't like the audio and video programs, you can find live trainers, courtesy of Internet videoconferencing, who will log on and help make sure that you exercise to the very end. Rates vary around the Internet, but generally range from $20 to $30 for an hour session. In these sessions, you see and hear the trainer — and the trainer sees and hears you. This is a great use of the wireless-enabled Web cameras that we talk about in Chapter 13.

Your Home Appliances

Most attempts to converge the Internet and home appliances have been prototypes and concept products — a few products are on the market, but we would be less than honest if we said that the quantities being sold were anything but mass market yet. LGE (`www.lge.com`) was the first in the world to introduce the Internet refrigerator — a Home Network product with Internet access capability — back in June 2000 (see Figure 19-2). It soon introduced other Internet-based information appliance products in the washing machine, air conditioner, and microwave areas. The Internet refrigerator has a 15-inch detachable LCD touch screen that serves as a TV monitor, computer screen, stereo, and digital camera all in one. You can call your refrigerator from your cell phone, PDA, or any Internet-enabled device.

Figure 19-2:
The LGE
Internet
Refrigerator
is wirelessly
enabled.

LGE also has an Internet air conditioner that allows you to download programs into the device so that you can have preprogrammed cooling times, just like with your heating system setbacks. Talk to your digital home theater to preprogram something stored on your audio server to be playing when you get home. It's all interrelated, by sharing a network in common. Wireless plays a part by enabling these devices to talk to one another in the home.

The Samsung (www.samsungelectronics.com) Digital Network Refrigerator is equipped with Internet access, a videophone, and a TV. In addition to storing food, consumers can send and receive e-mail, surf the Net, and watch a favorite DVD by using the refrigerator's touch-screen control panel, which also serves as a detachable wireless-enabled handheld computer. Pretty neat.

All this is still pricey — you may spend $6,000 or more on an Internet refrigerator. But the future is one where most appliances have a network interface (and predominantly a wireless one) on board, and prices come down fast.

With recent developments in radio frequency identification (RFID) and other technologies, you may indeed get to the point where your kitchen monitors all its appliances (and what's in them — "We need more milk.").

Your Musical Instruments

A wireless home backbone enables fast access to online music scores, like from www.score-on-line.com. Musical instruments are also growing more complex and wireless.

With ConcertMaster, from Baldwin Piano (www.baldwinpiano.com), your wireless home LAN can plug into your ConcertMaster-equipped Baldwin, Chickering, or Wurlitzer piano and play almost any musical piece you can imagine. You can plan an entire evening of music, from any combination of sources, to play in any order — all via a wireless RF remote control.

The internal ConcertMaster Library comes preloaded with 20 hours of performances in five musical categories, or you can create as many as 99 custom library categories to store your music. With as many as 99 songs in each category, you can conceivably have nearly 50,000 songs onboard and ready to play. Use your wireless access to your home's Internet connection to download the latest operating system software from Baldwin's servers. The system can accept any wireless MIDI interface. Encore!

You can record on this system too. A one-touch Quick-Record button lets you instantly save piano performances, such as your child's piano recital. You can also use songs that you record and store on floppy disk with your PC to use within editing, sequencing, and score notation programs.

Your Pets

GPS-based tracking services can be used for pets too! Just about everyone can identity with having lost a pet at some point. The GPS device's form factor can be collar-based or a subdermal implant. This device can serve as your pet's electronic ID tag; it also can serve as the basis for real-time feedback to the pet or its owner, and perhaps provide automatic notification if your dog goes out of the yard, for example.

Globalpetfinder.com is a typical example of a GPS-enabled system (www.globalpetfinder.com, $350). With this system, you create one or more circular virtual fences that are defined by a GPS location. Your home's address, for example, is translated by its online site into a GPS coordinate, and you can create a fence that might be 100 feet in radius. If your pet wanders outside this fence, you're alerted immediately and sent the continuously updated location of your pet, to the two-way wireless device of your choice — cell phone, PDA, or computer, for example. You can find your pet by dialing the collar's phone number, and it replies with the present location. If you're using a PDA with a graphical interface, such as a Treo 650, you can see the location on a street map. You have to pay a monthly subscription for the service — to cover the cell costs — which range from $18 to $20 per month. If your dog runs away often, go for the Escape Artist Peace of Mind plan!

The 802.11 technologies are making their way into the pet-tracking arena as well. Several companies are testing prototypes of wireless clients that would log on to neighborhood Wi-Fi APs and send messages about their positions back to their owners. Although the coverage certainly isn't as broad as cellular service, it certainly would be much less expensive. So, your LAN may soon be part of a neighborhood wireless network infrastructure that provides a NAN — *neighborhood-area network* — one of whose benefits is such continual tracking capability for pets.

Your Phones

True, many phones in homes now are wireless. (And, of course, cell phones are too.) But, remember that your wireless home network uses the same 2.4 GHz and 5.8 GHz wireless frequencies as your cordless phones do. When you factor in that your neighbor's phones and a bunch of other devices in home (like microwave ovens, wireless audio systems, Bluetooth phones, and more) are also on these frequencies, the throughput and usability of your wireless home networking system can get watered down pretty fast.

Enter your whole home 802.11 network. It makes sense to migrate your cordless phones, for example, to your wireless home network so that your wireless phones don't compete and interfere with your wireless home network; instead, you can get 802.11-based phones that ride over the same network in a seamless way. (Chapter 2 has all the details about the 802.11 protocol.)

To do this, you need to get an 802.11-enabled phone, which would work exactly like a cordless phone. In fact, you scarcely could tell the difference between the two. Only a few such phones are available now, but you may soon see many more home telephone products that support 802.11. You may also see 802.11 technology bundled inside your cell phone as well, although the early moves with cellular have focused on Bluetooth enablement, which we talk about in Chapter 15.

Much of the Wi-Fi Phone progress is being pushed by the voice over IP providers, like Vonage (www.vonage.com). Vonage users want to be able to roam around their homes while talking over the Internet, and Wi-Fi is a great way to do that. Vonage has also teamed with Wi-Fi hot spot service provider

Boingo (www.boingo.com) to allow you to take your home's Wi-Fi phone on the road so that you can make calls from anywhere that you can log on to the Internet via Wi-Fi. Trés cool.

For example, Vonage has an 802.11b-based Wi-Fi phone from UTStarcom (www.utstarcom.com) — the F-1000 — that includes three-way calling, call waiting, and call transfer. You can program as many as four different network settings on your phone, which makes it easier to log on to different wireless networks. Vonage also has announced phones from VTech (you may know VTech as the manufacturer of the phones under the AT&T brand). That phone, the IP-8100-2 (www.vtech.com), costs $149, but has a rebate from Vonage that brings it under $100 — the same price range as the UTStarcom phone. The Vtech phone operates in the 5.8GHz spectrum, which means that that it's geared more for the homebody (because most hot spots don't support anything other than 802.11b or g clients). Finally, ZyXel has its P-2000W VoIP Wi-Fi phone (www.zyxel.com, $100) based on 802.11b.

Even if you don't buy one of these newfangled Wi-Fi phones, you can still use your wireless network and broadband connection to make low-cost phone calls. VoIP providers can sell you something called an "ATA," or *analog telephone adapter*, that turns traditional analog phones into IP phones. Just plug your regular cordless or corded phone into the ATA, and you can place calls to any of a number of VoIP telephone companies (like Vonage) that carry your calls to their destination for low rates — less than the traditional long-distance carrier rates, for sure. Just plug your cordless phone into the adapter and call away.

Checking out new wireless gadgets

The merging of Wi-Fi and VoIP is a major movement in the telecommunications industry. You can expect that you will have many more options in the future to make phone calls over the Internet by using Wi-Fi devices. Here are three great places to keep track of the latest and greatest in new wireless products, including Wi-Fi phones:

✔ **Gizmodo** (www.gizmodo.com): Gizmodo tracks all the leading-edge gadgets of any type. This site is fun to visit, just to see what someone has dreamed up. As we write this chapter, there's a neat story about glow-in-the-dark light bulbs that still provide luminescence after they're turned off — that's emergency lighting! For your wireless fancy, all sorts of articles on new wireless wares appear each week; just be prepared that many are available only in Asia. Rats!

✔ **Engadget** (www.engadget.com): Engadget was founded by one of the major editors from Gizmodo. It largely mimics Gizmodo, but with meatier posts and reader comments for many articles.

✔ **EHomeUpgrade** (www.ehomeupgrade.com): EHomeUpgrade covers a broader spectrum of software, services, and even industry trends, but hardcore wireless is a mainstay of its fare as well.

You can't go wrong checking these sites regularly to see what's new to put in your home!

You can also make calls over your laptop with software from companies like Skype (`www.skype.com`) and Net2Phone (`www.net2phone.com`). We use Skype to call all over the world, and we love their cordless phone — the DualPhone (`www.dualphone.net`, $120) uses DECT frequencies, which means that it's more generally free from any interference because DECT isn't widely used in the United States. This phone plugs into your USB port on your PC and allows you to roam your house and call Ukraine whenever you want for free. It's pretty neat, we think. By the time you read this chapter, Skype probably will have launched its Wi-Fi phone. Check out its site for details.

Your Robots

Current technology dictates that robots are reliant on special algorithms and hidden technologies to help them navigate. For example, the Roomba robotic vacuum cleaner, from iRobot (`www.irobot.com`, $149-$349), relies on internal programming and virtual walls to contain its coverage area. The Friendly Machines Robomow robotic lawnmower relies on hidden wiring under the ground: `www.friendlymachines.com`, $1,100 to $1,500.

As your home becomes more wireless, devices can start to triangulate their positions based on home-based homing beacons, of sorts, that help them sense their position at any time. The presence of a wireless home network will drive new innovation into these devices. Most manufacturers are busy designing 802.11 into the next versions of their products.

The following list highlights some other product ideas that manufacturers are working on now. We can't yet offer price points or tell you when these products will hit the market, but expect them to come soon:

- ✔ **Robotic garbage taker-outers:** Robotic firms are designing units that take the trash out for you, on schedule, no matter what the weather — simple as that.

- ✔ **Robotic mail collectors:** A robotic mail collector goes and gets the mail for you. Neither snow, nor rain, nor gloom of night, nor winds of change, nor a nation challenged can stay them from the swift completion of their appointed rounds. New wirelessly outfitted mailboxes tell you (and the robots) when your mail has arrived.

- ✔ **Robotic snow blowers:** Manufacturers are working to perfect robotic snow blowers that continually clear your driveway and sidewalks while snow falls.

- ✔ **Robotic golf ball retrievers:** These bots retrieve golf balls. Initially designed for driving range use, they're being modified for the home market.

- ✔ **Robotic guard dogs:** Robots that can roam areas and send back audio and video feeds are coming to the market. These new versions of man's best friend can sniff out fires or lethal gases, take photos of burglars, and send intruder alerts to homeowners' cell phones. Check out the dragonlike Sanyo Banryu, the Mitsubishi Wakamaru, and others emerging even as we write this book.

- ✔ **Robotic gutter cleaners:** A range of spiderlike robots is available that can maneuver on inclines, like roofs, and feature robotic sensors and arms that can clean areas.

- ✔ **Robotic cooks:** Put the ingredients in, select a mode, and wait for your dinner to be cooked — it's better than a TV dinner, for sure.

- ✔ **Robotic pooper scoopers:** The units we have discovered roam your yard in search of something to clean up and then deposit the findings in a place you determine.

You're more likely to see humanoid robots demonstrating stuff at special events than cooking dinner in your kitchen. Products such as Honda's ASIMO (Advanced Step in Innovative Mobility, `world.honda.com/ASIMO/`) are remarkable for the basic things they can do, like shake hands and bow, but the taskmasters we mention in the preceding list can really help you with day-to-day chores.

Your Wearing Apparel

Wireless is making its way into your clothing. Researchers are already experimenting with *wearables* — the merging of 802.11 and Bluetooth directly into clothing so that it can have networking capabilities. Want to synch your PDA? No problem: Just stick it in your pocket. MIT Labs has been showing off some clothing that looks more like a Borg from *Star Trek* than anything practical, but all sorts of companies are working on waterproof and washerproof devices for wirelessly connecting to your wireless home network. We have even seen jackets that display advertisements on their backs.

Wireless technology will also infiltrate your clothing through radio frequency identification tags, or RFIDs, which are very small, lightweight, electronic read-write storage devices (microchips) that are half the size of a grain of sand. They listen for radio queries and, when pinged, respond by transmitting their ID codes. Most RFID tags have no batteries because they use the power from the initial radio signal to transmit their responses; thus, they never wear out. Data is accessible in real time through handheld or fixed-position readers, using RF signals to transfer data to and from tags. RFID applications are infinite, but when embedded in clothing, RFIDs offer applications such as tracking people (like kids at school) or sorting clothing from the dryer (no more problems matching socks or identifying clothes for each child's pile).

A technology of great impact in our lifetime is GPS, which is increasingly being built into cars, cell phones, devices, and clothing. GPS equipment and chips are so cheap that you will find them everywhere. They're used in amusement parks to help keep track of your kids. Some shoe manufacturers are talking about embedding chips in shoes.

Most GPS-driven applications have software that enables you to interpret the GPS results. You can grab a Web tablet at home while on your couch, wirelessly surf to the tracking Web site, and determine where Fido (or Fred) is located. Want to see whether your spouse's car is heading home from work yet? Grab your PDA as you walk down the street, log on to a nearby hot spot, and check it out. Many applications are also being ported to cell phones, so you can use those wireless devices to find out what's going on.

GPS-based devices — primarily in a watch form — are available that can track people.

The Gotcha! child-safety device (www.nsclocators.com, $59) is a two-piece, battery-powered system that consists of a clip-on unit worn by the child and a second, pager-size unit carried by the parent or guardian (see Figure 19-3). If the child wanders outside the adjustable safety zone, the system emits an alarm. The safety perimeter is set by the parent and can be as little as 10 feet and as much as 75 feet. The alarm tone also acts as a homing device to help a parent and child find each other after it has gone off — important for those subway rush hours in New York City! Gotcha! uses RFID as its wireless signal infrastructure. Many other person-locator products are on the market, such as a more removal-resistant unit from ionKids.com ($350) to a $900 GPS Kid Locator Tracker Backpack (www.spyshops.ca).

Having wireless fun with geocaching

Geocaching is an entertaining adventure game based around the GPS technology. It's basically a wireless treasure hunt. The idea is to have individuals and organizations set up "caches" all over the world; the GPS locations are then posted on the Internet, and GPS users seek the caches. Once they're found, some sort of reward may be there; the only rule is that if you take something from the cache, you need to leave something behind for others to find later. Check out what caches are near you: www.geocaching.com.

Want to find out more about GPS? Visit a couple of fun GPS tracking (pun intended!) sites, such as www.gps-practice-and-fun.com and www.gpsinformation.net.

Various possible monthly fees are associated with personal tracking and location devices. Some don't have any fees; they involve short-range, closed-system wireless signals. Some charge a monthly fee, just like a cell phone plan. Some charge per-use fees, like "per locate" attempts. Be sure to check the fine print when you're buying any sort of wireless location device to make sure that you don't have lots of extra fees that go along with it. (That's why we like 802.11-based products — because they're cheap and often don't have these fees; but then again, they don't have the range that some of these other systems do — you get what you pay for!)

Figure 19-3:
The Gotcha! lets you keeps a virtual leash on your kids.

Applied Digital Solutions (www.digitalangel.net) is really on the leading edge. The company has developed the VeriChip (www.adsx.com/prodservpart/verichip.html), which can be implanted under the skin for people in high-risk (think kidnapping) areas overseas. This chip is an implantable, 12mm x 2.1mm radio frequency device, about the size of the point of a ballpoint pen. The chip contains a unique verification number.

Although watches are a great form factor for lots of wireless connectivity opportunities, they have been hampered by either wired interface requirements (like a USB connection) or an infrared (IR) connection, which requires line of sight to a specific on-ramp. Expect these same devices to quickly take on Bluetooth and 802.11 interfaces so that continual updating — as with the Microsoft Smart Personal Objects Technology (SPOT) model (`www.microsoft.com/SPOT/`) — can occur. Heck, pretty soon, you won't have to miss your favorite TV show either. NHJ's VTV-101 TV wristwatch (`www.nhjapan.com/english/prod/vtv101/`, $179) has a built-in TV tuner that enables you to watch (pun intended) channels VHF 1–12 and UHF 13–62. The headphones act as the antenna. We're not sure what we think about that, but it probably isn't something to do at the dinner table!

Creating wireless connectivity via jewelry bears its own set of issues because of the size and weight requirements of the host jewelry for any wireless system. The smaller the jewelry, the less power the wireless transmitter can have to do its job. The less power, the shorter the range and the more limited the bandwidth and application of the device. These fancy watches still are living large when it comes to the size of beast you have to clamp on your wrist, but hey, if it means catching that basketball game you would normally miss, do you care?

Wearables are going wireless, and they're simply fun to research — MP3 sunglasses, Wi-Finder purses, GPS belts — you name it, someone has thought of it! Check out the Engadget wearables blog, at `wearables.engadget.com`.

Chapter 20

Top Ten Sources for More Information

*W*e have tried hard in this book to capture all that's happening with wireless networks in the home. However, we can't cover everything in one book, and so, in fairness to other publications, we're leaving some things for them to talk about on their Web sites and in their print publications. (Nice of us, isn't it?)

We want to keep you informed of the latest changes to what's in this book. So, we encourage you to check out the *Wireless Home Networking For Dummies* update site, at www.digitaldummies.com, where you can find updates and new information.

This chapter lists the publications that we read regularly (and therefore recommend unabashedly) and that you should get your hands on as part of your wireless home networking project. Many of these sources provide up-to-date performance information, which can be critical when making a decision about which equipment to buy and what standards to pursue.

The Web sites mentioned also have a ton of information online, but you may have to try different search keywords to find what you're looking for. Some publications like to use the term *Wi-Fi*, for example, and others use *802.11*. If you don't get hits on certain terms when you're searching around, try other ones that you know. It's rare to come up empty on a search about wireless networking these days. All sites listed here are free.

CNET.com

CNET.com (www.cnet.com) is a simple-to-use, free Web site where you can do apples-to-apples comparisons of wireless equipment. You can count on finding pictures of what you're buying, editor ratings of the equipment, user ratings of the gear, reviews of most devices, and a listing of the places on the Web where you can buy it all — along with true pricing. What's great about CNET is that it covers the wireless networking aspect of Wi-Fi as well as the consumer goods portion of Wi-Fi (such as home theater, A/V gear, and phones, for example). You can count on being able to find all sorts of products and ideas in one place. It's your one-stop resource for evaluating your future home wireless purchases.

Get started at CNET in its Wi-Fi Networking section, which at the time this book was written, was at http://reviews.cnet.com/Networking/2001-3243_7-0.html?tag=co. There, you find feature specs, reviews, and price comparisons of leading wireless gear. (CNET even certifies listed vendors, so you know that they pass at least one test of online legitimacy.)

What we especially like is the ability to do a side-by-side comparison so that we can see who has which features. By clicking the boxes next to each name, you can select that gear for comparison shopping. You can also filter the results by price, features, support, and other factors at the bottom of the page. Then just click Compare to receive a results page.

At wireless.cnet.com, the CNET editors provide feature stories focused on wireless use in practical applications. Overall, we visit this solid site often before buying anything.

CNET, like many other sites, now supports RSS feeds. If you don't know about RSS, you will soon: Most news and information sites offer RSS feeds to tell you what's happening on their Web sites. An *RSS feed* is an electronic feed that contains basic information about a particular item, like the headline, posting date, and summary paragraph about each news item on the site. You use a program called an RSS reader, such as NewsGator Online (www.newsgator.com) or any of dozens of other free RSS readers, to reach out and access these feeds regularly. You find RSS readers that load into your e-mail program, browser, and instant messaging program, for example. All these readers allow you to scan the headlines and click the ones you want to read. You could set up an RSS reader to access the RSS feeds of each of these sites in this chapter to stay current on everything wireless. We highly recommend RSS. By the way, the "Google" of the RSS world is the Syndic8 (www.syndic8.com) site. There, you can find a massive listing of user-submitted and Syndicat8-authenticated RSS feeds to which you can subscribe your RSS reader. Just enter your keyword in the Search area and Syndicat8 displays all the listings of available publications and sources with that phrase in their descriptions. Check it out!

Wi-Fi Planet

Wi-Fi Planet (www.wi-fiplanet.com/) is a great resource for keeping up with industry news and getting reviews of access points, client devices, security tools, and software. Look for the tutorial section, where you can find articles such as "TiVo and Wi-Fi — Imperfect Together" and "Used Routers Can Create Whole New Problems."

One of the more interactive parts of Wi-Fi Planet is its forum, where you can ask questions to the collective readership and get answers. (You can ask a question, and the system e-mails you with any responses — very nice.) The forum has General, Security, Troubleshooting, Interoperability, Standards, Hardware, Applications, VoIP, and WiMAX sections. The discussions are tolerant of beginners, but can get quite sophisticated in their responses. All in all, it's a great site for information. (Wi-Fi Planet also has RSS feeds!)

Broadband Wireless Exchange Magazine

The Broadband Wireless Exchange Magazine (www.bbwexchange.com) is a rapidly growing Web site dedicated to all things wireless, including coverage of lots of emerging products and services coming down the road. The site is a parent site for many sites-within-a-site. It started out covering fixed wireless topics for telephone companies and has grown to include all sorts of consumer, business, and industry content on wireless. If you're interested in just 802.11 products and services, the www.80211-news.com page is a good one, as are the firm's other sites on all aspects of wireless technologies. On any particular subsite, you find lots of information about industry news, new product announcements, buyer's guides, directories, and article listings.

This site is adding content and new capabilities daily, so it's hard to summarize in one paragraph. Suffice it to say that by the time you read this book, the site will probably have tripled in size. Definitely check it out. (Need we say it again? Broadband Wireless Exchange has RSS feeds as well).

The Wi-Fi Net News site (http://www.wifinetnews.com/) is a great site for finding out what's going on in the wireless world. You may have heard about *Weblogs:* They're link-running, rambling commentaries that people keep online about topics near and dear to their hearts. It's also called *blogging*.

Unless you want to track the wireless industry, though, you probably wouldn't want to check this site daily, but it's a great resource for when you want to see what the latest news is about a particular vendor or technology. We follow this site every day for interesting news and product or service developments.

Check out these other Weblogs about wireless topics: The Wireless Weblog (`wireless.weblogsinc.com`) and Daily Wireless (`www.dailywireless.org`). By the way, almost all weblogs offer RSS feeds!

PC Magazine

The venerable *PC* magazine (`www.pcmag.com`) is the go-to publication for PC users. This magazine regularly and religiously tracks all aspects of wireless, from individual product reviews to sweeping buyer's guides across different wireless segments to updates on key operating system and supporting software changes. If you have a PC, you should be subscribing to this magazine.

We really like the First Look sections of the publication, which offer you immediate insight on new product announcements and give you hands-on, quick reviews of the latest developments on the market. This site is great for the products you have heard were coming but were waiting to be ready. *PC* magazine is usually one of the first to review these products.

A one-year subscription (25 issues) runs only $25, and a two-year subscription (50 issues) is $50. You can subscribe to either electronic or print issues, which is nice if you want to catch up on your reading on the go but don't want to carry a bag of publications.

Electronic House Magazine

Electronic House (`www.electronichouse.com`) is one of our favorite publications because you can read lots of easy-to-understand articles about all aspects of an electronic home, including articles on wireless networking and all the consumer appliances and other non-PC devices that are going wireless. It's written for the consumer who enjoys technology.

Electronic House magazine includes articles on wireless home networking, wireless home control, and subsystems such as residential lighting, security, home theater, energy management, and telecommunications. It also regularly looks at new and emerging technologies using wireless capabilities, such as wireless refrigerators and wireless touchpanels, to control your home.

This monthly publication has a 13th issue, called the *Planning Guide,* that's available at newsstands. The magazine costs $19.95 per year. Back issues are $5.95 each or six issues for $30 (plus shipping), so you can catch up on what you have missed (we always love doing that). You definitely want to subscribe to this one!

Tom's Networking

Tom's Networking (www.tomsnetworking.com) is a free site with a slant toward slightly more techie users, but is a useful source for wireless advice nonetheless. You can read lots of practical tutorials on topics like "How To Crack WEP" (so that you can know how to better secure your wireless LAN) and things you would never find anywhere else, like "Building a BlueSniper Rifle — Part 1" (so that you can crack other people's LANs). You can read FAQs, track the most often read stories, get troubleshooting tips, and more.

Tom has some of the most detailed reviews of products on the Web, and he dissects them as he installs and uses the products. He opens up the boxes and tells you what's inside and why you should care, and he helps you troubleshoot your own installation. We like people like Tom.

He has a great companion site as well, Tom's Hardware Guide (www.tomshardware.com), that covers all types of networking and computing hardware.

Practically Networked

Practically Networked (www.practicallynetworked.com) is a free site run by the folks at Internet.com. It has basic tutorials on networking topics, background information on key technologies, and a troubleshooting guide. The site can contain some dated information in places, but it does have monitored discussion groups, where you can get some good feedback, and the reviews section gives you a listing of products with a fairly comprehensive buyer's-guide-style listing of features.

ExtremeTech.com

Ziff Davis Media has a great site at www.extremetech.com that has special sections focused on networking and wireless issues. There's heavy traffic at the discussion groups, and people seem willing to provide quick and knowledgeable answers. (You can find some seriously educated geeks on these groups.) Check out the links to wireless articles and reviews by ExtremeTech staff.

The site can be difficult to navigate because the layout is a little confusing. We recommend that you visit the OS, Software & Networking area, where wireless topics are covered in fair detail. And, if you're having a problem that you just can't seem to crack, check out the discussion groups on this site.

Network World

Network World (www.networkworld.com) is the leading publication for networking professionals, and although this site is geared primarily for businesses, it has lots of content about wireless because so much of the technology first appeared in commercial venues. The site has detailed buyer's guides that show the features and functionality of wireless LAN products — almost all of which is applicable for your home. Importantly, you can also search the site for more content on Wi-Fi and 802.11 as well as on Bluetooth. The publication has a large reporting staff and stays on top of everything networking-related.

Other Cool Sites

We can't list here all the sites we regularly visit, but lots of good information is out there. This section lists some other sites worth looking at.

Tech and wireless news sites

The following sites provide daily news coverage focused on the technology industry in general, or on wireless technologies in particular. We make them part of our everyday Web surfing routine — you may want to as well!

- ✔ **ZDNet:** www.zdnet.com
- ✔ **TechWeb:** www.techweb.com
- ✔ **SearchMobileComputing.com:** searchmobilecomputing. techtarget.com/

Fan sites

All the wireless products seem to have their own sets of fans. Some fans go a little further and set up Web sites geared toward telling all about their favorite products. The most popular brand of wireless gear has long been that made by Linksys (now a division of Cisco, the huge networking equipment vendor). So, it's no surprise that Linksys gear comes with its own unofficial support site, with forums, tips and tricks, and even links to specialized *firmware* that can make your access point do neat tricks, like act as part of a *mesh network* to expand the coverage of your Internet connection across several access points Check out the site at this URL: www. linksysinfo.org. If you have a different brand, don't despair. Do a Google search or check out some of the sites listed in this section for forums or vendor-specific pages, or go to www.broadbandreports.com and look in the forums there.

Industry organizations

The creation and maintenance of standards has driven wireless to very low price points and great interoperability. Here are some organizations pushing for change in wireless — each site has info about wireless and networks:

- ✔ **IEEE 802 home page:** www.ieee802.org
- ✔ **Wi-Fi Alliance** (formerly WECA): www.wi-fi.net
- ✔ **WiMAX Forum:** www.wimaxforum.org
- ✔ **Wireless LAN Association:** www.wlana.org
- ✔ **Freenetworks.org:** www.freenetworks.org

Roaming services and Wi-Finder organizations

As we mention in Chapter 16, a range of potential services are available that you can use to log on when you're on the road. Most of these have sections of their sites devoted to helping you find out where you can log on near you. Here are some of the more often mentioned services and initiatives:

- ✔ **Boingo Wireless:** www.boingo.com
- ✔ **Go Remote:** www.goremote.com
- ✔ **iPass:** www.ipass.com
- ✔ **JiWire:** www.jiwire.com
- ✔ **Wi-Fi HotSpot List:** www.wi-fihotspotlist.com

Local wireless groups

Many local groups are dedicated to offering free access around town for broadband Internet service. Here are some of the larger groups:

- ✔ **Austin Wireless** (Austin, TX): www.austinwireless.net
- ✔ **Bay Area Wireless Users Group (BAWUG)** (Bay Area, CA): www.bawug.org
- ✔ **Boston Area Wireless Internet Alliance** (Boston, MA): www.bawia.org
- ✔ **Houston Wireless** (Houston, TX): www.houstonwireless.org
- ✔ **Marin Unwired** (Marin County, CA): www.wifi-marin.org
- ✔ **NoCatNet** (Sonoma County, CA): http://nocat.net
- ✔ **NYCWireless** (New York, NY): http://nycwireless.net
- ✔ **Personal Telco** (Portland, OR): www.personaltelco.net
- ✔ **SeattleWireless** (Seattle, WA): www.seattlewireless.net
- ✔ **Southern California Wireless Users Group:** www.socalwug.org

Manufacturers

Some of these firms are more oriented toward business products, but many of them have great educational FAQs and information that are helpful for people trying to read everything they can (which we support!):

- **3Com:** www.3com.com
- ***Actiontec*:** www.actiontec.com
- **Alvarion:** www.alvarion.com
- **Apple:** www.apple.com/airportexpress
- **Buffalo Technology:** www.buffalotech.com
- **Cisco:** www.cisco.com
- **D-Link:** www.d-link.com
- **Hewlett-Packard:** www.hp.com
- **Intel:** www.intel.com
- **Intermec:** home.intermec.com
- **Linksys:** www.linksys.com
- **Macsense:** www.macsense.com
- **Microsoft:** www.microsoft.com
- **NETGEAR:** www.netgear.com
- **Proxim:** www.proxim.com
- **SMC Networks:** www.smc.com

Index

BUSINESS, CAREERS & PERSONAL FINANCE

0-7645-5307-0

0-7645-5331-3 *†

Also available:
- Accounting For Dummies †
  0-7645-5314-3
- Business Plans Kit For Dummies †
  0-7645-5365-8
- Cover Letters For Dummies
  0-7645-5224-4
- Frugal Living For Dummies
  0-7645-5403-4
- Leadership For Dummies
  0-7645-5176-0
- Managing For Dummies
  0-7645-1771-6

- Marketing For Dummies
  0-7645-5600-2
- Personal Finance For Dummies *
  0-7645-2590-5
- Project Management For Dummies
  0-7645-5283-X
- Resumes For Dummies †
  0-7645-5471-9
- Selling For Dummies
  0-7645-5363-1
- Small Business Kit For Dummies *†
  0-7645-5093-4

HOME & BUSINESS COMPUTER BASICS

0-7645-4074-2

0-7645-3758-X

Also available:
- ACT! 6 For Dummies
  0-7645-2645-6
- iLife '04 All-in-One Desk Reference
  For Dummies
  0-7645-7347-0
- iPAQ For Dummies
  0-7645-6769-1
- Mac OS X Panther Timesaving
  Techniques For Dummies
  0-7645-5812-9
- Macs For Dummies
  0-7645-5656-8

- Microsoft Money 2004 For Dummies
  0-7645-4195-1
- Office 2003 All-in-One Desk Reference
  For Dummies
  0-7645-3883-7
- Outlook 2003 For Dummies
  0-7645-3759-8
- PCs For Dummies
  0-7645-4074-2
- TiVo For Dummies
  0-7645-6923-6
- Upgrading and Fixing PCs For Dummies
  0-7645-1665-5
- Windows XP Timesaving Techniques
  For Dummies
  0-7645-3748-2

FOOD, HOME, GARDEN, HOBBIES, MUSIC & PETS

0-7645-5295-3

0-7645-5232-5

Also available:
- Bass Guitar For Dummies
  0-7645-2487-9
- Diabetes Cookbook For Dummies
  0-7645-5230-9
- Gardening For Dummies *
  0-7645-5130-2
- Guitar For Dummies
  0-7645-5106-X
- Holiday Decorating For Dummies
  0-7645-2570-0
- Home Improvement All-in-One
  For Dummies
  0-7645-5680-0

- Knitting For Dummies
  0-7645-5395-X
- Piano For Dummies
  0-7645-5105-1
- Puppies For Dummies
  0-7645-5255-4
- Scrapbooking For Dummies
  0-7645-7208-3
- Senior Dogs For Dummies
  0-7645-5818-8
- Singing For Dummies
  0-7645-2475-5
- 30-Minute Meals For Dummies
  0-7645-2589-1

INTERNET & DIGITAL MEDIA

0-7645-1664-7

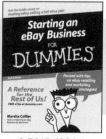

0-7645-6924-4

Also available:
- 2005 Online Shopping Directory
  For Dummies
  0-7645-7495-7
- CD & DVD Recording For Dummies
  0-7645-5956-7
- eBay For Dummies
  0-7645-5654-1
- Fighting Spam For Dummies
  0-7645-5965-6
- Genealogy Online For Dummies
  0-7645-5964-8
- Google For Dummies
  0-7645-4420-9

- Home Recording For Musicians
  For Dummies
  0-7645-1634-5
- The Internet For Dummies
  0-7645-4173-0
- iPod & iTunes For Dummies
  0-7645-7772-7
- Preventing Identity Theft For Dummies
  0-7645-7336-5
- Pro Tools All-in-One Desk Reference
  For Dummies
  0-7645-5714-9
- Roxio Easy Media Creator For Dummies
  0-7645-7131-1

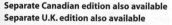

* Separate Canadian edition also available
† Separate U.K. edition also available

Available wherever books are sold. For more information or to order direct: U.S. customers visit www.dummies.com or call 1-877-762-2974.
U.K. customers visit www.wileyeurope.com or call 0800 243407. Canadian customers visit www.wiley.ca or call 1-800-567-4797.

SPORTS, FITNESS, PARENTING, RELIGION & SPIRITUALITY

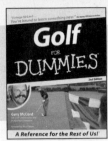

0-7645-5146-9

0-7645-5418-2

Also available:
- Adoption For Dummies
  0-7645-5488-3
- Basketball For Dummies
  0-7645-5248-1
- The Bible For Dummies
  0-7645-5296-1
- Buddhism For Dummies
  0-7645-5359-3
- Catholicism For Dummies
  0-7645-5391-7
- Hockey For Dummies
  0-7645-5228-7

- Judaism For Dummies
  0-7645-5299-6
- Martial Arts For Dummies
  0-7645-5358-5
- Pilates For Dummies
  0-7645-5397-6
- Religion For Dummies
  0-7645-5264-3
- Teaching Kids to Read For Dummies
  0-7645-4043-2
- Weight Training For Dummies
  0-7645-5168-X
- Yoga For Dummies
  0-7645-5117-5

TRAVEL

0-7645-5438-7

0-7645-5453-0

Also available:
- Alaska For Dummies
  0-7645-1761-9
- Arizona For Dummies
  0-7645-6938-4
- Cancún and the Yucatán For Dummies
  0-7645-2437-2
- Cruise Vacations For Dummies
  0-7645-6941-4
- Europe For Dummies
  0-7645-5456-5
- Ireland For Dummies
  0-7645-5455-7

- Las Vegas For Dummies
  0-7645-5448-4
- London For Dummies
  0-7645-4277-X
- New York City For Dummies
  0-7645-6945-7
- Paris For Dummies
  0-7645-5494-8
- RV Vacations For Dummies
  0-7645-5443-3
- Walt Disney World & Orlando For Dummies
  0-7645-6943-0

GRAPHICS, DESIGN & WEB DEVELOPMENT

0-7645-4345-8

0-7645-5589-8

Also available:
- Adobe Acrobat 6 PDF For Dummies
  0-7645-3760-1
- Building a Web Site For Dummies
  0-7645-7144-3
- Dreamweaver MX 2004 For Dummies
  0-7645-4342-3
- FrontPage 2003 For Dummies
  0-7645-3882-9
- HTML 4 For Dummies
  0-7645-1995-6
- Illustrator CS For Dummies
  0-7645-4084-X

- Macromedia Flash MX 2004 For Dummies
  0-7645-4358-X
- Photoshop 7 All-in-One Desk Reference For Dummies
  0-7645-1667-1
- Photoshop CS Timesaving Techniques For Dummies
  0-7645-6782-9
- PHP 5 For Dummies
  0-7645-4166-8
- PowerPoint 2003 For Dummies
  0-7645-3908-6
- QuarkXPress 6 For Dummies
  0-7645-2593-X

NETWORKING, SECURITY, PROGRAMMING & DATABASES

0-7645-6852-3

0-7645-5784-X

Also available:
- A+ Certification For Dummies
  0-7645-4187-0
- Access 2003 All-in-One Desk Reference For Dummies
  0-7645-3988-4
- Beginning Programming For Dummies
  0-7645-4997-9
- C For Dummies
  0-7645-7068-4
- Firewalls For Dummies
  0-7645-4048-3
- Home Networking For Dummies
  0-7645-42796

- Network Security For Dummies
  0-7645-1679-5
- Networking For Dummies
  0-7645-1677-9
- TCP/IP For Dummies
  0-7645-1760-0
- VBA For Dummies
  0-7645-3989-2
- Wireless All In-One Desk Reference For Dummies
  0-7645-7496-5
- Wireless Home Networking For Dummies
  0-7645-3910-8

HEALTH & SELF-HELP

0-7645-6820-5 *†

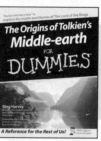

0-7645-2566-2

Also available:

Alzheimer's For Dummies
0-7645-3899-3

Asthma For Dummies
0-7645-4233-8

Controlling Cholesterol For Dummies
0-7645-5440-9

Depression For Dummies
0-7645-3900-0

Dieting For Dummies
0-7645-4149-8

Fertility For Dummies
0-7645-2549-2

Fibromyalgia For Dummies
0-7645-5441-7

Improving Your Memory For Dummies
0-7645-5435-2

Pregnancy For Dummies †
0-7645-4483-7

Quitting Smoking For Dummies
0-7645-2629-4

Relationships For Dummies
0-7645-5384-4

Thyroid For Dummies
0-7645-5385-2

EDUCATION, HISTORY, REFERENCE & TEST PREPARATION

0-7645-5194-9

0-7645-4186-2

Also available:

Algebra For Dummies
0-7645-5325-9

British History For Dummies
0-7645-7021-8

Calculus For Dummies
0-7645-2498-4

English Grammar For Dummies
0-7645-5322-4

Forensics For Dummies
0-7645-5580-4

The GMAT For Dummies
0-7645-5251-1

Inglés Para Dummies
0-7645-5427-1

Italian For Dummies
0-7645-5196-5

Latin For Dummies
0-7645-5431-X

Lewis & Clark For Dummies
0-7645-2545-X

Research Papers For Dummies
0-7645-5426-3

The SAT I For Dummies
0-7645-7193-1

Science Fair Projects For Dummies
0-7645-5460-3

U.S. History For Dummies
0-7645-5249-X

Get smart @ dummies.com®

- **Find a full list of Dummies titles**
- **Look into loads of FREE on-site articles**
- **Sign up for FREE eTips e-mailed to you weekly**
- **See what other products carry the Dummies name**
- **Shop directly from the Dummies bookstore**
- **Enter to win new prizes every month!**

Separate Canadian edition also available
Separate U.K. edition also available

Available wherever books are sold. For more information or to order direct: U.S. customers visit www.dummies.com or call 1-877-762-2974.
U.K. customers visit www.wileyeurope.com or call 0800 243407. Canadian customers visit www.wiley.ca or call 1-800-567-4797.

HAWKING®

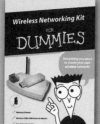